THE CREDIT UNION MOVEMENT

THE CREDIT UNION MOVEMENT

ORIGINS AND DEVELOPMENT

1850–1970

by

J. CARROLL MOODY

GILBERT C. FITE

UNIVERSITY OF NEBRASKA PRESS : LINCOLN

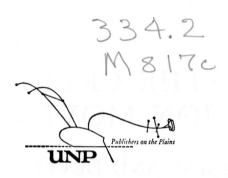

Publishers on the Plains

UNP

MANUFACTURED IN THE UNITED STATES OF AMERICA

Contents

A picture section follows page 180.

Preface

MOST AMERICANS ARE FAMILIAR with credit unions, and millions have utilized their services. Yet, few people know anything about the historical development of this important financial institution. Beginning with the establishment of the first credit union in New Hampshire in 1909, the credit union movement grew slowly until the eve of World War II. Subsequently, credit unions experienced a phenomenal growth until by 1970 they occupied a major place in the growing field of consumer finance.

Credit unionism grew out of a felt need. In the late nineteenth and early twentieth century many Americans recognized that proper credit facilities were simply not available for the mass of people. To meet this problem the founders of credit unionism in the United States imitated European and Canadian cooperators and turned to the establishment of cooperative credit societies. The founders of credit unionism in the United States possessed a combination of idealism and practicality characteristic of many American reformers. They believed that if people joined together in cooperative spirit and action they could solve the old problems of scarcity of credit and exorbitant interest rates. Their solution of credit problems fit their hope and vision that farmers, workers, and small businessmen could achieve better lives. At the same time, they believed that cooperative credit agencies must be operated in an efficient, businesslike way.

Perhaps first a word is in order in regard to what this book is not about. It is not an economic history of the role of credit unions in consumer finance. To deal with credit unions in this way and at this particular time would be premature. Indeed, it would be a consideration of current events rather than an exercise in history, because only since the 1950s have credit unions begun to handle a significant part of the nation's installment credit. Moreover, this study is not about individual credit unions, their founding or operation, or the thousands of volunteers and dedicated leaders who worked to make the movement succeed at the grass roots. Nor does it deal in any detail with credit union chapters and state leagues, except as these facets of credit unionism illustrate the failures and successes of the larger movement.

What this study does attempt to do is to trace and analyze the history of credit unionism as a national social movement. We have dealt primarily with the institutional growth of credit unionism. The social movement known as credit unionism gradually became institutionalized, and it is the development of the institution with which this book is mainly concerned. Therefore, much of the book considers the individual and associational efforts to found and expand credit unions throughout the United States, and the gradual enlargement of credit union services. In this connection it has been necessary to devote a good deal of attention to the founders and leaders of the movement. With this approach we hope that we have been able to add significant information on aspects of American reform, on the growing associational activities in society, and on the over-all development of cooperative enterprise in the United States and the world. In the end we try to assess the economic contributions of credit unions, raise some basic questions, and make some projections for the future.

We want to express our gratitude to all members of the administrative staff of the Credit Union National Association and the World Council of Credit Unions for their hearty cooperation in every phase of this project. The early interest and continued assistance of managing director J. Orrin Shipe, who first suggested the need for a scholarly history of credit unionism, have been especially appreciated. We are particularly grateful for the unrestricted use of all manuscripts and records dealing with the credit union movement which are located in the Bergengren Memorial Museum Library at Filene House in Madison, Wisconsin. Jerry K. Burns, historical librarian, went far beyond the ordinary call of duty to assist us in many ways. Mary Anne Dean, reference librarian, also gave unstintingly of her time. To E. R. Brann, director of historical projects at CUNA International, we extend our warmest thanks. He provided comfortable research quarters, suggested leads on fugitive materials, and paved the way for interviews with credit union pioneers, all of which were immensely helpful. We are also deeply appreciative to CUNA International for providing a grant for research and writing while this book was being completed. Others who were helpful to us include C. Fred Williams and Paul E. Mertz, and our typists Catherine Cox, Maryon Kaplan, and Peggy A. Hubble. Despite all of the assistance which we have received from others, we are entirely responsible for the material and views found in this book. To our wives, Carolyn and June, we express our heartfelt thanks, not for helping in this project, but just for being our wives.

J. Carroll Moody
January 4, 1971   Gilbert C. Fite

THE CREDIT UNION MOVEMENT

CHAPTER I

The Origins of
Cooperative Credit

THE ROOTS OF cooperative credit are obscure. Not only is adequate information lacking, but many currents of thought and the work of countless individuals flowed into the general stream of theory and practice out of which the movement grew. Then, too, cooperative credit has been part of the wider cooperative movement which developed earlier. Nevertheless, wherever cooperative credit appeared, it did so as the result of the growing complexities of modern economic life for both farmers and workers. The breakdown of feudalism freed European farmers from traditional obligations to feudal lords and gave them individual ownership of land. But their entrance into the individualistic, capitalist economy placed them in a position where money and credit became increasingly important. In addition, the industrial revolution brought about a similar change of relationships in the European towns, where small shopkeepers and skilled artisans began to lose the protections afforded by the guilds and were faced by an economic order characterized by growing competition and the need for greater capital. Cooperation of all types, therefore, can be looked upon as an attempt by agrarians, craftsmen, and other small producers to improve their position in a nonfeudal, modern capitalistic society. They were also concerned with restoring a spirit of community.

Concern for conditions associated with the industrial revolution led to two notable and widely publicized cooperative experiments in England. One involved Robert Owen's New Lanark mill community, in which the owners agreed to limit their returns on invested capital and to use whatever profits that might accrue for the benefit of the entire community. Called by some "utopian socialism," and by others "philanthropic paternalism," Owen and his colleagues hoped to reduce the hardships under industrial capitalism.[1] The second experiment, which

[1] John F. C. Harrison, "The Owenite Socialist Movement in Britain and the United States," *Labor History,* IX (Fall, 1968), pp. 323–37.

had greater success in that it reached more people and had a more lasting influence, was the organization of the Rochdale cooperative store in 1844. The group of workers who organized the Rochdale Society of Equitable Pioneers subscribed to shares, payable in small amounts weekly, in order to raise capital to buy goods at less than retail costs and sell them to their members at a saving. Members were paid 5 percent interest on their shares and were entitled to a proportionate division of the society's savings or profits at the end of the year. The Rochdale principles of co-operation included open membership to all; democratic control of the society, with each member having only one vote regardless of the number of shares owned; a limited interest on share capital; and the return to members of the cooperative's profits in proportion to their patronage. The example and principles of the Rochdale Pioneers profoundly influenced the cooperative movement in many countries of the world.[2]

During the 1830s and 1840s various kinds of socialist, utopian, and cooperative schemes also drew widespread attention in France. Frances Buchez founded cooperative associations for cabinetmakers and gold-smiths between 1832 and 1834, and in 1848 Louis Blanc prompted the government to contribute over a half million dollars to create national workshops for unemployed workers to be operated on a cooperative basis. At about the same time, Pierre Joseph Proudhon proposed a Bank of the People which, although not cooperative in the usual sense, implied a demand for fundamental changes in the field of banking, currency, and credit. None of these schemes succeeded, but they formed part of an emerging pattern of economic cooperation.[3]

The social reformers, communitarians, and socialists not only hoped to alleviate the distress caused by the industrial revolution, but they also wished to restore men of "honest toil" to their positions in society, to redeem a sense of community, and, in some cases, to convert capital-ism into another system altogether. To achieve these objectives it seemed essential to obtain greater control over banking and credit which had become so significant in the modern economic world. Banking had been known since ancient times, but even in their most advanced form in the nineteenth century banks served mainly the large merchant and pro-

[2] Florence E. Parker, *The First 125 Years: A History of Distributive and Service Cooperation in the United States, 1829–1954* (Superior, Wis.: Cooperative Publishing Assoc., 1956), pp. xiv–xvi.

[3] Donald S. Tucker, *The Evolution of People's Banks* (New York: Columbia University Press, 1922), pp. 15–16; Henry Cohen (ed.), *Proudhon's Solution to the Social Problem* (New York: Van-guard, 1927), *passim*.

ducer, leaving the small farmer and the urban craftsman at the mercy of the high-interest-rate moneylender.

In 1848, when Proudhon was launching his project for a Bank of the People, M. François Haeck in Belgium persuaded several individuals to organize a bank by each subscribing to one share. While some claim that the term "credit union" was first used in connection with Haeck's association, it consisted mostly of wealthier men and offered no solution to the credit problems of poor people. Therefore, this so-called credit union played no part in the development of the cooperative credit movement.[4]

The development of practical cooperative credit originated in Germany. Although the names of Hermann Schulze and Friedrich Wilhelm Raiffeisen are most commonly associated with people's banks, an important and influential figure appeared earlier in the person of Victor Aime Huber. An ardent Lutheran, Huber sought to create a "Christian communal life based upon economic reforms with the help of associated activity carried on in a spirit of Christian love." Beginning in 1844, he became the "evangelist in Germany of the gospel of cooperation," by publicizing and interpreting the cooperative ideas and experiments going on in England and France. In 1861 he published *Lectures on the Solution of the Social Problem* in which he discussed such topics as, "What a Loan Union May Accomplish" and "Credit Unions and Loan Unions." Huber believed that evil in the world resulted from defects of character, which stemmed from the "degrading pressures of poverty." He looked, therefore, to cooperative organizations to remove poverty. Moreover, when men worked for a common good rather than for self, he wrote, "their own horizons would be enlarged and their characters improved."

Although ethical and religious considerations motivated Huber, he did not believe that philanthropic and charitable acts would solve the problems of society, because they did "not necessarily help the unfortunate back to self-support and self-respect." The cooperative movement, on the other hand, provided a system of "self-help" which removed poverty, improved character, and eliminated evil. He believed that cooperative associations were primarily designed to aid the worker, but he did not preclude membership of the small proprietor or even the wealthy landlord. Overall, he thought that no class lines should be drawn for eligibility in such associations. Huber's writings were highly influential in Germany, but he personally founded only two associations. He showed

---

[4] Tucker, *Evolution of People's Banks,* p. 17.

little interest in the organization or actual operation of cooperative credit institutions.[5]

The development of practical cooperative credit societies was left to Hermann Schulze.[6] Schulze was born into a well-to-do family on August 29, 1808, in the village of Delitzsch, which later became part of Prussia. Young Hermann attended preparatory school in Leipzig, spent two years at the University of Leipzig, and then attended law school at Halle. In 1830 he took his law examination and received an appointment to the court in Torgau where he stayed for one year. During 1833 and 1834, he took another required law examination and served as an "apprentice" judge. Following these activities, he returned home to Delitzsch because of his father's serious illness. The elder Schulze served as *Patrimonial-Richter*, a combination of justice of the peace and southern country judge, and worked in a large territory surrounding Delitzsch. Hermann assisted his father for a time, took the final law examination in 1838, and three years later got the post of *Patrimonial-Richter* in a jurisdiction near his father's, where he served until 1849.

In 1846, a crop failure in Germany which brought great distress to the population, prompted Schulze to form a local committee which rented a grist mill and bakery and purchased grain at wholesale prices to distribute to the needy. The crop failure was followed by the severe winter of 1846–47, which produced even more suffering and political upheaval. Following a revolution in Berlin, the king announced elections for Parliament, and Schulze won the seat in his district. When he attended the sessions, he found so many other members named Schulze that he adopted the name Schulze-Delitzsch. He quickly became identified with the liberal members of the national assembly who were pressing for a constitution and reforms. This led, in 1850, to his being tried in court on the charge of high treason. Although acquitted, he had meanwhile lost his position as *Patrimonial-Richter*.

Two important events occurred for Schulze-Delitzsch during the hard times of the late 1840s. After losing his government post and while awaiting trial, he founded a "friendly society" for craftsmen to provide cooperative insurance against sickness and death. Soon thereafter, he organized a cooperative purchasing society for master shoemakers to buy leather at wholesale prices for members. But even then, the society had

    [5] *Ibid.*, pp. 20–28.
    [6] The discussion of Schulze-Delitzsch, unless otherwise noted, is based upon Tucker's *Evolution of People's Banks;* and Henry W. Wolff's *People's Banks: A Record of Social and Economic Progress* (London: P. S. King & Co., 1919), pp. 69–110.

to borrow funds to make their first purchase. Out of this experience Schulze-Delitzsch discovered the great need for credit among craftsmen and small shopkeepers.

In 1850 Schulze-Delitzsch founded his first cooperative credit society. Although his purchasing cooperative could have extended credit, he decided that the two functions, cooperative buying and selling and cooperative credit, should be kept separate. Therefore, he organized a loan association with an initial capital of $140 contributed by a group of friends. The features which distinguished this loan society from "charitable" loan associations of the past were that borrowers had to join the association and to contribute five cents a month toward its capital.

Soon after Schulze-Delitzsch organized his first loan association, he was acquitted of treason and assigned to a new judicial post in the small Polish village of Wreschen. Because of differences with the government, he resigned his post in 1851. Schulze-Delitzsch then had more time to devote to his cooperative activities. However, he discovered that during his absence his loan association had become moribund. A number of bad loans had been made and the society's wealthy contributors had withdrawn. On the other hand, a similar association at nearby Eilenburg, which had been organized by two friends, was prospering. Schulze-Delitzsch credited the Eilenburg society's success to the fact that it excluded wealthy patrons and required all members to contribute to the capital if they wished to borrow. Since the small investments of its members did not provide enough capital to meet all the demands for loans, the society borrowed money on the basis of "unlimited liability," which meant that all members were equally responsible for the debts of the association.

At first, Schulze-Delitzsch attempted to revive his loan association by asking municipal authorities to advance some working capital and offering them a voice in the administration of the society. When that request was refused, he reorganized the association on principles similar to those of the Eilenburg association. This task was accomplished in 1852 and almost immediately the membership rose from 30 to 150 and the association was able to raise all the capital it needed by pledging its joint liability.

Schulze-Delitzsch had settled on the principles which he thought were essential to the success of a cooperative credit association. Each member must pay an entrance fee of $2.50, and prove that he was capable of paying for one share, initially valued at $12.00, on installments. Members must deposit their savings in the credit society in order to provide working capital, and modest dividends were to be paid on these share accounts. If the association needed additional capital for loans, it should borrow from other financial institutions on the principle of unlimited liability, or, as Schulze-Delitzsch said, "all for one and each for all."

Loans granted by the Schulze-Delitzsch associations were not regular consumer credit in the twentieth-century sense. They were to be made for productive purposes. No loan, he emphasized, should have the appearance of a gift or charity. Moreover, the loans should be based on the character of the person borrowing rather than on collateral or chattel mortgages. "Your own selves and characters must create your credit," Schulze-Delitzsch wrote, "and your collective liability will require you to choose your associates carefully, and to insist that they maintain regular, sober and industrious habits, making them worthy of credit." Loans would be endorsed by two members, and would generally extend for three months. Another basic principle was open membership to all "worthy seekers after credit, not limited to any one occupation, or social class . . . ." An association which met these criteria became known as a people's bank, or a kind of savings bank managed by the depositors.[7]

Schulze-Delitzsch stressed democratic control of his people's banks. The supreme authority was the general meeting of the entire membership which followed the practice of only one vote for each shareholder regardless of the number of shares held. During the early months of his association's life, in order to educate people to their responsibilities, he insisted that all members participate in the routine affairs of the organization. Therefore, all members signed passbooks and promissory notes. From the beginning, however, there were subordinate committees. The *Aufsichtsrath,* or general committee, was elected annually by the general assembly. It consisted of the president, the treasurer, the secretary, and nine members. A bylaw adopted in 1853 prescribed that "all demands and propositions made to the union, particularly requests for loans, must be presented to the committee in writing. The committee is to decide on these matters in its meetings, is to provide for securing the capital necessary, the collection of what is due and is to keep business going in an orderly fashion." A smaller group, the *Vorstand* or executive committee, was elected from the general committee, and as time passed it began to transact most routine business, while the general committee became a supervisory and inspecting body. Thus, Schulze-Delitzsch out-

---

[7] Myron T. Herrick, *Rural Credits: Land and Cooperative* (New York: D. Appleton & Co., 1914), pp. 272–74.

lined the principles of operation and governance for his association which remained largely unchanged in subsequent years.

It is clear, as the outstanding writer on cooperative banking wrote, that, "Schulze had no scheme in his mind for the moral regeneration of mankind. Nor yet was he thinking of bringing about a workingmen's paradise." Moreover, he "had no intention of interfering in their private life, or educating them in morals. He rather sneered at 'Christian Socialists,' who troubled themselves about other people's moral well-being. Economy was enough for him. But the economy must be sound, resting upon self-help, production, and thrift." The first duty of a noncapitalist, Schulze believed, was to convert himself into a capitalist.

In 1853 Schulze-Delitzsch began traveling from town to town advocating the establishment of more people's banks. Henry W. Wolff described him as "a born economic missionary. His striking personality, his convincing eloquence, his invincible faith in his own cause, and his truly contagious enthusiasm made him an almost ideal propagandist." Wherever he went, new people's banks sprang up, often followed by other types of cooperative societies. By 1859 there were 183 people's banks with 18,000 members in Posen and Saxony.

As people's banks spread, Schulze-Delitzsch worked to provide cooperation within the movement. In 1854, for example, he began a regular column in a journal called *Deutsche Gewerbe Zeitung,* explaining his views on cooperation and reporting on the progress of the people's banks. Then in 1859 he called a convention of delegates from twenty-nine cooperative societies which met at Weimar. They decided to create a central office "to clear the way for business connections between the unions, for the exchange of mutual experience and an understanding about the common purpose." The delegates chose Schulze-Delitzsch manager of the office. By the end of the year, thirty-two of approximately two hundred cooperative organizations in existence had become affiliated. Within a few months, a second conference met and created a permanent organization, the *Nationalverein,* at Coburg. Schulze served as secretary, being compensated by the member societies. Despite the evolution of these "central" organizations, Schulze-Delitzsch insisted that each local society was autonomous in its basic functions.

Schulze-Delitzsch spent the remainder of his life as a member of the Prussian House of Representatives and of the German Reichstag, but his primary concern was always with the progress of cooperative credit. By 1864 he had participated in the organization of the Universal Federation of German Cooperative Societies, which embraced the older central organizations and the subordinate leagues. The next year the German Cooperatives' Bank, popularly called the *Soergelbank,* was organized to accept deposits of surplus bank funds, and to raise money to lend to co-operatives. A majority of the stock in this central bank was owned by the people's banks and the remainder by private individuals. Then Schulze-Delitzsch sought legislation giving legal status to his associations and finally succeeded in 1867. Only a year before his death in 1883, Schulze-Delitzsch published a book setting forth his ideas on laws for a new cooperative. The number of Schulze-Delitzsch banks continued to grow. By 1912 there were 1,002 people's banks in Germany, with a total membership of 641,000.

Even before Schulze-Delitzsch's death, a rival type of cooperative credit institution appeared in Germany. The head of the people's banks recognized them publicly in January, 1876, when he denounced two societies which had been officially registered in Neuwied. These societies were the creation of Friedrich Wilhelm Raiffeisen.[8] Although they were founded later than Schulze-Delitzsch's people's banks and grew more slowly, he viewed them as competitors to his own type of cooperative credit institutions. Schulze believed that the Raiffeisen banks followed practices that made them less safe than his own credit agencies, and he feared that if many of them failed, cooperative credit of all types might be dealt a fatal blow.

Raiffeisen was born on March 30, 1818, at Hamm in the Rhine Province. His father, who had once been a minister and mayor of the village, became an alcoholic and died when Friedrich was only eleven years old. Raiffeisen's mother was a devout Lutheran who imparted a strong piety to her son. Because his father's death left Friedrich and his mother in poor economic circumstances, college was out of the question. However, a local minister taught Friedrich on an informal basis. When Raiffeisen was seventeen years old he joined the army, where, after two years, eye disease forced him to retire from military service. He then took the civil service examination and rose from a clerkship to become mayor of Weyerbusch in 1846. Two years later, Flammersfeld and its thirty-three villages were added to his jurisdiction. In 1849 he married, and subsequently fathered seven children. His son Rudolph later succeeded him as head of his cooperative system, and his daughter Amelia became his

---

[8] The discussion of Raiffeisen, unless otherwise noted, is based upon Wolff's *People's Banks,* pp. 111–27; Herrick's *Rural Credits,* pp. 281–320; Helmut Faust, *Geschichte der Genossenschafts-bewegung* (Frankfurt: F. Knapp, 1965); and Heinrich Richter, *Friedrich Wilhelm Raiffeisen und die Entwicklung seiner Genossenschaftsidee* (Munich; 1966).

closest aide and confidant, rendering special service when he became partially blind.

In 1852 Raiffeisen became mayor of Heddesdorf, a borough of the city of Neuwied, but his failing eyesight and generally poor health plagued him constantly. Although he was re-elected mayor in 1863, the government refused to confirm his selection and he was forced into retirement on a small pension. He attempted to begin a new life by opening a cigar factory, and when that failed he began a wine agency and sold life insurance. Raiffeisen earned enough money to support himself until the end of his life, but meanwhile he directed most of his attention toward cooperative activities. Before he died in 1888, he was recognized by citizen and government alike for his services to the farmers of Germany, and those benefited increasingly used the name "good father Raiffeisen."

Raiffeisen's first cooperative venture was strikingly similar to that of Schulze-Delitzsch. He was profoundly moved by the suffering caused by the famine and hard winter of 1846–47, but where Schulze worked to aid the urban craftsmen and proprietors, Raiffeisen concentrated on helping the farmer. The famine, however, only dramatized the bad underlying conditions among farmers with which Raiffeisen had become concerned. The reforms that freed peasants from their feudal obligations and gave them their own land did not seem to improve their situation. Henry Wolff described farmers as a "half-starved population—ill-clad, ill-fed, ill-housed, ill-brought up [who] eked out by hard labour barely enough to keep body and soul together . . . ." Indeed, farmers were not prepared for a commercial-type agriculture. They did not have the money to pay for machinery, fertilizer, seeds, or livestock in order to increase their productivity and their income. Mortgages on land provided the basis of most rural credit, but mortgages were granted only to owners of large properties.

The typical small farmer, therefore, was at the mercy of profiteers. When he purchased land, he had to borrow from a high-rate money-lender who quickly foreclosed on the property if payments were not made on the day they were due. For money needed to buy seed and supplies, the farmer had to turn to loan sharks who often charged as much as 100 percent interest.

So it was not only the extraordinary distress caused by famine, but the general condition of the farmers that prompted Raiffeisen to try to help them. During the winter of 1846–47 he organized the *Brotverein*, or Bread Union, to distribute flour to the hungry, later building a bakery to sell bread to the destitute at low prices. Another association borrowed money and purchased seed and potatoes for planting, and sold them at a discount. Neither of these organizations was cooperative, however, because money was contributed or borrowed from the more fortunate for the benefit of the poor. In 1849, after Raiffeisen had become mayor of Flammersfeld, he started the Flammersfelder Auxiliary Union for the Support of Poor Farmers, which began its operations by purchasing cattle and reselling them to farmers on generous terms payable in installments. Later the society began to extend credit to farmers to improve their farms.

Still, Raiffeisen's society was not cooperative. It was composed of sixty well-to-do citizens of Flammersfeld, who pledged themselves jointly liable for the debts of the society. As a result, those who were liable controlled the society, deciding who should be admitted to membership and who would receive loans. On the other hand, members who were admitted so that they could borrow money contributed to capital and had no voice in governing the society. Nevertheless, the union appears to have freed many farmers from the grasp of the loan sharks and helped to put them on a better economic footing.

Raiffeisen did not organize his second union until 1854, when he moved to Heddesdorf as mayor. Called the Heddesdorfer Welfare Organization, the society revealed Raiffeisen's broad interests in Christian charity and welfare work. Besides the purposes of the Flammersfeld society, the new organization promoted the care and education of destitute children, hired "shirkers" and former criminals, and built libraries. The society was organized and operated like the first, except that Raiffeisen adopted the principle that profits were not to be distributed to investors until a reserve fund was established. In addition, the capital was unalienable and if the society was ever dissolved, it would be distributed for the benefit of the poor. The Heddesdorf society was followed by two more in 1862 and 1868, but it was not until 1874 that they became known outside their immediate localities.

In the meantime, Raiffeisen began to modify his views regarding the principles and methods of operating his societies. Probably the main reason for this change was that, although his earliest societies had succeeded, problems began to appear. Most of the public-spirited, wealthy men who had contributed capital to the loan societies out of the religious and benevolent enthusiasm imparted by Raiffeisen, began to lose interest because benefits only accrued to the poorer borrowers. He decided, therefore, to reorganize the society at Heddesdorf along the lines of the Schulze-Delitzsch societies, replacing charitable principles with the principle of self-help. There is no doubt that Raiffeisen was greatly influenced by the success of Schulze's organizations. In a letter of 1864, he wrote:

I was loath to give up the idea that cooperative societies should be based on charity without thought of self or pelf. I maintained my original idea in a letter to the well-known organizer, Mr. Schulze-Delitzsch, an efficient worker in economies, but experience compels me frankly to admit that such societies must consist only of the persons who personally need their help and thus have an interest in keeping them going.

With the object of preventing a repetition of the unfortunate experiences at Flammersfeld, I have resolved to allow the society here at Heddesdorf to be dissolved, and then to organize another society at an early date upon the new principles mentioned above. Already I have made most satisfactory progress, practically upon the model of the Schulze-Delitzsch associations. However, since the latter are formed mainly for cities and towns, I have made certain changes in the by-laws to adapt them to local conditions. So far I have obtained the signatures of about 300 reliable and industrious citizens of the district . . . .[9]

Thus, in 1864 Raiffeisen organized a new society known as the Heddesdorf Credit Union.

Although Raiffeisen adopted Schulze-Delitzsch's principle of self-help, there were fundamental differences between the two types of loan societies. Raiffeisen insisted that brotherly love and Christian principles motivated the credit union, while Schulze was mainly concerned with promoting economic self-sufficiency. Moreover, Schulze concentrated on urban workers and shopkeepers, while Raiffeisen devoted himself to helping farmers. Schulze also believed that membership should come from a large and economically varied area, but Raiffeisen preferred to restrict membership to a small district, preferably a parish.

To become a member of a Raiffeisen credit union a farmer applied and was admitted if his neighbors judged him to be of good character, industrious, and friendly. Although the credit union made no distinction between rich and poor, any person admitted to membership had to have tangible assets. In the case of a farmer who owned his own land, the assets were clear, but even a tenant was eligible if he owned livestock and equipment. For a number of years there was no share capital, as the societies raised money by borrowing on the joint liability of their members. Therefore, no dividends were paid. Interest was paid on deposits, however, and when a German cooperative law was passed in 1889

[9] Quoted in Herrick, *Rural Credits*, p. 259.

requiring capital, the Raiffeisen banks adopted only a token requirement of one share of $2.50 per member.

As in the case of the Schulze-Delitzsch associations, the governance of a Raiffeisen society was democratic. All members participated in the general meeting, each having one vote. They elected a committee of management to approve loans and to see that borrowers used the money specifically for the purposes set forth in the application, and to transact all other routine business of the bank. The council of inspection or supervisory committee was responsible for checking on the activities of the managers and reporting to the general meeting. Raiffeisen stressed volunteer work in all his unions, allowing compensation only to full-time cashiers.

The Raiffeisen credit unions grew slowly. Only six were in existence by 1862. Five new unions were added in 1868, twenty-two more the following year, but not until 1880 did a rapid expansion begin. At the time of Raiffeisen's death in 1888, there were 425 of his societies in Germany. Even before this spectacular increase, however, Raiffeisen faced the problem of creating regional and national organizations to bind his organizations into a whole, to promote their common purposes by providing a forum for the exchange of useful information, to supply legal and legislative advice, and to facilitate central banking services. The unions enjoyed no strong financial backing, and all unions suffered from time to time from a lack of adequate funds, or occasionally from surplus money. In 1872 he organized his first central association, the Rhein Agricultural Union Bank, to serve as a central banking institution and to oversee and control local credit unions. Other regional banks of this sort followed, and in 1874 he created a national organization called the German Agricultural General Bank of Neuwied. Unfortunately, the German laws did not allow one association to combine with another nor an association without shares to engage in banking.

Raiffeisen therefore dissolved his central banks, and in 1876 organized a new bank, called the Central Agricultural Loan Bank, as a joint stock company with its shares held in trust by officials. The following year the General Federation of Rural Cooperative Societies of Germany was organized to provide legal services, give advice, organize new societies, and disseminate information. Numerous other regional and central organizations were founded in ensuing years, but by 1905 all Raiffeisen societies had affiliated with the Imperial Federation of Agricultural Cooperative Societies, although they retained their membership in the Raiffeisen general federation. By 1913 the Raiffeisen societies withdrew from the imperial federation and relied entirely on their own central organization.

The Raiffeisen cooperative societies enjoyed a much larger growth than the Schulze-Delitzsch organizations. In 1913 there were 25,576 rural cooperative societies of all types in Germany, but 16,927 of them were credit societies. By 1915 there were 1,559 urban cooperative associations affiliated with the Schulze-Delitzsch Universal Federation, 980 of them being people's banks. Whereas Schulze stressed a purely business-like, self-help philosophy, the Raiffeisen societies emphasized their founder's moral and Christian principles. Recent historians of the Raiffeisen movement have concluded, however, that, in the mid-twentieth century, professional leadership became decisive in the affairs of the movement.[10]

The work of both great German cooperators made its impact not only on Germany, but on the rest of Europe as well. There was a direct connection between the founders of the cooperative credit movement in Italy and those in Germany. In 1864 Luigi Luzzatti, a twenty-three-year-old Italian scholar, visited Germany to study cooperation. He was greatly attracted to the ideas of Schulze-Delitzsch, and upon returning home he wrote a book on the subject, and then continued to expound his ideas as a professor of political economy at the University of Padua. In 1866 Luzzatti opened his first cooperative bank at Milan.

Luzzatti's people's banks bore many resemblances to those of Schulze-Delitzsch, but there were differences. When Luzzatti visited Germany, both Schulze and Raiffeisen still insisted that unlimited liability was a basic principle of operation, although the former later conceded that his societies should be given a choice between that and limited liability. Luzzatti, however, decided that Italians would never accept unlimited liability and from the beginning adopted limited liability. He also rejected Schulze's principle of high-priced shares to provide working capital, depending instead on money from small shares and from deposits to provide loan funds. Finally, he decided that officers of his bank should serve without compensation and that more officers and committees should be created so that members would be in closer contact with each other and the operation of their bank. As the banks increased in number and developed their operational methods, they became all-purpose banking institutions. They received deposits from, and extended credit to, nonmembers, but their principle of "character credit" followed the German model. A promissory note endorsed by one or two members was the

[10] See, for example, Richter, *Friedrich Wilhelm Raiffeisen,* p. 175.

preferred security, and Luzzatti adopted the motto of "capitalization of honesty." The clientele of the Luzzatti banks was much the same as that of Schulze-Delitzsch's—mainly small merchants and craftsmen. By 1909 the People's Bank of Milan was one of the largest banking institutions in Italy, with 70 unpaid officers and 100 salaried clerks. It numbered almost 25,000 members, had capital of nearly $2 million, and savings of over $32 million. At the same time, it served as a model for numerous other banks in Italy.[11]

The counterpart of Raiffeisen in Italy was Leone Wollemborg, who emphasized the establishment of cooperative banks for farmers. He began his first rural credit society in 1883 at Loreggia, a parish near Padua. Only thirty-two persons joined initially, but within eighteen months, ninety-six more took out membership. The organization had no shares or capital stock, accumulating its funds for lending from members' deposits and by borrowing on the principle of unlimited liability. No dividends were paid, and all profits were placed in a reserve fund to cover any losses and, when it became large enough, for general operations. The principles of the *casse rurali* were very close to those of the Raiffeisen rural unions: "The duty of the society [is] to promote all institutions likely to better, morally or materially, the condition of the inhabitants of the village, and to foster the foundation of cooperative associations for production, sale and consumption, by granting loans or opening cash credits to persons undertaking such enterprises." A member was required to be able to read and write so that he could participate wisely in the affairs of his association. The success of Wollemborg's first rural bank spread rapidly, and by 1913 there were over 2,000 rural banks in Italy, one-third of them nonsectarian and the remainder Catholic. Wollemborg founded a national federation to promote the spread of these institutions in 1887, but in 1909 a new central organization called the National Federation of Catholic Rural Credit Societies was organized as a central organization.[12]

Cooperative banking institutions soon made their appearance in other European countries. Austrians organized their first Schulze-Delitzsch

[11] Herrick, *Rural Credits*, pp. 346–54. See also Ettore Levi, *Manuale per le Banche Popolar: Cooperative Italiane, preceduto da una Memoria su Schulze-Delitzsch di Luigi Luzzatti* (Milan, 1886); Banca Popolare di Credit de Bologne, *La Banque Populaire de Credit de Bologne à L'Exposition Universelle de 1900 à Paris* (Bologne, 1900); Gustave François, "People's Banks in Italy," *Journal of Political Economy*, VII (Sept., 1899), 456–67.

[12] Herrick, *Rural Credits*, pp. 354–63..

society in 1858, and by 1913 there were 3,599 of these associations. The first Raiffeisen society was founded in 1886, with the number increasing to almost 8,000 by 1912. Farmers in France also experimented with cooperative credit societies.[13]

Surprisingly, cooperative credit made little headway in England where the Rochdale cooperative principles had originated. Nevertheless, Henry W. Wolff, chairman of the International Cooperative Alliance, became one of the strongest advocates of Raiffeisen-type cooperative banks. In 1893 he published an article on the subject in the *Economic Review,* and later the same year his book, *People's Banks: A Record of Social and Economic Success,* appeared. In 1895 he met the father of the Irish agricultural cooperative movement, Sir Horace Plunkett, and convinced Plunkett that his Irish Agricultural Organization Society should broaden its efforts to include cooperative credit societies. Despite lack of success at home, Wolff was an indefatigable propagandist for the movement. His *People's Banks* ran into several editions, he published innumerable articles, he spoke wherever a forum existed, and he carried on a voluminous correspondence with men who expressed an interest in or were identified with cooperative banks.[14]

Information about cooperative credit in Europe was not long in reaching the United States, which had always borrowed useful ideas and institutions from across the Atlantic. As early as 1864 in New York City several unions of German craftsmen organized a city-wide organization called the *Arbeiter-Bund.* While other organizations of this type concentrated on shorter hours, higher wages, or political activity, leaders of the *Arbeiter-Bund* were devoted followers of Schulze-Delitzsch. They sought to establish a bank and hospital, home-building societies, and producers' cooperatives, all according to Schulze's principle of self-help. They bought potatoes, tea, sugar, and coffee at cost and sold them to members at below retail prices, and also provided members with a $200 death

---

[13] *Ibid.,* pp. 456, 321–438; Tucker, *Evolution of People's Banks,* pp. 227–41.

[14] Jeannette Halford, "Mr. Henry W. Wolff and the Beginnings of the I.C.A.," *Review of International Cooperation,* XXIV (Aug., 1931), 286; Henry W. Wolff, "The Co-operative Banking Movement," *Economic Review,* VI (April, 1896), 193–204; and Herrick, *Rural Credits,* pp. 439–55. See also Great Britain, *Parliamentary Papers (Accounts and Papers: Commercial Reports,* Vol. LXVII), "Reports by Her Majesty's Representatives Abroad, On the System of Co-operation in Foreign Countries," Commercial no. 20 (1886); and "Reports from Her Majesty's Representatives Abroad on the Raiffeisen System of Co-operative Agricultural Credit Associations," Commercial no. 61 (1895).

benefit. The enthusiasts for Schulze-Delitzsch cooperatives, however, were soon pushed aside by the growing enthusiasm for the eight-hour day and European Marxism.[15]

Nevertheless, cooperative credit continued to receive attention. Reporting on the German people's banks in 1869, the *New York Times* concluded that "nothing in the various trials of cooperation for the working classes throughout the world has been so successful." The writer added that such societies were "apparently based on the fundamental laws of political economy," and could undoubtedly provide a peaceful alternative to "the great struggle which is agitating the civilized world between labor and capital."[16] That cooperation could ameliorate the violent struggles between employers and employees was a central theme of such favorable reports. Henry Villard wrote an account of people's banks the same year, in which he tied the "growing frequency of strikes and the continuous agitation of the labor question of late years in this country" to "our past and present fiscal policy" and to "the concentration of the leading branches of industry in the hands of large capitalists . . . ." Villard concluded that some method should be found of preventing the "extinction of the class of independent producers with small capital, in consequence of their inability to compete with large manufacturers . . . ." One remedy, Villard proposed, was the introduction of Schulze-Delitzsch credit banks.[17]

An attempt to introduce Schulze-Delitzsch societies occurred in Massachusetts in 1870. Samuel M. Quincy, a Boston attorney, and member of the Massachusetts General Court, translated into English extracts from a report of Schulze-Delitzsch called, *The People's Banks of Germany: Their Organization under the Recent Law.* His nephew, Josiah Quincy, a member of the Massachusetts senate, presented the report to the committee on banks and banking, along with a request that a law be enacted permitting the incorporation of such banks in the state. A Boston journal commented favorably on the idea and implied that people's banks could profitably be introduced into the United States. The following year, a senate bill provided for the incorporation of such societies, but in less than two months, Josiah Quincy, the chairman of the committee on banks and banking, informed the committee that such legislation was

15 David Montgomery, *Beyond Equality: Labor and the Radical Republicans, 1862–1872* (New York: Alfred A. Knopf, 1967), pp. 164–68.

16 *New York Times,* April 28, 1869.

17 Henry Villard, "People's Banks of Germany," *Journal of Social Science,* I–II (1869–70), 127–35.

unnecessary because he had discovered that such societies could be organized under existing laws. Quincy had, for example, participated in a reorganization of the Franklin Fund, which made small loans "to young merchants to be secured by mortgage on houses intended for their own occupation." Although Schulze-Delitzsch principles were not adopted by the Franklin Fund, the aims of the loans were similar to those of people's banks.[18]

Interest in cooperative credit in the United States did not die when the Massachusetts legislature failed to pass an enabling act. Political economists and other observers continued to write about the need for cooperative banking to keep the independent craftsman from disappearing and to reduce the conflict between capital and labor. Moreover, by the 1890s it had become clear that the absence of proper banking and credit facilities had forced the average man to turn to high-rate moneylenders and pawnshops. The 30 to 50 percent interest charged in these cases was referred to as "legalized robbery." "It is wrong that the poor should be robbed in the hour of their need and distress," wrote one author. "It is wrong that they should pay five or ten times as much for 'accommodation' as the rich and well-to-do." He called for institutions that would lend to all at 6 percent interest. "Hence, we propose bringing banking facilities to all classes—to the poor man as well as the rich man, to the workingman and the farmer as well as to the manufacturer and capitalist. We propose banks of the people, by the people, and for the people."[19]

But neither the Schulze-Delitzsch nor the Raiffeisen societies gained any immediate foothold in the United States, although various types of savings banks, and savings and loan associations appeared. But urban workers and the small farmers still complained about inadequate credit facilities. Commercial bankers catered to the already well to do, and no modern installment loan departments existed to meet their needs. Exactions of the pawnshops and loan sharks were the ubiquitous reminders

---

[18] Samuel Miller Quincy (trans. and comp.), *The People's Banks of Germany: Their Organization under the Recent Law* (Boston: Little, Brown and Co., 1870); "The People's Banks of Germany," *Old and New,* I (1870), 704–6; Massachusetts, *Journal of the Senate,* Feb. 17, 1871, p. 128, and April 4, 1871, p. 254; *Boston Evening Transcript,* April 8, 1870.

[19] Lee J. Vance, "Banks for the People," *North American Review,* CLX (Mar., 1895), 382–84. See also Richard T. Ely, "German Cooperative Credit Unions," *Atlantic Monthly* (Feb., 1881); and U.S., Department of Agriculture, Division of Statistics, *Cooperative Credit Associations in Certain European Countries and their Relation to Agricultural Interests,* prepared under the direction of Edward T. Peters, Misc. Series, Report no. 3 (Washington, D.C.: Government Printing Office, 1892).

that the mass of American wage earners and farmers were still without satisfactory credit institutions.

Cooperative banking gained its first permanent foothold in North America at the beginning of the twentieth century at Levis, a city located across the St. Lawrence River from Quebec. There, Alphonse Desjardins, a member of the Hansard staff, which reported debates of the House of Commons, established *La Caisse Populaire de Levis* on December 6, 1900. Born in Levis on November 5, 1854, Desjardins was a member of a large family. His father, François, had failed as a farmer at Saint-Jean-Port-Joli and had moved to Levis to seek other work. An illness soon overtook his father, and Desjardins's mother became the sole support of the family. Young Alphonse experienced the hardships of the poor, but his parents imparted strong moral and religious principles to their son, as well as seeing to it that he received an education. He attended parochial school in Levis, and from 1864 to 1870 was a student at Levis College. In the latter year, when he was only sixteen, he left college to help support his family. For a short period he joined the Canadian militia, but he returned to Levis where he became a member of the editorial staff of a local newspaper, the *Echo of Levis*.

In 1879, after a brief stint with a second newspaper, Desjardins began publication of the debates of the Quebec parliament. After eleven years the provincial government ceased its subsidy to Desjardins, and in 1891 he founded a daily newspaper at Levis, which he called *L'Union Canadienne*. This enterprise lasted only a few months, but Desjardins was almost immediately appointed to the staff which reported the proceedings of the House of Commons at Ottawa. He held this position until 1915, when he was forced to resign because of ill health.[20]

In his early years, Desjardins developed a strong attachment to his community. He was well known to most citizens of Levis, and was respected by them as an honest, hard-working, and responsible person. As a student at Levis College he participated in the cultural and religious life of his city, and as a journalist he became intimately aware of the economic and social problems of its citizens. Moreover, he developed a political philosophy of his own during these years. At a time when divisions appeared among Canadians, with some advocating closer ties and even union with the United States, while others debated provincial au-

[20] Hector MacPherson, "Co-operative Credit Associations in the Province of Quebec" (Ph.D. diss., University of Chicago, 1910), pp. 7–12; and "The Life and Work of Alphonse Desjardins, Founder of the Credit Union Movement," *Canadian Co-operator* (Nov., 1943), pp. 10–11.

tonomy versus national unification and centralization, Desjardins adopted as a motto for his newspaper—Before Everything Let Us Be Canadians.[21]

As a journalist, Desjardins had devoted much of his attention to the study of economics and social science, and he learned of the cooperative movement which had gained a strong foothold in Europe. He then became interested in adopting cooperative institutions in his native land. More specifically, however, he observed the lack of adequate banking facilities for the common wage earner, which caused many persons to turn to the high rate moneylenders. Although the plight of those who had fallen into the clutches of loan sharks were brought to his attention from time to time, in 1897 the Canadian Parliament began considering a law to outlaw usury. As a parliamentary reporter, Desjardins heard the testimony and debates on this bill. He was particularly horrified by hearing of a case in which an individual had been charged 1200 percent interest on a small loan. At that point, Desjardins decided to attempt to remedy such evils.

His brother, Napoleon, had already called Desjardins's attention to an article in the *Revue des Deux Mondes* about Rochdale cooperatives.[22] Upon investigating the extent of cooperative development in Canada, Desjardins discovered a few cooperative bakeries and one or two cooperative stores.[23] There is some evidence that he did learn of a very small, quasi-cooperative bank which operated at Rustico, on Prince Edward Island, but he did not mention it in any of his correspondence or other writings at the time.[24] At any rate, after a great amount of reading, Desjardins discovered the names of Europeans who were identified with the cooperative credit movement.

Early in 1898, he wrote Henry W. Wolff, probably the most noted writer and promoter of people's banks in Europe, inquiring about the principles and development of the movement. After a preliminary exchange, Desjardins informed Wolff that he had "made up my mind to

[21] "Alphonse Desjardins, II—His Political View," *Ontario Credit Union News,* X (Dec., 1949), 2, 7.

[22] "The Life and Work of Alphonse Desjardins," p. 11; Desjardins to Henry W. Wolff, June 6, 1898, Archives de la Fédération des Caisses Populaires Desjardins, Quebec (hereafter this collection is cited as Archives).

[23] Alphonse Desjardins, "Canada" (in Report of Proceedings, Fifth Congress of the International Co-operative Alliance, Manchester, England, July, 1902); Typescript in Bergengren Memorial Museum Library, Filene House, Madison, Wisconsin (hereafter cited as BMML).

[24] John T. Croteau, "The Farmers' Bank of Rustico: An Early People's Bank," reprint in BMML.

go into a thorough study of those institutions with a view of introducing the same in Canada." Desjardins was convinced "that the local circumstances are of such a character as to completely warrant me to go into the enterprise with the conviction that it will confer a great benefit on the people, who, being not in a position to go to our ordinary Banks, are obliged to subscribe to the terrible conditions imposed upon them by private money lenders."[25]

That same year Desjardins also wrote Charles Rayneri, director of the *banque populaire* of Menton, France, from whom he received a copy of Rayneri's book on people's banks. Subsequently, he requested a number of brochures about popular banking in France. Desjardins also wrote to other European cooperative credit leaders, including Luigi Luzzatti. As his knowledge of those institutions increased, and as confidence that he could introduce them into Canada grew, Desjardins began to preach the gospel of cooperation from the public platform, through the press, and in personal conversations with his many acquaintances.[26]

On September 20, 1900, Desjardins invited about a dozen friends to his home to present his plan for creating a people's bank in Levis. As he later wrote, he issued the invitations "not without hesitation, because, knowing the absolute ignorance of co-operative principles of the people whom I had invited, I saw reason to apprehend that my suggestion would be badly received." But he went ahead, explaining to them the ways in which people's banks had improved the lives of people of modest means in Europe and proposing that such an institution be organized in Levis. "To my great surprise," Desjardins wrote, "when I had thoroughly explained the matter, everyone present expressed himself willing and ready to take up the scheme."[27]

The small group which met at Desjardins's home appointed a committee to make a complete study of the subject by meeting every Monday and Wednesday evenings. Desjardins intended that those meetings would lead to the drafting of a constitution and the inauguration of a local people's bank. During the weeks of committee meetings, Desjardins also continued his correspondence with European cooperators and worked out the technical details for establishing a bank. The working committee, for example, became timid about organizing a cooperative financial concern since no law empowered them to do so. Desjardins's attitude, how-

25 Desjardins to Wolff, June 6, 1898, Archives.

26 Desjardins to Rayneri, Sept. 30, 1898; Desjardins to Luzzatti, June 15, 1900, Archives. MacPherson, "Co-operative Credit Associations," p. 12.

27 Desjardins, "Canada."

ever, was that in the absence of such a statute "everything that is not prohibited is permitted." He believed that once the bank had proved itself, Parliament would recognize its legal existence.

Desjardins also decided upon two fundamental principles for the operation of his bank that differed from some of the prevailing practices in Europe. He first decided that the dichotomy between urban and rural credit societies should not prevail in Canada. He determined to "unite as harmoniously as possible" the diverse characteristics of the *"Banque populaire"* and the *"Caisse rurale"* because "in a country as new as ours the economic situation of the population groups differs essentially in certain areas with that which is encountered in the old country . . . ." In the second place, Desjardins rejected the principle of unlimited liability, emphasizing that "our population is completely opposed to the idea of unlimited responsibility," and that he "would never have been able to acquire supporters if I had tried to have this principle accepted." Desjardins knew that Wolff zealously supported the principle of unlimited liability, but he asked "if, for the love of a principle, it is fitting to abandon all hope of implanting the institutions of credit in Canada . . . ."[28]

After a few meetings, the committee began drafting the constitution for the cooperative credit society and taking pledges for the first shares of stock. On November 22, after eighteen meetings, the bylaws were completed. On December 6, 1900, some one hundred citizens of Levis met and formally adopted the constitution and bylaws. They chose *La Caisse Populaire de Lévis* as the name for their new organization. The term *caisse* has no precise English equivalent, but Desjardins chose the term because it could be translated to mean credit society and was less objectionable than the word bank or banking. More than eighty persons signed the charter and subscribed for a total of two hundred shares.[29] The objectives of *La Caisse Populaire de Lévis* were to encourage economy and financial responsibility among members; to promote Christian and humane values; to combat usury; to provide capital for local individual enterprises; and to help borrowers achieve economic independence through self-help.

The *caisse populaire* opened for business on January 23, 1901. The first deposit amounted to only ten cents but by the end of the day total deposits stood at $26.40. In order to hold down expenses and because no member had the training necessary to manage the business, Desjardins handled all transactions himself without any fees or salary. "The office

[28] Desjardins to Wolff, Oct. 27, 1900, Archives.
[29] "Life and Work of Alphonse Desjardins," p. 11.

was kept in my own house," he later recounted, "the bookkeeping was done by myself, and whenever I was absent from town, by one of my family. All the members used to come to my place for the payment of their installments or shares, or to do any other transaction they had with the society." At first the office was open only on Saturday nights, but soon business was conducted three nights a week. By May, 1901, the *caisse populaire* claimed 840 members, who owned 2,750 shares, and had granted loans totaling $8,000.[30]

To become a member of the *caisse,* any urban or rural resident of Levis had to subscribe to at least a single five-dollar share and agree to pay for it at the rate of ten cents each week. In addition, he paid a small entrance fee, which went into the society's reserve fund. To be elected to membership, the applicant had to be judged as "honest, punctual in his payments, sober and of good habits, industrious and laborious." Once elected, a member could be expelled because he became bankrupt or insolvent, was convicted of a crime, because he "allowed himself to be sued for debt" or neglected to pay what he owed the association, or because he deceived the association "with regard to the use of borrowed moneys."

In order to borrow money from the *caisse,* a person had to be in "good standing" with the association, to have repaid all previous loans and not be in arrears in the repayment of a current loan. A committee of credit was responsible for approving or rejecting all loan applications. The constitution specified that the committee "shall always give the preference to smaller loans," and the borrower had to state in his application the exact purpose for which he intended to use the money. Although the applicant's character and record for financial responsibility were the most significant test of security for a loan, the committee of credit could, and did, require that the note be endorsed by one or two other members, who became responsible for repaying the loan if the borrower defaulted.

In addition to the committee of credit, the ruling body of the association were the members who in true cooperative fashion only had one vote each, regardless of the number of shares held. In reality, however, the executive decisions of the association were made by the council of administration, which consisted of nine shareholders elected by the general meeting of the shareholders. The council of administration admitted new shareholders, appointed and supervised employees, adopted bylaws

---

[30] Canada, House of Commons, *Reports of the Special Committee of the House of Commons,* to whom was Referred Bill No. 2, *An Act Respecting Industrial and Co-operative Societies* (Ottawa, 1907), Appendix no. 3, p. 108 (hereafter cited as *Special Committee Report*).

for the association, recommended the dividend rate, and controlled the reserve fund. From among themselves they elected a president, a vice-president, and a secretary, which constituted the "executive of the board." The committee of supervision consisted of three shareholders elected by the members. It was charged with watching over all the operations of the association.

The funds of the *caisse populaire* were to consist of investments by members in shares, deposits from members, entrance fees, earnings from loans, and "advances" made to the association by members or, "where the association fails to procure from the shareholders the necessary funds for its good working, then such advances can be made by non-shareholders." A reserve fund to "secure the soundness of the association" was to be established, equal to "at least double the maximum attained by the capital." All entrance fees and 20 percent of the net profits of each year were to go into the reserve fund. These resources could be invested. A "provident Fund" was also provided "to cover first extraordinary losses resulting from the operations of the association, and for other purposes." It was to be accumulated by setting aside 10 percent of the new proceeds of the year until the fund equaled half of the maximum capital. Thus, Desjardins's *caisse populaire* stressed the same principles as most earlier cooperative banks and credit associations.[31]

During its first six years, the *caisse* made loans totaling almost $200,000, and did not lose one cent. That record proved to Desjardins and other enthusiasts that the cooperative principle provided the necessary security. "The main security is the fact that the association is working within a small area and that everybody knows each other," he wrote, while "a second security is that everybody is interested by being a shareholder." The credit committee first evaluated an applicant's honesty, and then it decided whether to require endorsers. Interest on loans was fixed by the committee on administration, which took into account the general state of the money market, the rate being charged by banks, and the "legitimate remuneration to the thrifty who provide the funds." During the early years, interest rates were fixed at about 8 percent.[32]

The business of lending money produced profits for investors, although cooperators were reluctant to use the term. Likewise, Desjardins objected to the use of the word dividends because "it smells too much of commercialism . . . ." Instead, he adopted the term *boni* to apply to the payment of interest on deposits and dividends on shares. For the first six

[31] *Ibid.*, Exhibit No. 1, "Constitution of 'La Caisse Populaire de Levis,' " pp. 193–204.
[32] *Ibid.*, pp. 7–8, 11–13, 19.

years of operation, the *caisse* at Levis realized $5,800 in profits, $3,400 being diverted to a reserve fund, and $2,400 distributed as *boni*. The number of shares any one person could own was set by the general meeting in the beginning at $125, but the need for additional funds for loans caused the membership to raise the maximum to $250, then to $500, and by 1906 to $1,000. Dividends during the initial years of operation averaged 4 per cent. It could have perhaps been higher, but Desjardins adamantly insisted that until adequate reserves had been established dividends should be kept at a moderate level.[33]

Desjardins's absences from his home to continue his job as a reporter in the House of Commons at Ottawa, left his wife to manage the affairs of the association. After six years, however, the growth of the *caisse* and its financial condition caused the association to rent new quarters in the business district and to hire a manager. Desjardins, too, had always intended to use the *caisse* at Levis to prove that such associations were practical for Canada, but his conservative nature led him to move slowly in extending the experiment to other localities. However, within a year of the establishment of the *caisse* at Levis, another was organized in the neighboring rural parish of Saint Joseph de Levis. The third association began operation early in the year of 1905 at Saint Malo, near Quebec.[34]

The three societies existed at first without legal status, but Desjardins was determined to have them recognized in law. His work had won many warm friends in the Quebec legislature, and in 1906 it passed the Quebec Syndicates Act without a dissenting vote. The following year a bill modeled on that act was introduced into the Canadian House of Commons and referred to a special committee for hearings. Desjardins was the chief witness, but he had the support of Earl Grey, governor general of Canada, who was also president of the International Cooperative Alliance. His testimony in behalf of the bill is best summed up by his statement that "if a new Act is required to facilitate the multiplication of banks like that which Monsieur Desjardins, to his great credit, has established, the sooner that Act is passed the better." But the bill failed to pass as did a similar measure the following year.[35]

Nevertheless, the *caisse populaires* continued to grow; three were organized in 1907, eleven in 1908, and fifteen in 1909. By 1914 there were 150 cooperative banks in Canada serving urban workers, farmers, and

[33] *Ibid.*, pp. 20–22; Alphonse Desjardins, *The Co-operative People's Bank, La Caisse Populaire* (New York: Russell Sage Foundation, 1914), p. 40.

[34] MacPherson, "Co-operative Credit Associations," pp. 14–16.

[35] *Ibid.*, pp. 16–17; and *Special Committee Report*, pp. 89, 107–10.

miners. Desjardins was devoting himself wholeheartedly to organizing credit societies.[36] He boasted of their benefits and explained to a special committee of the House of Commons:

The poor people are . . . brought up to an astonishing level of education so far as economics are concerned. They know what is the nature of capital. They know its relation to the rest of the social life and thereby a good deal of prejudice is abated. Now when you go down into the details of it, one of the great advantages of co-operation is that it teaches people how to do their own business instead of relying upon a middleman . . . . You will find that it has taught people the great advantages of economy, thrift, saving, and above all, it has taught them the value of the cents, the small savings.[37]

Meanwhile, Desjardins had become involved in the cooperative credit movement in the United States. As mentioned earlier, the work of European leaders, such as Schulze-Delitzsch and Raiffeisen, had been known, but no effective experiment had been attempted along these lines. Desjardins's credit societies were known in the United States, but nothing had been done to duplicate the Canadian experiences before 1907. Desjardins was willing to assist in establishing cooperative credit associations, but the leadership would have to come from the United States if it were to be effective. The man about to emerge as the central figure in American credit unionism was Edward A. Filene of Boston. He became especially interested in cooperative credit during and after a trip to India in 1907.

[36] Desjardins, *The Co-operative People's Bank,* pp. 30–38.
[37] *Special Committee Report,* pp. 3–4.

CHAPTER II

The Origins and Early Development of Credit Unions in the United States, 1908–15

ON JANUARY 5, 1907, Edward Albert Filene, a wealthy forty-seven-year-old Jewish department store owner, set sail on his first trip around the world. For Filene this was "a dream coming true." [1] Here, at last, was an opportunity to study other peoples and institutions in the under-developed world at firsthand. This desire for information was something for which he had an insatiable thirst.

Filene was born in 1860, the second son of William and Clara Filene who were natives of Germany. He was named for the Prince of Wales who visited the United States that year. When he was five years old, Edward was injured in a fall which left him with a permanent limp and prevented him from engaging in many boyhood activities. He was graduated from the Lynn, Massachusetts, high school, and later attended a boys' school in his mother's home town in Bavaria where Edward "learned little and had a wretched time." In 1878, following months of intensive self-study, young Filene was admitted to Harvard. But before he could enroll, his father became ill and Edward had to go to work in the family clothing store which his father had opened in 1856, shortly after arriving in Boston. Edward quickly showed a marked interest and ability in business.

Filene was a shy, rather lonely young man. Besides his embarrassing limp, he developed eczema which did not respond to medical treatment. In moments of emotional stress, it reached acute proportions. Partly, at least, because of these factors, he saw very little of girls his own age and,

[1] "Trip Around the World: Edward A. Filene, 1907," scrapbook, entry for Jan. 5, 1907, BMML.

consequently, never married. Nevertheless, Filene developed a deep concern for others. Business and public service consumed his life, and his family in a very real sense became society as a whole.

By the time Edward joined the store in Boston on a full-time basis at age eighteen, his father had opened additional businesses in Lynn, Salem, and Bath. But Edward decided to concentrate the business in Boston, and by 1881 there was a single family store called William Filene, Merchant. By the end of the decade it was one of the most prominent business establishments in Boston, occupying five floors and a basement. Meanwhile, Edward's younger brother, Lincoln, had joined the enterprise which became known as William Filene's Sons Company, with full control in the hands of Edward and A. Lincoln Filene.

Essentially a women's clothing store, the enterprise prospered. Much of the success stemmed from Filene's merchandising and management practices, among which was his insistence that customers get full value for their money. He did not consider himself a particularly "good" or "moral" man, but he believed that fair treatment of customers was good for business. Likewise, he was an enlightened employer. He paid good wages and instituted many employee benefits far ahead of his time. These included installing lounges for relaxation, an employees' cafeteria, a savings and loan association, paid holidays, and free medical care. He also supported an employees' association that was given power to make rules for the store, including working hours and the determination of holidays. Moreover, Filene dreamed of someday turning the ownership of the store over to the employees.

Despite his growing prosperity, Filene lived simply, almost frugally. One luxury which he did permit himself was travel. In the mid-1880s he began to make trips to Europe. He not only purchased merchandise and studied European business practices, he also carefully observed European society and its problems. Moreover, he became interested in the international economy. Increasingly, his trips became fact-finding missions. In this connection he visited the offices of foreign officials, as well as American leaders. He corresponded with Woodrow Wilson, Georges Clemenceau, Aristide Briand, Ramsay MacDonald, Vladimir Lenin, Mahatma Gandhi, and Franklin D. Roosevelt. With increasing frequency, Filene published his ideas on social, economic, and political questions, and lectured widely to both popular and professional audiences.

Filene had a kind of false modesty which prompted him to say that, "I am a shopkeeper from Boston," but he was much more than that. He developed into an active, largely self-educated intellectual and internationalist who devoted large amounts of time and money to trying to solve human problems. There is a temptation to ascribe his view of the world and his strong sense of moral right to his being a Jew, but he received a sound education in rationalism from his father who "had become convinced that the faith of his fathers was so riddled with superstition as to be no longer worthy of credence . . . ." Nevertheless, while he did not practice his religion actively, he adhered to the basic principles of Jewish morality. Moreover, like many of his business contemporaries, he believed that financial success was only the means to the end of helping to build a better society.

Filene was a voracious reader, especially in the fields of history, philosophy, public affairs, and economics. He was familiar with the works of John Law, Robert Owen, Adam Smith, and David Ricardo. He was also a good listener. In the 1890s he joined the Liberal Club, where leading thinkers of the day, such as John Dewey, lectured. For years he attended summer conferences at Greenacres, New Hampshire, where speakers discussed great moral and philosophical issues. But Filene could not be satisfied in the world of contemplation. He was an activist. He looked upon ideas, as he did money, as instruments to solve great social problems.

Increasingly throughout his life, Filene sought to combine knowledge and money to improve the lot of people. He was not a revolutionary, but a progressive reformer. He believed that American institutions were basically sound, but that change was necessary in the nation's economic and social life. In the late 1890s he joined with other Bostonians, including Louis D. Brandeis, in the Public Franchise League to prevent private transportation and utilities companies from controlling the affairs of the city. He was instrumental in organizing the Boston Chamber of Commerce, and later the Chamber of Commerce of the United States and the International Chamber of Commerce. When he decided that all classes of citizens in Boston should be united to make it a place where everyone could live and prosper under good government, with ideal economic, social, and physical conditions, he organized Boston-1915 as a supercommunity committee to rehabilitate and unite the city to achieve those purposes. He was active in politics, usually behind the scenes as an adviser and financier. Filene had a lifelong interest in world peace, and supported organizations with that goal; he hired an engineer to design the simultaneous translator to be used in international conferences. His many and varied activities fit a pattern. He worked for what he considered the public interest. Since he did not believe that individual acts of charity could solve many problems, he contributed his resources mainly to discovering the causes of poverty, disease, and social distress, and then showing how to remedy the undesirable situations. Filene's round-the-world trip in 1907 and his growing interest in cooperative credit, reflected his desire for more information and his willingness to examine new approaches to old problems.

Filene reached Calcutta, India, in early February, eager to get into the Indian villages to study the cooperative movement about which he had heard. Because of transportation and language difficulties, he could not strike out on his own, so his travel agent, Thomas Cook and Son, suggested that he contact William Robert Gourlay, a member of the Indian Civil Service in the Province of Bengal, who had a close knowledge of the region. Filene and Gourlay met for the first time at the Grand Hotel.[2] Gourlay was a Scotsman who had been educated at Glasgow University and Jesus College, Cambridge. He entered the Indian Civil Service in 1897, and at the time he met Filene he was in charge of the cooperative credit societies in Bengal. Gourlay invited Filene to accompany him on a tour of the country districts.[3]

Filene engaged a car and a chauffeur and the three men set off through the rich, tropical countryside, visiting districts in which villagers had never seen an automobile. It was an arduous trip. The automobile broke down, they got stuck in a river bed, and the food and lodging were poor and even dangerous. But the journey provided a remarkable education for Filene. Never had he seen such poverty. "The average Hindu can save nothing," he noted in his journal, "and if the harvest fails famine kills more than a million." [4] As is true with most newcomers to India, Filene began to try to discover the causes for such mass destitution. He concluded that the ownership of land and adequate credit to develop the land were the basic needs of the villagers. Filene admired the Bengali peasant, seeing him as the honest and hard-working victim of an exploitive system. On occasions when the villager had to borrow money for a "grand celebration" such as a marriage in the family, he had to rely on the local moneylender who charged interest rates from 24 to 37.5 percent. Actually, rates were even higher.

---

[2] Adeline Gourlay to Roy F. Bergengren, Aug. 23, 1938, BMML (hereafter all manuscript material cited, unless otherwise noted, is found in BMML).

[3] Biographical sketch of William Robert Gourlay, typescript; and Adeline Gourlay to R. F. Bergengren, Aug. 23, 1938.

[4] "Trip Around the World: Edward A. Filene, 1907," entry for Feb. 8, 1907.

The one hope for the Indian peasant, according to Filene, was the Agricultural Cooperative Banks with which Gourlay was associated. The British government had persuaded groups of villagers to form associations to receive their meager savings. The government would then lend the association a sum equal to that deposited by the members. The association, in turn, loaned money to its members, most of the loans being from 5 to 25 rupees. Filene was impressed with the work of the associations and with their volunteer, unpaid officers.[5] He left India with a new appreciation of what he believed cooperative credit could do for poor people.

Moving on to the Philippines, Filene once again observed mass poverty among peasants who seemed always to be the victims of usurious moneylenders. He learned that there was a provision for an agricultural bank but that the difficulty of getting Torrens land titles required for loans by such an institution made it impossible to raise the necessary capital for such a bank. So, while the need for cooperative banks was very great among Philippine peasants, the prospect for their development was not bright.[6]

Soon after returning to the United States, Filene called upon President Theodore Roosevelt and told him about the Indian agricultural cooperative banks. He recommended that such institutions be introduced into the Philippines. Expressing interest, Roosevelt asked Filene to write him about the matter. Early in February, 1908, Filene wrote Roosevelt describing the Indian cooperative credit system and enclosing some literature which Gourlay had given him. Filene offered to go to Washington to talk again with Roosevelt, but nothing further developed. Nevertheless, it is clear that Filene's trip abroad had aroused a deep interest in cooperative credit and had given him an additional cause for which to fight.[7] Yet there is no concrete evidence that Filene was then deeply concerned about the problems of inadequate credit and excessive interest rates in Massachusetts.

There was another Bostonian, however, who had concluded that cooperative banking was a practical solution to credit problems. That was Pierre Jay. A man of unusual abilities, Jay had been appointed the first commissioner of banks for Massachusetts in April, 1906. Born in Warwick, New York, in 1870, Jay was a direct descendent of the first chief

[5] *Ibid.,* Mar. 3, 1907.

[6] *Ibid.,* Aug. 26, 1907.

[7] Filene to President Roosevelt, Feb. 28, 1908; Secretary to President Roosevelt to Filene, Mar. 2, 1908.

justice of the Supreme Court, John Jay. He attended Groton School and graduated from Yale University in 1892. From 1903 to 1906 he was vice-president of the Old Colony Trust Company in Boston. In 1906 the Massachusetts legislature abolished the old Board of Commissioners of Savings Banks and created a new Banking Department, headed by a commissioner of banks, who would exercise authority and supervision over all the banking institutions of the commonwealth. Jay was named to this new post.[8]

During the latter months of 1906, Jay was browsing in the Boston Public Library looking for something to read on the morning and evening train trips between his suburban home and his office, when he happened upon a copy of Henry W. Wolff's *People's Banks*. After reading this book, Jay began to search for more information on cooperative credit. The only other work he found, however, was the "Annual Report of the People's Bank of Milan." But he soon heard of the work of Alphonse Desjardins and initiated correspondence with him. Not only did Desjardins supply Jay with literature about cooperative banking, but he also put Jay into contact with European leaders of the movement. Early in March, 1907, Jay wrote Desjardins that such institutions contained "great possibilities of application in this country, especially in the older portions." [9]

Certainly there was a great need for better credit facilities for small entrepreneurs, wage earners, salaried employees, and farmers. Many among the poorer classes were forced to borrow from pawnbrokers, and from moneylenders known as "note-shavers." To avoid prosecution for usury, note-shavers loaned money on notes which bore the legal rate of interest but added fees for expenses and services which greatly enhanced the interest rate. Small loan companies, which first appeared in Chicago in 1870, supplied another source of extremely high-priced credit. They often charged interest rates ranging from 6 to 40 percent a month, and became known as "Shylocks" who forclosed on mortgages and garnisheed wages. The term *loan shark* had come to be associated with all of those who charged excessive interest rates. There had been some experiments with so-called philanthropic and charitable loan societies, and a few employers had provided savings and loan facilities within their companies to help employees, but these well-meaning efforts had not met the felt

[8] *New York Times*, Nov. 25, 1949; William H. Wellen, "The Story of the Writing of the First Credit Union Law," *Pioneer*, XXIV (May–June, 1959), 2 and 40.

[9] Jay to Desjardins, Mar. 4, 1907; Claude R. Orchard to Elbert K. Watkins (regarding interview Orchard had with Pierre Jay), Dec. 6, 1949; *Cleveland Credit Unionist* (Sept., 1949), n.p.

need of the vast majority of moderate and low income families. Could, Jay reasoned, credit unions supply this need?[10]

In March, 1907, Jay suggested to Desjardins that it might be profitable for him to visit Levis to observe the operations of *les caisses populaires*. The meeting between Jay and Desjardins, however, was not held until July 19, 1908, and it occurred in Ottawa, not Levis. The meeting was a great success. Jay wrote Desjardins the next day that their conversation "was most enlightening, and practical, on points which were doubtful in my mind. For one thing it has determined me to go ahead and try to bring these banks to notice in the United States—a thing I have had in mind for a long time, but have always hitherto felt a bit uncertain about." [11]

On November 22, 1908, Desjardins was in Manchester, New Hampshire, at the invitation of Monsignor Pierre Hevey, the priest of Saint Mary's Parish, to organize a *caisse populaire* among the Franco-American Catholics. Desjardins notified Jay that he was in the United States and suggested that he might visit Massachusetts. Jay immediately invited Desjardins to Boston, telling him that he wished to invite "certain persons" to meet him.[12] Desjardins arrived in Boston on November 24 and met with Jay and a group of "public-spirited citizens," among whom were Filene, Howard Coonley, Judge Abraham Cohen, Max Mitchell, Felix Vorenberg, and Henry B. Dennison. Desjardins told the group of his experiences in Quebec, explained the operation of *les caisses populaires*, and discussed with the Bostonians ways in which similar institutions could be introduced in Massachusetts. As one of the participants in the meeting later explained, "realizing the necessity of correcting the loan shark evil, they got together for the purpose of discussing ways and means to create legislation that would provide for small people's banks where a man of good character in modest circumstances could borrow money at reasonable rates of interest." [13]

As the bank commissioner of Massachusetts, Jay was required to submit an annual report to the legislature on the operation of his department. On December 15, 1908, he mailed a letter to about 150 major manufacturers in the state, telling them that he wished to include information about agencies "stimulating thrift," other than legally chartered

[10] David J. Gilbert, Walter S. Hilborn, and Geoffrey May, *Small Loan Legislation* (New York: Russell Sage Foundation, 1932), pp. 53–54, *passim*.

[11] Jay to Desjardins, Mar. 4, 1907, and July 20, 1908.

[12] Jay to Desjardins, Nov. 23, 1908; Desjardins to Jay, Nov. 23, 1908.

[13] "Broadcast by Felix Vorenberg, Former President and One of the Founders of Credit Unions in Massachusetts," June 24, 1933, mimeographed.

banks and trust companies. "Several employers of labor accept small deposits from their employees and allow interest thereon in order to encourage them to save," Jay wrote, "while in a number of cases the employees have formed associations among themselves, with remarkable success, to encourage saving and to provide their members with small temporary loans at reasonable rates." Jay asked the recipients of his letter to notify him if any such agencies existed in their firms, and what they thought about "the desirability of encouraging the organization of such associations, supplementary to, but of a smaller and more personal nature than, the savings and cooperative banks?" [14]

Jay received replies from only a few employers, but he was convinced that some sort of institution along the line of the *caisse populaire* was desirable in Massachusetts. Therefore, he appended to his annual report, a section which he called "Unauthorized Banking." Jay stated that some department stores allowed customers to deposit savings with them, usually paying 4 percent interest. Depositors were allowed to use the money for purchases or they could withdraw the money as they wanted it. Jay also discovered other types of credit agencies. These included a large number of stamp and school saving plans operating principally among children; eight cases in which manufacturers and other large employers received and allowed interest on deposits of employees; and five instances in which employees of a corporation had organized themselves into a "savings and loan association" which received deposits of its members and invested them in stocks and bonds, or in loans to members.

However helpful the practice of "in-factory banking" might have been, Jay did not think it a substitute for employees forming their own credit associations. He cited the Globe Savings and Loan Association, organized in 1892 and limited to employees of the *Boston Globe,* as a highly successful organization. It had been formed because employees had no place to borrow money except from loan sharks or corporations that loaned money on assignment of wages. Therefore, an employee-owned and -operated association would free employees from the clutches of loan sharks and remove the task of handling wage assignments from the employer. By January 1, 1909, the Globe Savings and Loan Association had loaned its members over $45,000, usually in amounts ranging from $1 to $25. Out of 600 employees, 444 were members, and they had deposits of $53,319 in the Association.

[14] Jay to Treasurer of ———, Dec. 15, 1908, printed.

Such an association gave ample evidence of the value of cooperative lending and savings institutions. As Jay put it:

The success of these voluntary associations as agencies, both for the stimulation of thrift and for the loaning of money to those who need to borrow, raises the question whether it would not be wise to provide by law for some form of organization through which persons of moderate means in favorable localities might associate themselves for these purposes, after the manner of the credit unions and people's banks of the European countries, India and Canada. These institutions have for their object the accumulation of savings among, and the extension of credit to, their members.

As to Massachusetts, he wrote:

What are known in Massachusetts as "cooperative banks," and elsewhere throughout the country as "building and loan associations," are excellent examples of the success of cooperation between savers and borrowers in an important but limited field. Their members are almost entirely salary and wage earners, who have joined together for systematic saving and for the owning of their homes. But inasmuch as all of their loans are secured, either on real estate or on the cash value of their shares, there is no need for selecting the members, no scrutiny is made of the object of loans made on the cash value of shares, and but little interest is taken by the members in the management of the institution. Furthermore they are of no service to those who have neither real estate nor shares as security, many of whom undoubtedly have legitimate need for loans. The existence of various individual and corporate loaners in every city and in many towns of the Commonwealth is indisputable evidence that there is a demand for loans which is not being supplied by existing banking institutions. Although some of the borrowing may be improvident, there can be but little doubt that much of it is the borrowing that comes of necessity.

Jay concluded by recommending that the legislature pass a law providing for the organization of credit unions under proper restrictions and supervision.[15]

Meanwhile, Jay invited Desjardins back to Boston to assist in drafting such a law. Remaining for several days as a house guest of Jay, Desjardins and his host, along with James F. Curtis, an assistant in the office of Attorney General Dana Malone, drafted the first credit union bill.[16]

[15] Massachusetts, Bank Commissioner, *Annual Report* (1908), Part I, *Relating to Savings Banks, Institutions for Savings, Trust Companies and Foreign Banking Corporations,* Public Document no. 8 (Boston: Wright & Potter Printing Co., 1909), pp. xlix, li, liii, and liv.

[16] Jay to Desjardins, Jan. 30, 1909; Wellen, "The Story of the Writing of the First Credit Union Law," p. 40.

On December 16, 1908, Jay passed on an invitation to Desjardins from the secretary of the Twentieth Century Club who wanted the Canadian to address that organization on February 20. Desjardins accepted the invitation, but on January 30, Jay broadened Desjardins's mission by inviting him to Boston on February 19 to testify before the Committee on Banks and Banking of the Massachusetts legislature. The committee, Jay stated, would "consider the question of whether it would be advisable to pass a law on the subject of cooperative banks in Massachusetts." [17]

The hearing before the Banking Committee occurred on February 19. Among the committee members was Calvin Coolidge of Northampton. Officers of several commercial and saving banks, as well as cooperative banks, testified at the hearings. They did not oppose a law permitting credit unions because they said such institutions would serve a different clientele, thus not competing with their businesses. Such institutions, moreover, would do much to help eliminate the high-rate moneylenders in the city. Desjardins was the principal witness, telling the committee of his institutions in Canada and answering questions. Filene and Vorenberg also made brief remarks. [18]

The Banking Committee encouraged Jay to draft a bill. By March 2, the bank commissioner had completed a revised draft and sent a copy to Desjardins for his suggestions. At the same time, Jay told Desjardins that he was resigning his position to accept a job with a bank in New York City, "so that it will be necessary for me to hurry the matter up in the Legislature, provided the Committee should consider the bill favorably, in order to make some progress on it before I leave." Desjardins did make some suggestions for revisions of the proposed draft and it was finally ready for submission to the Banking Committee. [19]

The legislative process went smoothly. On March 3, the executive committee of the Boston Merchants Association endorsed the credit union bill, and the Senate Banking Committee reported it out unanimously. The bank commissioner asked Filene, if he approved the measure, to write letters to his senator and representatives endorsing it. Filene immediately responded, telling his representatives: "As a large employer I have long felt that some provision should be made by which people of small means can, in case of necessity or distress, borrow at reasonable rates of interest and under thoroughly honest and fair conditions." Mean-

---

[17] Jay to Desjardins, Dec. 16, 1908; Jan. 30, 1909.
[18] Wellen, "The Story of the Writing of the First Credit Union Law," p. 40.
[19] Jay to Desjardins, Mar. 2 and 11, 1909.

while, Filene told Jay that if the law were enacted, he was "going to see to it that the advantages of such associations are made known throughout the state." [20]

The Massachusetts Credit Union Act became law on April 15, 1909. It defined a credit union as "a cooperative association formed for the purpose of promoting thrift among its members." The law required that at least seven persons apply for a charter to organize a credit union. Once incorporated, a credit union could receive the savings of members in the form of purchased shares or deposits, and make loans. The bylaws of most societies required members to pay a small entrance fee and buy one five-dollar share of stock to be paid for in installments. Credit unions were to be governed democratically with each member entitled to only one vote regardless of the number of shares owned. The members elected a board of directors which in turn chose a president and other officers. Members also elected a credit committee and a supervisory committee. The credit committee had to approve all loans, which must be for useful and beneficial purposes. Neither the directors nor members of the committees could receive compensation. Theirs was voluntary work.

Massachusetts was the first state in the nation to pass a general statute for the incorporation of credit unions. However, it just missed the distinction of having passed the *first* credit union law. On April 6, the New Hampshire legislature enacted a special act allowing the incorporation of the Saint Mary's Cooperative Credit Association.[21] Such an act had been necessary in order to give legal status to the credit union organized at Manchester by Desjardins some months earlier.

Even though Jay was now vice-president of the Bank of the Manhattan Company in New York City, he continued to follow closely the early developments in credit unionism. During the summer of 1909 he toured Europe and had two talks with Henry Wolff in London. Jay also informed Desjardins that the new bank commissioner of Massachusetts, Arthur Chapin, intended to issue a pamphlet explaining credit unions and giving advice on how to organize them. Chapin asked Jay to help write the pamphlet, and Jay in turn requested Desjardins's assistance. Jay continued to promote the credit union idea through correspondence

[20] James A. McKibben, secretary of Boston Merchants Assoc., to Filene, Mar. 3, 1909; Jay to Desjardins, Mar. 11, 1909; Jay to Filene, Mar. 23, 1909; *Acts and Resolves by the General Court of Massachusetts, 1909* (1909), chap. 419; Filene to Representative Thomas J. Grady, Mar. 26, 1909.

[21] New Hampshire, "An Act to Incorporate the St. Mary's Co-operative Credit Association," approved April 6, 1909.

and by distributing literature, such as a "blue book" containing the testimony Desjardins had presented before a Canadian legislative committee two years earlier. He passed out some of this literature at a meeting of the American Bankers' Association in Chicago in the fall of 1909.[22]

Jay took a rather conservative approach to "people's banking." When a Springfield, Massachusetts, publisher proposed that a publicity drive be undertaken to stimulate the organization of credit unions in many parts of the United States, Jay replied: "It is very desirable to have interest in this sort of banking stimulated, but I question the wisdom of getting a lot of associations started all over the country by people who do not know very much about the subject and without any state regulation or supervision to guide them. Nothing would give the system a blacker eye than to have it taken up generally, and then to have a lot of the associations fail." Jay wanted to prepare a model set of bylaws, written by himself and Commissioner Chapin, to guide the operations of new credit unions and to help them get started on sound principles. But, above all, he believed that the institution "is something which is going to be of use in the country, and I want to be sure that it progresses not too fast and always along lines which are conservative and which have proved satisfactory in their merits." [23] Jay need not have worried about credit unions springing up "like Topsy" around the United States, nor even in Massachusetts. With no agency actively promoting the movement, word about, and interest in, the new credit institutions spread slowly.

Filene had not yet become actively engaged in promoting the organization of credit unions, as he was in the midst of one of his first major public service efforts, Boston-1915. Enlisting the aid of Lincoln Steffens, the muckraking journalist, Filene set out to mobilize interests in Boston in an effort to conquer all the multitudinous problems affecting that urban community as well as most other cities of the country. The Boston-1915 movement organized leaders from all strata of Boston life into committees which were to take the lead in solving problems of slums, public health, crime, weaknesses in democratic government, and even to encourage cultural life. Although Filene favored the principle of cooperative credit, he now saw credit unions only as one additional device that could help a major segment of the population in his beloved city on the Charles. In October, 1909, he wrote Desjardins requesting him to prepare statistical tables and photographs illustrating the operation of *les caisses populaires.*

[22] Jay to Desjardins, July 3 and 23; Sept. 23, 1909.
[23] Jay to Herbert Myrick, Oct. 1, 1909.

Filene said he wanted to display this material at an exposition launching Boston-1915. Other than that, about all that Filene did during the first year that the new credit union law was in effect was to bring the matter to the attention of Paul U. Kellogg, the editor of the *Survey*.[24]

Without individuals or agencies actively promoting credit union development, the movement got off to a slow beginning. During 1910, only two credit unions actually came into existence. Like the Saint Mary's Parish credit union in Manchester, New Hampshire, however, the first credit union in Massachusetts owed more to the work of Desjardins than to those who later came to figure prominently in the United States development. Even before the Massachusetts law was enacted, Father J. B. Parent, a priest in Saint Jean Baptiste Parish in Lynn, invited Desjardins to address a gathering of his parishioners about *la caisse populaire*. The groundwork for a credit union was laid at that time and after the law was passed, Father Parent appeared before the Board of Bank Incorporation, on April 13, 1910, and applied for a charter. The charter was granted and *La Caisse Populaire* Saint Jean Baptiste began business on October 7, 1910. Like so many of the early credit unions, Saint Jean Baptiste began simply. Its capital on opening day of business was only $85. The organization was housed in the church's rectory and all duties were assumed by volunteers, Father Parent and Sister Marie Leocadia of Jesus. At the end of the first year of operation, the credit union had 105 members, paid up shares of $4,643, and outstanding loans of $4,048.[25]

By the summer of 1910 the Office of the Bank Commissioner had a pamphlet on credit unions, prepared mainly by Jay and Desjardins, ready to send out to all who asked for it. During that summer, Bank Commissioner Chapin also visited Desjardins in Quebec to inspect the operation of *les caisses populaires*.[26] In the fall Desjardins accepted an invitation to spend some time in Massachusetts organizing credit unions, principally among parish groups. On October 7, he spoke before a small meeting of the Women's Educational and Industrial Union. Not only did Desjardins visit the credit union he founded in Lynn, but he also expected that new organizations would result from his visits to New Bedford, Fall River, and Taunton.

Desjardins was assisted in his organizational efforts by the Industrial Relations Committee of the Boston Chamber of Commerce, of which

[24] Filene to Kellogg, Aug. 16, 1909; Filene to Jay, Aug. 16, 1909.

[25] "St. Jean-Baptiste Credit Union: The Oldest Credit Union in the United States," *Pioneer* (May–June, 1959), pp. 13–14; *Lynn* (Mass.) *Item,* Jan. 27, 1967.

[26] Jay to Desjardins, May 13 and Aug. 20, 1910.

Filene was chairman. John W. Plaisted, secretary of the committee, discussed strategy with Desjardins during the latter's visit to Boston. Plaisted reported to Filene that in Boston itself, a group of one hundred Italians were about ready to organize a credit union. Some of the prospective members had had experience with people's banks in Italy, thus providing competent leadership for the new organization. Plaisted emphasized that in the Boston vicinity emphasis should be placed upon showing how the new credit unions, honestly and carefully managed, could help people of small means. Besides this, of course, support should be given to organizing credit unions in other cities where Desjardins had already aroused some interest. At this time Plaisted believed that organizational work would be most successful if it were concentrated in communities and neighborhoods rather than in factories and industrial establishments. Some credit union supporters believed that Catholic parishes offered an especially fertile organizational field.[27]

Of paramount importance to the development of credit unions in Boston, and again as a direct result of Desjardins's autumn visit, was the organization of the Industrial Credit Union, sponsored by the Women's Educational and Industrial Union of Boston. Caroline Cook, an official of that organization, corresponded with Desjardins as early as 1909 concerning the purposes and experiences of the people's banks of Quebec. The Industrial Credit Union was granted a broad charter, enabling it to accept members from city residents and those working in the greater Boston area. It therefore had a very heterogeneous and cosmopolitan membership. Men and women of known honesty and industry were invited to become members, and, because "personal knowledge of the character of the members is essential," membership was restricted "to those of whom personal knowledge is possessed." In order to join the credit union, a person had to pay a fifty-cent admission fee and subscribe to at least one five-dollar share, which was payable in small weekly or monthly installments. Loans were limited to small amounts and could be repaid in installments.

The purposes for which loans would be made to members indicated the attitudes and objectives of the early credit unions. One industrial credit union announced that it sought to help members "get on a cash basis by paying up all indebtedness"; to assist members to buy tools or to begin a business; to encourage cash purchases and buying in larger quantities in order to save money; and to provide funds for education and practical training. Finally, the credit union was designed to permit

[27] Plaisted to Filene, Oct. 7, 1910.

borrowers to get funds at a low rate of interest "from an organization interested in their welfare and thus keep out of clutches of loan sharks and all other lending corporations organized for their own selfish profit." During the first ten years of its operation, the Industrial Credit Union loaned $330,000 to 2,210 borrowers. During that entire period it failed to collect only $292.43, a remarkable record which indicated that the credit union's insistence on knowing the character of its members produced good results.[28]

During 1911 the credit union movement in Massachusetts continued to develop slowly. For a time the Boston Chamber of Commerce provided the main organizational impetus. But in May, the Retail Trade Board of the Chamber of Commerce assumed an active role in promoting credit unions. Plaisted informed Filene that the board had appointed a committee, with Bank Commissioner Chapin as chairman, which would devote about six weeks organizing credit unions throughout the state. In June, H. L. Dillingham, secretary of the Credit Union Committee of the Chamber of Commerce, addressed a letter to state employers, inviting them to a meeting on June 8 to hear Desjardins explain the credit union system. But only seventeen credit unions were organized during 1911, and they served only 1,623 citizens in the entire state. These credit unions had assets of only $25,942, and shares averaged some $12 per member. Credit union development was, if anything, even slower in 1912 and 1913. Only nine credit unions were organized in 1912, and by the next year, the state had a mere thirty-four associations. There were only 4,577 citizens in the state holding credit union memberships, and total assets had reached a modest $180,923.[29] This was not an encouraging record.

Credit unions were not alone in attempting to combat the evils of exorbitant interest rates. Among its other aims and activities, the Russell Sage Foundation sought to deal with credit problems faced by the poor. Incorporated in 1907, the foundation was endowed with a gift of $10 million from Margaret Olivia Sage, widow of the multimillionaire Russell Sage. The foundation strove to improve "social and living conditions in the United States" through research, publication, and education.

In the summer of 1909 the foundation financed exploratory studies by Clarence W. Wassam and Arthur H. Ham in "the almost unexplored field of the hardships suffered by persons of small means when they

[28] *Ibid.*, June 2, 1911.

[29] Joseph L. Snider, *Credit Unions in Massachusetts* (Cambridge: Harvard University Press, 1959), Table I, p. 9, and Table II, p. 11.

needed a small loan." The evidence gathered by Wassam and Ham indicated that unregulated lenders exacted a heavy toll from borrowers in exorbitant interest rates and personal misery. The foundation became familiar with the work of the fourteen companies in the country, including the Provident Loan Society of New York, that were "philanthropic" in the sense that they loaned money at reasonable rates on chattel mortgages or pledges of personal property. These companies had joined together in June, 1909, and formed the National Federation of Remedial Loan Associations. The foundation decided to make a thorough study of what was being done by these organizations and thus employed Ham to direct the work. It created the Division of Remedial Loans in October, 1910.

The National Federation of Remedial Loan Associations turned over its executive functions to Ham and his division. The major tasks undertaken by the division during its first few years were the promotion of new loan associations, the improvement of those already in existence, the initiation of legislation in many states providing for the licensing and supervision of small loan companies, and the establishment of uniform interest rates. In addition to these activities, the foundation carried on campaigns "to enlighten the public as to the methods of loan sharks," utilizing public meetings, newspapers, magazines, and even a motion picture.[30]

As useful and important as these activities were, they did not do much to meet the special financial needs of low income persons. Therefore, the foundation engaged Cary W. Hayes "to make a study of the employers' loan funds and employees' cooperative savings and loan associations in the United States." Hayes began his work by contacting Pierre Jay who was now in New York, and Jay suggested that he write to Desjardins for information. On June 21, 1912, Hayes asked Desjardins for a copy of the Canadian reports on *caisses populaires* and for information about cooperative credit societies in other countries. He mentioned the credit union movement in Massachusetts, saying that it had advantages over similar societies in other states because credit unions were incorporated under the state banking law. Hayes emphasized that the foundation's study was preparatory to a campaign of expanding the organization of such societies. "If further study should justify it," he wrote, "it may mean a considerable extension of the Credit Union Movement in the United States." Desjardins replied promptly to Hayes's inquiry, sending published ma-

[30] John M. Glenn, Lilian Brandt, and F. E. Andrews, *Russell Sage Foundation*, Vol. I (New York: Russell Sage Foundation, 1947), p. 146.

terials and his own comments, and offering to help the foundation in its efforts to deal with the small loan problem.[31]

In July, 1912, Ham and John M. Glenn, general director of the foundation, conferred with Desjardins at Levis. This conference was followed by Desjardins's visit to New York in October to speak before groups interested in credit unions. Those meetings, Glenn wrote Desjardins, "inspired us to continue a consideration of the possibility of forming such associations in the U.S.A. and also to make us to proceed with greater caution, in order that we may be sure of taking the proper steps, if we decide to go into an active campaign." Ham seemed even more certain that the foundation would actively join the movement, as he wrote Desjardins: "We shall attempt to secure the passage of a satisfactory law in this state this year, to be followed by the organization of a credit union in a selected community for the purpose of experiment." [32]

Desjardins expanded his New York trip into visits to New Bedford, Fall River, Boston, and Lynn, Massachusetts. He also had an interview with the governor of Rhode Island who showed interest in credit unions and asked Desjardins to send him a copy of the Massachusetts law. While in Fall River, Desjardins himself organized yet another credit union. The Canadian offered the Russell Sage Foundation any help he could give it in its credit union campaign, saying he "would be exceedingly sorrow [sic] if you were to leave me aside, for then it would mean to me that my assistance would be worthless." [33]

In addition to its other interests, the Russell Sage Foundation became concerned about enacting a credit union law in New York. In November, 1912, Ham wrote Desjardins that before the foundation attempted to draft a bill and have it introduced in the legislature, he was going to visit Massachusetts to consult with the bank commissioner and other persons interested in the movement. Following the trip, Ham prepared the first New York credit union bill with the aid of Pierre Jay, Desjardins, and Leonard G. Robinson. Robinson was the general manager of the Jewish Agricultural and Industrial Aid Society which, beginning in 1911, had organized eighteen cooperative loan societies among farmers in New York, New Jersey, Connecticut, and Massachusetts.[34]

[31] Hayes to Desjardins, June 21, 1912.

[32] Ham to Desjardins, Aug. 27 and Oct. 25, 1912; Glenn to Desjardins, Oct. 23, 1912.

[33] Desjardins to Ham, Oct. 30, 1912.

[34] Ham to Desjardins, Nov. 11, 1912; Glenn, Brandt and Andrews, *Russell Sage Foundation*, pp. 147–48.

Before the bill could be introduced into the legislature, Senator Franklin D. Roosevelt of Dutchess County presented a measure providing for the incorporation of "purely agricultural credit unions," which was almost an exact duplicate of the rural credit union law in Massachusetts. Ham urged Roosevelt to broaden his bill to provide for both rural and urban credit unions. Desjardins approved of Ham's approach, saying that restrictions "are of a nature to damage ultimately the movement without any good at all." Ham decided, however, not to interfere with Roosevelt's agricultural cooperative bank bill because he believed that a regular credit union bill would be passed if it were introduced separately.[35]

The New York credit union bill was introduced in mid-March, 1913, and became law in May. During the hearings and debates, Roosevelt and the other sponsors of the agricultural bill agreed to withdraw their proposal and to support the Russell Sage Foundation measure.[36] Soon after passage of the law, the foundation began to receive numerous inquiries from corporations about organizing credit unions among their employees. The foundation decided that the organization of any credit unions should wait until a uniform set of bylaws had been drafted and published along with the provisions of the new law.[37] The first credit union in New York was organized in January, 1914, by employees of Bing and Bing, Inc. During the remainder of the year the foundation prepared a plan for credit union organization for the Mayor's Committee on Unemployment in New York City. Even though the foundation continued to take no active part in organizing credit unions, by September, 1915, nineteen credit unions were operating under the law, eleven of them being in New York City. This almost spontaneous development led Ham to conclude that "one or two experienced organizers could succeed in a comparatively brief period in bringing about the organization of a substantial number of credit unions." [38]

While support by the Russell Sage Foundation offered some general encouragement, the development of credit unions in Massachusetts languished. The movement needed an organization to actively promote the development of credit unions in the state. Reliance on informal committees, the bank commissioner's office, or even occasional forays into the

---

[35] Ham to Desjardins, Feb. 21, 1913, and Mar. 7, 1913; Desjardins to Ham, Feb. 24, 1913.

[36] Account of Carol D. Coombs in Roy F. Bergengren, *Cooperative Banking* (New York: Beekman Hill Press, 1931), p. 78.

[37] Ham to Desjardins, Sept. 30, 1913.

[38] Glenn, Brandt, and Andrews, *Russell Sage Foundation,* pp. 148–49.

state by Desjardins were not enough. The Greater Boston Credit Union, formed by a group of "wealthy, public-spirited" businessmen in 1911, had never functioned successfully. Consequently, on January 7, 1914, Filene and several of the organizers of the Greater Boston Credit Union—including Felix Vorenberg, a jewelry retailer; Max Mitchell, vice-president of the Cosmopolitan Trust Company; Summit Hecht, a wool importer; and David A. Ellis, a wool importer—formed the Massachusetts Credit Union. It was incorporated by the bank commissioner on January 22. The object of the association was to promote thrift among the people, especially in the Greater Boston area, to encourage the formation of credit unions, to give aid to the credit union movement, and to loan money to individual members, as well as to local credit unions. "The spirit of the corporation," said the charter, "is cooperative." In short, the new association was a credit union in its own right, but it was also to act as a central agency to help other credit unions, and it would assume responsibility for credit union promotion through publicity and organizational activities.

To become a member of the MCU, a person or a credit union submitted an application to the board of directors. Once accepted, the member paid a small entrance fee and subscribed for at least one share of stock which cost $5. Share investments could not be withdrawn before the end of five years without permission of the board of directors, except in the case of a member's death. Members could also make deposits in the MCU in sums of not less than $100 at any one time. Deposits could be withdrawn upon request, although the directors could require thirty days' notice of intention to withdraw funds. Interest on deposits was payable semiannually.

The capital, deposits, and surplus funds of the credit union were either to be lent to members or deposited in saving banks, trust companies, or national banks. The major purpose of the monies, however, was for loans to members. A borrower applied for a loan to the credit committee, a majority of which had to approve, and each application had to state the purpose for which the loan was being sought. Preference was given to requests for smaller loans. The rules provided a fine of two cents for each dollar due and unpaid on the first day of each month. A member could be expelled if he did not carry out his agreements with the cooperative, if he were convicted of a criminal offense, or if he deceived the corporation as to how he used the borrowed money. Reflecting the early concept of the credit union as an association of good citizens, a member also could be expelled "whose private life is a source of scandal, or who habitually neglects to pay his debts." [39]

The MCU opened its offices at 78 Devonshire Street in Boston within a few weeks after incorporation. It chose attorney William J. Stanton as its full-time general manager. Felix Vorenberg was elected president of the board of directors. After the first two months of business, February and March, 1914, $9,405 worth of shares had been purchased and there were $5,500 in deposits.

Stanton spent most of his time initially calling on officers of corporations, talking with employees, and meeting with other groups to promote the organization of credit unions. But progress was meager. Stanton very early found that "paternalistic" employers were a barrier to the organization of credit unions. One company official told Stanton that his company had made a practice of lending money to its employees at a low rate of interest and intended to continue doing so. Another executive said that whenever a worthy employee needed money, he would advance it without interest.[40]

At the first meeting of the MCU board of directors on April 1, 1914, Stanton was authorized to contract the printing and to stock various credit union business forms. These supplies would be sold at retail to small credit unions whose business did not warrant buying such supplies at wholesale. Another item of business was admitting the Lawrence Credit Union and the Salem Investment and Credit Union to membership. One of the major questions in the minds of the board members was whether the MCU could accept the deposits of other credit unions in the state. Augustus Thorndike, Chapin's successor as bank commissioner, wrote that, while he was not wholly satisfied that such a practice was absolutely legal, he would not object.

Three weeks later a joint meeting was held between the MCU board and the supervisory and credit committees which had been set up. The meeting had been called principally because the credit committee was ready to begin making loans and desired advice on procedures. It was agreed that interest rates should not exceed 6 percent a year and that the maximum loan would be $500, unless security was put up by the bor-

---

[39] Massachusetts Credit Union, "Bylaws of Massachusetts Credit Union," n.p., n.d. (hereafter all files pertaining to the Massachusetts Credit Union are in the BMML collection unless noted otherwise).

[40] Report of General Manager to Board of Directors, Massachusetts Credit Union, April 1, 1914.

rower in excess of that amount. The members of the three committees agreed that no distinction in granting loans be made between organized credit unions and individual applicants.[41]

After the joint meeting adjourned, the board of directors went into executive session. Stanton informed the board that he had attended a conference with the president of the Shawmut National Bank and two officials of the Chamber of Commerce. These men approved the credit union idea, but, according to Stanton, they thought "the work should be contributed to by a more interracial set of financiers and business men." They expressed appreciation of the "philanthropic and intelligent work of the gentlemen now constituting this organization" and did not think that it was a racial organization. Their suggestion, however, was that the board of directors be expanded to include "a number of people of other than the Jewish faith," so that it would "be easier to make the work general and to reach the outside public." Stanton told the directors that these sentiments were also shared by workers inside the credit union movement.[42]

This concern over Jewish domination of the MCU was not an expression of anti-Semitism, but a recognition that people of other faiths might be reluctant to become involved in an organization whose leadership was concentrated in a single religious faith. Filene's own interest in the credit union movement, he later explained, was partly motivated "because I wanted to fight an age old prejudice that all Jews were usurers." [43] A pamphlet published by the Massachusetts Credit Union Association, successor to the MCU, stated that the work of developing credit unions in Massachusetts "was started, financed and directed almost entirely by Jewish men who believed this among the most fundamental methods of helping their fellow men and who were thus effectively answering the historic accusation of Jewish usury." [44] Rabbi Harry Levi of Boston's Temple Israel declared that support of credit unions "helps to make the people realize that not all Jews are alike, that not all are bad, that not all are money lenders or usurers, that there are Jews who are ready to serve, to help, to give, to lend, not for what they can get out of it

---

[41] Minutes of Conference between Board of Directors, the Supervisory Committee, and the Credit Committee, MCU, April 24, 1914.

[42] Minutes, Executive Session, MCU Board, April 24, 1914.

[43] Filene marginalia on memorandum from Bergengren to Filene, April 13, 1933.

[44] "Massachusetts Credit Unions," pamphlet published by the Massachusetts Credit Union Association, ca. 1917.

but for the good they can thus do." [45] In any event, there was no desire to confine the credit union movement to the Jewish community. Therefore, the board of directors voted to appoint a committee, including Filene, to consider increasing the number of members on the board.[46] Broadening the leadership base of the credit union movement, however, did not come quickly.

MCU's organizational work made only meager headway. During April, Stanton organized only one new credit union, although four other authorizations were issued by the bank commissioner. Stanton reported, however, that his work would probably lead to the organization of twelve additional credit unions, and that he had made numerous worthwhile contacts. He did some follow-up work and observed several credit unions of different types that were already in operation.[47]

Most of the few credit unions in operation had some connection with men who were participating actively in the MCU. The Cosmopolitan Credit Union was organized among the employees of the Cosmopolitan Trust Company, whose president was Max Mitchell, treasurer of MCU; the Novelty Credit Union was formed by the employees of Felix Vorenberg, the president of MCU; and the employees of Nathan Sallinger, a member of the board, organized the Regnillas Credit Union. Although Stanton admitted that results seemed meager, he told the board in June, 1914, "the seed is being sown widely and the harvest is bound to come in due time." [48]

But people simply did not seem much interested in credit unions, and the summer of 1914 saw no significant progress in the movement. Although Stanton continued to present the idea to many individuals and groups, he met more rebuffs than favorable responses. He called his contact with the Boston Branch of the Remington Typewriter Company "a most decided failure." The manager told Stanton that he could not support credit unions because he did not think a man should ever borrow for personal reasons. Further, this executive said, if an employee became involved with a loan shark and his salary were assigned or attached, he would discharge him. One bright spot for the future, however, was Stanton's contact with postal employees, among whom there was a saying

[45] "The Work of the Massachusetts Credit Union," pamphlet published by the MCU, ca. 1916.

[46] Minutes, Executive Session, MCU Board, April 24, 1914.

[47] Report of General Manager to MCU Board, May 6, 1914.

[48] Ibid., June 3, 1914.

that a man could never become a member of the postal service until his name was on the books of some loan shark. During July, Stanton continued to make contacts, one of which was with the Boston School Teachers' Association. He also talked with leaders of the Armenian, Syrian, Polish, Greek, and Italian communities of Boston, but he still failed to generate any significant support for credit unions. By early September Stanton admitted that his summer's work had ended in failure. Moreover, war had broken out in Europe, and Stanton reported that the resulting "dullness of trade which it has caused may be unfavorable." [49]

To provide Stanton with some needed help, Max Mitchell engaged the services of Bert M. Harris, an energetic young man connected with the Roxbury Credit Union who had a good command of Yiddish. Mitchell agreed to pay Harris out of his own pocket and contribute his services to MCU to organize credit unions. Harris began work in November and by December he had organized one new credit union and had made many promising contacts. The MCU board voted to reimburse Mitchell the sixty-five dollars he had paid Harris during December, and to engage him for another month at the same salary. [50]

But Stanton ended the year by acknowledging that "the Unions have not been organized as fast as I expected or hoped for, but with the hard times and the European war with the general uncertainty attending it, I believe as good work has been done as could be fairly expected, and the work has been so thoroughly organized that very large returns may be fairly expected in the very near future." [51] During the year a mere sixteen new credit unions had been organized in the entire state, only part of which were the result of MCU's organizational work. In addition there were five liquidations, thus leaving only forty-five credit unions operating in Massachusetts at the end of 1914, four and one-half years after the law permitting credit unions had been passed. [52]

The Massachusetts Credit Union did not limit its efforts simply to organizing new credit unions, and this fact may explain in part why the development in Massachusetts was not more rapid. In a way, the MCU was the forerunner of the state credit union league, except that an individual credit union did not become a dues-paying associate in the MCU,

[49] *Ibid.,* July 1, 1914, Aug. 5, 1914, Sept. 2, 1914.
[50] Minutes, MCU Board, Dec. 27, 1914; Report of General Manager to MCU Board, Nov. 30, 1914.
[51] Report of General Manager to MCU Board, Dec. 27, 1914.
[52] Snider, *Credit Unions in Massachusetts,* Table X, p. 27.

but subscribed to shares on the same basis as an individual. The MCU attempted to provide a number of services for individual credit unions, such as stocking and selling business forms, providing advice and counsel in organizing and operating credit unions, maintaining contacts with state authorities on behalf of credit unions, assisting credit unions having difficulties in their operations or in danger of liquidation, and sponsoring general meetings of credit union officials at which matters of common interest could be discussed.

Because of its broader responsibilities, in May, 1914, Stanton suggested that the MCU should discourage loans to individuals and that applicants should be referred to other existing credit unions.[53] Some members objected to this recommendation because a few individuals were already members, while others raised the question as to whether it might be illegal under the society's charter to deny loans to individuals. Nevertheless, the following month the board voted to make no further individual loans. To serve this particular need a special committee organized the Trader's Credit Union on July 11, which was headquartered in the offices of the MCU. The Trader's Credit Union made loans chiefly to Jewish merchants in Boston and vicinity.[54]

The leaders of MCU thought of their organization as the guiding force behind the entire movement in Massachusetts, or as Filene put it, "the Massachusetts Credit Union as the mother union." [55] Thus, its work was to encourage the formation of individual credit unions, build public support for the entire movement, and to act as the guiding, coordinating force for credit unionism in the state. To achieve these goals, leaders of the MCU sought to persuade the various credit unions in the state to become affiliated with MCU. By the end of 1914, sixteen of the forty-five credit unions in the state were affiliated with MCU. Before a credit union was admitted to membership, it had to pass an inspection of its organization and business operations. MCU turned down the application of one credit union, and in several other cases, applications for membership were tabled until the board was satisfied that a particular credit union was operating according to the standards of the MCU.[56]

The MCU also assumed some responsibility for aiding credit unions to

[53] Report of General Manager to MCU Board, May 6, 1914.

[54] Minutes, Special Meeting of Members, MCU, June 15, 1914; Minutes, MCU Committee on Bylaws for the Traders' Credit Union, May 7, 1914; Traders' Credit Union Circular, n.d.; Minutes, MCU Board, Nov. 30, 1914.

[55] *Boston Post*, July 8, 1915.

[56] Minutes, MCU Board, April 1, 1914, and Dec. 27, 1914.

operate successfully. Soon after organization of the MCU, Stanton heard that a credit union organized in 1911 was preparing to liquidate because of numerous difficulties. Stanton straightened out the accounts and discussed ways of stimulating interest in the credit union so that new capital would be subscribed. With this help, the credit union assumed a new life. In another case a credit union in Lynn applied for admission into the MCU but was rejected by the board because of a bad report on its condition. Upon investigation, Stanton found that this credit union had been organized for over a year but that its affairs "were conducted in a very loose manner." Loans had been made freely and repayments were not prompt. Although the management was inexperienced, it was honest, and again Stanton made helpful suggestions.[57]

Intermittent contacts and advice by Stanton, however, was not the most ideal way to promote and teach good business practices among credit unions. Nor did occasional visits develop any sort of community interest among the individual organizations in the state. Therefore, early in the life of MCU, it sought to promote joint meetings of officers and representatives of credit unions. In September, 1914, Stanton told the board that he was arranging for a state convention of credit unions to be held during the week of September 23. When it turned out that arrangements could not be made for a state-wide meeting, Stanton invited the presidents, clerks, and treasurers of the various credit unions to meet in his office on December 10. Representatives of fourteen credit unions attended and showed great interest in this type of meeting. So successful was the gathering that a conference for members of credit committees was called for December 31 to discuss all phases of credit union work.[58]

The first general state-wide meeting of credit unions in Massachusetts was finally held at the Boston City Club on April 27, 1915. There were two hundred persons present. Felix Vorenberg, who served as toastmaster at this dinner meeting, reported that there were then fifty credit unions operating in Massachusetts of which twenty-two were affiliated with the MCU. Following Vorenberg's remarks, Governor David I. Walsh lavishly praised the movement: "This movement is going to be of more benefit to the masses of the people than even the savings banks and the cooperative societies, for every banking door in the Commonwealth is barred to the man who wants to borrow $25 without security. That's the greatest thing about this movement, it reaches a class the banks cannot reach. It will help all." Mayor James Curley attacked the loan sharks

---

[57] Report of General Manager to MCU Board, April 1, 1914, and June 3, 1914.

[58] *Ibid.*, Sept. 2, 1914, and Dec. 27, 1914.

operating in his city, and reported that a great number of city employees were in the clutches of the moneylenders. He said that he had ordered all employees to get out of debt by the first of May or visit a credit union. Arthur Ham of the Russell Sage Foundation told his listeners that they were "witnessing the beginnings of a movement of tremendous importance which is destined within a brief period to sweep over this country." Filene made a few remarks about his own role in the movement. Near the end of the meeting, representatives of the Jewish, the Irish-Catholic, the French-Catholic, the Italian and the industrial groups discussed informally the aims and purposes of credit unions.[59]

The following day, Arthur Ham wrote Desjardins that "a great deal of enthusiasm was shown which augurs well for the development of the movement in Massachusetts." Desjardins replied: "I hope that the enthusiasm whereof you speak will not cause that organizing union to fall into the error of thinking and doing only dry business, forgetting the most important feature of the question, I mean the social and educating aspect of Credit Unions. I warn you, my dear friend, about this danger for your own movement in New York State. I am myself obliged to fight here and there even in Canada this most deplorable error." But Ham assured Desjardins that the "social and humanitarian aspects of the work" were not being neglected and that the meeting had generated "much enthusiasm." [60] So far there had been too little of that important ingredient. The dinner did give credit unions some publicity, as several newspapers carried accounts of the meeting. One editor commented that credit unions deserved encouragement and were getting it "from men whose influence counts." [61]

One of these men was Filene. Following the Boston meeting, Filene began to take a much more active role in promoting the credit union movement. Along with Bank Commissioner Thorndike and Stanton, he helped to draft a set of principles for the operation of new credit unions. The eight principles were that credit unions must organize on a cooperative basis; form an association of men not shares, limit each member's shares, and allow each member only one vote; rigidly exclude thriftless and improvident borrowing; admit to membership only honest and industrious men and women; restrict operations to small communities and groups; make small loans, with frequent partial repayments; permit

[59] *Boston Transcript,* April 28, 1915; Address of Arthur H. Ham to First Annual Dinner, Massachusetts Credit Union, Boston, April 27, 1915, typescript.
[60] Ham to Desjardins, April 28 and May 6, 1915; Desjardins to Ham, May 1, 1915.
[61] *Boston Post,* May 2, 1915.

character and industry to be the main basis of credit; and require prompt payment of loans.[62]

Filene fully realized that success of the credit union movement depended on development of the cooperative ideal. In other words, the spirit behind the organization and operation of credit unions must be different from that of ordinary profit-making businesses. At the same time, however, credit unions must pursue sound business practices. Nothing could hurt the development of the movement more than the failure of credit unions which would cause members to lose their savings. While credit unions had recognition from the state and enjoyed the active friendship and support of leading political figures, official support could evaporate quickly if politicians saw they were backing a risky venture. Filene believed, however, that if credit unions followed the eight basic principles which he, Stanton, and Thorndike had outlined, the movement would develop along healthy and useful lines.[63] But in the middle of 1915, there were few signs to encourage credit union supporters. So far credit union development had languished under disinterest and some opposition by those benefiting from loan shark practices. Credit unionism gained some support from the reformism of the Progressive era, but it never achieved the position of a major reform which commanded widespread backing. It required better leadership and different economic conditions to make credit unionism a significant force in the nation's economic life. These conditions were still far in the future.

[62] Filene's Secretary to Stanton, June 14, 1915.
[63] *Boston Post*, July 8, 1915.

CHAPTER III

High Hopes and False Starts

WHILE A FEW individuals, the Massachusetts Credit Union, and the Russell Sage Foundation were working to improve credit facilities for urban workers, a related movement was underway to provide cooperative credit for farmers. For many years farmers had complained about the lack of both long-term and short-term credit, as well as high interest rates. Neither private bankers nor government had taken any action to meet the genuine credit needs of farmers. Was cooperative credit on the order of that found in Europe the answer?

Fortunately for those who were looking to new solutions for this old problem, Theodore Roosevelt occupied the White House. Roosevelt had a deep sympathy for farmers and for agriculture as a way of life. Not only had the city-born Roosevelt come to know farmers and their problems through his western visits, but his contact with Sir Horace Plunkett, the great Irish cooperator, had convinced him that agricultural difficulties deserved special attention. In regard to the specific problem of agricultural credit, Filene, following his trip to India in 1907, had urged the president to study the question of cooperative credit. In order to deal with a wide range of rural problems Roosevelt established the Country Life Commission in 1908 under the chairmanship of Dean Liberty Hyde Bailey of the College of Agriculture at Cornell University.[1]

The Country Life Commission sent out questionnaires to more than 500,000 farmers and rural leaders, held thirty public hearings, conducted many special investigations, and issued its report on February 23, 1909. Among its many conclusions, the commission reported that it had found a "lack of any adequate system of agricultural credit." The commission recommended that "a method of cooperative credit would undoubtedly prove of great service." About the only concrete action taken by Roosevelt on the problem of credit before he left the White House, however,

[1] For an account of the background and work of the Rural Life Commission see Clayton L. Ellsworth, "Theodore Roosevelt's Country Life Commission," *Agricultural History,* XXXIV (Oct., 1960), 155–72, and Joseph G. Knapp, *The Rise of American Cooperative Enterprise, 1620–1920* (Danville, Ill.: Interstate Printers and Publishers, 1969), pp. 110–20.

was to appoint the National Monetary Commission, which was charged with developing plans for a more satisfactory national banking and currency system. One of the commission's reports surveyed and commented favorably upon the *Landschaften* system of Germany, a cooperative plan for farm mortgage credit. This report stimulated discussion of, and interest in, introducing such an institution in the United States.[2]

The distinction for arousing American interest in cooperative agricultural credit belongs to David Lubin, the American delegate to the International Institute of Agriculture at Rome. As a small storekeeper in Sacramento, California, Lubin discovered that the farmer operated at great disadvantages, both in selling his own products and in buying commodities which he needed. When he later bought a fruit ranch, those problems became very real to him, but Lubin attempted to do something about them by participating in farmers' cooperative organizations. Lubin prospered financially and began to travel to Europe in the 1890s, where he studied European methods of farming and marketing. He became convinced that cooperative institutions, especially those devoted to credit, could be adapted to the needs of American farmers. He enlisted the support of several European leaders, including the king of Italy, in creating the International Institute of Agriculture which studied agricultural problems and disseminated information looking toward their solution.[3]

Even before Lubin joined the institute, he wrote President Theodore Roosevelt: "My studies and observations in Europe make me feel that the Raiffeisen and Schulze-Delitzsch system of cooperative credit associations would lift the Southern producer of cotton and tobacco from the payment of ten to one hundred percent interest, entailed by the crop lien system, and give him money at six percent. Your assistance is needed to aid in causing associations to be started in each cotton and tobacco state." Although Roosevelt took no action, Lubin encouraged the cooperative bureau of the institute to publish a report in 1910 outlining the operation of cooperative credit institutions in Europe. Lubin mailed thousands of these pamphlets at his own expense to farm leaders, businessmen, newspaper editors, and political officials throughout the United States. Lubin's mailing campaign brought requests for further information and calls for action. In April, 1912, he accepted an invitation to speak before the

2 Knapp, *Rise of American Cooperative Enterprise,* 110–12.

3 Herbert Corey, "David Lubin," *System,* XXIV (Nov., 1913), 526–27. For a full study of Lubin and his work see Oliva Rosetti Agresti, *David Lubin: A Study in Practical Idealism* (Boston: Little, Brown and Co., 1922).

Southern Commercial Congress which met in Nashville. Lubin led a special conference on farm financing which was set up during the congress. After a week's discussion, the congress adopted Lubin's suggestion that the Congress send a delegation, composed of two representatives from each state and from the Canadian provinces, to Europe to study various cooperative systems.[4]

Since 1912 was an election year, the Southern Commercial Congress decided to wait until a new president took office before launching the project. Both major party platforms, however, endorsed the idea of such an enquiry.[5] Moreover, President William Howard Taft had already shown interest in the credit needs of farmers. In the spring of 1912 he instructed the personnel of American embassies and ministries in Europe to gather information on "the forms and effectiveness of rural organizations" in the countries where they resided. That information was summarized in a report by Myron T. Herrick, ambassador to France, who had earlier expressed an interest in rural credit problems.[6] Herrick was a prominent Republican from Cleveland, Ohio, who had served as governor of his state from 1904 to 1906. In private life he had been president of a savings and loan company in Cleveland and his activity in banking organizations had led him to the presidency of the American Bankers' Association. On a trip to Europe in 1910 he had become interested in rural cooperative banking and had described his findings before a meeting of the ABA in 1911. He sponsored a resolution which called upon the ABA to appoint a committee to investigate the rural credit problem in the United States. The passage of this resolution probably had much to do with President Taft's interest in the subject.[7]

Herrick's report to Taft presented European rural credit institutions as well organized, and providing farmers with both short-term and long-term credit at interest rates lower than those prevailing in the United States. He noted that the most common means of obtaining short-term credit was through cooperative credit associations, and thought it "remarkable that the farmers of the United States have been so slow to

---

[4] Knapp, *Rise of American Cooperative Enterprise*, pp. 122–23; U.S., Congress, Senate, *Agricultural Cooperation and Rural Credit in Europe, Report of the American Commission . . .* , Senate Document no. 114, 63d Cong., 2d sess. (Washington: Government Printing Office, 1913), III, pp. 6–7 (hereafter cited as *Report of the American Commission*, with appropriate Senate Document numbers and dates).

[5] Knapp, *Rise of American Cooperative Enterprise*, pp. 123–24.

[6] President William Howard Taft to Governors of the States, Oct. 11, 1912, Senate Document no. 967, 62d Cong., 3d sess. (1912–13), p. 3.

[7] *Who's Who, 1918;* Knapp, *Rise of American Cooperative Enterprise*, p. 124.

adopt this system of banking for temporary loans on personal security." He noted, however, that only Massachusetts had enacted enabling legislation to provide for such cooperative credit associations. Herrick warned that this type of credit association seems "to be adapted only for localities where population is fixed and settled and welded together in close relation by community of interests." He also objected to the trend in Europe of state subsidization of these institutions. Not only did such subsidies violate the original principles of Raiffeisen and Schulze-Delitzsch, but it was inconceivable to him "that American farmers would accept such assistance from the Government and thus become a privileged class supported in part by the rest of the people." Furthermore, Herrick explained that short-term and long-term credit facilities were "inherently and irreconcilably separate and distinct," and thus required "separate lending institutions." He believed that long-term credit, based upon the security of land, was more complicated, and he recommended great care before settling on the *Landschaften* or a similar system. It seemed to him, on the other hand, that short-term, personal credit could be easily provided by adopting Raiffeisen-type cooperative credit societies. The state's only role, he said, should be to pass permissive legislation, relying exclusively on "local and voluntary effort" in the formation of such agencies. The personal credit societies should be composed of small, local groups of farmers, organized on the principle of unlimited liability, which would compel caution in membership selection. As far as a commission of enquiry was concerned, Herrick concluded that "very little now can be gained by further study of the European field," because American overseas representatives had already gathered "nearly all the material required on the working principles, business methods and achievements of farm and land credit systems." Herrick instead called for action.[8]

On October 11, 1912, President Taft publicly released Herrick's report, along with a letter to every state governor. He said that Herrick's report had convinced him that the Raiffeisen societies could be adapted to American conditions. Taft pointed out that the recently enacted Massachusetts credit union act was "a very good law" and that the organization and management of credit unions was "wonderfully simple, and the experience of the European countries shows that their success is practically inevitable where the environment is congenial to their growth and where proper laws are passed for their conduct." Taft summoned the

[8] *Preliminary Report on Land and Agricultural Credit in Europe,* Senate Document no. 967, 62d Cong., 3d sess. (Washington: Government Printing Office, 1912), *passim.*

governors to a White House conference on December 7, 1912, to consider the matter.[9] He urged the governors to take action, as he had already done in his letter and in certain public appearances. Speaking at Jamestown, New York, on October 26, he told his audience that he wanted "to put that seed into your mind so as to make your State Legislature take some action." [10]

Meanwhile, representatives of the Southern Commercial Congress worked to obtain congressional endorsement for its committee of inquiry, which had been named the American Commission on Agriculture Credit and Cooperation. Taft and House and Senate leaders agreed that Congress should set up an official committee to work with the American Commission, and to that end an amendment was added to the agricultural appropriations bill providing for the appointment of a United States commission, "to cooperate with the American Commission assembled under the auspices of the Southern Commercial Congress to investigate and study in European countries, cooperative land-mortgage banks, cooperative rural credit unions, and similar organizations and institutions devoting their attention to the promotion of agriculture and the betterment of rural conditions." Taft signed the bill into law on March 4, 1913, his last day in office.[11] Woodrow Wilson became president the following day and immediately appointed seven men to serve on the United States commission. He named Senator Duncan U. Fletcher of Florida, president of the Southern Commercial Congress, as chairman.

Both the American and the United States commissions sailed for Europe on April 26, 1913, and returned on July 25. David Lubin established the itinerary and arranged for the meetings and contacts between European agricultural leaders and members of the commissions. He called the commissions a "jury of enquiry" which would act as a "Grand Jury," as they listened to European cooperative leaders relate "their own experiences as members and co-operators of rural credit associations." [12] The main body of the commissions toured Italy, the Hapsburg empire, Germany, Belgium, France, and the United Kingdom. Subcommittees also visited Egypt, Russia, Switzerland, the Netherlands, Denmark,

---

[9] Taft to Governors of States, Oct. 11, 1912, Senate Document no. 967.

[10] *New York Times,* Oct. 26, 1912.

[11] Knapp, *Rise of American Cooperative Enterprise,* p. 124.

[12] "The Jury of Enquiry on the European Co-Operative Rural Credit Systems: Mode of Procedure of the American Commission . . . ," public letter, Lubin to Dr. Clarence J. Owens, Jan. 11, 1913, International Institute of Agriculture.

Norway, and Spain. The delegates gathered an exhaustive amount of data and opinion, and the commissions returned home with great enthusiasm and respect for what they had observed.[13]

Before the year was over, the two commissions issued a joint report which in some nine hundred pages brought together much of the information gathered in Europe. The recommendations of the commissions appeared the following year in a report to the American people. While commenting favorably on European agricultural credit systems, the report emphasized that the United States could not borrow those methods indiscriminately, but should "only take what seems best from Europe, adapt it to our conditions, and 'try it out.'" Moreover, the commissions agreed that the practices of government aid to credit institutions in Europe should not be extended to the United States. The role of the government, they reported, should be limited to investigating, informing, encouraging, and legislating. As to the question of whether government-fostered long-term credit agencies or cooperative short-term credit societies were antagonistic to commercial banks and private land mortgage banks, the commissions concluded that, in Europe, they are each "recognized as occupying a separate sphere. . . ." [14]

Like Myron Herrick, the report drew a sharp distinction between the methods and institutions providing long-term rural financing and those supplying short-term personal credit.[15] As for the former, both the majority and the minority on the American commission concluded: "In order that there would be a uniform and nationwide system of long-term credit, it would seem wise to secure the enactment of a federal law permitting the organization of farm land banks, either of the joint-stock or the cooperative plan, authorized to issue long time bonds secured by farm mortgages, required to do business on a narrow margin of profit, to allow payment of principal on the amortization plan, and carefully and fully supervised by the Federal Government." [16]

Turning to the question of short-term credit, the report concluded that, "the European experience seems to indicate that the cooperative form of furnishing credit is likely to be the ultimate method in America, for the very simple reason that credit will be furnished by private joint-

---

[13] *Report of the American Commission*, III, p. 7; Clarence J. Owens to Senator Duncan U. Fletcher, June 13, 1913, Secretary's Office: Incoming Correspondence, 1912–13, National Archives, Record Group 16, Tray 107.

[14] *Report of the American Commission*, Senate Document no. 261 (1914) Part 1, Vol. III, pp. 13, 27–28.

[15] *Ibid.*, p. 15.

[16] *Ibid.*, Senate Document no. 214 (1913), pp. 28–29.

stock financial institutions only for profit to the institution, whereas, under cooperative credit the members get the profits." Leaving an opening for more traditional private methods, however, the commission recognized that in some "favored regions" existing banks, in which farmers were stockholders, already were furnishing or could furnish short-term credit. In other areas it suggested that banks adopt a policy of extending the period of short-term loans from the usual thirty to ninety days to six months or longer.[17]

There was no doubt, however, but that the commissions favored the Raiffeisen-type cooperative credit societies, with the exception of the principle of unlimited liability. That feature, said the report, was not applicable to American agriculture because of the "general unwillingness of American farmers to trust one another," a reluctance by farmers to divulge their business to others, the fact that farmers resided in scattered residences compared to the compact rural villages of Europe, and their "traditional objection to becoming financially responsible for one's neighbors." With the exception of this feature, the majority on the commission (a minority report approved the long-term credit recommendations, but questioned the wisdom of short-term cooperative credit agencies) recommended that in the event existing banks were not able or willing to liberalize short-term credit, the states should enact laws permitting the organization of cooperative credit associations.[18]

The only immediate legislative result of the joint reports of the American commission and the United States commission was the passage of the Federal Farm Loan Act on July 17, 1916, and this measure dealt only with long-term mortgage credit. But the great interest aroused in cooperative short-term credit societies had produced some minor legislative results. Both Texas and Wisconsin passed rural credit union laws in 1913. These statutes however, were later considered "defective" by credit union leaders and had to be revised to bring them into line with accepted credit union principles. In the case of Texas, the commissioner of the State Department of Insurance and Banking wrote in 1920 that it did "not seem to have been well received by the people of this State. There have been but two rural credit unions organized in Texas. One of these liquidated before it transacted any business, and so far as we are advised, the other one has never done any business whatsoever."[19]

---

[17] *Ibid.*, Senate Document no. 261 (1914), III, pp. 16–18.

[18] *Ibid.*, p. 16; Senate Document no. 214, pp. 7–10.

[19] J. T. McMillin to E. E. Engelbert, Oct. 6, 1920, Department of Agriculture, NARG 83, Rural Credit Files (1913–19), Box 7.

The same year, Wisconsin's commissioner of banking reported that, "while several parties have investigated the law with a view to forming associations, none has been formed. It appears the law is impracticable." [20] The rural credits movement partially prompted passage of the New York credit union law in 1913, although it was broad enough to provide for both rural and urban credit union development. Two years later the legislatures of Oregon, South Carolina, and Utah all passed rural credit union bills, but they, too, proved ineffective.

The one successful law passed during the brief flurry of interest in rural cooperative credit came in North Carolina in 1915. John Sprunt Hill, a wealthy farmer, banker, and philanthropist, deserves much of the credit for passage and implementation of the act. Hill, who had been a member of the American commission, told a state convention of farmers meeting in Raleigh in August, 1913, of his experiences in Europe, and concluded: "The average small farmer either has no credit at all or is compelled to use such forms of high price credit as he can obtain from the country merchant, hence, a new agency, the co-operative society, must be created in each community to handle this new kind of banking business." [21] Hill organized the first rural credit union in the South at Lowe's Grove, North Carolina. Another "first" for North Carolina came when the state appropriated money to provide the Department of Agriculture with a full-time credit union organizer. By 1922 forty-six credit unions had been formed, although only twenty-nine were still in operation. Of the seventeen liquidations, however, all had been voluntary and without any losses to their members.[22]

The plan to establish credit unions to fulfill the personal and short-term credit needs of farmers never succeeded. While later analyses would ascribe this failure to the "nature of farming and farmers" or to other indigenous factors, much of the cause stemmed from the way in which credit unionism developed. It was essentially an urban rather than a rural movement. The leadership of the credit union movement was urban, and city workers, not farmers, were the most likely beneficiaries. Moreover, the nature of farming and the needs of agriculture did not fit the credit union pattern very well. Most farmers had small and irregular incomes which made it difficult to organize and operate a credit union. The

[20] Marshall Cousins to E. E. Engelbert, Oct. 4, 1920, *ibid.*

[21] John Sprunt Hill, "Co-operation and the Work of the American Commission in Europe" (Speech at the State Convention of Farmers, Raleigh, N.C., Aug. 27, 1913), unpaged.

[22] North Carolina, Department of Agriculture, Credit Union Division, *The Credit Union: The Way to Economic Betterment* (Raleigh, ca. 1936), pp. 1–2.

farmers who needed credit most had no money to invest in credit unions to provide the capital and loan funds for a viable society. Therefore, most credit union enthusiasts held out little hope for developing the movement in the countryside.

Meanwhile, organizational work at the national level proceeded slowly and unsystematically among urban employees. The Massachusetts Credit Union had appointed a publicity committee at its organizational meeting early in 1914, but it produced a few results. One approach to national publicity, however, was to get the credit union story before national conferences dealing with charity, welfare, and social work. In line with this aim, MCU named Jacob de Haas to attend the National Conference on Jewish Charities, held in Memphis, Tennessee, on May 7, 1914. De Haas told conference representatives that credit unions were the "most practical antidote for all that natural discontent which finds its expression through Socialism, and even more violent antagonism to the existing order of society." Moreover, he believed that the credit unions would "reduce the demands for charity," because, he said, people organized in a successful credit union would not need charity.[23] Following his address, de Haas discussed the movement with a representative of Julius Rosenwald of Chicago, and later met with leaders of the Southern Sociological Convention to consider the possible use of credit unions among southern Negroes. As a result of these meetings and discussions, de Haas told the MCU board of directors: "It is evident that the Credit Union is a new idea for the United States, that it appeals to people with business understanding rather than to social workers, and if a National Committee for the fostering of the Credit Union were started and capitalized, I feel that this movement could be made to cross from Massachusetts to California in two years." [24]

This was exactly what Filene was contemplating. In July, 1915, he told a reporter that the credit union promoters "are now beginning a definite propaganda to bring all the possibilities of the movement before the State and national officers of the big organizations of the country." Thinking even in international terms, he said that there was no reason why 15 million such societies could not be established throughout the world. Filene had assigned someone, probably Stanton, to draft a plan for spreading the credit union idea nationally. The plan was given to Filene around mid-July and it called for engaging an assistant for the general manager of MCU who should make it his job to contact leaders

[23] Minutes, MCU Board, May 6, 1914; *Jewish Charities,* August, 1914, pp. 17–19.
[24] Minutes, MCU Board, May 12, 1914.

of fraternal and religious organizations, factories and business firms, rural cooperative associations, social settlement houses, and country agricultural associations.

One result of this recommendation was the employment of George W. Elwell, an attorney who had been with the Boston Legal Aid Society, as field secretary for MCU's Propaganda Committee. Elwell began work on September 29, and concentrated on contacting the executive officers of "parent or head organizations" to interest them in credit unions. Initially, Elwell confined his activities to calling on business, labor, and professional leaders in Boston. He believed, however, that the committee should expand its activities to other cities in the state. The committee, in fact, had decided that fertile ground for credit union development could be found among city employees, particularly since the City of Boston Employees' Credit Union had just been organized and could serve as an example. Consequently, during October Elwell interviewed city treasurers in Worcester, Springfield, Fall River, New Bedford, Lawrence, and Lynn but was not encouraged by the response. Only in Cambridge and Lawrence did he believe it would be worthwhile to try to establish credit unions immediately.[25] After further interviews with the city officials, Elwell became even more discouraged. "I feel that we can hardly expect to find sufficient altruistic motives in cities outside of Boston," he wrote, "to warrant the hope that the city officials will take the initiative in starting the Credit Union among their employees." [26]

During November and December Elwell's hope of organizing credit unions among public employees, workers in certain businesses, and in the state Grange were dashed as one group after another pulled back after showing some initial interest. Despite this stepped up organizational activity the year 1915 ended in failure. During that year only twelve new credit unions came into existence, four less than in 1914. Moreover, there were ten liquidations during 1915, twice as many as the year before. By the end of 1915, there were forty-seven credit unions operating in Massachusetts, only two more than twelve months earlier.[27]

Why was the credit union movement, a simple self-help idea, so slow in gaining support? One Boston observer explained the situation by say-

---

[25] *Boston Post,* July 14, 1915; "Plan for Creating Channels for Spreading Credit Union Propaganda Nationally," memorandum, July 14, 1915; Elwell to Promoters of the Massachusetts Credit Union, Oct. 9, 1915; Minutes, Propaganda Committee, MCU, Oct. 22, 1915; Elwell to Promoters of the MCU, Oct. 30, 1915.

[26] Elwell to Promoters of the MCU, Nov. 6, 1915.

[27] Snider, *Credit Unions in Massachusetts,* Table X, p. 27.

ing that skepticism "meets every new financial venture in Massachusetts, a wise skepticism but one which too often failed when needed. . . . An astonishingly large number of people," the editor continued, had been taken in by "wildcat" banking and investment schemes, "yet a rational system such as credit unions met with a complete wall of distrust and dis-approval because it departed from the familiar financial methods." A second cause of failure, the writer thought, was that there had been no systematic effort to spread the movement. "What is everybody's business degenerates into nobody's business." [28]

The Boston *Transcript* editor was probably correct in saying that people had a natural suspicion of new financial ventures, but he obviously was not aware of the publicity and promotional work being carried on by MCU. Stanton and Elwell had learned that more fundamental factors than unawareness stood in the way of organizing credit unions. Many business and industrial firms already provided services which they thought made credit unions unnecessary. Various types of "employees' welfare clubs" or "mutual benefit societies" existed among employee groups, supplying savings and borrowing facilities. Some companies used the savings of their employees to increase the firm's business capital. What concerned Elwell was that the savings could be lost or impaired by business failure or through the manipulations of unscrupulous employers. In many cases employees did not know where their money was being invested; in others they knew but feared to complain because they were afraid of losing their jobs. Elwell believed that it would be unwise for the MCU to make this information public because it might cause suspicion of business firms that "are perfectly good with equally good fraternal societies." Stanton had found that heads of large firms were often en-thusiastic about credit unions until they learned that the deposits could not be invested in the company's business.[29]

Not only was there competition from employee-employer associations already in operation, but there was increasing rivalry from a new finan-cial institution, the Morris Plan of Banks, or sometimes called the "Morris Plan of Industrial Loans and Investments." This plan was the creation of Arthur J. Morris, a young Virginia lawyer, who had spent three years in Europe studying and observing industrial banking and the operations of peoples' banks. He formed his first company in 1910 at Norfolk, Vir-ginia, with a capital of $20,000. Although a private banking operation aimed at supplying consumer credit, the Morris plan was different

[28] *Boston Transcript*, Sept. 15, 1915.
[29] Elwell to Promoters of the MCU, Oct. 9, 1915.

enough from regular commercial and savings banks to interest a large number of people who were not served by traditional bank credit. By 1915 there were Morris plan banks in fifty-six cities, concentrated mainly in the South and the East. These banks had loaned over $23 million since the inception of the system.

The Morris plan banks presented competition to the credit unions because they offered small loans at lower interest rates than many borrowers could obtain elsewhere. Credit union leaders became worried over this development. Arthur Ham of the Russell Sage Foundation complained to Desjardins that the publicity surrounding the plan was deceptive and misleading, but that it capitalized on the interest in cooperative banking. He believed that the plan had "already gained so much ground that it is going to be difficult, if not impossible, to successfully check it." [30] Desjardins agreed that the Morris plan was nothing "but a huge moneymaking concern devised to insure to the promoters a good business proposition, at the expense of the public. . . ." [31] A few months later, Ham seemed to think that the Morris plan's danger to credit unions was past because people had learned that it was "purely a commercial enterprise that has been sailing under false colors." [32] But throughout Massachusetts, credit union promoters found that many people believed the Morris plan was taking care of credit problems.

Trouble with a competing organization was much less serious to the credit union movement than the growing unfriendliness of the Massachusetts bank commissioner. The first hint of this changing attitude came at the General Conference of Credit Unions held at Revere Beach on September 16, 1915. State Treasurer Charles L. Burrill praised the philanthropy of the MCU leaders, but then criticized the lending policies of credit unions. "A good many of the unions are holding simply a mass of paper," he said. Burrill also mentioned the number of credit unions that had liquidated, inferring that the societies had poor management. In 1914 and 1915 there had been fifteen liquidations, or 23 percent of the credit unions organized in Massachusetts since passage of the act. This compared to only two liquidations before 1914. Felix Vorenberg, president of MCU, agreed that more safeguards were necessary, but pointed out that only two credit unions had actually been liquidated by the bank commissioner. The others ceased operations voluntarily. Vorenberg be-

[30] Ham to Desjardins, Feb. 24, 1914.
[31] Desjardins to Ham, Feb. 28, 1914.
[32] Ham to Desjardins, May 15, 1914.

lieved that a majority of credit unions were managed "correctly." [33] It could not be denied, however, that management and operation of credit unions according to sound cooperative principles had become an increasing problem. For example, at the Revere Beach meeting, a local credit union president criticized some societies for charging more than 10 percent interest. To meet such problems, Judge Abraham K. Cohen proposed that no credit union should be accepted for membership in the MCU unless it permitted agency personnel to investigate its records and business methods. [34]

In November, 1915, Elwell reported that the bank commissioner tended "to hold up charters because of alleged incompetence of officers." Elwell did not deny that some credit union officials lacked the proper knowledge and experience to handle the business properly. He had even tried to recruit college graduates for credit union work, but without success. Moreover, he refrained from trying to form credit unions among employees who might have their charter refused. The matter of proper management had become so serious that Elwell warned MCU's staff to devote its main energies toward improving credit union operations. "Otherwise," he wrote, "it is entirely possible that we shall have no Credit Union law to work with after the coming session of the legislature has adjourned." [35]

When Elwell called on Bank Commissioner Augustus Thorndike on December 6, 1915, to discuss credit union problems, he did not receive a cordial welcome. Thorndike made it clear that he was very disturbed at the way credit unions had been operating. He told Elwell that in the future he intended to grant charters for new credit unions only when the "character and business experience of the proposed members, and the proposed field of operation, seemed to be such as to furnish reasonable guarantee of success." Thorndike was also critical of the MCU, intimating that the organization was responsible for forming some credit unions that later failed. If the MCU would spend as much time and effort developing and insuring sound business practices as it had to indiscriminate promotion, the credit union movement might achieve success and win his hearty approval.

Thorndike then explained his position in some detail. He charged that new credit unions were being formed among similar groups when the

---

[33] *Boston Herald,* Sept. 16, 1915.

[34] *Ibid.;* Minutes, Propaganda Committee, MCU, Oct. 22, 1915.

[35] Elwell to MCU Propaganda Committee, Nov. 13, 1915, and Nov. 30, 1915.

employees could just as well join an existing society. He also criticized
the organization of credit unions among employees of businesses that already had some kind of mutual benefit association. Moreover, he charged
that some loans had been made for purposes not allowed by law, indicating that the credit committees had not been fulfilling their duties or
that the applicants had falsified their applications. Thorndike even believed that malfeasance or fraud existed in some instances, but his main
criticism was that credit unions were too often governed by "their hearts
instead of their heads in making loans."

Elwell agreed that the operation of the credit unions in Massachusetts
had some weaknesses, and urged that the MCU should clearly point out
to credit unions what "dire results" might occur if they did not follow
sound business practices. Following his conference with Thorndike, Elwell made some specific recommendations to the MCU as to how the
quality of credit unions could be strengthened, thus reassuring the bank
commissioner. He insisted that the MCU should make certain that credit
and supervisory committees were capable and reliable, and that members
of these committees be held more strictly responsible for their decisions.
Elwell also believed that ways should be devised to reduce false state-
ments on application forms for loans. He emphasized that, while improving their operations, the leaders of the credit union movement should not
engage in any practices or push any policies which would antagonize the
bank commissioner.[36]

The day after reporting on his meeting with Thorndike, Elwell informed the MCU that one great difficulty with credit unions in the state
was the lack of uniform interest schedules. Furthermore, he believed that
some credit unions were charging exorbitant rates. While he recognized
the validity of different societies charging different rates, he objected to
the current inequalities and confusion. He explained that some credit
unions charged six dollars on each hundred-dollar loan payable at maturity. Others charged six dollars payable as a discount in advance. Still
others discounted the loans at 6 percent in advance, but then began receiving a true annual interest of more than 6 percent. "The strangest part
of this diverse number of systems," stated Elwell, "is that in every case
the Credit Union claims to be charging only 6%." He asserted that one
argument against the Morris plan was that it charged more than 12 percent interest, but that some credit unions were doing the same thing. But
credit union interest rates should not exceed 12 percent, Elwell argued,

[36] Elwell to Propaganda Committee, MCU, Dec. 6, 1915.

"and I mean 12% by strict accounting principles, and not in advance." [37]

But the MCU took no action on this matter. It did act, however, on one of the bank commissioner's objections which centered around the spending of credit union funds on advertising and public relations not provided for by law. In December, 1915, leaders of the MCU organized a separate agency known as the Massachusetts Maintenance Society "to support the Massachusetts Credit Union in its work of extending, systematizing and strengthening the credit union system." Elwell was asked to direct the activities of the new society. [38]

Credit unions also came under attack from another source. In January, 1916, a bill was introduced in the Massachusetts legislature, with the support of the bank commissioner, to eliminate the provision of the original credit union act which exempted credit unions from taxation. Critics said that they were not truly cooperative, nonprofit associations. The House Committee on Taxation heard testimony that credit unions were making good profits, paying liberal dividends, and, therefore, could afford to pay taxes. However, the proponents of the tax measure did not have sufficient data to press their point. Although eight credit unions had paid dividends of between 8 and 16.8 percent on share capital, twenty-seven of forty-five societies had paid no dividends at all in 1915. In any event, the legislature refused to change the tax-exempt status of credit unions.

Two other bills which might have affected credit unions were before the legislature in 1916. One provided that all savings and loan institutions must be audited by the bank commissioner, with the expenses being borne by the audited institutions. This would have been a severe burden on credit unions, especially the smaller societies. The other called for shifting the supervision of credit unions to the supervisor of small loans. Elwell, who was a registered lobbyist for the MCU, successfully worked to defeat both of these measures. [39] Following the disposal of these bills, a legislator introduced a measure restricting the organization of credit unions in areas already served by existing societies. Elwell called the bill "vicious and uncalled for" because it would provide monopoly positions

---

[37] *Ibid.,* Dec. 7, 1915.

[38] Maxwell Copelof, president, Massachusetts Maintenance Society, to Judge A. K. Cohen, Dec. 15, 1915; Letterhead of the Massachusetts Maintenance Society; Elwell to Propaganda Committee, MCU, Dec. 16 and 21, 1915.

[39] Elwell to Propaganda Committee, MMS, Reports for weeks ending Jan. 24, Feb. 2, and Feb. 10, 1916.

for existing credit unions, allowing them to refuse membership to "worthy individuals" who would have no recourse through organizing a new credit union. Moreover, he thought that leaders in control of a monopoly credit union might force members to support certain political policies. Elwell recommended that the MCU oppose the bill "with all the strength it can command." Fortunately, the bill's sponsor withdrew it, asking that consideration be deferred until the next session.[40] Thus, credit unions emerged unharmed from a legislative session which had threatened to place new restrictions on the movement. Much of the credit for this goes to Elwell. More important, however, was the fact that credit unions had not yet become important enough to generate either much opposition or much support.

Although Filene had remained in the background during this period, he had continued to assist the movement by contributing several thousand dollars to its promotional activities, lending his name to both the MCU and the maintenance society, and being moderately active in the affairs of both organizations. But he was not satisfied with the movement's progress. And with his passion for fact-finding and efficiency, he set out to learn why credit unionism remained in a rather stagnant condition. As he often did, Filene appointed one of his assistants to make a thorough study of the movement and to prepare a report for him.

The study was completed by March, 1916, and it was not encouraging. The problems facing the movement included continued hostility among some Massachusetts legislators and unfriendliness from the bank commissioner. The author of the report believed that, even though restrictive legislation had temporarily failed, "very little of it is really dead." He was certain that the attempt to tax credit unions would be revived. In regard to Bank Commissioner Thorndike, he had revoked some credit union charters and had denied charters to others. Moreover, he had ruled that one credit union could not borrow from another. The bank commissioner was also critical of credit unions for using their resources for promotional and propaganda purposes. Thorndike traced many of what he considered shortcomings in the movement to William J. Stanton, general manager of the MCU. The author of the report seemed to agree. He wrote that not only had Stanton failed to correct abuses in credit unionism, but accused him of inefficiency and of being a gossip who talked too much "about the affairs of the borrowers." Overall, the report did not present a very bright picture of the credit union movement.

What might be done? In a final section of his study, the unnamed

[40] *Ibid.*, Feb. 2 and 17, 1916.

author of the report proposed that the maintenance society employ an additional person on a half-time basis to study the operations of MCU and individual credit unions for the purpose of standardizing their business practices and accounts. The report also recommended limiting dividends to not more than 8 percent, and prohibiting credit unions from following any device which would let them exceed the legal rate of interest. Finally, the report suggested the discharge of Stanton.[41]

During the spring of 1916 several meetings were held by credit union leaders to consider the mounting problems within the movement. Filene gave a dinner for members of the Massachusetts Credit Union at the Boston City Club on March 10, where they heard Stanton discuss steps that should be taken to improve the situation. He emphasized that before undertaking more organizational work the MCU should make sure that the established credit unions were operating successfully. Perhaps feeling that he was under pressure for his past promotional work, Stanton told the audience that his two years' experience had made him

considerably less of an enthusiast in the matter of propaganda work than I was when I started. The big thing then seemed to be to organize unions, and more unions. Now I feel that we will be doing a very much larger work to first get in complete touch with all the system and its integral parts, find out its strength and its weakness, make the weak parts strong, build on a firmer foundation, eliminate any dangerous practices and, as early as possible, do away altogether with loose credits. Then, with a powerful and perfect machine, we can go ahead with measureless success.[42]

The following month Judge Abraham Cohen told a meeting of the maintenance society that he feared credit unionists might "lose sight of one of the fundamental principles of the system, and that is that they are formed primarily for the promotion of thrift." Cohen insisted that credit unions should stress the acceptance of deposits, and not simply emphasize low interest rates. Moreover, Cohen said that credit unions should be careful to conduct their business within the letter and the spirit of the law. They should be kept small and be composed of people who knew one another, he said. Under no circumstances should credit unions become profit-making institutions. Finally, Cohen emphasized that credit unions "should be conducted practically as philanthropic institutions."[43]

41 Unsigned Memorandum for Filene, Mar. 6, 1916.

42 William J. Stanton, general manager, MCU (Remarks at dinner given by Edward A. Filene, the Boston City Club, March 10, 1916), typescript in MMS Files.

43 Minutes, Massachusetts Maintenance Society, April 28, 1916.

Elwell, whose services were terminated in June, also wrote his reaction to recent trends in credit unionism. He frankly criticized the maintenance society for doing nothing to make the operations of credit unions safer. "I am aware that certain of the directors of the Massachusetts Credit Union are in favor of wholesale propaganda work," he wrote, "looking to the establishment of as many credit unions as possible throughout Massachusetts within the shortest possible time." But, he warned, new charters "will not be generally granted until the work of improvement has not only been undertaken in good faith, but also progressed to the point of showing real improvement in fact. I further feel that whatever activity the Massachusetts Credit Union may undertake in the future in the way of increasing public interest in the system, its success in actually creating unions must depend upon the previous assumption and successful discharge of the duty of supervision and improvement." Elwell asserted that this was clearly the attitude of the bank commissioner and the state treasurer.[44]

It was clear by the summer of 1916 that credit union leaders had been forced into a rather agonizing reappraisal of the movement. As a result of criticisms and discussions both within and outside credit unionism, Filene and other leaders decided to establish a new organization to provide fresh and vigorous leadership for the movement. Vorenberg, Filene, Cohen, and Mitchell supported the introduction and passage of a bill granting a charter to the Massachusetts Credit Union Association. The act was approved on April 13, 1917. The purpose of the MCUA was to "disseminate information in respect to the benefits of credit unions . . . ; to organize and assist in the organization of credit unions; to make loans to credit unions at a rate not exceeding six percent per annum and generally to promote and assist credit unions."[45] The bylaws of MCUA, adopted a month later, provided that members of the MCU and the maintenance society could become members of MCUA, as well as any other person, firm, corporation, association, or credit union. Funds for MCUA would consist of "all money which may be transferred to it by the Massachusetts Maintenance Society or the shareholders of the Massachusetts Credit Union," and dues from members and profits from loans. The first slate of officers elected were identical to the officers of the MCU. Vorenberg became president, Filene, Cohen, and Leon Strauss,

---

[44] Elwell to Propaganda Committee, MMS, Report for week ending June 10, 1916.

[45] *Massachusetts Acts* (1917), chap. 281, quoted in "You Should Know About Credit Unions," pamphlet (MCUA, n.d.).

vice-presidents, and Max Mitchell, treasurer.[46] Although the MCU and the maintenance society continued mainly as paper organizations, the MCUA became the agency which would direct the credit union movement in the future.

Even before formation of the MCUA, a campaign committee laid plans to raise $50,000 to develop the credit union movement. Team captains were appointed and daily luncheons were held to solicit the needed funds. It was agreed that only Jews would be asked for contributions, thus retaining the narrow religious and ethnic leadership and support of the movement. By the time MCUA began operating, however, only $25,000 had been subscribed, nearly all of it by Jewish Bostonians.[47] Also Filene moved to obtain a new manager for the movement. He wanted someone with the drive and ability to spread credit unionism in Massachusetts and to other states. One person who appealed to Filene was John Clark Bills, a Harvard law school graduate who was presently chief of the Bureau of Labor in Puerto Rico. After investigating Bills and arranging for him to visit with other credit union leaders in Boston, Filene said that he favored paying him $3,000 a year as a starting salary, with more later "if he succeeds and makes the Union financially able to pay such an increase." [48] Although Bills had some reservations about accepting the position, on March 10, he wrote Filene that he had decided to take up the new work. On March 21, the directors of the MCU and the maintenance society voted unanimously to retain Bills. Initially he became general manager of the maintenance society, but upon incorporation of the MCUA the following month he assumed the headship of that organization. Stanton was "demoted" to the position of clerk in the Massachusetts Credit Union.[49]

History has obscured the work of Bills and the MCUA. Nevertheless, he was no more successful in developing credit unionism than his predecessors. During 1917, only seven additional credit unions were organized in Massachusetts, while four more were liquidated. Thus there were only

[46] "Bylaws of the Massachusetts Credit Union Association," adopted May 28, 1917.

[47] Elwell to Josephine A. Bruorton, April 15, 1916; "Massachusetts Credit Unions," pamphlet (MCUA, ca. 1917), p. 3.

[48] Filene to Bruorton, Feb. 25, 1917; "An Analysis from Employment Department on John C. Bills, Jr.," Memo for Filene, Feb. 24, 1917.

[49] Bills to Filene, Mar. 10, 1917; Minutes, Special Joint Meeting, MCU and MMS, Mar. 12, 1917; Bruorton to Bills, Mar. 27, 1917; Vorenberg to Bills, Mar. 21, 1917; Bills to Filene, n.d., and Mar. 21, 1917; See "Officers of the MCU, July 1, 1917," in "Massachusetts Credit Unions," p. 5.

fifty-six credit unions in the state at the end of the year.[50] Although Bills was responsible for affairs only during part of 1917, the record in 1918 when he had full responsibility for credit union development was even worse. Only four new societies were chartered. The United States entry into World War I probably impaired the movement, but credit union difficulties went much deeper.

Some credit union supporters hoped that the government's emphasis on savings during the war would lend encouragement to credit unions. But the government did not choose to utilize credit unions in its war-financing. Nevertheless credit unions did join other Americans in emphasizing the need to save. IT IS PATRIOTIC TO SAVE became the official slogan of the MCU, and Stanton told a reporter for a Boston newspaper somewhat optimistically that "the billions of dollars from the millions of wage earners . . . will float the Liberty Loans and war savings certificates and enable the United States to win the war."[51]

Despite the scant success of credit unions during 1917 and 1918, Filene decided that there were enough societies in Massachusetts, New York, and North Carolina to warrant an attempt to organize a national movement. On May 31, 1919, he called together several prominent citizens to organize the National Committee on People's Banks. Attending the conference with Filene were George E. Roberts, former director of the mint; Governor T. W. Bickett of North Carolina; Warren S. Stone, grand chief of the Brotherhood of Locomotive Engineers; Major James M. Boyle of the Consolidated Coal Company, and Max Mitchell. The MCUA was also represented by three employees who had taken over the direction of credit union work in Massachusetts. These included Dr. W. F. McCaleb, who had succeeded Bills as managing director of MCUA; Bills, who remained in a minor capacity in the association while maintaining his private law practice in Boston; and Charles W. Birtwell, who had been appointed executive secretary of the MCUA. Other persons who accepted membership on the committee and lent their names to the movement were Governor David I. Walsh of Massachusetts; Albert Shaw, editor of *Review of Reviews;* Howard Coonley, a Boston manufacturer and vice-chairman of the U.S. Emergency Fleet Corporation; Charles A. Beard, noted historian and director of the Bureau of Municipal Research; W. W. Collier, former bank commissioner of Texas and vice-president of the State National Bank of San Antonio; Albert J. Beveridge, former senator from Indiana; Professor F. A. Cleveland of Boston Uni-

[50] Snider, *Credit Unions in Massachusetts,* Table X, p. 27.
[51] *Boston Post,* Nov. 25, 1917.

versity; Elwood Mead, chairman of the United States Land Settlement Board; Alphonse Desjardins, and Felix Vorenberg.

The objective of the NCPB was to spread credit unions throughout the country and to work for legislation which would permit state credit unions to take out federal charters. Roberts was elected chairman and Filene vice-chairman.[52] The group named McCaleb executive secretary and announced that he would maintain his office in New York City. Most of the funds for NCPB came from Filene, Mitchell, and Edward L. Doheny, president of Pan-American Petroleum and Transport Company of New York. Filene and Mitchell both contributed $12,500 in cash, while Doheny pledged $5,000, one-fifth on demand and the remainder as needed. By December $7,000 of the original contribution had been expended.[53]

During its short life this national committee was little more than a list of impressive names on stationery. Although prominent persons were willing to lend their names to the movement, they were unwilling to assume any active role or even to attend meetings. McCaleb personally carried on most of the work, which consisted of issuing a few pamphlets, obtaining some newspaper publicity, and making public speeches about credit unions. The bill which credit union leaders hoped that Congress would pass provided for the organization of "Federal People's Banks," which would be under the supervision of the Federal Reserve System. No people's bank could be organized in a city of more than 50,000 people or operate with capital of less than $200,000. Other than those restrictions, there was no mention of the size of capital or membership, except a provision that the banks would be "without fixed capital stock" and would confine their credit operations to members. Such banks could "receive savings of its members in payment of shares or on deposit," and could loan funds to its members or invest them. It could also receive deposits from nonmembers. Rates of interest could not exceed the local rate of the state in which the bank was located, except "where the maturity, face, or special conditions under which the loan is made shall be such as to warrant a higher rate." In such special cases, the rate had to be approved by the Federal Reserve Board. The bank could rediscount or borrow from any source, but for institutions having over $5,000 in capital, surplus and reserve, the aggregate amount of rediscounts and borrowings could not exceed the total of such assets. All loans to members of over $50 required security. Shareholders would enjoy limited liability. Finally, the bill pro-

---

[52] *New York Times,* June 1, 1919.
[53] McCaleb to Desjardins, Dec. 31, 1919.

vided that such banks were exempt from federal and state taxation, except for real estate holdings.[54]

McCaleb, Filene, and other credit union leaders discussed the merits and demerits of such legislation, but they might as well have saved their time and effort. By the last days of 1919 it was apparent that Congress would not enact any such legislation. The project was dead. Indeed, the entire credit union movement was at a standstill. Not only had McCaleb failed to get a national credit union bill passed, credit union organization under state laws was making no headway. Indeed, McCaleb, on the last day of 1919, wrote Desjardins that he had no plans to do anything other than try to organize some additional credit unions in Massachusetts and New York.[55] The Massachusetts Credit Union Association had practically nothing to show for nearly three years of work and the expenditure of thousands of dollars. Moreover, the attempt to establish credit unions among farmers had not succeeded, and some of the credit unions in operation were following questionable practices. Could the movement be made to succeed? This was the question that Filene was pondering.

[54] Memorandum of Main Points of a Proposed Federal Bill Prepared by National Committee on People's Banks, Dec. 27, 1919.

[55] McCaleb to Desjardins, Dec. 31, 1919.

CHAPTER IV

A National Credit Union Movement: The First Steps 1920–25

THE YEAR 1920 was a major turning point in the credit union movement. Prior to that time credit unions had made little progress in the United States. During the next decade, however, the movement made remarkable strides. It benefited from better management and organization, and also from the general industrial and financial trends of the 1920s.

During its early years, the credit union movement had suggested a moralistic progressivism, a philanthropic but not charitable approach to the credit needs of the urban small businessman and workingman; credit union leaders, however, had always taken a conservative, business-like attitude toward the role of credit unions. As Filene had told a Boston newspaper some five years earlier: "It is for the employer's interest as well as the employee's, because instead of having his workmen harassed by loan agents, he gets workmen, who, if they have to borrow in some emergency, borrow among the men with whom they are working and who will help them get on their feet and keep steady."[1] Thus credit unions fitted into the concept of welfare capitalism which so many industrialists adopted after World War I. Indeed, credit unions were well designed to play a role in a system which involved profit sharing, employee benefits, and company unions.

The growing prosperity of the decade also meant that people would have more money to save, and credit unions were consistently presented as thrift institutions. Moreover, existing banking and savings institutions were not designed for, nor did they welcome or appeal to, the small saver. At the same time, the 1920s saw the need for increases in consumer credit to supply people with money to buy automobiles, washing machines, electric refrigerators, radios, and other popular goods. In the role of pro-

---

[1] *Boston Post,* July 14, 1915.

viding funds for installment purchases, credit unions seemed to offer the consumer, businessman, and industrialist a means to encourage prosperity and facilitate the well-being of all in the New Economic Era.

Credit unions, however, could not play a significant role in the economy of the 1920s unless their numbers and resources were greatly expanded. In 1920, after a decade of development, there were only sixty-four credit unions in Massachusetts, and sixty-eight in New York. North Carolina registered thirty-three credit unions, but these were all rural organizations, and not typical of the movement. A credit union law had been enacted in Rhode Island in 1914, but by 1920 there was still only one credit union in that state. Additional laws had been passed in Utah, South Carolina, Wisconsin, Texas, Nebraska, and Oregon, but in most cases the statutes were either poorly written, designed only for farmers, or had not been utilized.[2] At any rate, no significant progress had been made by the beginning of the decade. Indeed, the credit union movement was sterile and stagnant.

No one recognized this situation more clearly than Filene. Yet, his interests were so widespread that he was unable to devote himself single-mindedly to rescuing the credit union movement in which he had invested so much time and money. What he needed was the "right" man, hopefully an expert who possessed the education, imagination, and initiative, to make the movement a success. Stanton, Elwell, Bills, and now Birtwell, had all produced only scant results in developing credit unions in Massachusetts. Then when he employed McCaleb to develop a national organization the result again was meager.

The National Committee on People's Banks had become a great disappointment to Filene. McCaleb's report for 1919, issued in January, 1920, showed neither past progress nor much hope for the future of cooperative credit. An article on people's banks had been prepared by McCaleb and published in the *Review of Reviews*, as well as reprinted and distributed as a pamphlet. He had organized several state committees, had drafted several versions of a federal credit union bill, and had enlisted the services of some "prominent men in both parties" who had promised their support in Congress. McCaleb also stated that "prominent bankers and men skilled in finance have been called to our aid so that we shall be able to muster strong representatives when hearings before committees are begun." But these activities were all that had come from Filene's expenditure of $12,500.

[2] Snider, *Credit Unions in Massachusetts,* Table X, p. 27; Bergengren, *Cooperative Banking,* pp. 100, 86–87, 96, 88–96.

To make matters even worse, Filene did not even favor pushing a federal bill, which was the major objective of the national committee.[3] In the fall of 1920, McCaleb resigned as executive secretary of the NCPB to accept the position of first vice-president and general manager of the Brotherhood Bank, in Cleveland, Ohio. Thus, the NCPB, which had been mainly a paper organization, did not have even one man to play an active role in national credit union development.

To discover what had gone wrong, Filene assigned an aide, Spencer Phenix, to make a complete study of the credit union movement. In August Phenix submitted his first report which concluded that the national and state committees organized by McCaleb "were composed, for the most part, of men without substantial influence or without great interest in the cause." A second report appeared in October and was no less critical of the movement. In a visit with McCaleb, the former secretary of the national committee admitted to Phenix that he had put the "wrong kind of men" on the national and state committees, but that there had been no alternative. One by one, McCaleb listed the names of those who had contributed little, if anything, to the movement. When he had finished, there were few names left. In addition, Phenix reported that only Filene and Mitchell had supplied any substantial funds, and since Mitchell was now deeply involved in his own business affairs—Mitchell's Cosmopolitan Trust Company had failed and was in the hands of receivers—the brunt of the financial responsibility had fallen to Filene.

Phenix recommended that no effort be made to revive the NCPB. If Filene did anything he should make a new start. Moreover, Phenix wrote that unless more money could be obtained, McCaleb's elaborate national plans should be abandoned. Credit unions, Phenix declared, represented a good cause, but they have "no dramatic nor compelling appeal to the general public. The movement grew very slowly in Europe and is growing slowly in Canada. The experience in Massachusetts would indicate that its growth would be slow in the United States." Further, he wrote, "that credit unions can succeed when they serve the selfish or personal interests of a group of men and women, but there must be a real demand if they are not to fail. The formation of credit unions in response to an artificially stimulated demand seems to me to be most unwise."

Thus, Phenix concluded that any further credit union work should be carried out in a different manner, concentrating on making Massachusetts a laboratory and model for other states to follow. Filene's closest

---

[3] John Glenn to Desjardins, Jan. 12, 1920. Glenn and Desjardins had also become opposed to seeking a federal act.

allies in the movement, Pierre Jay and Henry Dennison, another wealthy Boston businessman, seemed to agree with these observations. They acknowledged that credit union development would be slow, and that "the organization of the movement on any extensive and elaborate scale would probably not bring in returns commensurate with the cost." [4]

In light of the discouraging reports of Phenix, Filene might reasonably have abandoned the credit union movement. But he abhorred defeat. More important, he believed deeply in the principle behind cooperative credit. What he still needed was the right man to carry out the organizational work. Although he did not realize it, Filene's faith and patience were about to pay off. Sometime during the spring of 1920, a forty-year-old lawyer from Lynn, Roy F. Bergengren, called on Filene and said that he had heard the MCUA was looking for a new managing director. Filene had known Bergengren slightly as a result of Bergengren's work with one of the committees composing Boston-1915. Bergengren later recalled that after a few minutes' conversation, Filene offered him the job.[5] Among all of Filene's many personnel decisions, this was probably his wisest.

Roy Frederick Bergengren was born on June 14, 1879, in Gloucester, Massachusetts, the son of a Swedish immigrant physician, Frederick W. A. Bergengren. Dr. Bergengren practiced medicine in Brooklyn, returned home to Sweden for a time, then moved to Gloucester, where he also operated a pharmacy and invested rather heavily in real estate. He moved to Lynn, where his son graduated from high school. In 1903 Roy graduated from Dartmouth College. There was a notation in the Dartmouth yearbook accompanying his picture which read: "Class Member Most Likely to Succeed—in an Argument." After graduation, he entered the Harvard Law School, where he graduated in 1906. That same year he was admitted to the bar in Massachusetts, and began practice in Lynn.[6]

Bergengren never had more than a modest legal business. He barely collected enough fees to support his wife, Gladys Louise, an East Orange, New Jersey, school teacher whom he married in 1911, and a son and

[4] Spencer Phenix, "Memorandum for Mr. Filene, Relative to the National Credit Union Movement," Oct. 21 and 25, 1920.

[5] Roy F. Bergengren, *Crusade: The Fight for Economic Democracy in North America, 1921–1945* (New York: Exposition Press, 1952), p. 20.

[6] Commonwealth of Massachusetts, City of Gloucester, Certificate of Birth, Roy Frederick Bergengren; Barre (Vt.) *Daily Times*, Nov. 12, 1955; *Lynn* (Mass.) *Item*, Mar. 7, 1913; Charles Morrow Wilson, *Common Sense Credit: Credit Unions Come of Age* (New York: Devin-Adair Co., 1962), p. 38.

daughter. Serving mainly those too poor to pay for legal help, Bergengren's practice was described by one writer: "The shoe workers and other sweatshop victims needed help, and Roy Bergengren, Attorney-at-Law, gave them help. Unemployment was chronic. Tenements were deplorable. Bars were flourishing, as were the local loan sharks. Young Roy saw tenement homes raided bare by chattel mortgage foreclosures, and served clients who, since they were already paying interest at the rate of 25 percent per month on loan obligations, naturally couldn't pay lawyer fees." [7] Although Bergengren wanted to assist the needy, he concluded that law would not provide solutions to pressing economic problems, nor would it solve his own financial plight.

Consequently, with a growing distaste for law, Bergengren turned to other activities. During the Progressive era he became involved in the movement for the commission form of city government, and he and another attorney led a successful campaign to introduce that system in Lynn. Local citizens then prevailed on Bergengren to serve in the new government. In 1915 he was appointed commissioner of finance, a position which he held for two years.[8]

When the United States entered World War I, Bergengren volunteered for army service, although he was already thirty-eight years old. Appointed a captain of ordnance, he was assigned to a desk in Boston's First Army Base. His superiors rejected his request to serve on the western front and he never got overseas. Returning to Lynn after the armistice, he was determined to abandon law and find new employment. Bergengren and a fellow former army officer began manufacturing chocolate candy under a contract with a Boston confectionery firm. But sugar prices rose out of proportion to those of candy and Bergengren's first business venture soon ended in failure.

When he accepted Filene's offer to direct the MCUA, Bergengren had practically no knowledge of credit unions; he simply needed a job. Yet, there was something in the credit union movement that deeply appealed to him. Its principle of service, the effort to promote thrift, and the attempt to reduce exploitation of the poor—all touched his humanitarian spirit. He had always wanted to serve his fellow men and here seemed like a worthy opportunity. Besides, it would provide a better living for his family. Thus Bergengren threw himself into the credit union movement with intense energy and enthusiasm. Within a short time he took a small, struggling movement and gave it new life and vitality. Bergengren more

[7] Wilson, *Common Sense Credit,* p. 39.

[8] Interview with Mrs. Roy F. Bergengren, Sept. 29 and 30, 1967.

than any other man established credit unions in the stream of America's economic life.

The day after Bergengren had accepted his new job, he reported to Room 23 at 5 Park Square, a building in the Back Bay end of Boston Common, the home of the Massachusetts Credit Union Association. There he met Frances P. Habern, office manager and stenographer, and his predecessor Charles W. Birtwell. In long conversations with them, he began to learn about credit unions. He also consulted with Charles Donahoe, the manager of a credit union for employees of the New England Telephone and Telegraph Company, one of the largest credit unions in the state. Bergengren also read Myron Herrick's *Rural Credits,* which discussed the European antecedents of the movement, particularly the work of Raiffeisen and Schulze-Delitzsch.

Despite his lack of familiarity with credit unionism, Bergengren realized that it was essential for him to push the organization of new societies. On his first day at work he wrote a business executive friend urging him to organize a credit union among his firm's employees. Bergengren himself organized several credit unions in the Springfield area and he conceived the idea of having an organization of credit unions in a city or region which could function on the order of a state league, which he called a chapter. The first chapter was organized in 1920.[9] Largely as a result of Bergengren's persistent work, nineteen new credit unions were organized in Massachusetts in 1921, more than in any earlier year, and by the end of the year there were eighty-two credit unions in the state.[10]

Although Filene had assured Bergengren that his job would be mainly to expand the movement, a financial crisis faced the organization when Bergengren first arrived at his office. Failure of the Cosmopolitan Trust Company not only tied up MCUA funds, but threatened to embarrass the organization because of its ties with Max Mitchell, an officer of the MCUA and president of the bank. Besides not having money to meet the payroll, Bergengren found that the MCUA was in debt to the bank for $6,500.[11] Even though the directors of the MCUA agreed to solve this financial crisis, Bergengren assumed most of the responsibility. Within eight weeks he had eliminated the debt of the association and received, along with the other employees, his first paycheck for two months.[12]

[9] Bergengren, *Crusade,* pp. 35–39.
[10] Snider, *Credit Unions in Massachusetts,* Table X, p. 27.
[11] Spencer Phenix Memorandum for Mr. Filene, Oct. 25, 1920.
[12] Bergengren, *Crusade,* p. 37.

Even though he had erased the MCUA's debts, there was no future income in sight with which to continue operations.

At this point Charles Birtwell explained a plan for a new organization which would have a broader base and provide at least partial financial support for the movement. Up to this time the MCUA had been run by a small group of public-spirited citizens contributing to what they considered a good cause. Birtwell, however, believed that any effective organization for promoting credit unionism must include all credit unions in the state as members. This would give the movement broader support and be in the democratic spirit of true credit unionism. During the autumn of 1920 a number of Massachusetts credit union leaders considered Birtwell's ideas, and on October 1 Bergengren discussed the matter of forming a new organization to promote the establishment of credit unions with the MCUA directors.

Despite continued discussions, it was not until June 18, 1921, that delegates from many of the state's credit unions met at the Norton Boat Club in Worcester, to form the Massachusetts Credit Union League.[13] The purpose of the league was "to promote interest and cooperation between credit unions and members of credit unions." Credit unions were eligible for membership in the league upon application to the board of directors and payment of an entry fee of two dollars and the first year's dues, which were based on the assets of the union, the minimum being two dollars and the maximum thirty dollars. Membership entitled the credit union to two voting delegates at any general meeting of the league. Individual credit union members were eligible for membership in the league at annual dues of one dollar, but they were not entitled to vote. The first president was Frederick E. Cox of the Telephone Workers Credit Union of Boston. Frances P. Habern became the secretary-treasurer and, as such, the paid manager of the league.[14]

When the Massachusetts Credit Union League opened its office on July 1, 1921, Bergengren thought that his brief career as a credit union promoter might be finished. He had liquidated the affairs of the MCUA and had actually been approached by Howard Coonley, the president of a large manufacturing company, to take a job in the firm's personnel department. Hearing about Coonley's proposition, Filene asked Bergen-

[13] Joseph Campana, "Fifty Years of Credit Union Progress in Massachusetts, 1909–1959," *Pioneer*, XXIV (May–June, 1959), 10.

[14] Credit Union League of Massachusetts, "Bylaws of the Credit Union League," pamphlet (MCUL, ca. 1920).

gren to meet him. Filene told Bergengren that he wanted to "take one more chance" in organizing the credit union movement at the national level, and that he was prepared to provide the money to finance such an effort. Would Bergengren, Filene asked, head up a national campaign? As Bergengren later recounted the interview: "I had become thoroughly sold on the credit union idea and I had no illusions as to the dimensions of the job. It looked fascinating. We talked it over and we formed a partnership—without any papers. We decided that we must have a name and created 'The Credit Union National Extension Bureau.' We agreed that no one else should have anything to do with the Bureau; that he would put up the money . . . and that we would make plans which I would execute. I was given extraordinary latitude." Filene and Bergengren agreed on three main objectives: to get state laws passed permitting the chartering of credit unions, to organize individual credit unions, and to form a national association which could take over the promotion of credit unionism in the United States.[15]

Filene's ambitious plans challenged Bergengren, who was ready to accept the job. But first he wanted to make certain that there would be adequate financing. He told Filene that a conservative budget covering five years of operation would require $125,000 to $150,000, and suggested that Filene might persuade six men in Boston and New York each to guarantee $5,000 a year. Bergengren said that he should not be responsible for raising funds because this would monopolize his time, and even then he might not succeed. Therefore, he urged Filene to guarantee money for a five-year budget before he began the job.[16]

Bergengren was also concerned about his own financial rewards. He explained to Filene that he was forty-one years old, had a family and had devoted several years to "public service work," with small financial returns. Therefore, he wrote, "you can readily understand that I must positively settle down now to work which has in it a fairly permanent future. I no longer can gamble, as a young man could, with my years." He then proposed a five-year contract at a salary of $7,500 for the first two years, $8,500 for the next two years, and $10,000 for the final year. If Filene wanted him to try just one year on an experimental basis, the salary should be $10,000, "a sum which is probably in excess of the real value of the job, depending on just what progress could be made in the year."

[15] Roy F. Bergengren, "When a Credit Union Partnership Was Formed," *The Bridge*, III (Aug., 1938), 6–7.

[16] "Financing the National Work," Bergengren to Filene, Memo no. 2, April 16, 1921.

However demanding Bergengren's proposals may have seemed, Filene agreed and Bergengren went to work.[17]

The Credit Union National Extension Bureau opened its office in July, 1921, sharing the headquarters of the Massachusetts Credit Union League which had begun operations a few days before. The office was furnished with a few nondescript pieces of secondhand furniture and a typewriter which Bergengren had obtained from Filene's office. Frances Habern was Bergengren's only office assistant, while also serving as secretary of the Massachusetts Credit Union League. Whereas the Massachusetts Credit Union League was the formal organization representing credit unionism in the Bay State, the extension bureau was simply an arrangement between Filene and Bergengren to promote credit unions throughout the entire country. At the same time, Bergengren and Filene had a very close association with the MCUL, and regarded it as a kind of laboratory where they could carry on experiments in credit union development.

From this first day in office at the extension bureau Bergengren conceived his job as being chiefly concerned with getting laws passed in every state which would authorize the chartering of credit unions. He could find no textbook telling how to achieve this goal, nor had any college course shown him how it was to be done. But Bergengren's work with the legislation creating the Metropolitan Planning Commission, plus his legal training, gave him some of the necessary know-how. From the very beginning, however, the various legislative campaigns were the result of trial and error.[18]

CUNEB received a boost during its first year when the Massachusetts bank commissioner decided that the Telephone Workers Credit Union of Boston had become too large. That union served all employees of the New England Telephone and Telegraph Company, which covered all of New England except Connecticut. The commissioner suggested that the existing credit union be retained for those employees in Boston, and that additional credit unions be organized in Springfield, Worcester, New Bedford, and Lowell. In Massachusetts, credit unions were promptly organized, as was one in Rhode Island where a general law existed. In New Hampshire, however, there was no general law, so Charles Donahoe, with some assistance from Bergengren, pushed one through the legislature. Maine did not pass a general law that year, but Donahoe was

[17] "My Own Connection With the National Work," *Ibid.*, Memo no. 3, April 16, 1921.

[18] Bergengren, *Crusade,* pp. 41 and 48.

successful in persuading the lawmakers to grant a special credit union charter for telephone workers in that state.[19]

Bergengren fully realized that most legislatures would not pass credit union laws unless someone carried on an effective educational effort. Since there were few local persons on whom he could call, Bergengren saw that he must get out of his Boston office and publicize the movement at the grass roots. People throughout the country must come to share his enthusiasm and vision of what credit unions could be for the masses, and see that laws got enacted in their own states. With this in mind, Bergengren and his wife set out in late December, 1921, to visit several states. He concentrated on the southern and border states, feeling that they were "virgin territory and offered an early legislative opportunity." His main objective was to contact local persons to whom he could entrust the subsequent legislative campaigns.

Bergengren stopped in Washington and then proceeded to Richmond, Virginia, where he met with C. H. Morrissett, state tax commissioner, and Richard W. Carrington, a prominent local attorney. Bergengren was successful in convincing these two men of the great value of credit unions, and they became chiefly instrumental in the passage of the Virginia Credit Union Act in 1922. In Raleigh, North Carolina, Bergengren had the opportunity to discuss rural credit unions with John Sprunt Hill, the "father" of the credit union act in that state. The law in South Carolina had never been used, but Bergengren persuaded two professors at Clemson College to organize the first credit union in that state.

Filene had suggested that Bergengren contact Herbert E. Choate in Atlanta. Bergengren saw Choate, who introduced him to E. Marvin Underwood, a local attorney. Both of these men later aided immeasurably in securing the passage of the credit union law in Georgia. From Atlanta the Bergengrens traveled to Tennessee. In Nashville they contacted E. E. Miller, editor of the *Southern Agriculturalist,* who had long been interested in cooperative credit, and Dan McCugin, who was not only the football coach at Vanderbilt University, but also an attorney "who knew his way around the state capitol." Bergengren met several friends of the movement in Kentucky, and made his last stop in Indiana, where in Indianapolis he met Leo Kaminsky, an attorney who became known as the "father of the Indiana credit union act."[20]

A few weeks later Bergengren enlisted Filene's help to follow up his

[19] *Ibid.*, p. 52.

[20] *Ibid.,* pp. 53–55; Edward L. Field, *Virginia Credit Union League: History, 1922–1954* (Richmond: Virginia Credit Union League, 1956), p. 7

initial contacts. The two men left Boston for Atlanta in mid-February, 1922. Writing to his mother while enroute by train, Filene told her that the credit union movement was on the verge of success. Local merchants and civic leaders honored Filene at a dinner which both the mayor of Atlanta and the governor of Georgia attended. During dinner, Filene convinced the governor of the value of credit unions "so well that he came out for them in his speech . . . ." [21] The next day Filene discussed the benefits of credit unions with a Kentucky legislative committee and then he and Bergengren journeyed to Louisville. There Filene spoke before a luncheon meeting of the board of trade. Keying his remarks to the presumably conservative audience, Filene said: "Emergencies require savings or else class dissatisfaction follows. Groups of savers operate as schools to teach persons who have little that there is nothing essentially wrong in the possession of property." [22]

Filene's and Bergengren's efforts contributed greatly to the successful legislative campaigns of 1922. The Virginia legislature enacted the first credit union law in the United States that may be credited to the work of the CUNEB. A few weeks later Kentucky passed its credit union act. Passage of two state laws in so short a time represented a major accomplishment for the movement. Since most legislatures would meet the following year, Bergengren believed that 1922 was "an experimental year, and that the big job really starts with the 1923 session." Meanwhile credit unionists made some preliminary contacts on behalf of credit union organization in Connecticut, Pennsylvania, New Jersey, West Virginia, Vermont, Arkansas, Ohio, Illinois, Michigan, Minnesota, and Washington. [23]

During 1923 the pattern of legislative efforts followed that established the previous year. Once again Filene traveled widely to boost the movement. In February he spoke before the Chambers of Commerce in Toledo and Indianapolis. He also wrote an article for the *Illinois Journal of Commerce* in which he praised credit unions as a way for employers to promote the welfare of their employees, thus making them better workers. Bergengren was also active. He consulted local supporters, urging them to introduce credit union legislation, and conducted voluminous correspondence with those who were recommended to him as possible state

---

[21] Filene to Mrs. William Filene, Feb. 14, 15, and 16, 1922.

[22] Bergengren, *Crusade,* p. 57; *Louisville Courier-Journal,* Feb. 18, 1922.

[23] "In Re: Enlargement of Functions of the Credit Union National Extension Bureau," Bergengren Memorandum, Mar. 20, 1922.

leaders, or who had written for information about how to get a law passed.[24]

Despite a rather intensive effort by Bergengren and Filene, only Tennessee and Indiana passed credit union laws in 1923. However, lawmakers amended existing legislation in South Carolina and Wisconsin to bring it into line with accepted credit union principles. In Alabama, Michigan, Illinois, and Wyoming, credit union bills passed one house of the legislature. Bills in Arizona and Iowa received some support during the legislative sessions, but votes were postponed. Sponsors in Ohio withdrew their bill "when it seemed that enough preliminary work had not been done to warrant risking the possibility of rejection." Bergengren reported that "radicals" in Oklahoma opposed a bill there as being too conservative, while bankers fought a Pennsylvania measure because it had originated with a so-called radical group, the American Federation of Labor.[25]

The successful campaign for credit union legislation in Indiana characterized the legislative efforts in several states. Introduced in the senate, the measure was referred to the judiciary committee for hearings. However, small loan companies bitterly opposed the bill. Prospects of passage were very dim when the judiciary committee sent the bill to the committee on banks. Leo Kaminsky, who handled the Indiana campaign for CUNEB, wired Bergengren for assistance, and he and Filene hurried to Indianapolis. They attended a meeting of the Chamber of Commerce, and convinced several businessmen to testify before the banking committee in support of the bill. Luck may have played a part in the outcome when an influenza epidemic caused "the most obstreperous of the loan-shark adherents on the Committee" to remain in bed, and the committee reported the bill favorably to the senate. Once the bill passed both houses, it was, after some uneasy moments, signed into law by the governor.[26]

Bergengren found during his early efforts to get credit union legislation that the sources of opposition and support for credit unions were unpredictable. A Gary banker, for example, was one of the strongest supporters of the bill in Indiana, and in Georgia the bankers association issued a pamphlet stating that credit unions were agencies of "self-help" which deserved "more encouragement." Even better, the statement con-

---

[24] *Toledo Blade,* Feb. 20, 1923; *Indianapolis News,* Feb. 24, 1923; Edward A. Filene, "Usury, 'Greatest of Boot-Legging Businesses,' Finds Worthy Foe," *Illinois Journal of Commerce* (Mar., 1923), reprint, unpaged.

[25] "Legislative Activities 1923 up to and Including October 18, 1923," Bergengren Memorandum to Filene, n.d.

[26] Kaminsky's account quoted in Bergengren, *Crusade,* p. 59.

tinued, "it teaches the principles of banking to a class of people in whose lives, heretofore, banking has meant less than nothing." Yet in Connecticut, California, and Colorado, bankers spearheaded the opposition to credit union bills and initially succeeded in thwarting their passage.[27]

Looking back at the results of his first two years of legislative effort, Bergengren had every right to be encouraged. Five states had passed new credit laws, amendments had been added to two existing statutes, and a solid foundation had been laid for future campaigns in more than a dozen other states. Bergengren personally deserved much of the credit for this success, although in every state he had the assistance of attorneys, interested citizens, and legislators. Filene, too, gave liberally of his time, energy, and prestige. He talked personally with key people, referred Bergengren to friends in several states who could be helpful, and carried on correspondence with many prospective supporters. Moreover, Filene gave Bergengren general guidance and advice, and perhaps most important he financed CUNEB.

Extension bureau financing came almost entirely from the Twentieth Century Fund, a foundation established by Filene in 1919 under the name of the Cooperative League, whose purpose was to promote "the investigation and study of and providing instruction as to economic and industrial questions and aiding and improving the relations between employers and employees." In 1922, the name of the Cooperative League was changed to the Twentieth Century Fund and its purposes were broadened to include "the improvement of economic, industrial, civic and educational conditions." Filene contributed the entire endowment of the fund, and in 1928 signed over to it the income from all his holdings in the William Filene's Sons Company. Filene was president of the fund, but had only one vote along with the other directors.[28]

Filene required Bergengren to make periodic reports to the directors of the fund and to submit annual budgets. In March, 1922, after CUNEB had begun its various state legislative campaigns, Bergengren submitted a tentative budget and his first plan for organizing the bureau for effective work. He proposed to hire five full-time employees for the Boston office consisting of a publicity agent, a man "to do entirely organization and follow-up work after legislation has been secured in a given state,"

---

[27] Bergengren memo, "Legislative Activities 1923"; Georgia Bankers' Association statement quoted in Filene's "Usury," unpaged.

[28] Evans Clark, *Financing the Consumer* (New York: Harper and Brothers, 1931), pp. ix–x; Gerald W. Johnson, *Liberal's Progress* (New York; Coward-McCann, 1948), pp. 242–43.

and three stenographers. In addition, he suggested that ten local representatives be retained on a fee basis in the states where preliminary work had been done. Other items in the budget were to cover printing, postage and office supplies, and $4,000 for travel. Bergengren proposed expenditures of $19,740, exclusive of his own salary.[29] Filene rejected this budget as excessive and directed Bergengren to submit another. Bergengren then dropped his idea for more personnel, pared other expenditures, and came up with a budget of only $6,000 which was approved.[30]

The following year Bergengren again failed to get more liberal support. He was usually willing to trim his operational figures to meet demands of Filene and the fund, but he was unhappy about his own remuneration. The revised budget for 1923–24, for example, contained at the direction of Filene, a salary of $8,500 for Bergengren, who believed that the amount should be larger. He had, Bergengren explained to Filene, "made fairly good progress with a rather difficult job." Then he added:

One difficulty of all work of this sort—it has in it no definite future. The man who does this sort of work chances the future and few men chance it. . . . The credit union job is a big thing—worth doing whatever sacrifice be involved and so long as you will back the effort I shall go right along trying to get results. When I fail to get results I will know it before you will and will eliminate myself. When you feel that the work can no longer be financed through your effort, because of other work that there is to do, I shall do my best to keep the credit union work going forward. Meantime—I have a wife and two children—if the work is important enough to warrant a larger salary—I sure need it.

Bergengren not only complained about his own salary, but worried constantly about stable financing for the movement. Conversations with Filene and attendance at a meeting of the fund directors convinced Bergengren that he could count on money from that source for only two more years. Then what would happen? It would be impossible, he wrote Filene, "to make the credit union work self-supporting within that time. We will do extremely well if we get the legislative program out of the way in the next two years and there must be an extensive organization program before credit unions will of themselves support a national propaganda organization program."[31] While Bergengren worried about

[29] Bergengren, "In re: Enlargement of Functions of the Credit Union National Extension Bureau," Mar. 20, 1922.

[30] Bergengren to William H. Short, June 8, 1922.

[31] Bergengren to Filene, June 11, 1923.

finances, he did not let this concern deter him from his immediate goal of getting more state laws which would permit him to achieve the basic objective of organizing credit unions on a broad scale.

CUNEB had three bills pending in state legislatures in 1924, one of which was in New Jersey. In January, State Senator Arthur N. Pierson wired Bergengren to come to his office in Newark to help him draft a credit union bill. The genesis of the New Jersey law somewhat paralleled that of Massachusetts. A few years earlier employees of the Worthington Pump and Machinery Corporation organized a cooperative savings and lending institution. The organization became so large, however, that George Haines, who drafted the plan, decided that it should be brought under the supervision of the state banking authorities. Meanwhile, as he was drafting a bill to accomplish that purpose, Pierson heard of credit unions and arranged a conference which Bergengren attended. Subsequently, the senator interested J. Philip Bird, president of the New Jersey Manufacturers' Association, in the bill, and a meeting was held at the Newark Athletic Club on January 4, attended by Bird, Pierson, the bank commissioner, the head of the New Jersey State Chamber of Commerce, and others. Filene addressed the group and it was decided to push for a credit union act. With little opposition, the bill passed both houses of the legislature on May 1, and the governor signed it into law. Two southern states, Louisiana and Mississippi, also enacted laws during 1924.[32]

Besides pushing through three credit union bills that year, Bergengren made plans for a much bigger drive in 1925. Indeed, 1925 became the "biggest" legislative year in the history of the movement, with six states enacting credit union laws. Whereas most of Bergengren's attention had focused on the South during the first three years, by 1925 he turned his sights mainly to the Middle West. He decided to "make no piecemeal job of it," and legislators introduced bills in Ohio, Illinois, Iowa, Minnesota, and Michigan. By the end of the year all those states had enacted a credit union law except Ohio. Laws in Georgia and West Virginia added a bonus to CUNEB's efforts.[33]

Illinois, a populous, heavily industrialized state, was highly important for the credit union movement. The first step in the effort to get an enabling law passed there occurred in 1923 at a luncheon given for Filene by a Chicago attorney, Joseph H. Defrees. An influential group of men

[32] *Ibid.,* Jan. 7, 1924; *The Bridge* (June, 1924), pp. 1 and 4; Bergengren, *Crusade,* p. 68; and *The Bridge* (July, 1924), p. 1.
[33] Bergengren, *Crusade,* p. 77.

attended, including John W. O'Leary, vice-president of the Chicago Trust Company, and Wheeler Sammons, vice-president of the A. W. Shaw Company, both of whom were later identified with the national movement. As a result of this initial meeting, Senator Harold Kessinger of Aurora sponsored a bill in the Illinois senate. But the measure was a poor one, and it was vigorously opposed by the licensed moneylenders of the state. Both factors contributed to its defeat in the House of Representatives.

Looking toward more effective leadership for future legislative efforts in the state, Bergengren retained Willard King, whom he described as "a brilliant young lawyer who was fast moving up in an old, long-established firm in Chicago." King began working on a new draft bill, but was faced with a crucial problem. The state constitution provided that all banking laws had to be submitted to the people in a referendum, and experience had proven that it was almost impossible to have a banking law ratified by popular vote. Therefore, King had to draft a bill which contained no banking features. A reasonably good precedent was available in the Building and Loan Association Act which had been in operation for several years. Another constitutional difficulty was a provision that shareholders in corporations had to be given one vote in electing directors for every share of stock owned. This stricture violated the generally accepted credit union principle of one vote per stockholder regardless of the number of shares he owned. King solved this problem by providing in the draft that each credit union member would have one vote on all questions except the election of directors.

Once King completed the draft, Senator Kessinger again introduced it in the senate, and Representative Ralph E. Church sponsored the house version. But the measure again met strenuous opposition. Some legislators clearly represented the interests of the loan sharks, while others spoke for the building and loan associations. A few legislators were not too enthusiastic about the bill simply because it represented, in the words of Willard King, "a new-fangled idea." On the other hand, it received some strong support. In the first place, after the Cook County Bankers Association had adopted a resolution opposing the bill, King convinced the association that credit unions would really be an advantage to bankers. They would, for example, provide additional deposits for banks. In addition, John M. Glenn, secretary of the Illinois Manufacturers Association, and John Walker of the Illinois Federation of Labor issued a joint letter supporting the bill. King was not able to win the support of the Chicago Association of Commerce, which branded the bill as one "to permit a lot of ordinary people such as blacksmiths and bricklayers to go into the banking business, where they will certainly lose their money." Nevertheless the bill passed both houses and was signed into law by Governor Len Small on June 26, 1925.[34]

The story of the Iowa credit union act developed somewhat differently from that of Illinois. Bergengren got officials of the Iowa State Federation of Labor to urge Senator Charles J. Fulton of Jefferson County to introduce a credit union measure in the form of an amendment to the state banking act. As elsewhere the sponsors in Iowa were motivated by the high interest rate being charged by small loan companies. The bill was introduced too late in the 1924 session, however, to receive serious consideration. Again in 1925 Fulton introduced his bill, and then circumstances were more favorable. Numerous bank failures had led to great interest in new banking legislation, and the credit union bill was one of thirty such measures considered during the 1925 session. The bill passed the senate on March 5 by unanimous vote, and a few days later the house approved it. A recent historian of the Iowa Credit Union League explained the success of the measure in terms of "general ignorance on the subject of cooperative credit (rather) than to any strong support among the legislators for it." [35]

Despite general progress, there were failures during 1925. One of the most decisive defeats occurred in Ohio. There the powerful building and loan associations maintained a lobby in Columbus which openly fought the efforts of the credit union advocates. "When the lobbyist got tired," Bergengren later wrote, "he passed the cudgels over to the State Bankers Association, and they opposed our efforts with equally effective enthusiasm." So thorough was defeat that a credit union bill did not become law in Ohio until 1931.[36] Building and loan associations were also chiefly responsible for the defeat in 1925 of the credit union bill in Missouri. The California legislature passed the bill sponsored by CUNEB, but the governor vetoed it.[37]

Still, 1925 was a very successful legislative year for Bergengren. Six additional states had enacted enabling laws, bringing the total to twenty-

[34] Willard L. King, "How It All Began—35 Years Ago." *Credit Union Spotlight,* IV (June, 1960), 7; *The Bridge* (Aug., 1925), pp. 1 and 7.

[35] Rosemarie Bougie, *History of the Iowa Credit Union League, 1930–1956* (Des Moines: Iowa Credit Union League, 1958), pp. 8–9; *The Bridge* (April, 1925), pp. 1–2.

[36] Bergengren, *Crusade,* p. 77.

[37] *Ibid.,* p. 91.

four. Bergengren could look back only four years when there were only three such laws in the United States. He could and did take pride in his accomplishments. While the passage of state laws was important, they were only the means to the more important end of getting credit unions organized and in operation. Bergengren never lost sight of this basic goal. He constantly considered ways and means to organize credit unions, and spent much of his time in these efforts when he was not involved in legislative campaigns.

He firmly believed that nothing better illustrated the worth of the credit union idea than the operation of a successful local unit. Moreover, he thought it was necessary to organize a few credit unions in any state immediately after a law was passed in order to show that the law was being utilized. Seldom did Bergengren himself go into a state to organize a single credit union, but his counsel was usually evident through correspondence. He encouraged the organization of the first urban credit union in Kentucky in Louisville. Soon after the Wisconsin law was amended, two credit unions were organized, the first being the People's Rural Credit Union of Winter and the second, the Credit Union of the Employees of the City of Milwaukee. In Indiana Leo Kaminsky organized a credit union among the employees of Wasson and Company department store. This was the first credit union in the Middle West. Thus, in small numbers, credit unions began to spring up in each state where a law had been passed.[38]

The "small farmers of the South" attracted much of Bergengren's attention during his early efforts to organize credit unions. He pointed out in 1923 that credit unions had played a large part in the plans developed by rural credit advocates and had recently been taken up at the Conference of Southern Mountain Workers at Knoxville, Tennessee. To emphasize his great interest in the possibilities of service in that section, he called the credit problems of southern farmers "the greatest present credit union problem and the problem most promising of results."[39]

In order to push the organizational work early in 1924 Bergengren employed Angela Melville, a social worker in the southern Appalachians. Bergengren gave her the title of field secretary and a "roving commis-

[38] "Summary of Organization Work 1923 up to and Including October 18, 1923," Bergengren Memorandum to Filene, n.d.

[39] "Report of Activities of the Credit Union National Extension Bureau as of April 14, 1923," Bergengren to Directors of Twentieth Century Fund, n.d., p. 7 (hereafter cited as "CUNEB Report to April, 1923").

sion" to organize credit unions in Kentucky and later in Tennessee. He informed Filene of his choice, saying that he hoped that it might soon be possible to persuade a local citizen to take over the financing of the organizational work in Kentucky. Bergengren again justified his interest in the southern areas of the country, by writing Filene: "Credit unions are more needed among small farmers in the South than among any other class of people and the Southern Highland Region touches eight states in the South, in most of which we now have available legislation." Moreover, in addition to helping "the over two million people whose economic salvation depends upon some relief of this sort," Bergengren believed that credit unions organized by Miss Melville would "have a great human interest value and will supply us with a lot of new and very fine publicity material." [40]

Filene thought it was foolish to concentrate so much effort on southern mountaineers. "This Kentucky work is a fine charity," he wrote, "but of course not at all what I had in mind when you spoke of employing an organizer. I feel that here you are thinking with your heart not with your mind." Filene insisted that, after spending so much time and money to get state laws passed, broader efforts should be made to organize credit unions. Moreover, further work should be done to get laws in the other states. After these goals were accomplished, Filene said, "we can be generous to the Southern Mountaineers." [41]

Acknowledging Filene's criticism of his southern organizational work, Bergengren pointed out that the cooperative credit movement in the United States was much more complicated than it had been during the pioneer stage in other countries. He reminded Filene that Raiffeisen and Schulze-Delitzsch divided Germany between them, while Desjardins confined himself to one province in Canada. The United States movement embraced a much larger geographic area and faced multiple needs among both urban and rural workers. "I realize that you do not agree with me as to the importance of the agricultural end of our work," he wrote, "but, if there is anything that all present-day students seem to be agreed upon, it is that the farmer is in a desperate plight and that he needs help and that the farmer is at the foundation of our whole social and economic structure." Filene replied that he thought, "we ought to help farmers but first in due proportion to our means." [42]

[40] Bergengren to Filene, Jan. 24, 1924.
[41] Penciled comment in margin of *ibid.*
[42] Penciled comment in margin of Bergengren to Filene, April 9, 1924.

Bergengren's attitude stemmed in part from his romantic notion about the South and its people, particularly the mountaineers. But because Filene opposed concentrating organizational efforts in the rural South, Bergengren soon transferred Miss Melville from the mountains of Kentucky and Tennessee to New Jersey and other eastern industrial states. However, he never gave up his interest in rural credit unions, pointing with pride every time one was organized. Throughout the remainder of his credit union career, he continued to promote interest in rural cooperative development.

An early boost to the organization of credit unions came when the United States Post Office Department created its Service Relations agency to promote the welfare of postal employees. Fortunately, one of Filene's close friends, Henry L. Dennison, an active supporter of credit unions, was chosen to head the agency. Bergengren worked with Dennison to form credit unions among postal employees in Brockton and Springfield, Massachusetts. [43] Dennison reported, for instance, that the Brockton credit union had begun with 78 members out of 136 employees, but soon had 112 members, 43 of whom had borrowed a total of $2,675. By April, 1923, preliminary work was being done in other states to organize credit unions among postal employees. By the following year fifteen groups of postal employees in as many states were in the process of organizing credit unions. Dennison concluded that "the experimental stage is passed. . . ." [44] Endorsement by the Post Office Department, with the implied approval of the federal government, gave the credit union movement additional prestige which Bergengren hastened to exploit. By September 30, 1925, there were forty-four credit unions among postal employees, thirty-two of which reported a membership of 7,320, with shares and deposits of $258,000 and loans granted since organization of $591,000.[45]

Although organization of credit unions among some groups of public employees made good progress, Bergengren at first showed little interest in trying to establish credit unions among industrial workers. In his "five-year plan," submitted to the directors of the Twentieth Century Fund in January, 1924, he completely omitted industrial wage earners from the organizations and groups which he believed held a strong potential for rapid organizational work. Within a few months, however, he began

[43] "CUNEB Report to April, 1923."

[44] Henry L. Dennison to Members of Local Service Councils, Mar. 1, 1924, mimeographed.

[45] *The Bridge* (July, 1925), p. 1; (Oct., 1925), p. 2; (Nov., 1924), p. 1; (Dec., 1925), p. 7. *Monthly Labor Review*, XXII (Feb., 1926), 479–80.

to devote a great deal of time explaining the virtues of credit unions to industrialists and their employees. In April, 1924, he attended the annual convention of the Manufacturers' Association of New Jersey at the invitation of its president, J. Philip Bird. Through that meeting, Bergengren received encouragement from twenty-six out of the thirty representatives of some of the larger state industries to organize credit unions in their establishments, and left with the assurance that he had "the complete cooperation of the Manufacturers Association."[46]

Industrial credit unions became even more significant after such states as Illinois and Michigan passed enabling legislation. Many inquiries came into CUNEB headquarters from manufacturers in Michigan soon after that state enacted a credit union law. The first credit union in the state was organized among employees of the Mueller Brass Company at Port Huron.[47] In the fall of 1925, the Illinois Manufacturers' Association circularized its entire membership, calling attention to the new law and offering cooperation in organizing credit unions among industrial employees. As a result of this powerful support, the first credit union in Illinois was organized by a member of the association, the Belden Manufacturing Company of Chicago. In November Bergengren addressed a joint meeting sponsored by the Industrial Relations Association and the Manufacturers' Association in Chicago, called for the specific purpose of discussing credit unions. Bergengren later dubbed it "the greatest credit union meeting I ever attended." While in Illinois, Bergengren made his headquarters in the office of the Illinois Manufacturers' Association.[48] Thus, Bergengren quickly saw how valuable friendly industrialists and their trade associations could be in advancing the credit union movement.

Bergengren's experience seemed to show that great potential for organizing credit unions existed among almost any group with a common bond. Even before California had a credit union law, teachers in San Diego organized a kind of extralegal credit union early in 1924. A year later teachers in Detroit met to consider whether a credit union would benefit the 5,700 teachers in that city. Within a few months the Detroit Teachers' credit union was organized, and it became one of the largest credit unions in the country. Its success encouraged teachers all over the United States to organize local credit unions. One could never predict,

---

[46] Report accompanying letter from Bergengren to Filene, April 17, 1924.

[47] *The Bridge* (Aug., 1925), p. 7; (Sept., 1925), p. 1.

[48] *Ibid.* (Sept., 1925), p. 2; (Oct., 1925), p. 2; (Dec., 1925), p. 2.

however, what type of group would take up the credit union idea. In Mississippi the McComb Business Women's Club organized the first credit union and in Kentucky the employees of the Standard Printing Company took the lead. One great break-through came in North Carolina in the summer of 1925, when Harriet Berry organized two urban credit unions—one at the Southern Railway shops and the other in the Central Labor Union of Asheville.[49]

Despite rapid development of credit unions in a number of states, Filene's primary interest continued to be in the Massachusetts movement. He believed that "if we succeed in *largely* increasing the number of credit unions in Massachusetts . . . then that success in itself would boom the credit union in other states."[50] Bergengren agreed with Filene that more rapid development in Massachusetts would set a good example for other states. Yet, Bergengren did not want to sponsor a strong drive there because he believed that the Massachusetts Credit Union League should develop its own movement. As he wrote Filene: "anything we do in Massachusetts . . . should be done through the League in order to build up in the League a sense of leadership in this state." The league, however, had scant financial resources, and only one part-time employee in Miss Habern. Bergengren recommended to Filene that some wealthy patron be induced to finance a vigorous organizational campaign "through the League," but this effort failed.[51]

Indeed, 1924 and 1925 were two of the worst organizational years in the history of the Massachusetts movement, for only five new credit unions were formed in the state. By the end of 1925 there were no more credit unions in Massachusetts than in 1922, indicating that the state league had been ineffective as an organizing agency.[52]

The fact that credit unions were again having difficulties with the bank commissioner helps to explain some of the movement's slow growth in the Bay State. In 1923 Bank Commissioner Joseph C. Allen found many of the loose and unbusinesslike practices that his predecessors had complained about, and he appointed a person who had extensive supervisory experience to manage the credit union section of his office. As Bergengren reported, "from that time on everything having to do with the supervision of credit unions rapidly stiffened up."[53]

[49] *Ibid.* (May, 1925), p. 1; (July, 1924), p. 3; (Aug., 1925), p. 1.

[50] Filene's handwritten comments in margin of Bergengren to Filene, April 9, 1924.

[51] Filene's comments in margin of Bergengren to Filene, April 17, 1924.

[52] Snider, *Credit Union in Massachusetts,* Table X, p. 27.

[53] Bergengren to Filene, Dec. 20, 1924.

Publicly, Allen indicated no ill will toward credit unions, but he believed that a complete revision of the credit union law was necessary. Allen advocated several modifications of the statute which the movement opposed. One amendment would have limited a member's shares in a credit union to only $100, while another would have restricted loans to "small personal loans for remedial purposes." A third would have prohibited credit unions from making real-estate loans. Bergengren, who was a member of a commission appointed in 1924 to study revision of the credit union law, characterized these proposals as ones that "would have ended credit union development in Massachusetts," and he was successful in convincing the commission to reject Allen's amendments.

The new law, based upon the commission's report, satisfied credit union spokesmen, and the movement especially benefited from a provision that prohibited "any person, partnership or corporation from receiving deposits of money from members on account of shares or deposits and loaning the same in the way and manner of a credit union." Within only a few months after passage of the act, 156 such groups had received charters converting their organizations to credit unions.[54] With little organizational work of its own, therefore, the Massachusetts movement in 1926 enjoyed the greatest increase in new credit unions in its history. Bergengren's desire to protect the Massachusetts movement from unfavorable legislation, as well as his efforts to get individual credit unions in the state operating on an efficient basis, indicate his belief that Massachusetts was of "vital importance to the national program."[55]

One of the early problems that continued to face the movement was the question of interlending between credit unions. Filene had always believed that when a local credit union did not have enough loan funds, it should be permitted to borrow from other credit unions with surplus money rather than having to rely on commercial banks. This latter practice not only endangered the credit union in case the bank failed; it also made the credit union reliant on the very financial institutions which tended to exploit or ignore small borrowers. Moreover, with no provisions to lend to other credit unions, some organizations built up relatively unproductive surpluses. The Massachusetts law provided that surplus funds could only be deposited in savings or commercial banks, which meant as Bergengren explained, "decreased earning power and decreased usefulness." Bergengren informed Frederick E. Cox, president of the Massachu-

[54] Joseph Campana, "A Glimpse of the Credit Union Movement," *Pioneer,* XII (May, 1946), 20.

[55] "CUNEB Report to April, 1923," pp. 5–6.

setts league, that investment of surplus funds was becoming "increasingly bothersome," and recommended that a special committee make a careful study and propose a solution. He suggested the possibility of real-estate loans, and the cooperative buying of goods for members, but he admitted that "no carefully conceived plan has ever been worked out which could be recommended with safety." [56] Consequently, the solution to the problem of what a credit union should do with any surplus funds was left unsolved for several years.

Among his many activities connected with the credit union movement, Bergengren considered publicizing the national effort as one of his most important responsibilities. During his second year with the extension bureau, he wrote a twenty-four-page pamphlet in which he discussed the philosophy, history, and methods of operating credit unions. By the spring of 1923, 8,000 copies of the booklet had been distributed to interested persons throughout the United States. *Collier's,* one of the country's most widely read magazines, carried a major article on credit unions, which brought scores of inquiries to CUNEB from thirty-eight states. A number of other articles appeared in smaller agricultural and trade magazines. Bergengren's greatest publicity effort, however, was the writing of a full-length book entitled *Cooperative Banking: A Credit Union Book,* which was published by the Macmillan Company in 1923. He devoted almost the entire summer of 1922 to its preparation. *Cooperative Banking* became the first comprehensive study of the history, philosophy, and operation of credit unions in the United States.

To further publicize the movement, in June, 1924, Bergengren launched a four-page newsletter which he christened *The Bridge.* He selected this name because, as he wrote, "the credit union is in very fact —a bridge; it may be the bridge over which the tenant farmer travels the wide gap that separates him from ownership of the soil; it may be the way that opens the great broader possibilities for himself and his family." He added that "if credit unions, when logically developed on the broadest scale, educate great numbers of our people in the management and control of money; if they result in a better citizenship; if they serve as a great practical Americanization process—the credit union system will prove to be a bridge—over which, as a people, we may travel to a more perfect, a sound and a permanent democracy." [57] When Bergengren sent Filene a copy of the new publication, he explained: "I adopted this name—

[56] Bergengren to Cox, May 17, 1922.
[57] *The Bridge* (June, 1924), 1.

The Bridge—having in mind your suggestion of many months ago that it might be possible to develop some time a publication which would be primarily useful as a means of distributing information not only about credit unions but about allied subjects as well." The primary objective was "to indicate something of the national development in such fashion that a reader could get a general idea without any considerable reading." He intended to publish the newsletter on a four months' trial and if it succeeded, he would try to make it self-supporting. The immediate expense of publishing *The Bridge* was small. The first edition of 2,500 copies cost CUNEB only $76.[58]

Now the credit union movement had a publicity outlet of its own. *The Bridge* carried articles of popular interest on loan sharks and other credit problems, human interest stories on how credit unions had aided people in distress, and analyses of how credit unions fitted into the general economy. The paper reported on legislative campaigns and new state laws and the progress of organizational efforts. Special sections were devoted to the movement in Massachusetts and New York. Bergengren took justifiable pride in the publication, but his journalistic interests would cause him difficulties in the future.

Closely allied to his publicity work were Bergengren's efforts to obtain the endorsement of organizations whose support would aid his legislative and organizational work. During 1924 he sought increased support among bankers who in the past had both supported and opposed credit unions. Bergengren insisted that bankers should endorse the credit union system because "it would become a natural and normal supplement to the banking system promoting thrift among millions of people who save nothing, and caring for the credit requirements of the vast numbers of people who are bedevilled by the usurer." [59] In the spring of 1924 he and friends of the credit union movement appealed to the executive council of the American Bankers' Association in hopes that it might recommend endorsement to the full association. Bergengren supplied officials of the bankers' organization with CUNEB publications and copies of his book, *Cooperative Banking*.

Filene agreed with Bergengren's plan to approach the ABA, but warned that the whole matter might redound against the credit union movement. Bergengren was quick to reply that he was "by no means

[58] Bergengren to Filene, June 7, 1924.

[59] Bergengren, "Five Year Plan to the Directors of the Twentieth Century Fund," ca. Jan., 1924, p. C-3.

optimistic about the American Bankers Association," that he agreed "we are playing with a double-edged sword," but that it had been "almost impossible to avoid taking the matter up at this time." The general counsel of the ABA had been studying credit unions and building and loan associations. As a result, Bergengren thought that the ABA would make some sort of report during its next meeting. The work being done by pro–credit union people, therefore, had "been to decrease the possibility that this report so far as it affects credit unions would be necessarily adverse." [60]

When the executive council met on April 28, it discussed the credit union movement and then referred the question to its Savings Bank Division for further study. Bergengren immediately arranged a conference with the chairman of that committee and considered the results of the meeting favorable. He still thought, however, that the executive committee's reference of the matter to the Savings Bank Division was "most unfortunate," because credit unions did most of their banking business with commercial banks, which were more able to appreciate credit unions than bankers in the Savings Bank Division.

Later in the year Bergengren addressed 2,000 delegates to the American Institute of Banking meeting in Baltimore, at the invitation of the chairman of its Credits Conference. Bergengren told Filene that this was a most important occasion, as the institute carried on educational programs among younger bankers and acted as a "feeder" for the ABA. Bergengren not only told the delegates about the credit union movement, but he also spoke privately to the institute's president, "who is convinced of the value of the credit union and will help it in his home state," of California. Bergengren reported to Filene that the next issue of *The Bridge* would carry a cartoon picturing "bankers as fine and friendly fellows and indicate that the credit union movement is willing to march along with them, but will go it alone if necessary." [61]

Although the American Bankers' Association failed to endorse credit unions openly, the ABA did not at the time seem hostile to the movement. The editor of the association's journal invited Filene to write an article on credit unions, suggesting that his piece "might dissipate the belief that the credit union is a bank and otherwise show how they take care of people without bank credit." Filene submitted a rough draft of his ideas and asked Bergengren to prepare the article for him.[62] Bergengren

---

[60] Bergengren to Filene, April 26, 1924.

[61] *Ibid.*, Aug. 2, 1924.

[62] James E. Clark to Filene, Nov. 11, 1924; Filene to Bergengren, n.d.

warned Filene not to forget the old proverb, "Beware of Greeks bearing gifts." Still, he thought that the very fact that the journal had asked for such an article indicated a "state of mind" in the ABA "which we have been trying to create for a long time." [63]

Filene's article was entitled, "The Credit Union—a Crusader Against Usury." It was thoroughly conservative in tone, emphasizing that credit unions would "exercise a profoundly sane and sobering influence on the masses of people, at the same time bringing to them that increasing opportunity for self-development which will aim for an increasing prosperity." He challenged bankers to support the movement as a means to correct social discontent before it became serious, because "the time to defeat revolution is before it starts." Appealing to the self-interest of bankers, Filene insisted that the average wage worker had access to credit only at usurious rates. The average borrower, he suggested, "is willing to conclude that all interest is wrong," and "may easily be persuaded that all banking is wrong because he knows that banks deal in credit and yet, when he needs credit, the only source of credit open to him is the usurer." Thus, according to Filene, credit unions become a "natural and normal supplement to the present banking system," promoting thrift, eliminating usury, and educating people to understand the American economic system. [64] The Filene article gave the credit union movement its greatest exposure among bankers up to that time. However, most bankers were indifferent to credit unions because this type of financing was not sufficiently developed to provide any threat to their interests.

Securing the passage of state legislation, directing the organization of credit unions, publicizing the movement, and defending it from hostile attacks fully occupied Bergengren and the Credit Union National Extension Bureau from 1921 to 1925. These years were filled with both successes and failures, but Bergengren could point to more victories than defeats. Twenty-six states had enabling legislation by 1925 and hundreds of local credit unions had been organized under these laws. While tough problems still existed, by the middle 1920s a fair degree of momentum had been generated out of which a genuine national movement could develop.

[63] Bergengren to Filene, Nov. 17, 1924.

[64] Edward A. Filene, "The Credit Union—a Crusader Against Usury," *American Bankers' Association Journal*, XVII (Jan., 1925), 439.

CHAPTER V

Expansion and Consolidation, 1925-29

ALTHOUGH the early 1920s had witnessed substantial expansion of the credit union movement, progress fell far short of Bergengren's long-range objectives. Moreover, several disturbing problems remained unsolved. There was, for example, a need for better organization and more personnel to carry on the work, financing continued to be inadequate, and there were differences of opinion between Bergengren and Filene in regard to procedural policies and over-all priorities.

Bergengren felt severely handicapped by his small office staff of only three—himself, Miss Habern, who served as office manager on a part time basis, and Arthur N. Fernald, who carried the title of assistant secretary. The extensive field work so necessary to organize credit unions, to get credit union laws enacted, and to form state leagues was done mainly by Bergengren with the assistance of Angela Melville.[1] Bergengren's work load had become so heavy by 1924 that he told Filene that he could no longer submit the usual weekly reports. In order to lighten his own load and to increase efficiency, Bergengren wanted to employ "field secretaries" to carry on organizational work outside of Massachusetts, but he was unable to get Filene's approval for the additional expense.[2]

Most of Bergengren's administrative problems were associated with the perennial lack of money. In the long run Bergengren hoped that the financial burdens of credit union organization would be taken over by the state leagues. But this prospect, even in Massachusetts which had an active credit union association, was in 1925 some years away. Meanwhile, the financial problems persisted.

When Bergengren pressed for more funds, Filene insisted that he obtain local financial support. Bergengren agreed in principle and tried his best, but he succeeded in raising money only from John Sprunt Hill

---

[1] By the end of 1925 Bergengren was left with no aide in the field due to the resignation of Angela Melville as field secretary; *The Bridge* (Dec., 1925), p. 2.

[2] Bergengren to Filene, April 9, 1924.

in North Carolina.[3] Moreover, the Twentieth Century Fund, with Filene's complete backing, refused to commit itself to long-range financial support for credit union development. Although Bergengren prepared elaborate reports and exhibits to back his case before the fund's board, he complained to Filene of cavalier treatment, and accused the board of not giving serious consideration to the needs of the credit union movement.[4]

In May Bergengren asked for $37,882 to operate CUNEB in fiscal 1925, an increase of slightly more than $12,000 over the previous year. The rather large increase was to be used for the employment of three new field secretaries which he considered essential to advance the credit union movement. He urged Filene to support his budget, and argued that if it were approved, "we shall have no difficulty working out a plan which will assure the continuance of the work, and enable me to build up the modest personnel we need to carry on the work enthusiastically to completion." [5]

But Filene refused to agree. Rather than spending so much on organizational work, Filene believed that CUNEB should rely on national organizations to build credit unions among their members. Disappointed at Filene's stand, Bergengren replied that he would "cheerfully abide by your decisions and try to carry them out so long as I am identified with the Bureau." But he went on to explain: "Whenever there is a difference of opinion between those engaged in any undertaking, decisions have to be made. In the office here I consult on every important move with my associates but in the end always make up my own mind and take the responsibility. The Bureau belongs to you. In the past I have tried—with a measure of success—to carry its work on faithfully. The work is a great work—not fully appreciated as yet; were I to become suddenly the richest man in America I would be here tomorrow carrying it on for there is no greater project." [6] Then Bergengren added that, while he and Filene differed over how to "get quantity production of credit unions," they both might be wrong. Nevertheless, Bergengren knew that so long as Filene provided the money for CUNEB he would have to follow Filene's general advice.

Bergengren's continuing campaign to improve his own financial position was not much more successful than the effort to get additional money

[3] *Ibid.*
[4] Bergengren to Filene, Jan. 12, 1925.
[5] *Ibid.*, May 8, 1925, with draft of tentative budget attached.
[6] *Ibid.*, June 5, 1925.

to promote the credit union movement. Believing that his position would not be needed after a national association began to promote the organization of credit unions—a development which he foresaw within three years—Bergengren pled with Filene for higher pay which would mean greater personal security. He faintly threatened Filene by mentioning the possibility of taking up other work, and at the same time emphasizing how much he had done for the movement. On one occasion Bergengren wrote to Filene that, when he had completed his credit union work, he might become involved in promoting "international cooperation to prevent future wars. . . ." [7] But again Filene turned down Bergengren's request for a raise from $8,500 to $10,000 a year. After making further pleas, however, in 1925 Bergengren did get an increase for the year of $500, the first he had enjoyed since 1920.[8]

Bergengren never let his differences with Filene over money matters interfere with his commitment to the credit union cause. His fertile mind was constantly seeking to devise improved methods and procedures which would boost the credit union movement. In January, 1926, he submitted a long memorandum to Filene in which he outlined his plans for the extension bureau during the coming year. For the first time Bergengren raised the matter of getting national legislation which would permit the organization of credit unions under a federal charter. Such a law, he wrote, would enable supporters to organize credit unions in those states where the legislatures would not pass enabling legislation because they were "either hopelessly reactionary or too much boss-controlled." In the second place, individual credit unions could be more easily organized in those thinly populated states west of the Mississippi where state campaigns could hardly be justified. Thirdly, organizers in states which had enabling legislation might choose whether it would be most beneficial to organize under state or federal law, "thereby minimizing the effects of state administrative hostility." Bergengren was convinced that the movement had the necessary support "to make a real campaign." Moreover, he thought that the Coolidge administration would not be "too hostile" because the administration favored cooperatives and the president was from Massachusetts, "the pioneering credit union state." [9]

Besides favoring the passage of a federal credit union bill, Bergengren declared that the extension bureau's most essential work in 1926 should

[7] *Ibid.*, Nov. 17, 1924.

[8] Draft of tentative budget, May 8, 1925; Bergengren to Filene, June 5, 1925.

[9] Bergengren, "Memorandum to Mr. Filene Having to Do with the Work of the Bureau during 1926," Jan. 12, 1926 (hereafter cited as Bergengren, "1926 Plan").

be to organize new credit unions, an activity "to which all else is subordinate." In pursuit of this goal, Bergengren wrote that the bureau was circularizing national organizations to obtain the names of their directors and to find out when their conventions would be held. He hoped that organizations such as the Kiwanis, Rotary, Lions, the American Legion, the YMCA and YWCA, the Chambers of Commerce and the American Bankers' Association would be among those who would provide publicity for the movement, as well as actually to direct some organizational work among their local units. In getting down to specifics, however, Bergengren recommended concentrating organizational work on such groups as the postal and railroad workers, and municipal and public utility employees.

To push the work of organizing credit unions, Bergengren again urged the employment of field secretaries. He recommended dividing the country into four organizational zones with a field worker responsible for activities in each zone. In illustrating the need for field secretaries, Bergengren pointed out that the large meeting of credit unionists in Chicago the previous year had achieved no concrete results because there had been no effective follow-up work. "Had it been possible immediately after the Chicago meeting to leave an organization secretary in Illinois for two months," Bergengren explained, "an Illinois league would have been assured in 1926." He recognized that four field workers would require greater funds for the work in 1926 and 1927, but Bergengren was convinced "that in the end such an expansion of the organization work would be a dollar and cents economy."

Finally, Bergengren hoped that more state credit union leagues could be organized. He considered only the Massachusetts league a success, although New York and Indiana also had state leagues. He wanted to add at least two leagues to the group during 1926 and the best possibilities, according to him, were in Louisiana, Georgia, and Illinois. Once enough state leagues had been organized, forming a national association would be the next step in the national credit union development. Bergengren hoped that such an association could be organized in 1927, but he estimated that it would take "five years to bring the credit union national development to the point where an effective, self-sustaining national organization will be possible."[10] Such were Bergengren's plans and recommendations for 1926 and the years immediately ahead.

After considering Bergengren's suggestions, Filene wrote a long response in which he outlined how he thought CUNEB should proceed. He

10 *Ibid.*

rejected the idea of pushing federal credit union legislation, because, as he put it, a national law might interfere more than it would help. Although he admitted that he might be wrong on this issue, Filene told Bergengren not to "go ahead in trying to get federal legislation until we have agreed." He urged Bergengren to give first priority to organizing credit unions in the twenty-six states where enabling laws existed, and to seek the passage of statutes in the other states. He wrote that, if needed, a federal law could be obtained after the formation of a national association of credit unions.[11]

Although Bergengren favored getting the support of national organizations whenever possible, he did not have much faith in using them to build the credit union movement. Filene, on the other hand, believed that high priority should be given to working with the Chamber of Commerce of the United States, the American Bankers' Association, farm and labor organizations, and cooperative associations. He recommended that CUNEB representatives solicit invitations to address the annual meetings of various organizations, and meet with the directors and executive committees "to sell the credit unions to them." Filene also believed that these organizations or associations should be persuaded to appoint a credit union committee "whose work it will be to start new Credit Unions." The bureau's success in 1926, he wrote, "should be measured by the number of credit unions we get started. The number of Credit unions we get started depends upon the kind of work we do. The field is very large—unlimited, practically, for our purpose."

As a second priority, Filene advocated appointing a public relations man to formulate an effective publicity campaign. He suggested that such a person might also become editor of *The Bridge*. Thus Filene's objectives were twofold, publicity and organization. Those two activities, he wrote, "ought to take all our time, strength and money and nothing else should be done unless we have a surplus available for other things." Filene told Bergengren that he was anxious to "come to an agreement as soon as possible on the 1926 program," as he was sailing for Europe in May.[12]

The differences between Bergengren and Filene centered mainly around the means to the end, not the end itself. They both favored organizing as many credit unions as possible and extending the movement nationwide. Their arguments were over how best this could be done. While Bergengren placed his faith in the employment of field secretaries

---

[11] Filene to Bergengren, Jan. 29, 1926.
[12] *Ibid.*

to help him carry on the organizational work, Filene wanted to give the movement greater publicity by hiring what amounted to an advertising manager. Moreover, Bergengren had no confidence that organizations such as the Chamber of Commerce could be persuaded to "greatly expedite the work," as proposed by Filene.

Nevertheless, Bergengren presented a plan of action somewhat along the lines suggested by Filene to the Twentieth Century Fund's board of directors in April, 1926. A few days later Filene asked him to submit a more detailed prospectus for the year's work. Bergengren reacted strongly to Filene's letter. He clearly resented the implication that he had been operating without a proper plan of action. Bergengren insisted that he must have authority and power to act on his own. In defending his record, Bergengren reminded Filene that "when I took on the credit union work it was after McCaleb had had a year at it and turned out nothing but an empty file." While Bergengren admitted that "the Bureau is just as much your property as your house in Otis Place and you have the absolute right to do with it what you will," he emphasized that the credit union movement now concerned both of them. "I have given too much to it," Bergengren wrote, "know too much about it, have sacrificed too much for it and care too much about it to so reform myself that I can successfully follow out a plan for carrying the work on unless I am sure that the plan conforms with the needs of the national development." Bergengren again outlined what he considered the most effective methods to advance the credit union movement.

Most of all, Bergengren seemed to resent Filene's accusation that he had lost his modesty, efficiency, and loyalty. He reminded Filene that he had always given credit to Filene rather than taking it himself. "As regards modesty," Bergengren wrote, "you should know by this time that I don't give a single, solitary damn about my own connection with this work so far as attempting to establish a reputation." In regard to efficiency, he told Filene that he worked long hours, had taken only two vacations in four years, and that he had spent $1,000 from his own pocket to publish *Cooperative Banking*. Finally, Bergengren said that he had been absolutely loyal to both the movement and to Filene. He concluded his letter by inviting Filene to give him an operational plan which he could carry out. However, he added: "the credit union development will long outlive both of us; we are cellar builders—putting in foundations—and I am pledged to get those foundations in to the best of my ability; not pledged to you, but pledged to myself." [13]

13 Bergengren to Filene, April 12, 1926.

Bergengren won his controversy with Filene, as he usually did. His mild threat to abandon the movement coupled with his flattery of Filene's own leadership role was enough to prevail. But Bergengren gained his position in the credit union movement by producing results, something that Filene thoroughly respected and admired. It was difficult to argue with Bergengren's success, and certainly Filene did not know of any other man who could do as well. The source of Bergengren's strength was achievement, and, as he often reminded Filene, the results had come at bargain basement prices. Bergengren's firm posture toward Filene, on whom he had to depend for funds, indicated that he had gained a large measure of self-assurance in directing the credit union movement. This confidence stemmed from his wide acquaintance, from his knowledge of how to organize credit unions, how to conduct a legislative campaign, and how to get publicity. But more than being an evangelist, Bergengren was also becoming a kind of philosopher for the movement.

One of the challenges before credit unionists in the 1920s was not only to define a credit union, but to determine the relationship of credit unions to the broader cooperative movement, and to resolve where credit unions fitted into the total economy. There was general agreement that a credit union was a type of banking institution, that it was cooperatively owned and operated, and that its primary purposes were to promote thrift through savings of members and to provide a source of small loans at reasonable rates of interest. As Bergengren wrote: "The credit union is based on the theory that the banking system needs supplementing by the development of a plan which will specialize in the smallest individual units of savings and, at the same time, concern itself with problems of small credit, collectively of great importance, but individually so small that existing banking facilities cannot cope with them except in substantial loss. As the lack of legitimate credit always results in the practice of usury it may be said that the credit union seeks to promote thrift and to eliminate usury." [14]

Credit unions were clearly cooperative institutions. They operated on the Rochdale principles of open membership, democratic control by members, limited return on share capital, and net savings returned to members in proportion to their patronage.[15] But how should credit unions relate to other cooperative enterprises, such as producers' and consumers' cooperatives? Some credit union pioneers viewed credit unions as the "financial arm of the cooperative movement." Many early

[14] Bergengren, *Cooperative Banking*, pp. 2–3.
[15] Parker, *The First 125 Years*, p. xv.

credit unions organized cooperative buying plans for such commodities as coal, using members' savings to purchase supplies at wholesale and allowing members to borrow from the credit union to purchase their winter's supply at below retail prices. Some of the first credit unions in North Carolina were connected with farmers' marketing cooperatives and the funds of members were used to finance those enterprises.

Bergengren was highly sympathetic to the entire cooperative movement, and at times he envisioned credit unions as an important aspect of the larger cooperative system. Filene shared this view to a large extent. But in practice Bergengren did not apply this philosophy to his credit union activities. He and other credit union leaders viewed the movement as one with its own integrity and special field of service. They did not consider it very important that credit unions should have a close relationship to other cooperative enterprises. Indeed, they viewed credit unions as a supplement to, rather than an integral part of, the larger cooperative movement in the United States.

As credit unions spread among employees of industrial firms, public agencies, and transportation and communication corporations, too much emphasis upon the cooperative nature of the movement seemed dangerous because to be successful credit unions needed the approval and cooperation of management. The need for support by economic conservatives, whether they were businessmen, bankers, trade-union leaders or legislators, prompted Bergengren to avoid anything which appeared to threaten the traditional private enterprise system. Bergengren wrote that the credit union movement must be "sufficiently conservative to be economically sound,"[16] two concepts which were closely associated in his mind. In other words, credit unions had their own specific functions to perform apart from the general cooperative movement, and they must perform these functions in a conservative, businesslike way.

Bergengren also viewed the credit union movement as a conservative political and social influence. He emphasized that credit unions represented the best principles of Americanism—they were democratic, they were self-help institutions, they aided citizens in achieving a better life, and they contributed to strengthening the nation's economy. As Bergengren saw the credit union movement: "It has to do with problems which are national in scope and which are crying for solution; the problem of the wage worker in the crowded city, who, without credit goes to the usurer and who, without savings, is the sort of raw material out of which bolshevism is manufactured. It is true that the world is in the midst of a

16 Bergengren to Filene, May 1, 1923.

conservative reaction but it is conservatism on trial after a state of uncertainty and unrest and the apparent failure of radicalism of a sort in
England and near anarchy in Russia." And then Bergengren continued,
"conservatism is distinctly on trial and if the people of the United States,
particularly in our cities, are to become so satisfied with our constitutional institutions that they will improve them in the long run rather
than destroy them there must be thrift and savings and the benefits of
thrift. There must be applied democracy as distinguished from theoret-
ical democracy." [17]

Thus Bergengren conceived credit unions as agencies to help forestall
radical change by making each person's lot in society better and more
secure. Ultimately, he believed that credit unionism could contribute to
the elimination of poverty and other ills which plagued society. This was
high idealism, but it was a vision which he imparted to many of the
pioneer leaders of the credit union movement.

One of the main goals of CUNEB was to get additional state laws
passed which would permit the organization of credit unions. While little
progress was made in 1926, partly because few legislatures met, the next
year saw three important states—California, Missouri, and Alabama—
enact credit union statutes. The California law came largely as a result
of the work of Leo H. Shapiro, a San Francisco attorney. Shapiro had
become interested in credit unions in 1922, and for the next five years he
pushed for the enactment of such a law. He had to overcome public indifference as well as the outright opposition from the Building and Loan
League of California.[18]

Passage of the Missouri law was also the result of nearly a half a decade
of work. In 1922 Bergengren initiated correspondence with John F. Case
of the State Board of Agriculture and editor of the *Missouri Ruralist*. Case
invited Bergengren to discuss the credit union movement in both 1925
and 1927, and also put him in touch with a Jefferson City law firm which
took over direction of the legislative campaign. But it was not until the
1927 session that credit union supporters could overcome the opposition
of the building and loan associations and get their law enacted.[19] The
credit union law in Alabama must be credited largely to a public-spirited
citizen of Birmingham, W. V. M. Robertson, Jr. Having first read about
credit unions in 1922, Robertson immediately contacted Bergengren and
said he hoped to promote credit unions in his state. After several unsuc-

[17] *Ibid.*, Jan. 12, 1925.
[18] *The Bridge* (June, 1926), p. 1; (April, 1927), p. 1.
[19] *Ibid.* (May, 1927), pp. 1 and 7.

cessful attempts Robertson finally won the day and the credit union bill became law on September 16, 1927.[20]

Bergengren left most of the legislative work to others in 1926 and 1927. In keeping with both his own and Filene's priorities, Bergengren spent most of his time organizing credit unions. This involved traveling long distances and holding numerous meetings. He nearly always traveled by train, and later in his book, *Crusade*, wrote about his organizational tours under the chapter title "All Night in a Day Coach." During one of these trips in the spring of 1926 into the Midwest he traveled 4,500 miles in twenty-one days.[21] A typical day for Bergengren involved spending several hours in an industrial plant talking with company officials and employee groups about the advantages which they would enjoy if they organized a credit union. At the end of one day, he wrote that he had "explained the credit union from A to Z to four individuals separately and at two meetings—six presentations all told." [22] Sometimes he succeeded, other times he failed; in this case all of his meetings were in vain.

In both his writings and speeches, Bergengren used human interest stories to win support for the movement. He emphasized how credit unions could help individuals, especially the poor. For example, he published a story in *The Bridge* about an Italian immigrant and his young wife who, after landing in New York, set up housekeeping in a one room flat. Manuel secured a job as a laundry worker at a salary of $30 a week, and soon joined the credit union where his uncle was a member. When Manuel and his wife were expecting their first child, they decided that they needed larger living quarters. With his uncle's endorsement, Manuel obtained a $400 loan from the credit union, $250 of which was invested in furniture and the remainder put aside to pay medical costs. The couple also moved into a four-room apartment at a monthly rental of $40; however, there was enough room for two boarders whose payments covered Manuel's rent and left him a small balance. Out of Manuel's earnings, he took $8 each week to repay his credit union loan. Bergengren concluded his story by reporting that the baby had been born and was being brought up in what Manuel called "American style." [23] The reader could conclude that without the credit union Manuel might have turned to a life of crime, become dependent upon public charity, or he might have fallen prey to "radicals" preaching revolution. As it was, the credit

20 *Ibid.* (July, 1926), pp. 1 and 7; (Oct., 1927), pp. 1 and 8.
21 *Ibid.* (June, 1926), p. 10.
22 Bergengren, *Crusade*, p. 90.
23 *The Bridge* (Sept., 1924), p. 7.

union had saved him from any of those awful fates. Bergengren also related accounts of how credit unions had saved workers from the grasp of
the loan sharks and how they had provided financial counseling for persons who needed assistance in straightening up their financial affairs.[24]

Regardless of how hard Bergengren worked, it was impossible for him
to make anywhere near as many contacts as were necessary if the credit
union movement were to show rapid expansion. Since Filene would not
approve paid field secretaries, Bergengren turned to credit union enthusiasts who would do part-time organizing work. During 1926 he enlisted several individuals who greatly aided the movement both at the
time and in the later years. One of the most important recruits was
Thomas W. Doig, a stenographer in the office of the Minneapolis postmaster and treasurer of the Minneapolis Postal Employees Credit Union.
As early as the fall of 1925 Doig wrote Bergengren that he was becoming
"more than ever enthused with the credit union idea." By early 1926
Doig was actively organizing credit unions and predicting the early organization of a state credit union league in Minnesota.[25] Others who
enlisted in Bergengren's "crusade" were Timothy O'Shaughnessy and
Joseph DeRamus of the Rock Island Railroad, Ralph Long who worked
for the Wabash, Clarence Howell of the Detroit Teachers' Credit Union,
and Claude Clarke, a Cleveland attorney.[26]

As helpful as they were, volunteer organizers had definite limitations.
They could only take limited time away from their regular jobs, which
meant that they had mainly evenings and weekends for credit union
work. Nevertheless, as a result of work by Bergengren and volunteer organizers, scores of credit unions were organized in 1926 and 1927. Among
these in 1926 were the credit unions formed among the employees in the
shop of the Chicago, Rock Island and Pacific Railroad which Bergengren
hoped would serve as a "laboratory experiment" to show company officials how beneficial credit unions could be; and two Catholic parish
credit unions, one in Ames, Iowa, and another in Racine, Wisconsin. By
1927 Bergengren was saying that the movement's experimental stage was
over. No longer, he said, was it necessary to organize and operate credit
unions mainly to demonstrate their general usefulness. "The way should
be cleared for the quantity production of credit unions," he wrote.
"There should be a credit union in every post office, enough credit

[24] *Ibid.* (Sept., 1924, and Oct., 1924), p. 7.
[25] *Ibid.* (Sept., 1925), p. 8; Doig to Bergengren, Jan. 7, 1926.
[26] Bergengren, *Crusade*, p. 92.

unions on railroads to serve all railroad men, a credit union for school teachers in every city, a parish credit union in every parish where there are folks who need to save and who, from time to time, need credit and have no credit resources available for their use at fair rates of interest." [27]

To Bergengren this prospect was not unrealistic. Credit unions, he wrote, were "snowballing" among important groups of workers. By October, 1927, there were eighty-three postal credit unions in the major cities of the nation, an increase of thirty-five since April, 1926. These credit unions had 16,257 members, assets of over $1 million, and had loaned $3 million. Less than five years earlier the first postal employees' credit union had been organized with eight members and assets of only $50. Bergengren was particularly proud of this record, asserting that postal credit unions had "produced some of our best credit union leadership and have sweetened the lives of hundreds of thousands of men who, in and out of season, go about the beautiful job of uniting people who are far apart and depend on Uncle Sam to be forever carrying their messages, one to another." [28]

Railroad workers provided another excellent field for organization. In July, 1926, Bergengren formed a credit union among the employees of Local No. 136 of the Brotherhood of Railway Clerks in Kansas City. He also organized workers in Locals No. 438 and No. 542 of the same union in Decatur, Illinois. Thomas Doig organized railway workers in Minnesota and by September, 1928, there were eight credit unions in the Twin Cities serving employees of the Great Northern, the Soo Line, and the Northern Pacific.[29]

There were a number of "firsts" in credit union organization during 1927. The first credit unions were organized in Utah, Nebraska, and Missouri among the postal employees in Salt Lake City, Omaha, and Kansas City. Leo Shapiro formed the first credit union under the new California law among the municipal employees in Los Angeles. At Saint Catherine's High School in Racine, Wisconsin, the first high school credit union in the world began business. Its primary purpose was to encourage students to save systematically and to permit them and their parents to begin saving for college expenses. With the exception of one faculty member, the directors were all high school students. A credit union was also organized among the employees of the Parker House

[27] *The Bridge* (Oct., 1927), p. 4.
[28] Bergengren, *Crusade*, pp. 116–17.
[29] *Ibid.*, p. 109; and Doig to Bergengren, Feb. 11 and 18, 1927.

Hotel in Boston, the first of its kind in the credit union movement. The president and treasurer were Negroes.[30]

To maintain this momentum and to accomplish even more, late in 1927, Bergengren planned a massive organizational campaign to take place during January, 1928. He called it "Expansion Month." He hoped that such an effort would meet Filene's demand "that we mass-produce credit unions." [31] Also Bergengren wanted to experiment with enlisting the services of members to organize additional credit unions. His plan called for paying any credit union member who organized a new credit union a fee of twenty-five dollars, plus expenses. Bergengren saw at least three advantages in this approach. In the first place, it would provide training for local credit union leaders and prepare them for subsequent work in the state leagues and national association. Secondly, the fees would actually be less than the amount paid to local attorneys, or the cost of field secretaries. Finally, the expenditures would be made to people who needed the money and it would be kept "in the credit union family." [32]

The goal established for Expansion Month was 20 new credit unions in each of twenty states, or a total of 400. Bergengren, however, underestimated the magnitude of this task, and twice extended the time until the campaign ran through May. Even then the goal was not met. Nevertheless, the effort was a qualified success as 271 new credit unions were organized. Seven states met their quotas. Actually, in this period of less than five months more credit unions had been formed than had been organized throughout the United States from 1909 to 1921.[33] That situation told a great deal about the strength of the movement. The campaign was important, too, because Bergengren found some thirty-three men who proved their ability to organize credit unions. Some of these individuals had already been active in credit union work in their states, including Doig, Long, Donahoe, O'Shaughnessy, King, Kaminsky, and Shapiro. But others—Earl Rentfro, a clerk in the Rock Island freight office in Kansas City; Hubert M. Rhodes, an employee in the Raleigh, North Carolina, post office; and W. O. Vickery, a postal employee in Birmingham—were relatively new recruits. A cynic might charge that

---

[30] Stories on these credit union "firsts" are found in issues of *The Bridge*, June-Oct.,1927 and July, 1928.

[31] Bergengren, *Crusade*, pp. 120–21.

[32] Bergengren to the Trustees of the Twentieth Century Fund, April 1, 1929, pp. 3–4.

[33] Bergengren, *Crusade*, p. 121; *The Bridge* (April, 1928), p. 6.

these men were attracted only by the fees which they earned, but their subsequent service to the credit union movement proved their genuine commitment to credit unionism. Bergengren also played an important role in the Expansion Month campaign, by visiting seventeen towns and cities and personally assisting in organizing 29 credit unions.[34]

The ever-widening scope of the credit union movement was reflected not only in the number of local units, but in the variety of firms and agencies in which credit unions were being organized. In the private sector, credit unions were becoming increasingly common among railway, telephone, and factory workers, while teachers and postal and municipal workers were among the public employees forming credit unions. By the late 1920s it had become clear that rural credit unions had little future. They simply could not provide the kind of credit which farmers needed. Even in North Carolina where the rural credit union movement had made some progress during World War I, the new credit unions being organized there in 1927 and 1928 were mostly among urban workers.

In assessing the situation at the close of Expansion Month, Bergengren recognized some weaknesses in the movement. One thing was clearly evident—many of the new credit unions had been hurriedly organized without, as he put it, "much time for preliminary development of interest or for instruction." Bergengren saw that a too rapid, mushroom-type growth which resulted in weak and poorly organized credit unions would ultimately lead to a high percentage of failure. This might discredit the entire movement. Thus Bergengren called for a period of consolidation during which all credit unions would be placed on a sound operational basis. Besides, he explained, people expected a great deal from credit unions and their management. "It is amazing to what abnormally high standards credit unions are held up," he wrote. "We have to be more above suspicion than Caesar's wife. We are obligated to operate with greater efficiency than has ever been required of any business organization." [35] But Bergengren was confident of the movement's future. Indeed, he had a touch of predestination in his thinking when it came to credit unionism. While admitting that CUNEB had sort of "muddled through" with relatively few mistakes, he thought this was due "to the fact that there seems to be something more or less inevitable about this whole credit union business. Nothing in the long run can stop the orderly progress of credit unions in the United States, because that progress is so

34 Bergengren, *Crusade*, p. 121.
35 *The Bridge* (May, 1928), p. 4.

consistent with the American conception of government and economics." [36]

Filene, who constantly gave close scrutiny to the credit union movement, expressed his views about the future of credit unionism in June, 1928. In a letter carried on the front page of *The Bridge,* he wrote that the movement had "reached the end of Chapter I and was ready for Chapter II." The next stage, he explained, was the organization of state leagues, so that the leagues could "move forward together to the organization of the National Association of Credit Union Leagues—that the national development may be permanently self-sustaining." [37] Bergengren agreed wholeheartedly with Filene on the objectives of establishing state leagues and the eventual organization in the near future of a national association of credit unions.

But the prospect of forming state leagues, as well as a national association, was not at all bright in 1928. Only the Massachusetts league was a viable organization. According to Bergengren, it "represented over 100,000 people and is self-supporting, with a permanently employed secretary and assistant secretary, and with full direction of the work in this state." [38] Besides Massachusetts, Bregengren believed that leagues in only three states showed much promise. These were the Minnesota league, organized mainly by Doig in 1927; the association in Georgia which had grown out of the Atlanta Association of Credit Unions, and the Indiana league which was still in its infancy. Bergengren had little hope for the New York league because he thought it was faulty in conception, organization, and operation.

In September, 1928, Bergengren submitted a plan to Filene for the development of state leagues. He recommended that a league be organized in any state which had fifty credit unions. To that end, he retained Joseph Campana, who had been active in the Massachusetts movement, to head a campaign known as "Recruit Month" to "bring the ten states outside of Massachusetts with the largest number of credit unions up to fifty as quickly as possible." Bergengren proposed to turn over the sale of bookkeeping supplies to each league as soon as it was established in order to give the new organization some concrete function. As a league became stronger it would gradually assume the entire work of directing the movement in a state.[39] By April, 1929, the most promising states for

[36] *Ibid.*

[37] *Ibid.* (June, 1928), p. 1.

[38] *Ibid.* (Feb., 1927), pp. 1 and 10; (May, 1927), p. 5.

[39] Bergengren to Filene, Sept. 18, 1928.

the development of new leagues or the expansion and strengthening of those already established were Illinois, Georgia, Indiana, Iowa, Minnesota, Missouri, North Carolina, Michigan, and Virginia.[40]

However important the organization of state leagues and a national association may have been, Bergengren was also considering the prospects and importance of international credit unionism. He viewed credit unions as one force which would create "cooperation and understanding" both at home and abroad. A world-wide credit union movement, he wrote, could make for "international good will," and it might even eliminate war. "Any agency," he wrote, "which makes folks in one national unit realize how like they are to folks in another national unit and how well they can get along together, performs a great service." [41]

Bergengren's study and work with CUNEB had made him increasingly aware of the international cooperative credit movement. His reading had acquainted him with the work of Raiffeisen, Schulze-Delitzsch, and Desjardins. Also he routinely received inquiries from people in different parts of the world about credit unions in the United States. These came from as far away as the Philippines and Moscow. The mailing list of *The Bridge* included addresses in London, Foochow, Geneva, Paris, Honolulu, and Madras. He regularly corresponded with people in Canada and Mexico. Thus Bergengren looked forward with enthusiasm and excitement to a trip to Europe in the summer of 1928 which Filene had persuaded the Twentieth Century Fund to finance. While in Europe Bergengren visited the scene of Raiffeisen's work in Neuwied, Germany, observed the operations of Raiffeisen and Schulze-Delitzsch societies, and visited cooperative credit organizations in Switzerland, Czechoslovakia, Denmark, and Sweden. One of the major results of his European trip was that from then onward Bergengren envisioned a much closer relationship between American credit unions and similar organizations throughout the world. It gave him much more of an internationalistic outlook.

Whatever Bergengren's interest may have been in the international credit union movement, he had immediate problems at home. One of these concerned his office personnel. Bergengren was still operating mostly with his original staff—himself, Miss Habern, and Arthur Fernald, although in April, 1927, the Twentieth Century Fund board approved employment of a field secretary. Campana was appointed to that position the following year. His work involved visiting existing unions and helping

[40] Bergengren to Trustees of the Twentieth Century Fund, April 1, 1929, p. 4.
[41] *The Bridge* (Christmas, 1928), p. 1.

them with their operational problems. He also aided in organizing new credit unions, thereby taking some of the burden of the field work off Bergengren.

The extension bureau's staff problems increased greatly when Arthur Fernald resigned as assistant secretary. Fortunately, however, Bergengren was able to employ Agnes Gartland, an accomplished stenographer, bookkeeper, and office manager, who, according to Filene, possessed "an alert, inquisitive and well trained mind and, above all, the latent capacity for high devotion and loyalty to a cause which she found worthy of her best effort." She became assistant executive secretary and remained with Bergengren for many years.[42]

Although he had relented and allowed Bergengren to employ a field secretary, Filene continued to insist that the movement needed more publicity. Early in 1928 he again recommended that a speakers' bureau be established. Filene thought that such a bureau should consist of men with ability to present the credit union message from material prepared by CUNEB. He envisioned speakers going around the country addressing various groups and then being followed by organizers who would capitalize on the interest created by the publicity agents. "We can get ten times more results if we let the world know what 'C.U.' has and is accomplishing," Filene wrote.

Filene also called for the creation of "an honorary society within the credit union movement to which men and women would be admitted for exceptional service." Bergengren announced the creation of such a society early in 1928 which he dubbed the Founders' Club. The sole requirement for membership was that a person organize at least one new credit union. The organization was to promote interest in a national credit union association which would be organized around a nucleus of state leagues and the Founders' Club.[43]

It was unfortunate that New York State did not provide greater support for the credit union movement. In the beginning, prospects for credit union development in New York appeared good. The Municipal Credit Union for New York City began business on January 1, 1917, and quickly made a remarkable record. Within a year it had 600 members, assets of $20,500, and had loaned more than $22,000.[44] Later in the year Arthur Ham organized the New York State Association of Credit Unions which soon had thirty affiliated members. The association's main objec-

---

[42] Filene notes dated Feb. 1 and 4, 1928.

[43] *The Bridge* (May, 1928), p. 6; (Sept., 1928), p. 14.

[44] Municipal Credit Union of New York, "Announcement at the Close of the Year 1924."

tive was to publicize the credit union movement and to deal with legislative matters. However, by the end of World War I the credit union movement in New York was moribund. When Bergengren later attempted to strengthen the movement in the Empire State, control there by the Russell Sage Foundation hampered his efforts. At one time it appeared as though the foundation might become a major financial backer of the national movement, but this support never materialized. Relations between Bergengren and foundation officials were fairly cordial during the early 1920s, but tension was never very far below the surface. Bergengren was displeased with credit union development in New York and he blamed this on the foundation's failure to promote credit unionism actively and aggressively. In June, 1927, he publicly criticized the movement in New York, asserting that credit union development "would have been prodigious had it followed normal credit union lines." The problem, as he saw it, was that the early credit unions in the state were mainly organized within racial groups without territorial limits. Thus they became "a highly specialized form of racial bank with little if any resemblance to the credit union." He referred to the heavy Jewish composition of most credit unions. Worst of all in Bergengren's view, the foundation was not giving much guidance or direction to the movement in New York. Some new leadership and reorganization after 1925 had helped a little, but the New York Credit Union League, which had been organized in 1922, still limped along without much effect or influence.

Convinced that he should assist in strengthening the movement in New York, Bergengren decided that he should go into New York and organize credit unions "of the right sort." He wrote in April, 1928, that he planned to make three short trips to the state in order to organize between ten and twenty credit unions.[45] Officials of the Russell Sage Foundation quickly let it be known that they did not want Bergengren in the state. They viewed his prospective organizing work as a dual effort and one which infringed on their territory. John Glenn of the foundation wrote to Filene complaining about Bergengren's activities and insisted that the head of CUNEB "will not listen to any requests from us and will not pay any attention to our judgment, but insists on acting entirely on his own initiative without realizing the importance of cooperation."[46] But Bergengren defended his action by telling Filene that the foundation had failed in trying to promote credit unions in New York. It had simply not done anything worth-while, according to Bergengren. He had al-

[45] Bergengren to Leon Henderson, April 12, 1928.
[46] Glenn to Filene, May 3, 1928.

ready formed seven credit unions in New York and had good prospects of organizing eight more. This, Bergengren wrote, would "constitute more credit unions of the right sort for New York State than the Russell Sage Foundation has been able to accumulate in fifteen years of supposedly continuous credit union interest and activity."[47]

Although Filene said he would back Bergengren "in any position which judgment tells you is the best to take," foundation officials warned Bergengren to stay out of New York. With both sides critical of the other there was little hope that any cooperation would result. And it did not. Arthur Ham complained that Bergengren did not know the meaning of cooperation. As, he wrote, "the starving poet in the city garret writes beautifully about spring in the country, that fact probably qualifies Bergengren as a credit union expert."[48] This kind of carping could do the movement no good.

Despite the rivalry and competition over who was the head of the credit union movement in New York, one thing was certain—the movement had been weak there almost from the beginning. The Russell Sage Foundation, which had assumed the task of promoting credit unionism and continued to guard its position jealously, had not been successful. Part of the reason for this was that the foundation concentrated on both credit unions and uniform small loan legislation to meet the problems of usury, but in taking on so much it had done neither very well.

In contrast to the situation in New York, Massachusetts presented an encouraging picture. Indeed, Massachusetts had everything that New York lacked—an effective state league, a growing number of local credit unions, vigorous leadership, and grass roots support. By the end of 1928 there were over 98,000 members in 296 separate credit unions in the state which had assets of over $15 million. In that year 47,000 people borrowed almost $12 million from credit unions in Massachusetts.[49] The state league performed a number of essential tasks. It sold bookkeeping supplies, served as a lobbyist, organized new credit unions, and through meetings and training sessions it helped to develop uniform business practices among the local credit unions. The Massachusetts league provided the kind of example which Filene hoped would spread to other states. Bergengren, however, saw even a greater role for the Massachu-

---

[47] Bergengren to Filene, May 10, 1928.

[48] Memorandum of Ham to Glenn, June 14, 1928.

[49] Snider, *Credit Unions in Massachusetts*, Table X, p. 27; Table I, p. 9; Table III, p. 14; *The Bridge* (July, 1927), p. 3.

setts league. He hoped that it would initiate new projects and programs to expand and broaden the activities of credit unions.

The problem of what to do with surplus funds in the hands of credit unions remained unsolved. Without a central bank for credit unions, Bergengren explained in December, 1928, some credit unions were building up surpluses far in excess of loan demands by their members. To deal with this problem Bergengren proposed establishing an investment trust which would be "ultra conservative in type," and which would "guarantee the maximum return which is consistent only with the maximum safety." Credit union treasurers could invest in the trust and professional managers would administer it. The trust should be, according to Bergengren, governed by a board of directors "of unquestioned standing in financial circles, whose established standing and capacities will give faith to the credit union investing public." [50] Filene was interested in the investment trust, but, as was his nature, he refused to approve the plan. Nevertheless, the Massachusetts league appointed a committee to organize such a venture, but before it could be finalized the stock market crash destroyed any interest in this kind of investment arrangement.

As a result of his trip to Europe in the summer of 1928, Bergengren became enthused about consumer cooperation or what he called "collective buying." He believed that cooperative purchasing of the necessities of life was a proper function of credit unions. One credit union manager told Bergengren how his local unit had purchased 4,000 tons of coal for resale to its members at a savings of about $1.25 a ton. Other credit unions were already buying such items as gasoline, oil, furniture, and groceries for their members at great savings. Bergengren envisioned a credit union league which would handle the purchases and sales for its members as producing more savings "per annum through the use of their collective buying power than they now get in dividends." He urged Filene to make a study of how a chain of cooperative stores, such as existed in Sweden, might afford the "next logical step" in credit union development in the United States. He thought that eventually collective buying might "include life insurance as well as all sorts of things which credit union members need in common." [51] But again no action was taken to implement this idea.

Bergengren also proposed establishing a cooperative printing plant, controlled initially by CUNEB but eventually to be turned over to a

[50] Bergengren, "Memorandum re Investment Trust," Dec. 12, 1928.
[51] Bergengren to Filene, Sept. 18, 1928.

national credit union association. This plant would print all of the business forms and promotional literature used by the movement.[52] Joseph Campana prepared a plan for this project which Bergengren submitted to Filene. Campana's report indicated that the Massachusetts league and CUNEB spent almost $14,000 for printing in 1928, an increase of 40 percent over each of the previous two years. Campana estimated that great savings could be made by these organizations if the movement had its own printing establishment; but nothing was done.

Consideration of establishing a central bank for credit unions, an investment trust, cooperative retail stores, and a printing plant reflected Bergengren's restless search for ways to strengthen and expand the services of credit unions. His ideas, however, were far ahead of the movement's strength and ambitions in 1928. Moreover, his suggestions were often not well thought out and he seldom had concrete plans for implementation. To a businessman like Filene such lack of precision was intolerable. Also, Filene continued to insist that the major and almost exclusive task of the movement was to get laws in every state and to increase the number of credit unions throughout the country. Other projects, he thought, should not divert the movement from these immediate and most important goals. If such projects were implemented and then failed, the entire movement would be discredited. Yet, in the years ahead, credit union leaders implemented many of the so-called idealistic projects conceived by Bergengren and other credit union pioneers.

Bergengren faced another busy legislative year in 1929 when most state lawmakers were in session. As a result of efforts that year, five new state laws were enacted—in Arizona, Kansas, Maryland, Montana, and Florida. Moreover, friends of the credit union movement obtained amendments to defective laws in Texas, Utah, Oregon, and Wisconsin, bringing the statutes in these states in line with generally accepted, sound credit union principles.[53] Besides getting new and revised legislation in 1929, credit union advocates successfully resisted attacks on the movement in several states. The State Banking Department in Tennessee proposed an amendment to permit it to charge the same examination fees for credit unions as for commercial banks. Such charges would have driven small credit unions out of business. The Tennessee credit unions rallied against the amendment, CUNEB retained a local attorney to

---

[52] *Ibid.*, Dec. 12, 1928.

[53] *The Bridge* (Jan., 1929), p. 8; (April-May, 1929), pp. 7, 9, and 10; Bergengren to the Trustees of the Twentieth Century Fund, April 1, 1929; and *The Bridge* (Aug., Sept., and Oct., 1929).

oppose the bill, and it was never reported out of committee. More serious was a bill introduced in Michigan which would have drastically restricted secured loans, and limited credit union organization to groups of employees of a common employer. However, credit unions in the state, aided by a CUNEB-retained attorney, were able to defeat the bill.[54] These actions demonstrated that strong opposition still existed to the credit union movement.

Despite a highly successful legislative year, there were failures and disappointments. For several years the building and loan associations had successfully thwarted all efforts to enact a credit union bill in Ohio. In 1929, however, Claude Clarke met with representatives of the associations and convinced them not to oppose credit union legislation. But when victory appeared in sight, the state bankers association took up the campaign against the bill and it ultimately died in the House Rules Committee.[55] In Washington, where the governor had twice vetoed credit union bills, a measure was prepared which the governor agreed to sign if it passed the legislature. But now the bill got bogged down in the legislative process and adjournment came before any action was taken.[56] The legislatures of Arkansas, Idaho, and Pennsylvania refused to enact credit union bills in 1929, mainly, Bergengren believed, because the extension bureau had not done adequate work.[57] Nevertheless, success had been so great in recent years that Bergengren predicted that legislative work would be completed in one or two more sessions. By the end of 1929 some thirty-two states had credit union laws. They contained about 80 percent of the nation's people.

As usual, Bergengren divided his time in 1929 between legislative and organizational work. He organized a number of credit unions in Texas, Kansas, and elsewhere. He also received active assistance from several organizers, most of whom received the $25 fee for organizing a new credit union. Between early 1928 and late 1929 more than fifty organizers received some $4,000 in payments. Thomas Doig organized more than forty credit unions and Bergengren described him as "a seasoned organizer," who was "rapidly equipping himself for leadership." [58]

Bergengren believed that one of the most important developments in the movement in 1929 was the open support given by two Roman Cath-

---

[54] *The Bridge* (April–May, 1929), p. 6.

[55] *Ibid.*

[56] *Ibid.*

[57] Bergengren, *Crusade,* p. 138; *The Bridge* (April–May, 1929), p. 6.

[58] *The Bridge* (Aug., Sept., and Oct., 1929), p. 6; Bergengren, *Crusade*, p. 142.

olic organizations—the National Catholic Welfare Conference and the Central Bureau of the Catholic Central Verein of America. Father John A. Ryan, director of the Department of Social Action of the Welfare Conference, wrote Bergengren in October, saying that credit unions "should make an unusually strong appeal" to Catholics because they relied "mainly upon mutual confidence, fraternal sentiment, honesty, good faith and knowledge of one another's needs and capacities." In October, 1929, the Rural Life Conference met in Des Moines and voted to organize the Parish Credit Union National Committee, with head-quarters at the office of the National Catholic Welfare Conference in Washington. For three years Bergengren had worked for just such an endorsement.

Bergengren told Filene that the Roman Catholic endorsement brought to CUNEB "tremendously important supporting strength, certainty of very definite cooperation in organization, and an assurance of a diversity of credit unions which, while in no way interfering with our industrial development," would ensure the movement of "not carrying all of our eggs in the industrial basket." Filene urged Bergengren to make the same type of effort among the various Protestant denominations. Bergengren assured him that he planned to do so. But Bergengren thought that Catholics offered a better possibility because they had "a discipline which results in church attendance and church identity which I know from much experience to be sadly lacking within the church with which I am personally affiliated." Nevertheless, as parish credit unions developed slowly during the next few years, Bergengren also made efforts to bring about a corresponding Protestant development.

Development of individual credit unions continued to emphasize the need for more state leagues. According to Bergengren, Minnesota, North Carolina, and Illinois had reached fifty credit unions, the number thought necessary to organize a successful state league. Prospects were also good, he said, in Alabama and Georgia. Bergengren hoped that as soon as there were fifteen state leagues, a meeting could be called to form a national association.

By 1929, Bergengren was being more precise about the functions and purposes of the state leagues. Among the four broad responsibilities of a league, the first was to provide "an offensive and defensive alliance" to deal with high-rate moneylenders who were hostile to credit unions, and bank commissioners who did not understand the role of credit unions. Besides beating down legislative assaults, state leagues could constantly work to amend and improve credit union laws. Secondly, leagues were necessary, Bergengren said, for the "interchange of ideas and experiences." League meetings, the development of area chapters, the holding of managers' conferences, the development of social interchange, and meeting with state officials and others interested in the credit union movement were all important objectives for a state league. In the third place, since credit unions had "business transactions of common importance," state leagues could work out the variations in the business practices demanded by different state laws. Finally, Bergengren said, each league, along with a national association, would "be a clearinghouse for research and information; its job will be to develop the credit union plan to its maximum capacity for service." [59]

During 1929, however, league development continued to move slowly. A few credit unions joined together and called themselves a league, but generally they did not fulfill the criteria established by Bergengren for a "viable" organization. During January, Filene took a vacation trip to California, combining relaxation with his many interests, including credit union work. He spoke before several credit union meetings in Los Angeles and San Francisco. As a result, the California Credit Union League, Southern Branch and the Northern Chapter of the California Credit Union League were formed. In June, Bergengren attended a meeting of sixty-six delegates at Kansas City, Missouri, presided over by Earl Rentfro, where a chapter was organized. Later that month a similar chapter was formed in St. Louis. A few weeks later Missouri credit unionists organized a state league with Rentfro as president. [60]

Despite the growing number of leagues, they had done very little actually to improve the operation of local credit unions. However, the Massachusetts league was an exception. In 1929 it turned its attention to the more technical aspects of credit union management. Leaders in Massachusetts recognized that if credit unions were going to be successful in the long run they must be operated efficiently. The league held a training session in March, 1929, attended by representatives of fifty credit unions.[61] This was only the beginning of what finally developed throughout the movement as a more sophisticated type of management training.

The Massachusetts league also showed its maturity when it notified Filene in October that "the time has come when the Credit Union League of Massachusetts feels it can stand on its own feet financially by paying its own expenses." Expressing gratitude for Filene's subsidies

[59] *The Bridge* (April–May, 1929), p. 8.
[60] *Ibid.* (June–July, 1929), pp. 1–2 and 6.
[61] *Ibid.* (April–May, 1929), p. 3.

and help, league officials asked Filene to withdraw his financial support on December 1. Bergengren had envisioned in the beginning a strong, unified, self-sufficient organization which would develop the movement in Massachusetts. Although this looked like a great achievement, the day would come when credit unionism in Massachusetts would become too strong and independent for Bergengren's liking. Nevertheless, the league had fulfilled the original objectives which Bergengren and Filene had set for it.

By the beginning of 1930 a substantial part of Filene's and Bergengren's objectives for the credit union movement had been achieved. Indeed, the decade of the 1920s had witnessed a remarkable advance in credit unionism. Thirty-two states now had credit union legislation, most of the laws coming after 1920. There were 1,100 individual credit unions organized among a wide variety of workers. According to Filene, these credit unions had assets of approximately $45 million, and did a yearly loan business of some $60 million. This was still a far cry from what the credit union pioneers envisioned, but it was a strong start. There was no longer any doubt about the viability of the movement, but wide opportunities for expansion still remained. The principal tasks ahead were to organize more credit unions and state leagues, to establish a national association of credit unions, and to get Congress to pass a federal credit union law

CHAPTER VI

Credit Unions and the
Great Depression

WHEN BERGENGREN returned from Europe in the late summer of 1928, he observed that "everyone from the bootblack on the corner to the captain of industry was playing feverishly" on the stock market.[1] But, like most Americans he had no idea what was ahead for the economy. Within a little more than a year, following the stock market crash, the nation entered a major depression.

What effect would the growing unemployment and hard times have on the budding credit union movement? Would, as Bergengren wrote, credit unionism completely collapse? That seemed like a distinct possibility. Typically, credit union members were industrial workers, railroad and utility company employees, school teachers, postal workers, and others of modest incomes. When their wages were cut, or they became unemployed, they had no money to save for credit union operations. Many people even had to withdraw their investment in shares, weakening the capital structure of credit unions even further. As credit union funds dwindled, the people who most needed credit to buy the necessities of life found their source of money dried up.

Under these conditions Bergengren and other credit union leaders had little more to offer than to advise operating credit unions "to ride out the storm." He urged local units to accept even the smallest amounts when people had so little to save; to make the most efficient use of every cent loaned; to seek competent leadership and to encourage people to believe that they could handle their own money; and to "point out that better times were coming when, with more of our own money, . . . we could do more and more important things with it." [2] But this kind of counsel was of little more value to credit unions than was Hoover's advice to the nation that prosperity was just around the corner.

[1] Bergengren, *Crusade*, pp. 136–37.
[2] *Ibid.*, p. 151.

127

However discouraging the prospects appeared for credit unions, the depression turned out to be a boon rather than an impediment to the movement. In the first place, this was due to the poor record of other financial institutions. Hundreds of banks were unable to weather the depression and closed their doors. In 1931 alone, some 2,298 banks suspended operations and the following year the number was still high, reaching 1,456. With billions in deposits wiped out, people lost faith in banks. Credit unions also failed during the depression, but the best figures available indicate that their record of solvency was much superior to that of banks. Bergengren took pride in contrasting the closing of banks with the steady organization of new credit unions. In December, 1931, for example, he stated that 512 banks had closed the previous month while at the same time thirty new credit unions had been organized.[3]

The depression may also have helped the credit union movement by stimulating the cooperative ideal in the United States. As the depression deepened with its industrial stagnation, bank failures, and widespread unemployment, the competitive system came under sharp attack. Critics took business to task for its selfishness and lack of public concern, while many speakers and writers praised the cooperative motive of service. Moreover, the depression put citizens in a mood to try different approaches to their credit problems. The credit union movement undoubtedly benefited from a widespread desire to depart from traditional practices and to experiment with new systems.

Although the total number of credit unions continued to grow during the worst of the depression, a substantial number did fail. One of the basic problems was that as late as 1929, some 40 percent of credit union loans were for real estate purchases.[4] With unemployment and declining real estate values some credit unions suffered heavy losses. Others lost money which they had deposited in closed banks, while some suffered from the loss of investments in securities. In one case, a credit union bought a block of securities from the bank's portfolio on the advice of the banker with which the credit union did business. Within three months, the securities had depreciated in value by 60 percent.[5] Finally, credit unions suffered losses when small borrowers were unable to repay their loans.

The situation in Massachusetts, where statistics are the most reliable, illustrates how the depression hurt credit unions. Between 1929 and

---

[3] Bergengren to Robert L. Moore (assistant to Filene), Dec. 31, 1931.

[4] Snider, *Credit Unions in Massachusetts,* Table IV, p. 15.

[5] Bergengren, *Crusade,* p. 192.

1933, the number of credit unions in the state dropped from 299 to 282, or 5.7 percent; credit union membership declined from 107,000 to 102,-000 or 4 percent; and credit union assets fell 25 percent from $16 to $12 million.[6] Considering the severity of the depression, however, this record was not bad.

On the other hand, there were continued successes in the movement. Despite a drop in employees on the Rock Island Railroad from 42,000 in the 1920s to about 30,000 in 1933, all of the credit unions among the railroad's workers were operating successfully.[7] Assets of credit unions in Minnesota grew from $600,000 to $755,000. The treasurer of the Chicago Municipal Employees' Credit Union wrote Bergengren in 1932 that "in spite of delayed pay days, salary reductions, layoffs, and added burdens on members now obliged to contribute to the support of unemployed relatives, we are going steadily ahead."[8] Reports such as this prompted Bergengren to boast to Filene that "the credit unions have come through the industrial depression better than any form of banking in the United States."[9]

But credit union gains did not come easily. One of Bergengren's continuing problems was to get budgetary support to finance the movement. In 1929, the last predepression year, the Twentieth Century Fund appropriated $50,000 for credit union work. This was $12,500 less than Bergengren requested. He not only wanted more money with which to push the legislative work, but he wanted to buy a five-story building near Boston's financial center. The structure, he wrote Filene, "would make a dignified headquarters for the cooperative credit development in the United States."[10] Bergengren believed that such a building would serve as a symbol of the national credit union movement and would encourage the formation of a national association of credit unions. Even though the building was probably a bargain at $50,000, the matter was dropped after the stock market crash. Headquarters remained at 5 Park Square.

Bergengren's main need was for additional funds to finance a field staff of "the four best men in the credit union movement" to help in the legislative and organizational work. Once a national association of credit unions was formed, Bergengren thought, these men could be shifted to

---

[6] Snider, *Credit Unions in Massachusetts*, Table XI, p. 29.

[7] Bergengren to Filene, Sept. 13, 1933.

[8] Bergengren, *Crusade*, p. 180–81, 192.

[9] *Ibid.*, p. 151.

[10] Bergengren, "Memorandum re Proposed Building Devoted Exclusively to the Credit Union Development and Mr. Filene's Outside Activities," October 9, 1929.

various departments of the new organization. He estimated that four field secretaries would cost $30,000 a year.[11] Bergengren failed to get enough money to hire four field organizers, but his 1930 appropriation was raised to $65,000, an increase of $15,000. This permitted him to employ Thomas Doig on a full-time basis and place him in charge of a new Midwest headquarters at Minneapolis—the first organizational expansion of CUNEB.

Doig had become one of the outstanding volunteer credit unionists in the country. When Bergengren offered him a full-time position, Doig at first refused. He said that he was thoroughly "sold on the credit union as a helpful human agency," but for personal reasons preferred not to make a change.[12] Bergengren, however, appealed to Doig's sense of adventure and belief in the importance of credit unions, and said that he had arranged it so that Doig could continue to live in Minneapolis. This did it, and on January 21, 1930, Doig wrote that he and his wife had decided "to cast our lot with you." Doig was to concentrate on organizational work in Minnesota, Missouri, Iowa, Indiana, Illinois, and Wisconsin.[13]

Throughout 1930 and 1931, Bergengren spent considerable time arguing with Filene and officials of the Twentieth Century Fund over finances. The $65,000 which he received in 1930 permitted him not only to support Doig and the Minneapolis office, but to spend $8,300 on volunteer organizers. Despite the depression, however, printing costs and office expenses were higher. But Bergengren wanted more money for 1931, saying that the organization of additional credit unions would be costly. Moreover, he wanted to support three new state leagues as "laboratory experimental leagues," in order to learn how to develop a state league so that it would be self-supporting. Minnesota, Iowa, and Missouri had opened league offices with full-time managing directors, but Bergengren thought CUNEB should assist them if they could not meet their expenses. CUNEB, Bergengren wrote, had already formed the League Central Committee, a voluntary association of executives of the existing state leagues. This committee had taken over the business of providing business supplies to leagues, but CUNEB had to finance the operation. Bergengren kept telling Filene that, with proper support, the credit union movement would soon be strong enough to maintain a national associa-

[11] *Ibid.*

[12] Doig to Bregengren, Jan. 8, 1930.

[13] *Ibid.,* Jan. 16, 1930; Bergengren to Doig, Jan. 18, 1930; Doig to Bergengren, Jan. 21, 1930; *The Bridge* (Jan., 1930), p. 1.

tion, which in turn would gradually take over the responsibility of financing credit union growth.[14]

Filene did not waste any time telling Bergengren that neither he nor the Twentieth Century Fund would provide an expanded budget. While Filene admitted that CUNEB could use $100,000 advantageously in 1931, he informed Bergengren that only $50,000 would be available.[15] While Bergengren seemed to accept this decision, he kept pressing Filene for more money, both for the movement and for himself. Despite his idealism and concern for credit unionism, Bergengren constantly sought more money for himself. He saw no contradiction between service to the movement and improving his own financial position. At times Bergengren grew angry and said things which he later regretted, but Filene soothed Bergengren's ruffled temper by assuring him that there was no hostility between them. Nevertheless, Filene said that the $50,000 budget must stand.[16] Bergengren continued to nag Filene and to present a broadly expanded budget for 1931, but Filene was unyielding to Bergengren's threats and emotional outbursts. He simply recommended that Bergengren cut expenses. One saving, Filene said, would be to dismiss Doig and close the Midwest office.[17] While Bergengren only got $50,000 for 1931, he was determined to spend it as he thought best. He refused to shut down Doig's office, arguing that he was "the best man by far as yet developed in the credit union movement." [18]

Bergengren's situation was complicated by the Twentieth Century Fund's attempt to exert greater influence over credit union activities. In May, 1931, the directors requested Bergengren to submit a plan of action for CUNEB for 1932 and 1933 for their approval. They announced that there should be no deviation from those plans and policies without approval of the fund's president or executive committee. Bergengren submitted a long report, but he resented what he considered interference by fund officials. Moreover, Bergengren did not get along very well with Evans Clark, the executive director of the fund. He believed that Clark was not really loyal to the credit union movement, and, besides, Bergengren resented the fact that Clark made a higher salary than he did.[19]

As the depression worsened, the annual battle of the budget continued.

[14] Journal of Credit Union National Extension Bureau, entries for 1930; Bergengren to Filene, June 7, 1930.

[15] Filene to Bergengren, Jan. 31, 1931.

[16] Bergengren to Filene, Mar. 20, 1931; Filene to Bergengren, Mar. 21, 1931.

[17] Bergengren to Filene, Mar. 24, 1931; Filene to Bergengren, Mar. 26, 1931.

[18] Bergengren to Filene, Mar. 27, 1931.

[19] Ibid.; Clark to Bergengren, Nov. 2, 1931.

Bergengren never missed an opportunity to emphasize what his office had been unable to do because of limited funds. When Filene, for example, requested certain statistics on the movement, Bergengren replied that there had never been funds to gather data.[20] Bergengren took this opportunity to ask for $100,000 in 1932, telling Filene that the opportunity for the rapid development of credit unions would never again be as great as it would be during 1932. Annoyed by this constant pressure, Filene penciled in the margin of Bergengren's letter: "When will the credit union become self-supporting?" Rather than expect any increase in funds to promote credit union work, Filene told Bergengren that he should utilize the national publications and news media to publicize credit unionism. Two days later Bergengren got his allocation for 1932; it was $50,000.[21]

The Credit Union National Extension Bureau received a bad shock when the Exchange Trust Company of Boston failed on April 25, 1932. This froze all of CUNEB's remaining operating funds of $4,500. Filene was thoroughly annoyed at Bergengren for ignoring his earlier suggestion of removing CUNEB's money to another bank. Nevertheless, Filene arranged with the Twentieth Century Fund to rebudget the amount of money which the bureau had lost.[22]

Another aspect of the growing tension between Bergengren and Filene and fund officials was Bergengren's insistence that the Twentieth Century Fund should support a National Credit Union Association once it was formed. Bergengren regularly predicted that the organization of a national association was only a year or two away. He believed that the fund should provide financing for an association over a period of at least five years. When fund spokesmen, as well as Filene, refused to give him assurance on this point, Bergengren persistently but vainly kept repeating his request. Filene also rejected his demand for a larger appropriation for 1933 so that more organizers could be hired. The Twentieth Century Fund, with Filene's approval, appropriated $50,000 for the bureau in 1933. Filene said that Bergengren should not be permitted to exceed the budget.[23]

Neither the depression nor the wrangling over money to support the

[20] Bergengren to Robert L. Moore, Dec. 31, 1931.

[21] Bergengren to Filene, Jan. 25, 1932.

[22] Bergengren to Filene, April 25, 1932; R. L. Moore to Evans Clark, April 25, 1932; Bergengren to Clark, April 26, 1932; Bergengren to Filene, April 27, 1932; Filene to Bergengren, May 2, 1932.

[23] Bergengren to Filene, Mar. 17, 1933 [Filene's comments written in margin].

bureau's work stood in the way of steady gains for credit unionism. At the beginning of 1931 there were still sixteen states which did not have laws authorizing credit unions. During the next two years, laws were enacted in six important states and the District of Columbia. One of the difficulties confronting credit union advocates during these years was the fact that every legislature was flooded with bills designed to deal with the economic emergency. Under these circumstances, credit union bills generally received low priority from lawmakers.[24] In some cases, however, credit union legislation won new backers because credit unions seemed to provide a possible way of helping people who were suffering from the depression.

Bergengren considered it especially important when the Ohio legislature finally passed a credit union bill in 1931. This was the culmination of nearly a decade of effort. Previous bills had been defeated by the commercial banks and the states' building and loan associations, but in 1931 Bergengren found new allies in L. B. Palmer, president of the Ohio Farm Bureau Federation, and Murray Lincoln, a cooperative leader, and other influential citizens.[25] While Bergengren was not completely satisfied with the measure, he wrote that "a half loaf was far better than no bread at all." [26] Lawmakers in Arkansas and Colorado also passed credit union legislation in 1931. When it appeared that there was no chance to enact the bill in Arkansas, Earl Rentfro, manager of the Missouri Credit Union League, went to Little Rock and was largely responsible for getting favorable legislative action.[27] In Colorado, Bergengren retained a local attorney to push credit union legislation, and, with the support of prominent persons as well as the National Catholic Welfare Council, the legislation was easily adopted.[28]

Besides the passage of three state laws in 1931, there were some additional legislative gains. Professor John R. Commons, University of Wisconsin economist, wrote an amendment to that state's law which provided for a state appropriation for the work of organizing credit unions. The law specified that a full-time organizer would be attached to the office of the State Banking Department. Following the passage of this law, a group of credit union leaders in the state recommended that Charles G. Hyland, manager of the La Crosse Fire Department Credit

24 Bergengren, *Crusade*, p. 166.
25 *The Bridge* (June–July, 1931), p. 2.
26 *Ibid.*
27 *Ibid.*, pp. 2–3; Bergengren, *Crusade*, p. 171.
28 *The Bridge* (June–July, 1931), p. 3.

Union, assume the new post in the Banking Department. This recommendation was promptly approved. Bergengren characterized Hyland as one who "believed in credit unions and organized them with the zeal of a Raiffeisen. . . ." This was no exaggeration, for within a few weeks Hyland had organized twenty-four new credit unions in Wisconsin.[29] Hyland eventually became a national figure in the credit union movement. Also in 1931, the legislatures in Tennessee, Indiana, and New York amended their credit union laws, and harmful tax bills were defeated in Minnesota and Alabama. The major failures came in unsuccessful legislative campaigns in Washington, Oklahoma, Pennsylvania, and Connecticut.[30]

Bergengren, however, was not discouraged by these defeats. He simply prepared for the next legislative sessions. In Washington, CUNEB had been trying to pass a credit union bill ever since 1925, only to have the measures vetoed by the governor who, Bergengren said, had "a hook-up with the small loans business." But in 1932 Governor Roland H. Hartley was defeated and when the lawmakers gathered in 1933 they found such widespread support for a credit union law that it passed with little opposition. The story was much the same in Pennsylvania and Oklahoma.[31]

It was clear by the early 1930s that credit unions had picked up substantial political strength. One source of support came from the three major farm organizations. By 1933 the Farmers' Union, the National Grange, and the American Farm Bureau Federation had all endorsed the credit union movement.[32] The practical effect of this can be seen in Washington, where Albert S. Goss, a prominent Grange leader, supported the credit union law, while in Oklahoma Tom Cheek, president of the state Farmers' Union, and W. Pat Murphy of the State Department of Labor were among the prominent men giving support to credit union legislation. Indeed, in several states farm and labor leaders provided key help in getting credit union laws. In any event, by 1933 one of the extension bureau's primary objectives, "to get the laws," had been achieved. There were credit union laws in thirty-eight states covering 95 percent of the nation's population.

Meanwhile, a serious move began in Congress to pass a credit union

---

[29] Bergengren, *Crusade*, pp. 172–73; *The Bridge* (Aug.–Sept., 1931), p. 1, and (Christmas, 1931), p. 5.

[30] Bergengren, *Crusade*, pp. 166–68, 172; *The Bridge* (June–July, 1931), p. 3.

[31] Bergengren, *Crusade*, p. 213; *The Bridge* (Christmas, 1933), pp. 3 and 8.

[32] Bergengren to Evans Clark, Feb. 15, 1933; Bergengren to Filene, Nov. 4, 1931.

law for the District of Columbia. Senator Arthur Capper of Kansas and Representative Gale H. Stalker of New York introduced bills in 1930. Senator Capper sent copies of his bill to many influential leaders in Washington; Filene contacted friends in the capital, while Bergengren followed up these leads with letters and personal visits. Filene was especially anxious to get a law permitting credit unions in the District of Columbia because he believed it would help to quicken the interest in credit unionism throughout the country. As he wrote: "then the Congressmen and Senators will be interested in their [credit union] development in their own states and districts." But Congress took no action on the measure in 1930. The next year both houses passed a credit union bill, but it died in "the jam at the end of the session." [33]

Early in 1932, Senator Capper again introduced his bill in the Senate, and Representative William P. Connery of Massachusetts sponsored it in the House. The Capper-Connery bill was similar to the credit union legislation passed in the various states. Its stated purpose was to promote thrift among members and to create a supply of credit at reasonable rates of interest. The bill permitted as few as seven people in the District of Columbia to form a credit union which would be capitalized by selling shares at ten dollars each. There were to be five directors, and credit and supervisory committees. The officers were to be a president, vice-president, clerk, and treasurer, none of whom could be paid for their services. No unsecured loan could exceed fifty dollars and every loan had to be approved by a majority of the credit committee. Interest rates were to be limited to not more than 1 percent a month on the unpaid balance.

Despite opposition from the District Bankers' Association and the problem of obtaining time to consider the measure, the Senate took up the bill on March 11. Senator L. J. Dickinson of Iowa argued that consideration of the credit union legislation should be delayed. As he put it, "there is a feeling on the part of some of the banking institutions in Washington that it would be detrimental to have this additional element enter into the financial atmosphere of the city [Washington] at this time." However, Senator J. J. Blaine of Wisconsin made a stout defense of the credit union bill. He insisted that its passage would help people who could not borrow from regular financial institutions. Every citizen's group in the district, he declared, favored the measure. Senator Capper argued for

[33] Percy Brown to Filene, July 9, 1930 [Filene's marginal note dated Aug. 12, 1930]; Bergengren, Report to Twentieth Century Fund Directors, May 21, 1931.

Senate passage because there was "an overwhelming sentiment in this city, especially among the Federal employees and labor groups" for its enactment. Following acceptance of some amendments, the Senate passed the measure on April 11.[34]

The House did not take up the bill until June 13. There it was presented as a poor man's bill which would help those who were being exploited by loan sharks. Representative Connery declared that the sole purpose of the legislation was to "do away with the loan sharks in the District of Columbia and allow Government employees and other residents of the District to borrow money at a reasonable rate." Connery told his colleagues that small loan establishments were charging up to 36 percent interest in the capital city. This seemed to convince the House that credit relief was both desirable and necessary.[35]

Passage of the measure in the House on June 13 completed the campaign for a credit union law covering the District of Columbia. The only other problem was to make sure that President Hoover signed the bill. Bergengren wrote to Hoover's secretary, Theodore G. Joslin, emphasizing the measure's importance to federal employees.[36] On June 21 Senator Capper visited with the president about the matter and Hoover signed the bill later the same day.[37] This was a major victory for the movement because it indicated congressional approval of the principle of credit unionism. It also gave added prestige to a development which still needed a great deal of public support if it were to be genuinely successful.

Another potential aid for credit unions provided by Congress in 1932 was their inclusion among the financial institutions and associations which could borrow funds from the Reconstruction Finance Corporation. Bergengren and Filene did considerable lobbying to persuade Congress to include credit unions in the bill. Bergengren did not think that credit unions really needed the aid of such an agency, but he thought the RFC would provide credit unions with "a sort of insurance policy against prolongation of the depression." Besides having something to fall back on, he believed that it was advantageous to have Congress recognize credit unions in this fashion. But Bergengren hoped that credit unions would get "through the depression without need for this or any other artificial help."

[34] U. S., Congress, Senate, *Congressional Record,* 72d Cong., 1st sess., 1932, LXXV, Part 5, p. 5738; Part 7, pp. 7888–90.

[35] House, *ibid.,* Part 12, pp. 12866–71.

[36] Bergengren to Joslin, June 20, 1932, and June 21, 1932, Container No. 1-E/400, Herbert Hoover Library, West Branch, Iowa.

[37] *Washington Post,* June 24, 1932; Joslin to Bergengren, Hoover Library.

This hope was realized. Up to 1941 only five credit unions had borrowed a total of $600,000 from the RFC, all of which had been repaid.[38]

International aspects of credit unionism received additional impetus in 1932 when the parliament of Nova Scotia enacted a law permitting the operation of credit unions in that province. The year before Bergengren had been asked by Father James J. Tompkins to visit Nova Scotia and talk with the people about forming credit unions.[39] The conditions among farmers, fishermen, and industrial workers in eastern Canada had been bad even during the generally prosperous 1920s, but now they were deplorable. During the 1920s Dr. M. M. Coady, a Roman Catholic priest and educator, and Angus MacDonald, who later became a leader in the Canadian credit union movement, had attempted to improve social and economic conditions in Nova Scotia. Their work became known as the Antigonish movement. One of the goals of this group was to promote cooperation along Rochdale lines among the people of the province. Bergengren's invitation to visit Nova Scotia resulted from the Antigonish leaders' desire to establish cooperative credit institutions. During his stay in Nova Scotia, Bergengren explained the benefits of credit unions to several groups of farmers and fishermen. Soon afterwards, the Antigonish leaders asked Bergengren to draft a credit union bill. It was Bergengren's measure which the Nova Scotia parliament enacted into law.[40] Bergengren's work in Nova Scotia, as well as his assistance in organizing the first credit union at Welland, Ontario, the year before, repaid in a small way the efforts of Desjardins who did so much to bring credit unionism to the United States more than two decades earlier. This was the kind of international cooperation which credit union leaders believed was necessary to carry the gospel of cooperative credit to people all over the world.

Bergengren hoped that the beginnings in Nova Scotia would provide a "model development" for the spread of credit unions to other Canadian provinces. Furthermore, he saw the world-wide growth of credit unions as "a kindergarten of understanding on the part of a group of ordinary people of the necessary and inevitable interrelation of the peoples of the world." [41] Bergengren even considered changing the name of the Credit

[38] Bergengren to Filene, Jan. 21, April 27, and Feb. 15, 1932. See RFC table in the appendix of Broadus Mitchell, *Depression Decade: From New Era through New Deal, 1929–1941* (New York: Holt, Rinehart and Winston, 1947), pp. 442–43.

[39] Bergengren, *Crusade*, p. 176.

[40] Moses M. Coady, *The Social Significance of the Cooperative Movement* (New York: Cooperative League of the U.S.A., 1945), pp. 3 ff.

[41] CUNEB Quarterly Report, June 22, 1933; Bergengren to Filene, April 27, 1932.

Union National Extension Bureau to the Credit Union International Extension Bureau.

Beyond his work in Canada, Bergengren corresponded with leaders and promoters of cooperative credit on a world-wide basis. In 1932 he wrote to interested parties in the Philippines, Switzerland, and Great Britain urging the establishment or expansion of a system of cooperative credit. He claimed to have had a hand in setting up a cooperative bank in Palestine.[42] Yet, in the early 1930s anything resembling a genuine international credit union movement remained in the unforeseeable future.

Although the enactment of state laws permitting the formation of credit unions had been largely achieved by 1933, the real work of organizing successful credit unions still remained. Moreover, it was highly important for CUNEB to help increase the operational efficiency of credit unions. Since credit unions were run by unpaid volunteers who had little if any financial experience, it was absolutely necessary that they adopt simple, sound, and uniform business practices if they were to succeed. Thus, passage of credit union laws only provided the starting point for expanding cooperative credit in the United States. Citizens had to organize credit unions and then see that their institutions operated efficiently. Bergengren and other credit union leaders had an important part to play in achieving both of these goals.

In the actual organization of credit unions, Bergengren and Filene continued to disagree on the best methods to pursue. As he had for years, Filene insisted that Bergengren seek the endorsement of national, civic, and business organizations which in turn, he hoped, would encourage the formation of credit unions among the employees of the affiliated firms. Bergengren, on the other hand, continued to see little hope for support among the spokesmen of business and industry. In April, 1932, during the depths of the depression, Bergengren sharply attacked Filene's position: "I believe I am right when I say that the failure of the Chamber of Commerce of the United States, and the failure of the American Bankers' Association, and the failure of every organization of businessmen or bankers to produce anything approximating constructive leadership and patriotic direction, either to avoid or to mitigate the evils of the industrial depression through which we are passing, is the most conspicuous fact connected with the depression."[43]

[42] Bergengren to Filene, April 27, 1932; Bergengren, *Crusade*, p. 194; *The Bridge* (Aug.–Sept., 1931), p. 1.

[43] Bergengren to Filene, April 27, 1932.

Critical of, and impatient with, some of Filene's views, Bergengren proceeded to develop the work of organizing credit unions as he thought best. He believed that the movement must be flexible and varied in its approach. He insisted that an appeal should be made to both rural and urban workers, to community groups, and to church parishes. Moreover, Bergengren emphasized that each individual credit union must be formed on a solid foundation. This meant properly educating the individual members, having persons in charge who know how to file the charter with state authorities, who could formulate and see that bylaws were adopted, and who could guide the elections for officers and committees and set up the books. These functions required the leadership of experienced and intelligent people, Bergengren wrote. The organization of a credit union, he believed, was akin to removing an appendix, "a technical matter calling for a measure of skill on the part of the operator." Indeed, Bergengren spent so much time organizing individual credit unions that Filene accused him of wasting effort that might have been better used in the broad administration of the organizational campaign. But Bergengren defended his work and boasted that "no credit union I have organized has ever been through a process of involuntary liquidation . . . ." [44]

Bergengren, however, always recognized that he could not do the job alone. He continued to employ paid organizers and expenses for this purpose in 1931 and 1932 averaged more than $6,500 a year.[45] None of these so-called volunteers did more effective work than Claude R. Orchard, who began working for Armour and Company in Omaha, Nebraska, in 1903. Over the years, Orchard became intimately acquainted with the financial problems of Armour employees, many of whom were poorly educated blacks and immigrants who worked for seventeen to eighteen cents an hour. He saw poor, ignorant packing-plant workers caught up in the grip of loan sharks who exacted exorbitant interest rates.

Orchard first heard of credit unions in 1929 from Henry Meyer, a lawyer whom Bergengren had sent to Nebraska on an organizational mission. Over dinner Meyer convinced Orchard that a credit union was the answer to the needs of Armour employees. Shortly afterward, they organized a credit union for Armour workers. Company officials were so

---

[44] Bergengren, "Final and Immediate Objectives of the Credit Union National Extension Bureau," Report to the Board of Trustees of the Twentieth Century Fund, May 21, 1931; Bergengren to Filene, Jan. 30, 1931.

[45] Journal of Credit Union National Extension Bureau, entries for 1929–33.

impressed with the result that they freed Orchard temporarily so that he could travel to other Armour plants to form credit unions. By 1931, there were seventeen credit unions in Armour facilities and by 1933 the number had grown to seventy.[46] This kind of dedicated and effective organizational assistance was a major factor in credit union growth during the depression.

Despite the general gains of credit unionism, Bergengren and other organizers continually had to stress both the philosophy and practical benefits which employees and employers could derive from cooperative credit. That is, there was a constant selling job to be done. The advantages which appeared so obvious to credit union advocates were by no means so plain to others. Therefore, Bergengren emphasized that workers who were freed from severe financial worries and who stayed out of the clutches of loan sharks were much more efficient. Employers would also benefit, he said, if they did not have to deal with garnishments or wage assignments to creditors. Credit unions also encouraged thrift among workers and discouraged borrowing for frivolous purposes. Filene appealed to employers on broader economic grounds. He argued that when employees borrowed to buy refrigerators, radios, automobiles and other consumer goods they helped the total economy. "Consumption must be financed," he said, "if there is to be general prosperity." [47] Thus, credit unions were not only helpful to individuals but to the entire economy. Whatever validity this position may have had, it was not yet widely accepted in the early 1930s.

Besides devoting his efforts to organizing credit unions, Bergengren continued to emphasize the importance of forming state leagues which would provide the basis for a national association of credit unions. By the end of 1930 there were eleven state organizations referred to as "leagues." However, only the Massachusetts league met the Bergengren standards of being financially self-sustaining and carrying on a full range of organizational, legislative, and auxiliary services. Believing that at least fifteen strong state leagues were necessary to form the basis of a national association, Bergengren set out in 1930 to strengthen the so-called paper leagues. He drew up a uniform set of bylaws for leagues to adopt and began an organizational campaign by holding meetings in Minnesota, Iowa, Illinois, and Indiana.[48]

[46] Interview with Claude R. Orchard, Miami, Florida, August 10, 1968; CUNEB Quarterly Report, June 22, 1933.

[47] Edward A. Filene, "The Spread of Credit Unions," *Survey*, LXV (Nov. 1, 1930), 180–81.

[48] Bergengren to Filene, Mar. 13, 1930; *The Bridge* (Feb.–April, 1930), p. 12.

In June the Minnesota league was reorganized under Bergengren's by-laws. It opened an office with a full-time secretary on October 1.[49] Leaving Minneapolis, Bergengren and Doig went to Des Moines where they met with forty-eight delegates from twenty-four credit unions. After considerable maneuvering and some delay, the Iowans adopted the uniform bylaws, raised some money to finance a state office, and voted to seek a $2,000 loan from CUNEB.[50] Then Bergengren visited with delegates from Missouri credit unions in Kansas City and another state league was formed. He also helped to form state leagues in Illinois and Indiana. Nearly 50 delegates from throughout Indiana met on Leo Kaminsky's lawn in Indianapolis where they voted to reorganize the state league.[51] During the fall of 1930, Bergengren and Doig organized leagues in North Carolina, Virginia, Georgia, Alabama, and Michigan.[52]

This seemed like a remarkable record, but the appearance was more impressive than the reality. Within a year Bergengren reported that all of the new leagues were "operating in a tentative way," and that none of them really had "enough credit unions to make effective league operation possible." [53] By the spring of 1932, Bergengren reported that only five states, Massachusetts, New York, Minnesota, Missouri, and Illinois, had leagues "operating on a self-sustaining basis." This was far short of the fifteen which he thought was necessary before a national association could be formed.[54]

Bergengren was also concerned about expanding the services of individual credit unions. By 1929 he expressed the hope that soon a credit union member could deposit his savings, obtain a needed loan or take out insurance at his credit union office.[55] Massachusetts credit unions pioneered in handling insurance. In 1930 the manager of the Plymouth Cordage Company at Plymouth, who had organized a credit union for his employees, established an agency for Savings Bank Life Insurance in his credit union. Within a short time the credit union had issued life in-

[49] "The Minnesota League Meeting," *The Bridge* (Midsummer, 1930), p. 2.

[50] "The Iowa League Meeting," *ibid.,* p. 3; Bougie, *History of the Iowa Credit Union League,* pp. 13–18.

[51] "The Illinois League Meeting," *The Bridge* (Midsummer, 1930), p. 5; "The Indiana League Meeting," *ibid.,* p. 159.

[52] Bergengren, *Crusade,* pp. 159–60.

[53] Bergengren, "Final and Immediate Objectives of CUNEB," May 21, 1931; Bergengren to Robert L. Moore, Dec. 31, 1931.

[54] CUNEB Quarterly Report, June 22, 1933.

[55] Bergengren, "Memorandum for Executive Committee for Meeting, November 29, 1929," Nov. 23, 1929.

surance policies to its members totaling $400,000. The Massachusetts league promoted this plan among other credit unions in the state. Bergengren believed that this was "the beginning of an association . . . of the credit union and life insurance." [56] The Illinois state league provided borrowers protection insurance for credit union members and acted as an agent for a bonding company.[57]

A further service set up in Massachusetts was establishment in 1932 of the Central Credit Union Fund. Any credit union in the state could gain membership by investing at least $50 in the corporation. The maximum investment was set at $20,000 or 2,000 shares, but no credit union could invest more than 5 percent of its total assets. The Central Credit Union Fund lent money to local credit unions and also placed surplus funds in investments which were legal for savings banks. All earnings above reserves and administrative expenses were to be distributed in the form of dividends to member credit unions. A board of directors elected by the members managed the fund which was under the general supervision of the State Banking Department. Bergengren was elected as the first president of the Central Credit Union Fund.[58]

In 1930 Bergengren formed the League Central Committee to take over the business of handling credit union supplies from the Massachusetts league. The new agency was to sell supplies to leagues at cost, which in turn would sell to member credit unions at a small profit. Agnes Gartland managed the League Central Committee's supply business. The business did not prosper, however, and in 1931 Bergengren had to borrow $4,000 from Filene to keep it solvent. Later, business picked up and the loan was repaid.[59] The expansion of services for credit unions in the early 1930s foreshadowed the work which would later be performed by a national association.

A continued difficulty facing Bergengren was his rivalry, and even conflict, with the Russell Sage Foundation over the development of credit unions in New York. Bergengren considered the foundation's Division of Remedial Loans as a rival to the credit union movement, and he resented the foundation pushing its uniform small loan bills at the same time credit union measures were being considered. Also Bergengren

[56] Bergengren, *Crusade,* pp. 161–62; *The Bridge* (May, 1930), p. 3.

[57] *The Bridge* (Christmas, 1931), p. 10.

[58] Bergengren to Filene, May 3 and 19, 1932; Massachusetts Credit Union League, "A Central Fund for Massachusetts Credit Unions" (Boston, 1932).

[59] "The League Central Committee," *The Bridge* (Christmas, 1930), p. 2; Bergengren, *Crusade,* pp. 182–83.

thought the foundation was ineffective in getting legislation to control loan sharks. He wrote Filene that the foundation, with a million dollar budget, had been campaigning for laws limiting interest on small loans to 42 percent for six years longer than Bergengren had been seeking credit union laws, yet "we have our laws in 32 states, against their laws in 19 states." [60] Moreover, Bergengren believed that there was a "hook-up which increasingly exists between the 42% lenders operating under the Russell Sage Bill and the banks, resulting in opposition to our legislation by banks for the protection of 42% private lenders." [61]

Bergengren explained how this worked in a later letter to Filene:

In this county seat there is one bank which owns a 42% loan company across the street from the bank. The farmer brings to the bank what little money he has. When he comes to the bank for credit, he is told that the industrial depression prevents the bank from making any short-term loans, and he is sent to the 42% loan company. The bank loans its money at 10% to the 42% company (which belongs to the bank) which in turn loans the farmer money at 42%. There is no business, large or small, in the United States which could operate on 42% credit . . . . There is no worker in the United States who can afford . . . to pay 42% for credit."

Bergengren said he did not want to quarrel with the foundation, but predicted that eventually the 42 percent credit structure would fail "because it is completely un-American and violates all economic law." [62] Filene warned Bergengren not to attack the foundation's work, partly because it would arouse the opposition of the vested interests operating under the Uniform Small Loans Laws in some of the states where credit unions were getting started.[63] Filene did not wish to create any unnecessary opposition to credit union development. But Bergengren continued at odds with the Russell Sage Foundation until it later withdrew from credit union work.

What bothered Bergengren most was the Russell Sage Foundation's continued control over the credit union movement in New York. He had found it impossible to cooperate with the foundation which, he wrote, had "botched, mismanaged, and improperly conducted" the credit union movement in the state.[64] Although Bergengren had earlier organized some credit unions in New York, in 1930 he decided that a branch office

[60] Bergengren to Filene, Mar. 27, 1931.
[61] *Ibid.*, Mar. 20, 1931.
[62] *Ibid.*, Nov. 4, 1931.
[63] Filene to Bergengren, Dec. 8, 1931.
[64] Bergengren to Filene, April 30, 1930.

of CUNEB should be opened there. At about the same time the Russell Sage Foundation dropped its financial support for the movement and CUNEB financed the new office on Forty-Second Street.[65] To manage this new headquarters which he called the Eastern States Department, Bergengren employed Basil B. Mallicoat who went to work on May 30. Mallicoat later recalled that Bergengren wanted "an outsider to straighten out the nasty New York situation." [66]

This arrangement, however, did not work out. Mallicoat soon became ill and was replaced by Dora Maxwell, who had worked with the Consumer's Cooperative Credit Union. Also, Sidney Stahl left the Sixth Avenue Credit Union and became manager of the New York league. Under new leadership the credit union movement in New York began to make sound advances. Bergengren reported in 1932 that Dora Maxwell was rapidly organizing new credit unions "of the right sort." Miss Maxwell was especially successful in gaining support from New York farm groups as well as Governor Roosevelt and Henry Morgenthau, Jr., who headed a commission to investigate the crisis in agriculture caused by so many bank failures. One upstate New York fruit grower referred to CUNEB as "the central organization of the Raiffeisen banks in America." [67]

Despite Bergengren's optimistic picture of the situation in New York, the credit union movement was considerably weaker in the state in 1932 than in 1929. The number of credit unions had declined from 125 to 113 and the amount in loans had dropped from more than $18 million to only $5.5 million. Yet, a foundation for sound future growth was being laid.

The credit union movement continued to meet opposition from employers who saw it as a competitor for their own financial plans for their employees. For example, officers of a textile corporation opposed the organization of a credit union among its workers because it was about to launch a program of employee stock purchases and did not want any competition for funds. In another plant the personnel director opposed Bergengren's efforts to organize a credit union because this official owned stock in a bank which loaned money to some of the firm's employees. In some other instances employees themselves opposed credit unions be-

[65] *The Bridge* (Jan., 1930), pp. 1–2; Bergengren to Filene, Mar. 13, 1930; Sidney Stahl, "History of the New York State Credit Union League," typescript, p. 2.

[66] *The Bridge* (Feb.-Mar.-April, 1930), p. 6; (May, 1930), p. 1; (Jan., 1931), p. 2; Mallicoat to E. R. Brann, July 2, 1961; Stahl, "History of the New York State Credit Union League," p. 2.

[67] Bergengren to Filene, Jan. 20, 1932.

cause they loaned a few dollars to fellow workers at exorbitant interest rates and did not want to lose this income.[68]

Another difficulty was getting the cooperation of officials in subsidiaries of large companies because no one wanted to take the responsibility of authorizing a credit union. Labor turnover in the mass production plants also created problems of organization and operation of a credit union, since success depended to some extent on a stable membership. But despite such obstacles, by 1933 credit unions existed among employees of some of the country's largest and most powerful corporations.[69]

Bergengren never lost his zeal for organizing rural and parish credit unions which were typical of the cooperative banking development in Europe. Most farm leaders, however, did not believe that credit unions were really fitted to meet the needs of rural people. As M. S. Winder, executive secretary of the American Farm Bureau Federation wrote in 1933, farmers were not obtaining credit from small loan companies at excessive rates. Yet, when a survey was made in one Iowa county it was found that 20 percent of the American Farm Bureau Federation's members were borrowing at rates up to 42 percent. Revelations of this kind helped to bring official support to the credit union movement from agricultural leaders, but only a few credit unions were formed among farmers.[70] For example, in Nebraska, where the Farmer's Union urged the formation of credit unions, only two societies were organized in 1932.

Bergengren had shown an interest in parish credit unions for several years, but only a small number had been organized before 1930. That year, according to Bergengren, parish credit union development finally began "in a systematic and deliberate fashion." In 1930 some fifty parish credit unions were organized, partly because of the work of Doig, who spent considerable time in that type of organizational work. But, overall, progress was slow. Doig met opposition from local bankers, parishioners who were suspicious, as one priest wrote, of "anything a pastor tries to start," [71] and from other sources. There was a great deal

[68] Roy F. Bergengren, "Riding the Credit Union Circuit," *Survey*, LXV (Nov. 1, 1930), 140; Bergengren, *Crusade*, pp. 174–75.

[69] Bergengren, "Riding the Credit Union Circuit," pp. 14–141; Bergengren, CUNEB Quarterly Report, June 22, 1933. By December, 1933, twenty-nine credit unions existed in plants of Swift and Company, with 8,546 members and assets of $165,900. There were also three credit unions in Standard Oil Company facilities and two in DuPont plants. *The Bridge* (Christmas, 1933), pp. 4–5.

[70] Winder to Bergengren, Sept. 16, 1933.

[71] Rev. C. M. Nellen to Doig, Feb. 7, 1930; Doig to Nellen, Feb. 9, 1930.

of sheer indifference to the movement. Nevertheless, the continued attempts to reach all types of borrowers and savers indicated the broad scope which the credit union pioneers had for the movement.

To create enthusiasm and to overcome opposition, Bergengren was always seeking ways to publicize credit unionism. In September, 1932, he hit upon the idea of having Filene tour the Midwest to visit with credit union leaders and to make public speeches on cooperative credit.[72] Such a trip would not only give the movement valuable publicity, but Filene would get a clearer picture of the progress actually being made. Besides meeting with credit union supporters, he and Bergengren agreed that Filene would discuss the best way to form a national association.

During the fall, Filene and one of his assistants, Charles W. Wood, prepared nine addresses, plus a number of lesser talks. Bergengren suggested that the speeches deal simply and directly with credit problems because as he said, "people today are hungry for knowledge as to how to solve the problems with which they are sorely beset." [73] Meanwhile, Bergengren traveled throughout the Midwest preparing the way for Filene's trip.

Filene, Bergengren, and Lillian Schoedler, Filene's secretary, arrived in Indianapolis from Boston on January 12, 1933. That day he addressed the Advertising Club on "The Business Need of Financing the Masses"; later he talked on "What and Why Is Credit" before the Indiana Credit Union League. During the next twenty days he made thirty-six speeches in twelve cities, including Chicago, St. Paul, Madison, Des Moines, and St. Louis. He spoke before credit union groups, businessmen's organizations, university student and faculty gatherings, labor, church and farm groups, and three state legislatures. He also made several radio talks. In addition to dwelling on topics dealing with money and credit, Filene dealt with such subjects as "High Wages as a Remedy for Unemployment" and "Religion in the Machine Age." But whatever his topic, Filene had one central message; the American economy needed new and different arrangements for the production and distribution of goods, new agencies of finance, and a much greater concern for social welfare. Unless basic changes occurred, Filene repeated, the future of capitalism was in doubt.[74]

This message proved highly popular to people who were weathering

[72] Quoted in Lillian Schoedler, "Edward A. Filene's Trip into the Middle West, January 12–31, 1933," Trip Books, Filene Collection (hereafter cited as "Midwest Trip Book").

[73] Bergengren to Filene, Nov. 9, 1932.

[74] Filene, "Midwest Trip Book."

the third winter of depression. Moreover, Filene's remarks took on added significance since they came from a wealthy businessman and philanthropist. Hundreds came out to hear the Boston merchant—Bergengren estimated that at least 5,000 credit union members met Filene at these meetings—and radio and newspaper reporters spread the message among thousands of unseen readers and listeners. The Filene meetings produced remarkable enthusiasm and demonstrated what Bergengren called "a genuine outpouring of affection for Mr. Filene." [75]

The highlight of the trip was the testimonial dinner given for Filene by the Illinois Credit Union League in Chicago on January 14, 1933. An overflow crowd of about 1,000 persons gathered in and outside of the grand ballroom of the La Salle Hotel. When Timothy O'Shaughnessy introduced Filene, the crowd rose to its feet, the band began to play, and people stamped their feet and cheered. Someone held up a credit union banner and the crowd began to march "about the great room, passing Mr. Filene in review and behaving about as sensibly as do the delegates at a national political convention when the favorite son has been nominated." Visibly shaken, Filene wept as he told Bergengren: "You didn't tell me it was like this." [76]

This amazing demonstration of devotion to Filene, "father of the credit union movement," was best described by a reporter for the Decatur, Illinois, *Sunday Herald*. He wrote:

I have seen a good many demonstrations but nothing that quite equalled that given the founder of the credit union movement in Chicago. It was not the volume of the cheering nor the duration that impressed. It was the spontaneous love of disciple for a master. Eyes glowed and the faces of people were rapt as they leaped to their feet to greet a little man whom many in the back part of the room could not see. There was a spiritual fervor in the attitude of these folks from parishes and farms, from factories and stores, from railroads and shops, towards a man who, for the most part, had been almost a legendary figure in the background of a movement that promises to become a great economic force in this country . . . . Known at home and in the capitals of the world, holder of citations and decorations of European governments for meritorious public service, Mr. Filene was visibly touched by these demonstrations by the plain people to whom he had given only an idea.[77]

Besides generating enthusiasm for credit unionism, Filene's trip had another important result. The day following the testimonial dinner a

[75] Bergengren, *Crusade*, pp. 203–4.
[76] *Ibid.*, pp. 205–7.
[77] *Ibid.*, p. 208.

number of key credit union leaders met in his Chicago hotel suite where they discussed the matter of organizing a national credit union association. Although the details of what transpired at this meeting are not known, the discussions did create additional support for a national organization of credit unions.[78]

Altogether, Filene's trip was a huge success. It capped a difficult period of credit union development, but one in which the movement had continued to make good progress. By 1933 most states had laws authorizing credit unions, at least five states had effective leagues, and Bergengren had been able to set up a Midwest office with Doig in charge and an eastern states headquarters in New York. Moreover, despite the depression hundreds of additional credit unions had been organized and were operating successfully. In 1932 Bergengren made a survey of credit unions and found 1,700 compared to only 1,100 in 1929. His figures were higher than those given by the Bureau of Labor Statistics, which gathered data on all kinds of cooperative societies—the bureau reported 974 credit unions in 1929 and 1,612 in 1932—but either set of statistics shows great gains for the credit union movement in terms of the number of societies. The picture was much different when viewed from the viewpoint of loans, as they dropped from $54 million in 1929 to $16 million in 1932.

Thus, it is clear that however worthy the achievements of the credit union movement were, it had not yet made any great impact on the nation's credit structure. Bergengren and other credit union leaders, however, were not discouraged. They had a vision and dream for the future which they fully believed could be achieved with more time and effort. They were convinced that the idea of service, helping the man of small means, would eventually win them widespread support and that someday credit unions would supply a really important part of the nation's consumer credit needs.

[78] *Ibid.*, pp. 208–9; Filene, "Midwest Trip Book."

CHAPTER VII

The Federal Credit Union Act

THE INAUGURATION of Franklin D. Roosevelt came only a few days after Filene completed his triumphal tour of the Middle West. No political event could have pleased Filene more. As a Democrat who had contributed more than $3,000 to his party in 1932, he believed that the new and more service-oriented capitalism which he desired had no chance under Republican leadership. Filene saw in Roosevelt's election a public rejection of exploitation and "irrational selfishness." What the business community must be more concerned about, he wrote, was high wages, full employment, and employee security which were essential for the nation's prosperity. Filene applauded Roosevelt's criticism of the "unscrupulous money changers," and telegraphed the president that the inaugural address "fully came up to our expectations." [1]

The mounting banking crisis had created a critical situation for many credit unions. As the number of state banking holidays increased in late 1932 and early 1933, credit unions found their funds tied up in closed banks. Bergengren advised local credit unions on actions which might exempt them from the various laws and even suggested that, as a last resort, credit unions should rent safe deposit boxes where they could keep enough cash to make small loans. He also thought that local societies might open postal savings accounts in the name of the credit union treasurer so that business could proceed on a limited scale.[2] But these were obviously unsatisfactory approaches to the basic problems of credit unions in a crumbling financial structure.

While Bergengren pondered just how to protect credit union operations, the entire situation suddenly changed when President Roosevelt implemented a nationwide bank holiday on March 6, 1933. Bergengren was "astounded" and "caught off balance" by the inclusion of credit unions in the holiday. He objected to including credit unions because

---

[1] Filene to Roosevelt, Nov., 1932; Edward A. Filene, "The New Capitalism," *Annals of the American Academy*, CXLIX (May, 1930), 3–11; Filene to Roosevelt, Mar. 4, 1933.

[2] Bergengren to Filene, Feb. 27, 1933; CUNEB, "Memo No. 9—To All Credit Unions in States Where There Is Now a Bank Holiday," Mar. 1, 1933.

this implied that credit unions were banks, a definition which Bergengren rejected. Moreover, there had been no runs on credit unions, so he thought there was no need to close them.[3]

Under the Emergency Banking Act, banks and other financial institutions were to be reopened if they were found to be sound. At first Bergengren feared that credit unions would be the last institutions examined by banking authorities, and therefore the last to reopen. This fear, however, proved groundless. Bergengren later admitted that "when the banks which were allowed to resume threw wide open their doors again, to the best of my knowledge every credit union resumed normal business, most of them having found some way of getting along without banks during the holiday." [4]

Once the crisis was over, Bergengren gave his assessment of the effect of the bank holiday on credit unions around the country. Because credit unions had been dealt with in the same manner as banks, he insisted that they should play an important part in any consideration of reorganizing the banking system. Bergengren believed that credit unions had performed their greatest service to members during the bank holiday. He urged credit unions to guarantee that their funds would be used to the best advantage, and called on the movement to consider establishing a central state depository for reserve funds. He also suggested that credit unions should be tied into the Federal Reserve System. Finally, he explained that state credit union leagues should be organized and strengthened at once because they had been "found to be so very valuable in this period of difficulty." [5]

Bergengren did not permit the depression nor the banking crisis to deter him from what had become a major objective—the enactment of a federal credit union law which would allow the incorporation of credit unions in any state or territory. He had mentioned this possibility to Filene as early as 1920, but they had agreed at that time to concentrate on state legislation.[6] But during the following decade, national legislation became increasingly necessary to Bergengren. A federal law, he argued, would permit the organization of credit unions in states which had refused to pass such legislation. Moreover, there was some possibility that other states might repeal their credit union law as West Virginia had done in 1931. A federal statute would also be useful for a basis of organ-

[3] Bergengren, *Crusade,* p. 211.

[4] Bergengren to Filene, Mar. 10, 1933; Bergengren, *Crusade,* p. 212.

[5] CUNEB, "Memo No. 12—Credit Unions and the Bank Holiday," Mar. 20, 1933.

[6] Bergengren, *Crusade,* p. 220.

ization in those states which had weak or defective laws. In other words, "a federal credit union law would be," as Bergengren wrote, "a sort of blanket insurance policy for all our state laws, giving us an alternative method of organization." Finally, when credit unions formed a national association, Bergengren wanted "a completed legislative job, with a United States in which organization was possible everywhere." [7]

In April, 1932, Bergengren informed Filene that he had discussed with Senator Morris Sheppard of Texas "the matter of a bill which would permit credit union organization under Federal jurisdiction." He assured Filene, however, that he would talk over the question with him before proceeding. Still in doubt about such a move, Filene warned Bergengren not to press the matter until they had agreed "that the dangers are not too great." [8] Just what "dangers" Filene had in mind, he did not say.

Filene was cool to the idea of seeking a federal credit union law, not so much on principle, but because he had different priorities for the movement. As early as 1930 he urged that credit unions should concentrate on financing installment purchases. As the depression worsened, Filene became more insistent that credit unions emphasize short-term consumer loans rather than advancing long-term credit on real estate mortgages. Filene looked upon credit unionism as one of the props for the "new capitalism." That is, he believed credit unions had a role to play in stimulating consumer buying power. One helpful move, Filene said, would be to create central credit sources in each state "to get a better coordination of credit unions and make it possible to pool surpluses and use such surpluses in ways approved by the credit unions." [9]

While Bergengren did not disagree with Filene, he simply believed that federal legislation should have first priority. A few days after the bank moratorium in March, 1933, Bergengren wrote to Filene that he planned to go to Washington where he would discuss federal legislation with senators and representatives. He believed the time was ripe to get such a law through Congress. But again Filene warned Bergengren not to proceed until they had agreed on a "written plan of exactly what Federal help we want." [10]

Late in March Bergengren outlined for Filene in considerable detail

---

[7] *Ibid.,* pp. 220–21; Bergengren to Filene, April 27, 1932.

[8] Bergengren to Filene, April 27, 1932. Filene's reaction written in margin.

[9] "Installment Payments," Filene Memorandum, Feb. 14, 1930; "Suggestions for President's Report by Mr. Filene at Twentieth Century Fund Meeting as Regards Credit Unions," Jan. 12, 1932; Filene to Bergengren, Oct. 6. 1932.

[10] Bergengren to Filene, Mar. 10, 1933. Filene's comments written in margin.

why federal legislation was desirable and what the law should include. He reminded Filene that twelve states still had no credit union law and that the population of some of them was so small it did not warrant an effort by CUNEB to obtain a state statute. A federal law, he said, would open up the way for organizational work everywhere in the country. Moreover, Bergengren believed that a federal credit union act would lead to a closer relationship between the federal banking system and credit unions. He foresaw the funneling of some federal credit resources to the ultimate borrowers through credit unions. Also if credit unions had federal charters they would be free from discrimination by unfriendly state banking departments. Bergengren further thought that if credit unions operated under federal control they would more likely be permitted to set up their own central banks or clearinghouses. Finally, he believed the time to act had come because after economic conditions improved, he saw bankers resuming more influence and resisting anything favored by credit unions. Get the legislation in a time of emergency, he argued.

Bergengren proposed that a careful effort be made to get administrative support, as well as nonpartisan backing in Congress for his bill. He already had the endorsement of Senator Sheppard, Democrat of Texas, and Senator Capper, Republican of Kansas. Democrat Connery and Republican A. P. Andrew in the House had also pledged support. So Bergengren had the beginning of solid nonpartisan support in Congress and he depended on Filene's contacts with Roosevelt and other federal officials to get help from the administration. Furthermore, Bergengren proposed mobilizing a grass-roots campaign among credit unionists in every state, asking them to put pressure on their congressional representatives.

Bergengren asked Filene, who was planning a trip to Washington to discuss several matters with President Roosevelt, to try to determine the feasibility of getting federal legislation at that time. If the drive were successful, Bergengren wrote, it would "do more to make possible the organization of our National Association in 1934 than could any one accomplishment . . . ." [11] As it turned out, Filene was unable to see Roosevelt. But even if he had visited with the president there is no indication that Filene planned to bring up the question of federal legislation. At least there is no mention of this topic in the memorandum which he prepared for his prospective conference with Roosevelt.[12]

[11] Bergengren Memorandum for Filene, [March] 1933.
[12] Filene Memorandum, "Matters to Take Up With the President," April 3, 1933.

Nevertheless, while in Washington on April 8, 1933, Filene participated in a radio broadcast over the National Broadcasting Company network, sponsored by the Brookings Institution. Entitled "The Problem of Consumer Credit," the program consisted of a conversation between Filene and Isador Lubin. After discussing the need for credit to increase the purchasing power necessary to buy the great output of American industry, Filene argued that credit unions were the ideal agencies to provide consumer finance.[13]

Despite Filene's lack of enthusiasm for a federal credit union law, he and Bergengren had agreed on the general form of legislation by the end of April. The main features included federal incorporation of credit unions and the establishment of a Credit Union Central Fund in each state which would have rediscount privileges with the Federal Reserve Banks. Filene insisted that the bill must be drawn "tight enough so as not to weaken or interfere with the basic principles of credit unions." He especially feared restrictive federal supervision as well as excessive charges for examining the business affairs of credit unions.[14]

Bergengren had already written to Senator Sheppard on March 11, 1933, saying that the special session of Congress would no doubt enact important banking legislation, and that "in the new banking plan there should be credit unions for small communities, operating under Federal supervision." A week later Bergengren went to Washington where he and Senator Sheppard developed three bills for introduction during the special session.

The cooperation between Bergengren and Sheppard was a natural one. For years the senator had been interested in cooperative banking, especially short-term credit for farmers. Moreover, Sheppard had been deeply influenced by the Populist and Progressive traditions. As a young congressman, he introduced an income tax bill in 1906, and he regularly assailed the tariff and the trusts. After election to the Senate in 1913 he supported programs of rural credit and actually introduced a bill modeled on the German *Landschaften* system. In 1915, he proposed to investigate a system which would provide short-term personal credit for farmers. Since Sheppard believed that land-mortgage credit was not enough to meet farmers' needs, the idea of utilizing credit unions to pro-

[13] "The Problem of Consumer Credit," Economics Series Presentation no. 20 (Chicago: National Broadcasting Co., 1933).

[14] "Alternative Suggestions Re Federal Credit Union Legislation," Bergengren Memorandum, April 29, 1933; "Summary of Proposed Federal Legislation Authorizing the Organization of Central Credit Union Funds," Memorandum signed by Filene and Bergengren, n.d.

vide personal credit to farmers, as well as others, strongly appealed to him.[15]

The first and most important of the three bills was S. 1639 which permitted federal incorporation of credit unions and the operation of state central credit agencies. The second measure relaxed the restrictions of the postal savings system for the benefit of credit unions, and a third bill would give credit unions deposit and borrowing privileges in the Federal Reserve Banks.

Senator Sheppard introduced these measures on May 1. The bills were referred to the Senate Committee on Banking and Currency which in turn sent them to a subcommittee chaired by Senator John Bankhead of Alabama. Bergengren immediately urged credit union supporters to write and wire their congressional representatives on behalf of the legislation. Filene did not play a major part in mobilizing support for the bills, although he did write Senators Thomas P. Gore of Oklahoma and Carter Glass of Virginia, asking them to endorse the measures. He also wrote Louis M. Howe, Roosevelt's chief aide, suggesting that the credit union bills become a part of the administration program. Such action, he wrote, "would not only ensure its passage at this session, but would bring additional strength and support from the people to the President." But, at best, Filene's request for help from the administration was lukewarm, as he said that he did not want to ask Howe "for any favor for the bill, or for myself or Mr. Bergengren." [16]

The Bankhead subcommittee held hearings on the credit union legislation on June 1. Both Bergengren and Sheppard testified on behalf of the measures. Although no opponents appeared in person, several critical letters from various government agencies were introduced into the hearing. The Post Office Department opposed S. 1641 which would have allowed credit unions to use the postal savings system because, as the acting postmaster general wrote, it would be "contrary to the true mission of the Postal Savings System."

E. R. Black, governor of the Federal Reserve Board, opposed S. 1640 which would permit credit unions to make deposits in, and to borrow from, federal reserve banks. Black argued that if such privileges were

---

[15] Lucille Sheppard Keyes, "Morris Sheppard," mimeographed MS (Washington, 1950), pp. 52, 105–10, 122–24; U.S., Congress, Senate *Congressional Record,* 63d Cong., 3d sess., 1915, LII, p. 2940.

[16] Filene to Gore, May 17, 1933 (identical copy sent on same date to Glass); Filene to Howe, May 17, 1933.

extended to credit unions, they would also have to be given to building and loan associations. Since the Reconstruction Finance Corporation could loan money to credit unions, Black did not see any need for the Federal Reserve System to extend such help. Moreover, he explained that it would be expensive and burdensome to service credit unions. Black also opposed the section of S. 1639 which would have allowed central credit unions to rediscount financial paper with the Federal Reserve Banks. The Federal Reserve Act, he said, intended that only commercial and agricultural paper should be used in rediscount operations. The paper of central credit unions would not be of this nature. Secretary of the Treasury William H. Woodin agreed with these views. Black neither opposed or supported the federal chartering of credit unions. He professed inadequate information and therefore did not make a recommendation.

Dean Acheson, writing for the Treasury Department, opposed enactment of the entire legislative package. He pointed out that credit unions were "in their very nature small local associations which should be supervised and regulated by State law." Acheson held that the Treasury Department knew of no good reasons for enacting the Sheppard bills, and argued that they were unnecessary and inadvisable. The Treasury Department, he concluded, strongly opposed passage of the measures.[17]

The opposition of the Federal Reserve Board, the Treasury, and the Post Office Department, especially to S. 1640 and S. 1641, made it unlikely that they could be passed. This still left a good possibility that S. 1639, authorizing federal charters for credit unions, might be enacted. It was important that there was no very strong opposition to this part of the legislative package. Therefore, Bergengren received assurance that S. 1639 would be taken up in January, 1934. There was simply not time to consider the bill so near the end of the special session in June.

From the time the special session adjourned in mid-June until the opening of the seventy-third regular session in January, 1934, Bergengren maintained close contact with Senator Sheppard. Moreover, credit unionists around the country continued to bombard their representatives and senators on behalf of federal legislation. Filene, however, virtually ignored the legislative goal, and concentrated on getting federal aid and subsidies for credit unions so they could be more effective in stimulating

[17] U.S., Congress, Senate, Committee on Banking and Currency, *Federal Credit Union System: Report to accompany S 1639*, 73d Cong., 2d sess., 1934, S. Rept. 555, pp. 5–8 (hereafter cited as S. Rept. 555).

consumer purchases. Bergengren opposed Filene's activities because he feared that the kind of government assistance desired by Filene would endanger the credit union bill and violate true cooperative principles upon which credit unions were based.[18]

Although he was unable to visit with Roosevelt in September, 1933, Filene arranged to meet with Secretary of Commerce Daniel Roper, Jesse Jones, director of the Reconstruction Finance Corporation, and Hugh S. Johnson, head of the National Recovery Administration. Prior to the meeting, he asked both Bergengren and Evans Clark to give him their ideas as to how credit unions could best cooperate with government agencies to stimulate consumer purchasing power and thereby become a more vital part of the general recovery program. Bergengren replied that credit unions could play a larger role in economic recovery if more societies were formed and if they used their funds for consumer-type loans. While Clark favored a campaign to increase the number of credit unions, he argued that credit union resources were too small to make any significant economic impact. Clark proposed "government credit on a large scale to *all* the existing consumer agencies *on condition* that they loan the money at low rates . . . ." [19]

Filene, however, believed that with government help credit unions could be expanded fast enough to be of genuine help. Credit unions, he wrote, "will get credit out much faster than can be done by the other consumer credit organizations who must take time to investigate all their applicants who are unknown to them, which the credit unions, being composed of people who work together, can and will grant credit without delay to all properly entitled to it." [20] Therefore, Filene asked Bergengren to prepare a statement which he might use in his forthcoming conference with government officials. Knowing Filene's views, Bergengren wrote what he knew would be acceptable to Filene. He recommended a federal appropriation of $100,000 to help carry on an organizing campaign and RFC loans to new credit unions to enable them to begin advancing credit immediately. The plan also called for the president to create a Consumer Credit Committee, with Filene as chairman and Bergengren the other member, to administer the federal funds.

After Filene presented his ideas, Jesse Jones said that, while more credit unions might be helpful, no public funds could be used to promote

[18] *The Bridge* (July, 1934), p. 2.

[19] Roper to Filene, Sept. 15, 1933; Bergengren to Filene, Sept. 2, 1933; Clark to Filene, Sept. 16, 1933.

[20] Filene's comments written in margin of Clark to Filene, Sept. 16, 1933.

their organization.[21] But Filene was not deterred. He wrote Roosevelt: "Shall the plan fail because $100,000 is not available in order to put it into operation?" [22] After being turned down by other government officials, he appealed to Louis Howe. All Howe could suggest was that some government agency might loan CUNEB the money, a proposal which Filene quickly rejected. When Roosevelt finally read Filene's letter to Howe, he scrawled a note in the margin: "Louis, help him find the money and put it through." [23] But nothing was done and Filene's repeated pleas for government aid to implement his consumer purchasing program through credit unions were to no avail.[24]

Meanwhile, Bergengren, who had little faith in getting federal funds, was busy promoting the organization of credit unions in the usual way. He also continued to work for passage of his federal credit union law and the establishment of a national association of credit unions. These had become the basic goals of credit unionism.

When Filene could get no federal financing for credit unions, he sent a check for $20,000 to the treasurer of the Twentieth Century Fund "to be used for a special Credit Union extension plan and campaign to help the National Recovery Program with the understanding that it must be used for this special plan" or returned.[25] It was unclear to anyone connected with the fund just what "special plan" Filene had in mind. Percy Brown, Filene's chief aide, informed Evans Clark that once the differences between Bergengren and Filene had been resolved a definite plan to use the $20,000 would be forthcoming.[26]

But by early 1934 Bergengren and Filene had reached a temporary impasse on how to proceed. Bergengren was unalterably opposed to Filene's attempt to obtain federal funds to organize credit unions and provide operating capital. Filene instructed Percy Brown to advise Bergengren that unless he agreed to an organizational campaign in cooperation with federal agencies, Filene would make no additional contributions to the movement above those coming through the Twentieth Century Fund. The $20,000 would be available only if Bergengren agreed with Filene. Brown urged Filene not to create further differences

---

[21] Jones to Filene, Sept. 21, 1933.

[22] Filene to Roosevelt, Sept. 21, 1933.

[23] Roosevelt's comment in margin of Filene to Louis M. Howe, Oct. 13, 1933, OF706, Franklin D. Roosevelt Library.

[24] Filene to Jones, Oct. 13, 1933; Filene to Hugh Johnson, Oct. 14, 1933; Filene to Jones, Dec. 7, 1933; Jones to Filene, Dec. 2, 1933.

[25] Filene to Henry Bruere, treasurer of the Twentieth Century Fund, Dec. 23, 1933.

[26] Clark to Filene, Dec. 26, 1933; Brown to Clark, Dec. 27, 1933.

between him and Bergengren by issuing such an ultimatum, but Filene rejected any compromise.[27]

Unable to convince Bergengren that he was right, Filene decided to take his case to the country's credit union leadership. In January and February, 1934, he took what he called a "cross-country New Deal study tour" to "see how the New Deal was going over in the United States." He appealed to credit union leaders in Chicago, St. Louis, Kansas City, San Francisco, Los Angeles, Houston, Atlanta, and elsewhere, arguing that his ideas of federal aid should be implemented as a means of strengthening the movement and increasing consumer buying power.

In his public addresses Filene emphasized the relationship of credit unions to the New Deal and to economic recovery. He explained that people "must continue to save and to lend." But, he added, "America is growing up, and the credit unions are growing up; and the time is here when we must learn to save and to lend in ways suitable to this new age, which may be very different from the ways of our credit union childhood." In a Keynesian vein, he insisted that the masses should not be saving their money, but spending it. If consumers save their incomes, he said, "instead of buying things which they want and need, . . . they will be creating unemployment in the industries manufacturing those things." Unemployment would result in less buying power and create more joblessness until "nobody's job is safe." He advocated policies which would "bring to the masses such a wealth of buying power that they will be able to purchase and to enjoy the things which we are now so abundantly able to produce." [28] Besides talking in general terms about the importance of greater consumer purchasing power, Filene discussed privately his ideas for credit union development with movement leaders.

Bergengren acted quickly to counteract Filene's direct appeal to credit unionists. He wrote to his friends in the movement insisting that such policies as loans from the RFC and federal funds for organizational work would generate legal difficulties and be contrary to the "basic credit union cooperative principles." The conflicting appeals by Filene and Bergengren for support throughout the movement proved that Bergengren, not Filene, had the real grass-roots support. Doig backed Bergengren as did most other active credit unionists. Earl Rentfro wrote Filene that the executive committee of the Missouri Credit Union League was

27 Brown to Filene, Jan. 4, 1934.

28 "Report of Edward A. Filene's Cross Country Study Tour, January-February, 1934," Trip Books, Filene Collection.

unanimous in its view that the principles of self-help should not be weakened and that the "introduction of government money would undo much that has built up the intense loyalty to you and to the credit union movement." Rentfro urged Filene to permit Bergengren to place another organizer in the field and to agree that any organizational campaign would only "be administered through and under the direct supervision of the existing credit union agencies." [29] The final blow to Filene's efforts to win popular backing came in March, 1934, when the leading credit union spokesmen from nine states signed a letter endorsing Bergengren's approach to the movement's development. These leaders rejected Filene's effort to get direct government help, and emphasized the need for him to back an organizing campaign.[30]

Filene may have been rebuffed by rank-and-file credit union leaders, but he still controlled the purse strings. He refused to release the $20,000 until Bergengren agreed to his general plan of action. But by early 1934 Bergengren was again concentrating on a federal credit union bill and he told Filene that he would have no definite plan for using the $20,000 until after he completed that work. If he had the money, Bergengren said, he would use it to employ an additional organizer, to establish a publicity department and to pay for forming a national association of credit unions. This was unsatisfactory to Filene. But there was a postscript to the argument. Bergengren told Filene that he wished Filene would refrain from stating that he had made an additional appropriation for credit union work. This, Bergengren said, was not true because the money could not be used. With some bitterness, Bergengren concluded that the movement had lost a great deal "through your unwillingness to back our efforts at this time . . . ." [31] Thus Filene's conception of a close relationship between the New Deal and the credit union movement ended on a bitter note.

Meanwhile, Bergengren and Senator Sheppard had been actively pushing their federal credit union law. Neither man believed that Filene's dream of ending the depression by greatly increasing consumer purchasing power through credit unions was realistic. But they both believed that a federal law permitting the incorporation of more credit unions would provide a long-range program of aiding the consumer and the entire economy. Despite a great deal of work, neither Bergengren

[29] Bergengren to John L. Moore, Feb. 1, 1934; Rentfro to Filene, Feb. 12, 1934.

[30] T. J. O'Shaughnessy *et al.* to Filene, Mar. 18, 1934.

[31] Bergengren to Filene, July 17, 1934.

nor Sheppard were very optimistic about the possibility of getting their bill enacted. Early in 1934 important administration measures still held the legislative spotlight.

Nevertheless, on March 20, the Committee on Banking and Currency issued a favorable report on a somewhat modified S. 1639. The main section of the bill provided for federal incorporation of credit unions. There was to be no relationship between credit unions and the Federal Reserve System, a change which satisfied the FRB and the Treasury Department. One of the main arguments for this connection was that the right to make deposits in Federal Reserve Banks would protect credit unions from losses because of bank failures. However, the report said, this seemed unnecessary because of the establishment of the Federal Deposit Insurance Corporation, an implication that federally incorporated credit unions would be covered by FDIC. This turned out to be untrue and remained a controversial issue in future years.[32]

On March 29, Senator Sheppard got a provision of the bill approved eliminating the section which called for taxing credit unions, but he was unable to obtain any further action. Bergengren was doubtful if the bill could be passed at that session, and informed Percy Brown that "much legislative experience has taught me . . . that a bill which is filed in the House as a bald-headed, blue-eyed Scandinavian baby, comes out of the Senate . . . as an old, black-eyed Chinaman with his black hair in a braid . . . ."[33]

On April 25, when the bill was brought up again, Senator Alva B. Adams of Colorado asked to postpone consideration. But Senators David I. Walsh of Massachusetts and Alben Barkley of Kentucky joined Sheppard in praising credit unions. Barkley asked Adams to withdraw his objection, but the Coloradan refused. Consequently, supporters of the legislation were unable to get the unanimous consent necessary to consider the measure at that time. Adams asked why a federal law was needed when credit unions operated under "very exemplary State legislation." As the bill was passed over, Sheppard told his colleagues that the measure sought "to solve a great national problem in the only way it can be solved—by making available to people of small means credit for provident purposes through a national system of cooperative credit."[34]

Despite their recent differences, Bergengren called on Filene to write

[32] S. Rept. 555, p. 9.
[33] Bergengren to Brown, April 7, 1934.
[34] *Congressional Record,* 73d Cong., 2d sess., 1934, LXXVIII, pp. 7259-61.

Adams, urging him to support the credit union measure. Filene not only wrote Adams, but he suggested that Bergengren contact former Governor William E. Sweet of Colorado, who had once been a member of CUNEB's National Advisory Committee. Sweet did not try to influence Adams directly, but advised Bergengren to enlist the support of credit unionists in Colorado, especially those in labor unions with whom Adams "stands high." Within a few days Adams began to receive a large number of communications in regard to the credit union legislation from his constituents.[35]

Besides gaining additional support, Bergengren and Sheppard had another problem. That was to decide what federal agency would administer the proposed law. A. S. Goss, a former Grange leader and one of the early backers of credit unions in the state of Washington, was now Land Bank Commissioner in the Farm Credit Administration. Goss suggested that credit unions would find a welcome administrative home in that agency. Sheppard amended the bill to provide for this administrative arrangement and the Senate passed the measure by unanimous consent and without debate on May 10.[36]

The next day the bill went to the House where it was referred to the Committee on Banking. With only two exceptions it was still virtually in the same form as that drafted by Bergengren. Anticipating a tougher battle in the House, Bergengren had arranged several weeks earlier for a petition to be circulated in Alabama on behalf of the measure and forwarded to Henry Steagall, chairman of the House Banking Committee. Bergengren also called Earl Rentfro, one of his most trusted and effective lieutenants, to Washington to help get the bill passed. Rentfro assumed responsibility for the active lobbying among congressmen.

Four major tasks faced Bergengren and Rentfro. First, they needed Roosevelt's endorsement of the bill because without it the measure had little chance to pass with so many administration-backed bills pending in Congress. Secondly, the bill had to be completely redrafted so that it "would fit in with the over-all machinery of the F.C.A." Third, Steagall had to be persuaded to report the bill out of committee. And finally, the bill had to be passed by the House, acted upon again by the Senate, and

---

[35] Percy Brown to Filene, April 25, 1934; Bergengren to Filene, April 27, 1934; Filene to Adams, April 27, 1934; Sweet to Bergengren, April 28, 1934; Bergengren to Brown, April 30, 1934.

[36] Bergengren, *Crusade*, p. 225; John T. Croteau, "The Federal Credit Union System: A Legislative History," *Social Security Bulletin* (May, 1956), p. 1.

signed by the President. All this had to be accomplished during the three or four weeks remaining before adjournment.[37]

The FCA assigned one of its attorneys to assist in redrafting the Senate-passed bill, a task accomplished within a few days. During this time Bergengren worked hard to obtain Roosevelt's endorsement of the bill. On the surface, this would seem easy. Not only had Roosevelt sponsored the original credit union act in New York, but as late as 1929 he had expressed his interest in credit unions. Speaking at a meeting of the Georgia Credit Union League, he told his audience: "I have a sort of hunch that we owe a duty to our fellow citizens not to violate the biblical injunction against usury . . . . I am glad to say that credit unions through-out the United States have the fine record of never closing their doors. It is a mighty fine thing." Still, supporting a principle was not the same as backing a particular piece of legislation.[38]

Again Bergengren urged all those officials who had become interested in the credit union measure, particularly Frederic C. Howe, consumers' counsel for the Agricultural Adjustment Administration, and officials of the Farm Credit Administration who were already committed to the bill, to support the measure in every way possible. In addition, Filene wrote the president and also talked with his son, James. The younger Roosevelt promised to call his father and urge him to endorse the bill.[39] The next day, May 22, Roosevelt asked Secretary of the Treasury Henry Morgen-thau if he thought "we should make a definite effort to have this bill taken up and passed by the House." [40] Some two weeks later Frederic C. Howe wrote the president that he was greatly interested in the bill. Its passage, he said, would free borrowers from the loan sharks (Howe claimed that he knew of interest rates as high as 1000 percent); it would "promote decentralized, small scale, industrial, mercantile, craft and other activities, leading to the employment of labor and the development of self help;" and it would aid other groups.[41]

Roosevelt's decision on whether to back the bill would be determined largely by Henry Morgenthau's recommendation. But the president was obviously sympathetic to the measure. He wrote his Treasury Secretary on June 6: "I really believe in the usefulness of these Credit Unions.

[37] Ibid.

[38] The Bridge (June–July, 1929), p. 6; Bergengren, Crusade, p. 141.

[39] The Bridge (July, 1934), p. 2; Percy Brown to Bergengren, May 21, 1934.

[40] Roosevelt, "Memorandum for the Secretary of the Treasury," May 22, 1934, OF706, Roosevelt Library.

[41] Frederic C. Howe to Roosevelt, June 5, 1934, OF706, Roosevelt Library.

Would you please take it up with the Congressional Committees concerned and see if we can get it passed without opposition in the closing days?" [42] After referring the bill to two aides for study, Morgenthau approved the measure, provided the section permitting organization of state central credit unions was deleted. He then referred the bill to W. I. Myers, governor of the FCA. Myers gave the bill to an aide who, with Bergengren, began yet another revision. Once that was finished, Myers referred it for final approval to his administrative assistant, Herbert Emmerich. Fortunately for Bergengren, Emmerich was a member of a credit union and presumably sympathic to the bill. However, Emmerich remained skeptical until he telephoned Goss and FCA Deputy Governor W. Forbes Morgan for their opinions. With their approval, Emmerich and Myers sent FCA's endorsement of the bill to Morgenthau. Morgenthau then notified Roosevelt that the measure should receive administration support. [43]

Roosevelt moved quickly and urged Steagall to see that the bill received a quick and favorable hearing from his committee. Despite presidential backing, time was running out for Bergengren because by June 13 the adjournment of Congress seemed imminent. Bergengren had doggedly pursued Steagall during the days in which efforts were being made to obtain administration backing. He later recalled that he saw Steagall "so often during the trying days . . . that it is a wonder he did not kick me out of the Capitol. I can still give an accurate inventory of everything in his outer office, where I sat, wearing out his furniture, day after weary day." [44]

On June 13 Steagall sent for Bergengren, who, with Rentfro, hurried to the chairman's office. Steagall and another member of the Banking Committee began to put the two credit union men through the "third degree," asking, "what do you mean by coming in here at almost the last day of the session with this new thing that none of us ever heard of?" Bergengren was prepared for this tactic, and reached in his pocket for a copy of the petition from Steagall's Alabama constituents. "I stood up and, holding tight to the top sheet, let all the other sheets, which were pasted to it, unfold like an accordion. There were sheets still unfolded when it hit the floor." Then Bergengren explained that congressmen had been sent all kinds of material on the bill. At that point Steagall turned to

[42] Roosevelt, "Memorandum for the Secretary of the Treasury," June 6, 1934, OF706, Roosevelt Library.

[43] *The Bridge* (July, 1934), p. 2.

[44] Bergengren, *Crusade,* p. 227.

his colleague and said: "It's no use, Jack. This man has been pestering us with this bill ever since I can remember. If you haven't read it, it's your fault." [45]

The next day, June 14, the committee reported the bill favorably, but only two days remained before Congress would adjourn. In that short time, the House had to act and the Senate must approve the House version of the bill. Still, Bergengren thought that the chances were much improved. He wrote Filene on June 15: "A week ago our chances were about 1 in 100; yesterday morning 1 in 50; last night and now 1 in 5. I shall be agreeably surprised if the bill passes." [46]

Meanwhile, Bergengren and his fellow credit unionists had mobilized as much pressure as possible on congressmen. On May 14 he had written to all representatives, calling their attention to S. 1639 which had been recently passed, and urging them to support it. "The enactment of this bill will be completely consistent with everything Congress is doing to hasten industrial recovery," Bergengren wrote.[47] One congressman who became convinced of the bill's value was Wright Patman of Texas. On June 8 he wrote all Democratic members of the Banking Committee that he believed the bill "should be enacted without delay. It will serve a useful purpose all over the Nation and especially in communities not served by small banks. I am sold on this legislation one hundred percent." In effect, an alliance was formed between Sheppard and his fellow Texan to secure passage of the credit union act.[48]

On June 16 newspapers predicted that Congress would adjourn by nightfall. At 7:15 P.M. Steagall walked onto the floor of the House and received recognition from Speaker Henry T. Rainey. Steagall asked for unanimous consent so that the credit union bill could be considered by the House as a committee of the whole. There were no objections and the chair allotted thirty minutes for debate. Steagall told his colleagues that the bill had passed the Senate unanimously, that the newly revised measure had the unanimous approval of the House Banking and Currency Committee, and that the administration had endorsed it. No one voiced opposition to the measure, although there were some questions

[45] *Ibid.,* pp. 227–28.

[46] Bergengren to Filene, June 15, 1934.

[47] Bergengren, *Crusade,* pp. 228–29; *Congressional Record,* 73d Cong., 2d sess., 1934, LXXVIII, Part 2, pp. 12218–26.

[48] Patman to Congressman Jeff Busby, June 8, 1934 [same letter sent to all Democratic members of the House Banking and Currency Committee on same date]; Patman to Steagall, June 8, 1934; see also Sheppard to Patman, June 11, 1934, and Patman to Sheppard, June 16, 1934, Subject File: Legislation-Federal, BMML.

about the nature of credit unions, their operations, and the proposed administration of the act. Before the time allowed for debate had expired, the House passed the bill with only two dissenting votes.[49]

The battle, however, was not yet won. The bill had to proceed through the enrollment office and then go back to the Senate. Bergengren frantically grabbed his old friend Congressman William Connery from the floor of the House and persuaded him to rush the bill out of the clerk's office. Connery complied and the bill reached Senator Sheppard at about 8:30 P.M. Now strategy counted, as Sheppard told Bergengren that he could either have the bill referred to a conference committee to resolve the differences between the original Senate-passed bill and the House version, or he could bring it to the floor to ask for unanimous consent to pass the bill, "as amended *unread.*" It was too late for a conference committee, so Sheppard approached another fellow Texan, Vice-President John Nance Garner, who was presiding over the Senate and arranged to present the bill. In order to do so Sheppard had to interrupt a senator who was discussing air mail contracts. Bergengren recounted that he and Rentfro "stopped breathing" at that point, realizing that "had one Senator raised his voice against the bill, our long, hard campaign would have collapsed in defeat." No one objected, however, and within two hours, Bergengren and Rentfro were on a train to Boston with their task successfully completed.[50]

Two days later, Governor Myers of the FCA notified Budget Director Lewis Douglas of the FCA's recommendation that Roosevelt approve the credit union act. Douglas concurred, and the president signed the measure on June 26, 1934.[51] In the euphoria of the moment, the relationship between Filene and Bergengren took a turn for the better. Roosevelt sent the pen with which he signed the bill to Filene, but the Bostonian forwarded it to Bergengren, saying that the "pen clearly should have gone to you. You did the work, without which the Bill could not have passed . . . ."[52] Equally generous, Bergengren told Filene that there "could have been no Credit Union National Extension Bureau had you not imported the credit union idea originally, and through these many years which have contained many discouragements and disappointments

[49] Bergengren, *Crusade,* pp. 228–29; *Congressional Record,* 73d Cong. 2d sess., 1934, LXXVIII, Part 2, pp. 12218–26.

[50] Bergengren, *Crusade,* pp. 229–31.

[51] Myers to Douglas, June 18, 1934; Douglas to Marvin McIntyre, June 25, 1934; Croteau, "The Federal Credit Union System," p. 1.

[52] Filene to Bergengren, June 27, 1934.

sustained your interest and enthusiasm, and backed them very liberally." [53] Actually, however, Filene played only a minimal role in getting the federal law. It was a Bergengren triumph but one in which Filene also took pride.[54]

The stated purpose of the Federal Credit Union Act was to promote thrift and provide credit for "provident and productive purposes." Any seven persons could form a society, take out an organization certificate which, when approved by the governor of the Farm Credit Administration, became the credit union's charter. These federal credit unions could lend and borrow money under policies determined by a board of directors and other elected officers. In purpose and organization, the federal law was much like the various state statutes and the law for the District of Columbia. Looking back a few weeks after the law's passage, Bergengren wrote Filene that it "was the greatest single step forward in the history of the credit union movement." [55] He believed that placing its administration in the Farm Credit Administration was especially favorable because that agency would provide "a very sympathetic and cooperative administration with which we can work easily and intelligently . . . ." [56]

Despite his confidence in the Farm Credit Administration, Bergengren realized that it would be tremendously important to get the right man to head up the new Credit Union Division of FCA. It would be tragic, he wrote, if the administrator were hostile "to everything which we have been trying to accomplish." [57] Bergengren feared that the new officials might create a system of dual credit unions. As he put it, the Washington office "could develop federal credit unions as a competing system with state-chartered credit unions," or it "could make them a part of the greater whole." Bergengren wanted to make sure that credit unionism grew as a single, integrated movement on the basis of societies with both state and federal charters.[58]

The matter of the new director of the Credit Union Division took on greater seriousness for Bergengren when he learned that representatives of the Russell Sage Foundation, his old rival, had suggested Nat C. Helman, an attorney for the New York league, to head the new agency.[59]

[53] Bergengren to Filene, June 27, 1934.

[54] Filene to Morris Sheppard, June 18, 1934.

[55] Bergengren to Filene, June 21, 1934.

[56] *Ibid.*, June 15, 1934.

[57] *Ibid.*, July 20, 1934.

[58] Bergengren, *Crusade*, p. 234.

[59] Herbert Emmerich to Rolf Nugent, June 21, 1934, Russell Sage Collection, Library of Congress, Washington, D.C.

But Governor Myers of the FCA asked his first assistant, Herbert Emmerich, to serve as the first director of the Credit Union Division with
the idea that Emmerich would hire an assistant who could later become
director. Bergengren had already discussed the matter with Emmerich
so it came as no surprise when Emmerich asked Bergengren to recommend several men for the post. Bergengren submitted a list of six or
seven major credit union leaders, any one of whom he believed was emi-
nently qualified. He later claimed that Doig topped the list, but at the
time he wrote Filene that he had not recommended Doig because he was
needed more elsewhere in the movement.[60]

Emmerich soon authorized Bergengren to open negotiations with those
on his list. On July 16 Bergengren sent Claude Orchard in Omaha a
telegram telling him that he was first choice for the $4,600 a year job.
Orchard accepted at once, but raised a question about giving up his
pension and seniority rights at Armour & Company in case the credit
union job did not become permanent. Bergengren advised Orchard to
apply for a year's leave of absence. He recognized that the $50,000 ap-
propriation for administration might be cut off in the future, or that
jurisdiction over credit unions could be transferred to another agency.
But if that happened, Bergengren explained, the national association
should be "swinging along in good shape," and it would "be tickled to
death to absorb you in that work if anything conceivably did happen to
the Federal work."[61]

Whatever his nagging doubts may have been about the permanency of
the new position, Orchard said he would take it if offered. He amply
demonstrated the proper "credit union spirit," so much desired by
Bergengren, in his acceptance letter: "I hope the 'Assistant Director'
will be permitted a chance to get out into the field," he wrote, "to actually set up a few key credit unions and [have] the opportunity to train
organizers both paid and volunteer. That would be a fine sort of a job for
me."[62] Two days later Emmerich wired Orchard inviting him to Washington for a conference. Orchard arrived in Washington on July 23
where he first met with Emmerich and then with Myers. Following that
meeting, Orchard received the appointment.[63]

[60] Bergengren to Filene, July 20, 1934; Bergengren, *Crusade,* p. 234.

[61] Bergengren to Orchard, July 16, 1934 (telegram); Bergengren to Orchard, July 16, 1934.

[62] Orchard to Bergengren, July 17, 1934.

[63] "Early Days of the Federal Credit Union Program," transcript of tape recordings of
interviews with officials of the Federal Credit Union Section, Washington, D.C., June, 1964,
p. 28.

Although Orchard did not take office until August 20, he quickly established the philosophy and procedures for the new agency. He obtained Emmerich's approval for a policy of actively encouraging the organization of both federal and state credit unions. The type of charter would be determined "by the wish of the Credit Union itself, in the light of the cost of organization and the workability of the State Law involved . . . ." Orchard agreed that only federal credit unions could be established in states which had no state credit union law, but that there would be "no attempt in the other states to urge the use of the Federal Law where the State Law will serve the same purpose." The FCA, he said, would be just as concerned with organizing credit unions in states which had credit union laws as it would in those "which must use only Federal Charters." One of the main goals would be greatly to increase the number of credit unions in the United States.[64]

Thus, Orchard moved promptly to carry out Bergengren's wishes of avoiding a competing system of credit unions. He further showed his allegiance to a unified national movement when he bade his colleagues at Armour & Company farewell. He had "little patience," he said, with those who questioned "the necessity of State Leagues and a National Association," because the "defense of this fine agency is only possible through organization." [65] In Orchard the movement had an experienced credit union man who was thoroughly imbued with the philosophy of the movement's pioneers. Credit unionism was fortunate to have him administering the new law.

[64] Orchard to Emmerich, July 27, 1934; Emmerich to Orchard, July 30, 1934.
[65] *Armour Credit Union News,* IV, (Aug. 16, 1934).

CHAPTER VIII

The Meeting at Estes Park

PASSAGE OF THE federal credit union act in June, 1934, completed the first of the long-range tasks which Bergengren had set for himself fourteen years earlier. The second goal, that of creating large numbers of credit unions in every state so that self-sustaining state leagues could be organized, had been partially achieved. There were approximately 2,500 credit unions in thirty-eight states and the District of Columbia with about 450,000 members. Bergengren claimed that five effective leagues existed, but, except for Massachusetts, none was completely self-supporting. Nevertheless, Bergengren determined to move ahead and complete the final goal of the Credit Union National Extension Bureau—the establishment of a national association.

Creation of a national association seemed more necessary than ever to Bergengren because of his worsening relations with Filene and the Twentieth Century Fund. A headstrong and independent person, Bergengren wanted to set his own course, and he chafed at having to justify his plans and actions to Filene. He became increasingly restive when Filene opposed his organizational plans and when money so crucial to the movement's development was not forthcoming. Indeed, when Filene pushed his scheme for federal aid to credit unions, Bergengren came close to severing connections with his "boss." Publicly, he remained completely loyal to Filene. In his writings and speeches, Bergengren referred to Filene as the founder, financial supporter, and head of the movement. But this reflected the appearance, not the substance, of the relationship between the two men. Only the continued need for Filene's money and the bad publicity that a break with the founder of the movement would have brought kept Bergengren from going it alone.

Thus, to assure his own independence, to make the credit union movement self-reliant, and to enhance credit unionism throughout the country, Bergengren moved swiftly to form a national association. As early as late 1933, he had used the occasion of Filene's tour through the Midwest to discuss the formation of a national association with credit union leaders. Then during the annual meeting of the Illinois Credit Union League

169

in March, 1934, in Chicago, the matter came up again. Leaders from nine states were present and, after some discussion, Claude Orchard suggested that a meeting be held at Estes Park, Colorado, in August. Those present promptly passed a resolution which read: "The meeting is called for the purpose of enjoying a vacation and incidentally there will be a discussion and a meeting of minds and an exchange of ideas on whether or not there shall be a National Association and other questions necessarily involved." [1]

The call for such a meeting that day was not unexpected by anyone in the hotel room. Bergengren had always urged the organization of a national association in his speeches and writings. It was the logical outcome of a growing movement. Yet, he wanted to be sure that he had grass-roots support. Once Bergengren received the approval of the major leaders in Chicago, he sought the opinion of every credit union in the nation. On March 24 he sent all credit unions a memorandum that summarized the current position of the movement, and asserted that the time had come "when we should organize our own National Association." Attached to his own views was a questionnaire asking if the credit unions were willing to join state leagues and pay reasonable dues, if the board of directors of the credit unions favored the organization of a national association, and how such an association should be organized, managed, and financed.[2] By sending out questionnaires, Bergengren claimed that "we have eliminated in advance any possible criticism that the Estes Park meeting went ahead to formulate plans for our National Association without taking into account the opinion of the credit unions in the United States." [3]

On April 9, Bergengren sent notices to seventy credit union leaders in twenty-seven states, inviting them to the Estes Park meeting in August. He wanted a truly representative group from the movement, and began his list by including the president and executive officer of each state league. Next, he included "all of those outstanding leaders who have contributed in a major fashion to the national development, being careful to have representatives present from (a) the parish development; (b)

---

[1] "Recollections of Claude E. Clarke on the Estes Park Meeting," undated typescript, Subject File: Estes Park Meeting, BMML; Bergengren, "Plans for Estes Park Meeting." Memorandum accompanying Bergengren to Filene, July 5, 1934.

[2] CUNEB Memo no. 18, March 24, 1934, with attached Questionnaire, Filene Collection: Clippings and Pamphlets, 1934.

[3] Bergengren, "Plans for the Estes Park Meeting."

the chain industrial development; (c) the postal development." In addition, the group included some personnel officers of corporations who were interested in credit unions, several attorneys who had cooperated with CUNEB, and a few of the outstanding credit union organizers.[4]

Perhaps anticipating criticism from Filene and others about how the list of invitees had been determined, Bergengren asserted that "this is not a convention; it is in no sense an attempt to bring together a certain number of delegates from each credit union state. It is rather to be compared with the original Constitutional Convention of the United States, which was an attempt to get together a group of outstanding men who could exchange views on a national constitution, with the thought in mind that if they agreed on such a constitution it would be submitted to the states for ratification." Therefore, he made no attempt to invite representatives from every state that had a credit union law.[5]

In order to make the most of a four-day meeting, Bergengren indicated that the delegates would be given draft copies of a constitution and bylaws in advance. He was preparing one version, and Edward Norman of the New York league had another. Once the matter had been thoroughly discussed, Bergengren anticipated that the delegates would approve a constitution and bylaws which would then be submitted to credit union groups for ratification. He planned to spend October organizing additional state leagues which would act as the ratifying agencies.[6]

Bergengren notified Filene of his plans for the Estes Park meeting on April 16, 1934, about a week after he mailed invitations to other credit union leaders. He urged Filene to attend the meeting and invited suggestions about the matters which should be discussed.[7] Filene asked Percy Brown, his chief assistant, to see that a "thoroughly good plan" was developed for a national association, and then informed Evans Clark of the Twentieth Century Fund about the Estes Park gathering. Filene told Clark that he did not think Bergengren should proceed to organize a national association without the assistance of men who had the necessary experience in "organizing large financial institutions." Filene was especially concerned about preserving democratic procedures, protecting invested funds of credit unions, and keeping what he called "self-seeking and grasping interests" from getting control. He told Clark to get expert

---

[4] Ibid.
[5] Ibid.
[6] Ibid.
[7] Bergengren to Filene, April 16, 1934.

help, perhaps from an economist, and prepare a plan for the new association. This should be done at once, Filene wrote, before Bergengren got "too far along in his own planning." [8]

Filene also sought to keep a rein on Bergengren by controlling appropriations for credit union work. For months Bergengren had been urging Filene to commit the Twentieth Century Fund to a pledge of $25,000 to support a new national association the first year with the amount declining $5,000 annually for the next four years. After some discussion, Filene and Clark agreed to Bergengren's request in May, 1934, providing that the three men agreed on the plans for the national association and the control of expenditures.[9] Shortly afterward, the directors of the Twentieth Century Fund promised to appropriate $25,000 a year for CUNEB so that it could continue to operate while the national association was establishing itself and becoming self-supporting. It was clear that Bergengren believed it would be three to five years before a national association would be strong enough to assume the functions performed by CUNEB. Moreover, his request for continued support for the bureau indicates that he was not sure just where he would fit into the work of the national association.[10]

But Bergengren had more immediate financial problems in the early summer of 1934. The campaign for a federal credit union law had been so expensive that the bureau's appropriation was exhausted. In order to keep the work going and to pay the expenses of some delegates to Estes Park, Bergengren asked Filene for a special grant of $5,000.[11] Filene replied that he would not advance anything until Bergengren had submitted a detailed account of expenditures of the legislative campaign in Washington and produced a proposed budget for the Estes Park meeting. In regard to Estes Park, Filene said that, as president of CUNEB, he had "a definite responsibility for its acts, even though you may assume the major responsibility." [12]

On July 10, Filene notified Bergengren that he would attend the Estes Park meeting. At the same time he approved $2,500 to pay the expenses of some delegates. These actions, however, did not indicate any improvement in the relations between the two men. Indeed, throughout July, just a few weeks before they were to go to Estes Park, Filene and

[8] Filene's comments written in margin of *ibid;* Filene to Clark, April 25, 1934.

[9] Memorandum by Filene, May 5, 1934; Percy Brown to Clark, May 9, 1934.

[10] Bergengren to Filene, May 13, 1934.

[11] *Ibid.,* June 21, 1934.

[12] Filene to Bergengren, June 25, 1934.

Bergengren engaged in a steady flow of controversy and criticism of one another. Filene disliked Bergengren's choice of delegates, he insisted that any constitution and bylaws developed at Estes Park must be approved by the Twentieth Century Fund or all future financial help might be eliminated, and he complained that Bergengren was trying "to cut off the Credit Unions from all connection with the 20th Century Fund and myself." [13]

Filene feared that Bergengren wanted a "showdown" and that it might come at Estes Park. Consequently, on July 19 he wrote him a long letter which combined bitterness with a plea for cooperation. Filene said he was anxious to avoid any rupture "after all these years of common work for a great movement," but he accused Bergengren of acting as if CUNEB was his "private property, and I was a 'big bad wolf' trying to hurt your lambs." He charged that Bergengren refused to share his plans and ideas and ignored his suggestions. Moreover, Filene argued that the federal act had been passed because he had interested Roosevelt in credit unions as a means of alleviating hard times. Whether or not Bergengren agreed with Filene's plan for federal aid, many credit union people, Filene wrote, favored it. Moreover, Filene was annoyed at Bergengren's constant requests for more money and then refusing to consult with him on how to use the funds. Despite his complaints, Filene's letter ended on a compromising note. Within two weeks, he said, they would be leaving for Estes Park. They should be thinking about the "big questions" that would be coming up rather than arguing over past or current issues.[14]

Bergengren replied that he hoped they could work together at Estes Park, but he insisted that credit unionism must be organized and directed by those within the movement. He rejected Filene's idea of relying on outside experts to provide advice and leadership. As Bergengren put it, "nowhere in the United States outside of the credit union movement is there any expert assistance which can help us in . . . determining our own basic form of organization in setting up our own machinery, and in making it function." He urged Filene to abandon his plans for government assistance and bringing in experts, especially bankers, and warned that such action would be "extremely unpopular, if it is seriously advanced to our credit union leadership." [15]

This continued acrimony did not deter Bergengren from his prepara-

[13] Filene's comments written in margins of memoranda accompanying Bergengren to Filene, July 5, 1934.
[14] Filene to Bergengren, July 19, 1934.
[15] Bergengren to Filene, July 20, 1934.

tion for Estes Park. On July 21, he mailed final instructions to the forty credit unionists who had accepted his invitation. In this letter he emphasized the serious responsibility for the advancement of credit unions which rested upon the delegates. He urged them to think in broad national terms "as citizens of the United States." This advice may have been given to offset Filene's criticism that all states would not be represented at Estes Park. Since Bergengren had received replies to his questionnaires, he included some of the suggestions which had been returned on the matter of organizing a national association so that delegates could consider the various ideas before the meeting.[16]

Meanwhile, Bergengren developed his own draft of a constitution and bylaws for the prospective national association. Calling it the Credit Union National Association, or CUNA, he stated that the principal purposes of the association would be to foster the credit union movement in the United States and to support the "cooperative credit movement abroad." Organizationally, Bergengren recommended that the association be composed of state leagues and groups of credit unions within states which did not yet have leagues. The association was to be democratically controlled through a general meeting of credit union delegates to be held every three years. A board of directors would manage the association. Bergengren's constitution provided that the association would be financed by dues "based on a per–credit union member basis" as designated in the bylaws, and by CUNA business activities, grants, and gifts.

The bylaws developed by Bergengren provided that the board of directors would consist of one person from each affiliated state who would be elected by the state league. The board would elect its own officers including a president, four vice-presidents representing districts of the country, a secretary, a treasurer, and a managing director. These officers would comprise the executive committee which would meet at least every fourth month. The real executive authority was to be placed in the hands of the managing director, whose duties would cover general management of the association. Other administrative officers were to be an assistant general manager and heads of the various service departments. Bergengren suggested that the association be financed by assessing each credit union member ten cents a year. He called for beginning operation of the association as soon as delegates from fifteen states had agreed to

[16] Bergengren to "Dear Fellow Credit Unionist," July 21, 1934. This document contains the first use which the authors found of the name Credit Union National Association.

the constitution and bylaws. These representatives would then elect a board of directors which in turn would name a managing director whose sole task would be to obtain the ratification of the constitution and by-laws by credit unionists in other states. On the delicate question of Filene's position in the new association, Bergengren suggested that he be made "president emeritus." Such were Bergengren's plans for the organization and administration of CUNA.[17]

Filene anxiously awaited a copy of Bergengren's draft which arrived in late July. Earlier he had asked Evans Clark to prepare suggestions for a constitution and bylaws which he might take with him to Estes Park. But on July 23 Clark wrote Filene saying that he wanted to see Bergengren's work before drafting anything himself. After seeing Bergengren's proposals, Clark wrote Filene that both he and Frederic Dewhurst, the Twentieth Century Fund's staff economist, believed that Bergengren's constitution and bylaws were "a well worked out and able draft." Clark implied that there was no need for him to draw up separate suggestions.[18]

Filene, too, seemed generally pleased with Bergengren's work. Nevertheless, relations between the two men remained somewhat tense in the days just before the Estes Park meeting. Again it was Percy Brown who acted as mediator. Brown explained to his boss that Bergengren had been under a heavy strain and, even though he was nervous and irritable, he was "the same Bergengren that you have always trusted and had confidence in." He urged Filene to go to Estes Park "to listen and advise on request . . . . You are highly respected and admired by Credit Union people and they will listen to you, but not necessarily follow you." They were more likely, Brown said, to follow Bergengren. Brown ventured that Filene had hurt his prestige among rank-and-file credit unionists by pushing so hard for federal aid to credit unions and his continued emphasis on obtaining expert financial advice for the movement. Bergengren interpreted this as bringing bankers into the organization. "The very name 'banker' is a red flag to many people," Brown wrote, "and probably more so to Credit Unionists than others. Undoubtedly," he continued, "Credit Unionists feel superior to bankers, and I would dislike to see your cause injured by making an issue of something which can better be fought out with a chance of winning, at a later date." [19] In

---

[17] Bergengren, "Suggested Constitution and Bylaws, Credit Union National Association," n.d., Subject File: CUNA Constitution and Bylaws.

[18] Clark to Filene, July 26, 1934. Filene's comments in margin.

[19] Brown Memorandum for Filene, July 24, 1934.

notes on the margin of Brown's memorandum, Filene wrote that the principal difference remaining between himself and Bergengren was the matter of obtaining "expert financial advice." He did not mean that "regular bankers" should be brought into the movement, but rather "a liberal college or university professor of finance" who had practical experience.[20]

Despite his general satisfaction with Bergengren's draft of a constitution and bylaws, Filene prepared a lengthy statement of his own for use at Estes Park. Entitling his remarks, "Planning Safe Growth for Credit Unions," he admitted that credit unionists should develop their own organization and business practices, but that they should seek the help of "fact-finders" who could advise on national and world economic developments and offer predictions about the future. Filene seemed to be calling for the services of intellectuals from among the social scientists.[21]

Brown also drafted a conciliatory letter which he hoped that Filene would mail to Bergengren. This Filene did on July 25. He said that he would take part in the Estes Park deliberations "just as any Credit Union member who is invited, but not as one who has financed and promoted Credit Union work and not as President of the Credit Union National Extension Bureau." He further promised not to press his point of view beyond making a strong argument and if the majority disagreed he would yield "gracefully." Filene agreed that both men had been under severe strain which had contributed to their disagreements, but differences, he said, helped colleagues to clarify the issues. Filene offered to "wipe the slate clean" and continue to work for their common goals. "You think I am dogmatic and I think I am too," Filene continued, and "I think you are self-centered and over-concentrated and resistant to suggestions, and I think you will agree that this is true, but both of us forget sometimes why these things are true, what pressure of work has done to throw us off balance. I should like to start all over and it is not easy for me to say so."[22]

Bergengren accepted the proffered truce, and said he felt "very certain that we can both contribute effectively to the proceedings without any substantial differences of opinion." He also eloquently expressed his thoughts about the movement at that crucial juncture:

[20] Filene's comments in margin of ibid.

[21] Filene, "Planning Safe Growth for Credit Unions; Possible Statement for Estes Park Discussion, August 5–11, 1934," n.d.

[22] Filene to Bergengren, July 25, 1934.

In the midst of what seems to be, both nationally and internationally, a vast confusion of thinking on social, political and economic matters, I am convinced that we have in the credit union one basic principle of economic cooperation on which the masses of the people can eventually unite, and in the process solve so many of the problems which are now bedevilling them that what we have done, and what we shall do, will together constitute, in the end, a vast contribution to the well-being of our day and generation. I am not, for example, simply using pleasant sounding words, with no other objective than to see how they look, when I have written into this constitution, as one of our objectives, the development of better international understanding. It will come probably long after I am dead, but there will be a day when those persons whose economic lot has been improved by the cooperative system in various parts of the world will appreciate that by working together in similar spirit, most international difficulty can be eliminated. I may be all wrong about it, but I sincerely believe that what we are going to do at Estes Park will have extraordinary consequences, and I feel sure that you will agree, after meeting our fifty leaders who will be there assembled, that they have the fundamental virtues of heart and mind which will be necessary if they are going eventually to realize the great objectives which you made first possible when you brought the credit union to America a quarter of a century ago.[23]

This was the type of broad vision and confidence which had always appealed to Filene.

Moreover, the two men really agreed on most essentials for the future of the movement. Both believed that credit unions should begin providing life insurance for their members, and that the national association should own and operate a life insurance company for this purpose. This company, they agreed, should be managed on an ultraconservative basis and operate on cooperative principles. They also thought that the national association should provide additional services such as selling fidelity bonds, and someday even automobile and fire insurance.[24] Because of Filene's conciliatory letter and the fact that their agreements were far more fundamental than their disagreements, much of the rancor of the past few months no longer existed when Filene and Bergengren left for Estes Park.

On Sunday morning, August 5, 1934, a number of delegates, mainly from the East and Midwest, left Chicago on the Rock Island Railroad for Denver. Their travel had been scheduled by Timothy O'Shaughnessy. Both Bergengren and Filene were present, and the long trip gave them time to discuss credit unionism with the other delegates. They

[23] Bergengren to Filene, July 26, 1934.

[24] Filene to Bergengren, July 3, 1934; unsigned memorandum, "Credit Unions and Life Insurance," July 6, 1934; note by Filene, July 9, 1934.

arrived in Denver on Monday, after which they boarded special buses for the YMCA conference grounds at Estes Park where Claude Orchard had arranged for accommodations. There they met the other delegates and their families who had arrived by automobile. At the camp they found a beautiful and relaxing setting, with mountain peaks framing the valley in which several individual cabins surrounded a large common lodge.[25]

The fifty-two delegates came from twenty-one states and the District of Columbia. Illinois had the most representatives with twelve, while Massachusetts had five and New York and Iowa four each. There were three delegates from Missouri and Minnesota, and two each from Ohio, Texas, Colorado, Wisconsin, and California. Michigan, Tennessee, Washington, Arkansas, Indiana, Nebraska, Alabama, Oregon, North Carolina, Kentucky, and the District of Columbia each had one delegate.

The majority of delegates, or thirty-four, came from states of the Midwest. There were no representatives of the Russell Sage Foundation or, except for Filene, from the Twentieth Century Fund. The Farm Credit Administration had no official representation, although Orchard was present. Neither the *caisse populaire* nor any of the new credit unions in Canada sent delegates. Most of those at Estes Park had been closely associated with the development of credit unionism in the United States. The largest single group, fourteen delegates, were affiliated with credit unions in industrial and communication firms, while eight were postal employees, six railroad workers, three public school teachers, and one each from parish and community credit unions. Ten delegates represented state leagues. Besides Bergengren and Filene, all of those associated with CUNEB were present—Doig, Maxwell, and Gartland; Claude Clarke, a Cleveland attorney who worked for the bureau in Ohio, was also there. The two delegates from Wisconsin were both state employees. E. G. Hampton was in the State Banking Department and Charles Hyland was associated with that department as a credit union organizer. Three delegates belonged to management, and four were women. Overall, the delegates were truly representative of the nation's credit union movement.[26]

[25] Bergengren, *Crusade,* pp. 238–39; "Report of Edward A. Filene's Western Trip, Summer, 1934," Trip Books, Filene Collection.

[26] "Credit Union Conference, Estes Park, Colorado, August 7–11, 1934," delegates list; Bergengren to E. K. Watkins, Mar. 29, 1954, Subject File: Estes Park Meeting.

The meeting opened at 9:00 A.M. on August 7, and during the next four days the delegates convened twice a day for from two to three hours. At the opening session, Ben F. Hillebrandt, president of the Missouri Credit Union League, was elected chairman, and Agnes Gartland, secretary. The delegates also adopted procedural rules to help facilitate the orderly flow of business. The tone of the meetings was serious as representatives recognized the important step they were about to take in launching a new national association of credit unions.

Although there were at least five drafts of constitutions and bylaws, those prepared by Bergengren and Timothy O'Shaughnessy drew the greatest attention. Most delegates were not initially committed to any particular plan of organization, but they tended to support Bergengren's views because of his leadership in the movement. While O'Shaughnessy advanced his ideas with vigor, he declared that the Illinois group would "accept any plan that can be shown to be superior to the one which we propose." After all of the debate, some of it so heated that there was need for "much cooling off on the porch," Bergengren's draft of the constitution and bylaws for CUNA remained basically intact.[27]

Membership in the association was confined to state leagues, although a provision was included to allow groups of credit unions in states where there were no leagues to affiliate with CUNA. One major compromise with O'Shaughnessy was the provision of permitting each state additional national directors for each one hundred credit unions to a maximum of five. Bergengren's idea of having four districts with a vice-president from each was enlarged to five. The delegates also dropped Bergengren's proposal for an assistant managing director.

There were also very few modifications in the bylaws brought to Estes Park by Bergengren. The main change was on the matter of how CUNA would be supported. Bergengren had suggested that each credit union member would pay ten cents a year until the fourth annual meeting. However, the revised draft called for allowing the board of directors to assess and collect dues, but the board would determine this on the basis of "the number of individual credit union members affiliated with credit unions which are directly or indirectly members of the Association." This provision left the question open as to whether the association would be supported almost entirely from the profits of subsidiary activities, such

[27] Jerome K. Eldridge to E. K. Watkins, June 3, 1954; Andrew J. Percival to Watkins, June 22, 1954; Claude E. Clarke, "Recollections on the Estes Park Meeting," Subject File: Estes Park Meeting; Bergengren, *Crusade*, p. 240.

as the sales of life insurance, security bonds, and printed supplies.[28] This was the approach of O'Shaughnessy and his supporters.

Where did Filene fit into the deliberations? He generally followed Percy Brown's advice "to listen and advise on request." He made a major address at the opening of the conference, and delivered a short talk at the closing session. He participated as any other delegate and made no effort to dominate the proceedings. He did get one of his major objectives written into the bylaws, a provision calling for the creation of a department of statistics within CUNA.[29] Filene did not, however, receive the title he wanted. Bergengren had suggested that Filene be made president emeritus of CUNA for life with full voting powers as an ex officio member of the board of directors. But Filene objected to this designation because it implied that he was "retired or finished." He clearly wanted to become the first president of CUNA and sought to get his title changed to *founder-president*. The most he could get at Estes Park was the substitution of *founder* for *president emeritus*.[30]

The revised drafts of the constitution and bylaws were completed on August 10. Bergengren suddenly decided that the documents should be signed on parchment, and he and his wife toured several nearby mountain towns searching for the proper material. They finally located what a local printer claimed to be parchment, and brought it back to Estes Park, where all fifty-two delegates affixed their signatures to the historic documents. That night the delegates and their families assembled for a farewell dinner, short speeches, and group singing. Most of those present felt a deep sense of satisfaction at having at last developed the organizational framework for an association which hopefully would advance the credit union movement to new heights of usefulness and service. Moreover, they had accomplished this in a very short time.

The next important task was to get the constitution and bylaws ratified. Upon his return to Boston from Colorado, Bergengren lost no time in making preparations for this work. Getting existing state leagues to ratify the new documents was no great problem, but a much greater task was to get additional leagues organized and affiliated with CUNA. Unless this were done CUNA would be little more than a paper organiza-

---

[28] Credit Union National Association, "Constitution and Bylaws," 1934; Bergengren, "Suggested Constitution and Bylaws, Credit Union National Association," n.d., Subject File: CUNA Constitution and Bylaws.

[29] CUNA Bylaws (1934), Art. I, Sec. 2(i).

[30] Lillian Schoedler to Filene, Mar. 28, 1937; Claude Orchard to E. K. Watkins, June 3, 1954.

Edward A. Filene (left) and Roy F. Bergengren, pioneers in the credit union movement, in the early 1930s.

Roy F. Bergengren (1879–1955), first managing director of Credit Union National Association, the man who created the framework of the worldwide credit union movement and who served as the movement's first full-time chief executive from 1921 to 1945.

F. Hermann Schulze-Delitzsch (1808–
1883), German urban cooperative
credit founder.

Friedrich Wilhelm Raiffeisen (1818–
1888), German rural cooperative
credit founder.

Alphonse Desjardins (1854–1920),
founder of the Canadian cooperative
credit movement and first credit
union in the United States.

Staff members of the New York Municipal Credit Union, one of the oldest credit unions serving municipal employees.

Study session for prospective credit union members in Jamaica.

The home of Texaco P.A.W. Federal Credit Union, Port Arthur, Texas, one of the newer buildings housing hundreds of credit unions.

Filene House in Madison, Wisconsin, home of the World Council of Credit Unions, Credit Union National Association, and CUNA Supply Cooperative— as it looked in the 1960s.

Spanish-speaking directors of CUNA International, listening to the simultaneous translation of proceedings at the 1968 National Board meeting in Madison, Wisconsin.

President Harry S. Truman at dedication of Filene House in 1950.

Managing Director J. Orrin Shipe receiving a pen from President Lyndon B. Johnson after the signing of the "Truth in Packaging" law, November 3, 1966.

tion. At that time there were still only five state leagues—Massachusetts, New York, Illinois, Minnesota, and Missouri—that were nearly self- sustaining and which employed professional personnel. Credit unions in Alabama, Georgia, Indiana, Iowa, North Carolina, and Virginia con- ducted some of the activities of a league, but they had no paid employees. The organizations in California and Michigan were leagues in name only. Nevertheless, credit unions existed in thirty-eight states and the District of Columbia, where local laws had encouraged their formation, and now the new federal law opened up the way for organizing credit unions anywhere in the country. This was the foundation on which Bergengren had to work.

Bergengren saw two approaches to the task ahead. One, as he ex- pressed it, was "a hasty ratification by the ten states most apt to ratify, and an attempt to immediately launch the national association there- after, depending primarily on a subsidy." The other alternative was to bring the matter of CUNA "officially before every credit union in the United States, and to present it on the basis of adequately financing the national development through substantial dues paid by state organiza- tions." Bergengren favored the second approach because he believed that no national association could be successful without the backing of credit unions all over the United States. He knew this was the most difficult path. It would be time-consuming and would require a great physical effort. But, with his chief aides Doig and Gartland, he believed success could be achieved.

As Bergengren viewed the matter, one of the main problems of organ- izing state leagues was that of destroying the habit of dependency in credit union thinking. Credit unions had been receiving services for many years from CUNEB and had been asked to contribute nothing in the way of financial aid. "I know the credit unions well enough," he told Filene, "to know how difficult it is going to be to get them to compre- hend the desirability of making such financial sacrifice as is necessary in order to support strongly a National Association." He asserted that those credit unions that had maintained "abnormal" dividends of 7 to 10 per- cent during the depression were the least willing to cooperate with state leagues, while credit unions paying "normal" dividends were the most cooperative. Bergengren explained that he was determined to "break down this selfishness which has been creeping into many of our larger credit unions, and to bring home to them, so forcefully that they will not hesitate to cooperate, that the National Association will be of proportionately greater service to the larger credit unions than to the small ones." He had already urged, for example, that new credit unions organized under federal law limit their dividends to 6 percent.

Bergengren's tactics were first to secure ratification from the five viable leagues. Then, he had Agnes Gartland send copies of the new constitution and bylaws to every credit union in the United States known to the bureau. He and Doig divided the states among themselves and determined to hold meetings in thirty-three states between September and December. At these meetings, Bergengren announced that his first objective would be to persuade credit union representatives, whether few or many, to organize a state league and pledge to support it financially. Only then, he said, would he present the constitution and bylaws of CUNA for consideration.[31]

By October 20, all the organized leagues, except Massachusetts, had ratified the constitution, along with newly organized leagues in Colorado, Tennessee, Mississippi, Louisiana, Texas, Arkansas, Georgia, North Carolina, Kentucky, Ohio, Michigan, New Jersey, and Wisconsin. Eleven of the state leagues promised to support the national association by pledging annually one-half of one percent of their assets. Doig was responsible for most of the organizational work, but Bergengren planned November meetings in Rhode Island, Washington, D.C., Indiana, California, Arizona, South Carolina, and Virginia.[32] In late November, Bergengren wrote Filene: "When someone writes the history of the credit union movement a hundred years from now, the fact that Tom and I have induced thirty-three states to ratify the national constitution and bylaws, in the process organizing over twenty new state leagues, between the last week of September and Thanksgiving week, will be—I think— rated as possibly the major achievement of the Credit Union National Extension Bureau." [33]

Strangely enough, the Massachusetts league, oldest in the United States, presented the greatest problem for Bergengren. Late in October, he and Hubert Rhodes attended a meeting of the league directors and urged them to ratify the Estes Park documents. He soon found himself under attack from such state leaders as Charles W. Harvey, a past president of the league, and William Wellen, current president. Bergengren believed that criticism arose because of the belief that the delegates to the Estes Park meeting had been "hand picked." Several directors

---

[31] Bergengren to Filene, Sept. 10, 1934.

[32] Bergengren to the Members of the Estes Park Conference, Oct. 20, 1934; Bergengren to Filene, Oct. 22, 1934.

[33] Bergengren to Filene, Nov. 30, 1934.

thought that Felix Vorenberg and Harvey should have been invited. As a result, even though Bergengren believed that he had enough votes for ratification, the opposition prevented any vote from being taken. Angered by the results of the meeting, Bergengren charged that for years the league had suffered from poor leadership and that Massachusetts was about "the only state where the credit union movement is not progressing in typical fashion." He predicted that the rejection of the constitution would prove "a blessing in disguise" because it would demonstrate the need for new leadership to many credit unionists in the state. Ominously, he wrote to Filene that he had "long been in favor of disrupting the league." [34] In his frustration Bergengren contradicted everything he had said earlier when he held up the Massachusetts league as an exemplary organization.

Harvey explained to Filene that the Massachusetts league favored a national association but it would not ratify the constitution and bylaws until certain objections were met. He charged that Bergengren had not appointed delegates to the Estes Park meeting who were representative of the Massachusetts league. Bergengren's recent claim, Harvey wrote, that Massachusetts was represented by five delegates was a subterfuge, because most of them came from the CUNEB office and had a "national viewpoint" rather than a particular concern for credit union problems of the state. Harvey made it clear that part of his objection to the national association involved personalities, particularly the place in history to be occupied by Filene, Pierre Jay, and Vorenberg. He suggested that the article in the bylaws recognizing Filene as founder of the movement did an injustice to others. It was, he wrote, "only natural for them to feel hurt that they should be forgotten." Why not, Harvey asked, change that provision to read that "Edward A. Filene associated himself with Bank Commissioner Pierre Jay, Felix Vorenberg, and others, and organized the first Credit Union Law in the United States in Massachusetts in 1909." [35]

The problem of historic recognition had faced Bergengren earlier and perhaps he could have handled the delicate problem better than he did. In April, 1933, Vorenberg telephoned him and complained that many people were concerned about Filene getting all of the credit for the movement. Vorenberg insisted that he, too, had started credit unions. To quiet this criticism, Bergengren suggested to Filene that he might see Vorenberg and try to straighten out any misunderstanding. Filene, how-

---

[34] *Ibid.*, Oct. 22, 1934.
[35] Harvey to Filene, Nov. 1, 1934.

ever, refused, claiming that he had brought Vorenberg into the movement after it was started, and that he "did not work hard and showed little real interest and had nothing to do with the national organization work." [36] Bergengren, however, remembered history somewhat differently, and he told Percy Brown that when he was employed as managing director of the old Massachusetts Credit Union Association, Vorenberg was not only president, but "guaranteed the financing of the Association if I would undertake the work." Probably as a result of the dispute, Vorenberg delivered a radio address in June, 1933, claiming that the credit union movement was born out of a discussion held by Howard Coonley, Abraham Cohen, Max Mitchell, Henry Dennison, Pierre Jay, Edward Filene, and himself.[37]

The controversy subsided somewhat until after the Estes Park meeting, when Vorenberg sent Filene a copy of his earlier radio address. His accompanying letter stated:

The amount of work and time given to the Credit Union System, by me and others, since its inception in 1909 needs no publicity as the records speak for themselves. As president of the first Credit Union in Massachusetts, for over four years, I gave more time to the Movement than anyone else in Massachusetts, and while my financial participation did not match yours (and for good reasons) yet my contribution of time was most important . . . . I do not care about having my name mentioned in the Constitution of the National Association, yet for historical reasons the names of all its founders should appear. I am also surprised that even your own State has not been mentioned, despite the fact that Massachusetts was the first State to make Credit Unions possible." [38]

In spite of Vorenberg's disclaimer of wanting to be honored by the national association, Bergengren charged that Vorenberg's son had been at the league's meeting "to see to it that Harvey did what he had doubtless been told to do." [39]

Harvey told Filene, however, that there were more substantive reasons why the league had not ratified the CUNA documents. He objected, for example, to the provision giving the board of directors sole power to determine which league would be recognized in states where two ex-

[36] Bergengren to Filene, April 13, 1933. Filene's comments written in margin of Bergengren to Filene, May 16, 1933.

[37] Bergengren to Brown, April 21, 1933; "Broadcast by Felix Vorenberg, Former President and One of the Founders of Credit Unions in Massachusetts," June 24, 1933, mimeographed; *Boston Herald,* July 1, 1933.

[38] Vorenberg to Filene, Oct. 15, 1934.

[39] Bergengren to Filene, Oct. 22, 1934.

isted. He wanted the bylaws changed to insure that the league which would be recognized must comprise a fair proportion of the credit union members in the state. This was particularly desirable, he said, since Bergengren "threatens to start a League of his own in Massachusetts if the Credit Union League of Massachusetts does not join, and that this new League would be recognized as representing Massachusetts."

Harvey also opposed the provision that would not allow a league's withdrawal from CUNA to become effective until the next annual meeting of the national directors after notice to withdraw had been received. Such a provision was unfair, he said, because if the directors at their first meeting set dues at ten cents per member, Massachusetts could not afford to pay, yet it would be obligated for approximately $10,800 even if it withdrew. He suggested, therefore, that the bylaws be amended to allow dues obligations to end within thirty days after a withdrawal notice had been received by CUNA. Moreover, he argued that, since Massachusetts was entitled to only three national directors out of fifty-eight while paying over 16 percent of the total national dues, the assessment was out of proportion to representation.

Harvey also objected to the representation of Massachusetts, as part of the northeast district, on the executive committee. He claimed that the area contained at least 50 percent of credit union assets and 33 percent of the membership, yet the bylaws gave the district only one vice-president, or 20 percent of the total. He said that it was not practical for the Massachusetts league to affiliate with CUNA until the dues question was decided, especially since Massachusetts had so few representatives on the board. Finally, he opposed the provision that the bylaws were to become effective when only ten states had ratified them, requiring any changes to be approved by a two-thirds vote of the directors. Harvey said that a "true spirit of cooperation" would have prompted the Estes Park delegates to allow any state that indicated its intention to join the naional association to be represented on the first board, and that the bylaws would then have been ratified by a majority of the directors at the first meeting. This procedure would have allowed Massachusetts to affiliate and then work to change objectionable provisions in the documents.[40]

Meanwhile, the directors of the Massachusetts league held another meeting to consider ratification. Bergengren reported that eight directors voted to ratify and four opposed the question. But then, according to Bergengren, Harvey succeeded in recessing the meeting, "and with much

[40] Harvey to Filene, Nov. 1, 1934.

political business of swapping votes, etc., got a sufficient switch in sentiment so that on the re-assembling of the meeting there was a ballot
against ratification." In subsequent meetings, Bergengren charged,
Harvey "packed" the house "to prevent the credit unions from getting
any true conception of the situation."

To meet this challenge, Bergengren assembled representatives of
fifteen Massachusetts credit unions at the Boston City Club on the
evening of December 4. Those attending represented the Boston and
Albany Railroad credit union, the New England Telephone and Telegraph Company, the credit unions in Swift and Company, Armour and
Company, the Plymouth Cordage Company, the DuPont Viscoloid
Company, Standard Oil, the Lynn American Legion Post, and credit
unions of municipal employees and public school teachers. These credit
unions had several thousand members and assets of about $3.5 million.
After discussing the Massachusetts situation, they voted to incorporate
a league to be known as the Raiffeisen Associates, adopted bylaws,
named a board of fifteen members, and elected officers. They then ratified the national constitution and bylaws, and elected Edward Shanney
national director from Massachusetts. Bergengren told Filene that he
had not taken this step until he had tried all other methods to bring the
old league into the association. He was personally "delighted beyond
measure at what we have done," because "for the first time in years the
credit union movement in Massachusetts is going to be in the hands of
the kind of credit union leaders who are making the credit union movement so successful in other states." He also believed that when all the
credit unions in the state learned the truth about the dispute, a vast
majority of them would affiliate with the new league. "I believe that at
this moment our organization is the stronger organization of the two," he
wrote Filene, "and that within six months it will be practically the only
truly representative central organization of Massachusetts credit
unions." [41]

The establishment of two credit union groups in Massachusetts demonstrated the problem which had plagued the cooperative movement in
the United States almost from its beginning. It was simply a matter of
cooperators refusing to cooperate. Different ideas as to procedures and
organization, jealousy over who should get credit for achievements, and
personality conflicts were among the factors which not only showed up
in Massachusetts credit unionism, but in the general cooperative movement.

[41] Bergengren to Filene, Dec. 5, 1934.

Bergengren's hope that his rival group would soon prompt other credit unions to oust the leadership of the Massachusetts league and bring about unification did not materialize. Nevertheless, his action at least spared the national association the embarrassment of having no affiliation in the pioneer credit union state. Several of the issues raised by the Massachusetts league, however, continued to plague CUNA in the months ahead, as other leagues threatened to disaffiliate. By the end of 1934, however, thirty-four states and the District of Columbia had ratified the constitution and bylaws, and thirty of those states had required the organization of new leagues or the reorganization and strengthening of existing paper leagues. Bergengren and Doig had accomplished a monumental task in only four short months.[42]

This activity, of course, pointed toward the first meeting of the national board of directors and turning over the functions of the extension bureau to CUNA. There still remained a myriad of unsettled questions, not only for the new directors, but also for Bergengren and Filene. One of the most immediate involved Bergengren's own role in credit unionism. Many times in the past, he had told Filene that he was unsure of his future in the credit union movement, and he usually raised this question when he was pressing Filene for a higher salary. After Estes Park, however, he told Filene "that it may be best for all concerned for me and for the Bureau to pass out of the picture together."[43] Based upon past experience, there is evidence to suggest that once again Bergengren was "fishing" to see if Filene had plans for him in some other capacity. Filene, however, immediately urged Bergengren to remain with the movement, because "having done so much of the pioneer work, you are clearly entitled to some of the fruits of the maturity of such work and plans."

Filene told Bergengren that he hoped to be named president of CUNA for at least one year. He wanted the presidency, he wrote, because he planned "to put a chain of cooperative department stores across the country, and that position would have been useful in this project, which I believe will be most beneficial to the credit-unionists who can get the profits out of the goods they buy in this way without involving credit unions in cooperative distribution, which I believe cannot compete successfully in the present day if organized in the individual or small groups in which the credit unions would have to organize at present." He also thought that the movement might benefit from having a "successful

---

[42] "Leagues Admitted to Membership in Credit Union National Association," typescript.
[43] Bergengren to Filene, Oct. 11, 1934.

businessman" at its head. However, Filene said he would support Bergengren if he wished to be the first president.

Filene believed that Bergengren should become the managing director of the new association. In spite of Bergengren's feeling that all "credit-unionists should work for nothing, or for small salaries," Filene thought that such a big job should pay at least $20,000 a year so that a man's "family cares do not interfere with his work." He suggested, therefore, that Bergengren accept a salary of $20,000 from CUNA and then return a portion of it to the movement until such time as the association was financially stable. As an alternative, Filene suggested that Bergengren accept only the salary he thought was right in principle, and he or the Twentieth Century Fund would underwrite the difference between it and $20,000. That portion would be for services as editor of *The Bridge*.[44]

By the end of the year, Bergengren again brought up his problem. He assured Filene that the amount of the salary was not the main question, but the source from which it came. The reason he questioned whether or not he should continue with the national association, he said, was that his work up to now had required "something of a dictatorship," and that he was not certain that "temperamentally or otherwise I am the right man to undertake to build a superstructure on the very splendid foundation" already laid. He thought that the editorship of *The Bridge,* or head of the movement's projected mutual life insurance company, might suit him much better than managing director of CUNA.[45] On January 2, 1935, Bergengren visited Filene to discuss finances for the bureau, the national association, and himself. He insisted that he should not be on the credit union payroll so that he could retain his independence. Bergengren suggested that Filene continue to pay his salary of $15,000 annually for three years, from which he would pay the salary of Agnes Gartland. Filene agreed to Bergengren's plan, but limited the term to one year.[46]

The second major unfinished business involved the closing out of the Credit Union National Extension Bureau, which had been active for more than thirteen years, and setting up new offices for the Credit Union National Association. Bergengren and Filene were both interested in seeing that the transition went smoothly. There never seemed to be any question that the offices of the new national association would be moved

[44] Filene to Bergengren, Oct. 15, 1934.

[45] Bergengren to Filene, Dec. 29, 1934.

[46] Percy Brown to Filene, Dec. 31, 1934, with addendum dated Jan. 2, 1935; Filene to Evans Clark, Jan. 5, 1935.

away from Boston. Yet, Bergengren recommended to Filene in December, 1934, that headquarters remain at 5 Park Square at least until the following summer, when the work of the bureau was slowest. The bureau was still involved in organizational and legislative matters and it would continue until CUNA was organized and operating.[47] Filene agreed, and requested the Twentieth Century Fund to appropriate $25,000 to continue the work of the bureau through the transition period. He acknowledged that this expenditure had not been contemplated, but he thought the fund directors would agree "that we cannot afford to risk the future of the Credit Union movement after having spent so much time and such large sums on it, by allowing a situation to exist where its work might be taken over by selfish interests." [48]

In regard to the permanent location of CUNA's offices, Bergengren argued that considerable room would be required and that the work could be carried on more comfortably and efficiently if the headquarters were not in a major city. Moreover, he preferred some spot in the Midwest.[49] Percy Brown informed Filene that Bergengren favored Madison, Wisconsin, but suggested that any site chosen should be centrally located, and served by adequate rail and air facilities. In January, 1935, Bergengren and Filene agreed that the association would remain in Boston as long as necessary and that a thorough investigation be made of various locations for the permanent offices. Filene indicated that a college town might be best, but that a location on a main railroad line near Chicago would be preferable.[50]

By early 1935, a number of people began showing interest in seeing that CUNA's offices were established in their cities. The president of the Kansas City Power and Light Company, for example, wrote Filene early in January on behalf of interests in Kansas City. Glenn Frank, president of the University of Wisconsin in Madison and a former employee of Filene's, also wrote Filene, saying he did not know "another place in the United States where the atmosphere would be more congenial to this particular enterprise and where the movement itself would have greater and more sympathetic support." Filene replied that he liked the "democratic atmosphere of the University, and the general progressiveness of Wisconsin," but that Madison was neither centrally located nor a recognized rail center. However, Filene said that he was

[47] Bergengren to Filene, Dec. 29, 1934.
[48] Filene to Evans Clark, Jan. 5, 1935.
[49] Bergengren to Filene, Dec. 29, 1934.
[50] Brown to Filene, Dec. 31, 1934, with addendum dated Jan. 2, 1935.

willing to consider Madison even though he had "only one vote," and not "directly or indirectly any control." Frank replied that all conditions were favorable in Madison, including a "splendid climate and delightful summers," and that location in a smaller city would allow a head-quarters building to "stand out as a monument to a splendid idea," rather than in a large urban center where it "would be lost in the midst of numerous skyscrapers." [51]

The arrangements regarding future financing of the movement and the location of a headquarters would, of course, have to receive the approval of the new CUNA board of directors which was scheduled to meet in January, 1935. But neither Bergengren nor Filene anticipated that their recommendations would be rejected. They still were the most powerful forces in credit unionism. However, the situation where two men largely controlled the credit union movement was nearing an end. So far credit unionism in the United States had been dominated by the work and personalities of Filene and Bergengren. Over a period of four-teen years Bergengren, supported by Filene's money, had taken a small, struggling, largely local movement and organized it into a national economic force. Bergengren had organized so well that despite future problems the movement was nearly strong enough to continue on its own. Perhaps Bergengren and Filene sensed that forces outside their control would soon threaten their power and influence. In any event, they entered the transitional period between the closing out of CUNEB and the organization of the Credit Union National Association with dedication to credit union principles and a harmony of purpose seldom experienced in recent years.

[51] Joseph F. ("Jep") Porter, president of Kansas City Power and Light Co., to Filene, Jan. 11, 1935; Frank to Filene, Jan. 21 and 28, 1935; Filene to Frank, Jan. 25, 1935.

CHAPTER IX

Launching the Credit Union National Association

EARLY IN JANUARY, 1935, Bergengren issued the call for the first meeting of CUNA's board of directors to coincide with the annual meeting of the Missouri Credit Union League in Kansas City. On the same day, he met with Filene to discuss the many problems relative to the transition from CUNEB to the national association. Following the conference, Filene instructed Evans Clark to arrange a meeting of the Twentieth Century Fund directors so that a final plan for financial support of the credit union movement could be approved. Filene wanted $25,000 appropriated for CUNA for the 1935–36 fiscal year, $2,500 of which would be used to pay expenses of directors who attended the Kansas City meeting. He also suggested that a final appropriation of $25,000 be made to the extension bureau, with $15,000 of that amount going to pay Bergengren's salary, even though he would soon become managing director of CUNA.[1]

Filene was as vitally interested in the first board meeting as he had been in the Estes Park Conference, and he urged Bergengren to plan for it carefully. Filene still worried about possible dangers to the movement, and insisted that Bergengren draft a memorandum summarizing the threats that might confront credit unionism during the next few years. Bergengren replied that the greatest problems were internal. He saw the matters of persuading credit unions to join state leagues and then getting the state leagues to affiliate with the national association as two of the major challenges. Bergengren charged that the bureau had "done so much for the credit unions without charge that they have become, to a certain extent, dependent on charity." Contributing to this psychology, he said, was the fact that many credit unions were interested in maintaining high dividends that they would try to eliminate dues and finance the national association through borrower's insurance which would be

---

[1] Bergengren to Filene, Jan. 2, 1935, copy of mimeographed letter sent to all CUNA directors; Filene to Clark, Jan. 5, 1935.

191

paid for in the expense of loan service. Bergengren predicted that only a minority of credit unions would join their leagues and the national association at the outset; not many societies, he wrote, had smart and broad-minded leaders who understood the importance of a central organization and who were prepared to make the necessary financial sacrifices. A smaller minority of credit unions, "managed by very narrow-minded men," would join the state and national organizations, but would seek the advantages of the central association without being burdened by dues. Finally, he saw the majority of credit unions holding back until CUNA developed "such specific services that the leaders of these credit unions can figure out arithmetically that they are losing money by refraining from joining the State Leagues and the National Association."

Bergengren also believed that the movement was plagued by "bad thinking" among many credit unionists. He charged that some leaders, such as those of Massachusetts, were no longer interested in organizing new credit unions, being satisfied with the number which could support a state league. In addition, he had found that managers of state leagues were unwilling "to do the drudgery incidental to organizing new credit unions." Such attitudes were deleterious, he said, because the future of the credit union movement depended on attaining a large membership and huge assets. Another problem, according to Bergengren, was that some leaders wanted "to manipulate and exploit the credit union movement for their own benefit." Some, too, were guilty of "sectional thinking" and refused to look at the movement from a national point of view. Finally, he thought that there was too great a tendency to be "niggardly in the matter of payment of our personnel," and to look upon anyone who wanted to work for the national association as being "inspired only by a desire to get a soft job." Bergengren insisted that he would take no money from the national association, but that the amount of his salary should be included in the budget to establish the principle of paying decent wages. "If the National Association is turned over to unambitious and incapable people, who will work for nothing," he declared, "it will fail miserably in my judgment."

Bergengren also saw some external dangers to the movement, although he minimized them. He recognized that small loan agencies might work to repeal state credit union laws or cripple them with amendments. He also believed that the nation might "swing to the right" politically; this could endanger the federal law. These problems could be met, however, by a strong and watchful national association that had already established friendly relations with state legislators and congressmen of both political parties. Moreover, Bergengren believed that the federal government itself might someday enter the small loan field. Then, too, there was always the possibility that commercial banks might "wake up and establish an effective small loans system."

But Bergengren contended that credit unions could meet all of these possible difficulties with hard work and proper dedication:

> The credit union work calls for unlimited industry, tremendous sacrifice, vision, courage and the ability to absorb punishment. We will have to contend with petty jealousy, the inclination to exploit stupidity, lack of vision, and, in the end, the result will be about as it is in all other concerns of life—the eternal struggle between good impulses and bad impulses produces results which, at any given time, mark the advance or retreat of civilization. Our prayer, it seems to me, should be for vision, courage and the capacity to take it.[2]

Unlike Filene, Bergengren believed that a strong organization of credit unions, with "right-thinking" leaders, would go a long way in meeting future problems.

The first step toward building an effective national association was to get as many credit union groups affiliated with the organization as possible. Even before the first board meeting, Bergengren circularized all credit unions and pointed out the advantages of membership in CUNA. He emphasized that the national association would protect credit unions from adverse legislation and taxation, and that it would provide centralized services to credit unions. Appealing to credit union pride, he suggested that credit unions would eventually become "the largest organization of working people in the United States and the strongest organization financially . . . ." Moreover, credit unions were truly American, in that if they formed a powerful organization, it would "be patriotic, conservative in the right sense, and yet intolerant of a continuation of obsolete anachronisms in our economic system . . . [and] a bulwark against a Fascist dictatorship on the one hand, and a Communist dictatorship on the other . . . ."[3]

Bergengren also prepared a list of activities which he believed should be authorized by the board of directors and undertaken by the national association. The most important, he thought, was the development of a

---

[2] Bergengren to Percy Brown, Jan. 18, 1935, with accompanying memorandum, "Suggestions Relative to the Difficulties with which the Credit Union National Association Will Be Confronted."

[3] Bergengren to Filene, Jan. 23, 1935.

printing and supply department which would provide credit unions with all their bookkeeping forms and act as a central purchasing agency for everything "from pen points to adding machines." Two additional service departments which CUNA should establish, according to Bergengren, were a statistical branch and a department to furnish surety bonds for credit union officers. He also believed that a monthly magazine was more essential than ever "in order to bind credit unions and credit union members together." Other activities which Bergengren projected for the national association included both protecting and perfecting existing state and federal credit union laws, cooperating in strengthening state leagues, and continuing to organize individual credit unions. Regarding the latter function, however, Bergengren believed that "within a year the organization program can be almost one hundred percent transferred to the State Leagues and the Federal Credit Union Section." CUNA should also seek a law from Congress making possible the organization of banks of discount in each state, and the national association itself should establish a central bank when legislation permitted.[4]

Before the directors met in January, 1935, there was a great deal of discussion about establishing an insurance company. Bergengren favored providing borrowers' protection coverage, but he was extremely hostile toward supporting the national association from insurance profits as proposed by the O'Shaughnessy group in Illinois. Moreover, he insisted that the premiums for insurance coverage should be paid by the credit union and not the individual borrower. "Just as soon as we start adding to the cost of loans service, no matter in what terms we disguise it," Bergengren wrote, "we start destroying our own fundamental justification for existence." More important than borrowers' protection, he argued, CUNA should set up a mutual life insurance company to supply life insurance to all credit union members at cost. Bergengren agreed with Filene, however, that this subject should be referred to a special committee of the directors and not decided at the initial meeting.[5]

The first CUNA board of directors met on January 27, 1935, in Kansas City, with representatives present from thirty-four state leagues and the District of Columbia.[6] The first order of business was to elect a president of CUNA and the results were never in doubt. The thirty-

[4] "Activities which Should be Authorized by the National Association," memorandum by Bergengren accompanying *ibid.*

[5] *Ibid.*; Bergengren to Filene, Dec. 29, 1934; Percy Brown to Filene, Dec 31, 1934.

[6] Minutes, Board of Directors, CUNA, Jan. 27–29, 1935, pp. 1–2.

seven directors cast a unanimous vote for Filene just as Percy Brown and Bergengren had planned. In putting Filene's name in nomination, Bergengren told the directors that he was not acting out of sentimentality, but for practical and selfish reasons, since Filene would give the movement prestige with businessmen, legislators, and other important people.[7]

Filene's election as president was the last act of unanimity at the meeting. When the nominations were opened for vice-presidents representing the five districts, Nat Helman of New York and Timothy O'Shaughnessy of Illinois began their attack on the new constitution and bylaws. Both men objected to what they considered underrepresentation of their states on both the board of directors and the executive committee. Helman was able to persuade the directors to appoint a committee to consider a revision of the bylaws, but O'Shaughnessy's proposal to delay the election of officers until the committee reported was not accepted. Bergengren told the directors that it was time for a showdown on the issues because the bylaws had been carefully written at Estes Park and accepted by all the leagues. He argued further that enough compromises had already been made. Clarence Howell of Michigan supported this position, and sarcastically asked for separate geographical districts for "the great state of Massachusetts and the great state of New York." Al Dodd reminded the group that a credit union member in his state of Colorado would be paying the same dues as a credit union member in Massachusetts or New York.

In the midst of controversy over representation and dues, the directors proceeded to elect vice-presidents. John L. Moore, Hubert M. Rhodes, and Earl Rentfro were elected to represent the western, southeastern, and the south central districts respectively. E. L. Shanney of the CUNA-sponsored Massachusetts league and Helman entered a runoff election for the northeast central district, and Claude Orchard and O'Shaughnessy contested for the north central post. Shanney and Orchard were elected, proving the power of the Bergengren forces.[8]

It was no surprise to anyone when Claude Clarke of Ohio nominated Bergengren for managing director, but Bergengren's frank response may have caused some dismay. He warned the directors that they should not be under any delusions "about the leopard changing his spots." Despite some criticism of his past work, he announced that, if elected managing director, he would follow the same principles which he had developed in

[7] *Ibid.*, pp. 5–7.
[8] *Ibid.*, pp. 8–13.

CUNEB. Moreover, he would be the manager in both name and fact. He intended to appoint department heads because, he said, someone had to be responsible. "In our democracy we have learned one thing this last decade—that is, that democracy without discipline is no good. A man of this sort has got to have discipline—it has got to be a sort of autocracy." Finally, he told the directors that, "if I take this job, you must bear in mind that I will have all of the weaknesses I have ever had, and I shall fight for the things which we have set down as the policies of the movement." Filene stepped in at this point and told the directors that if the movement did not want Bergengren, he would consider it a great personal favor. Filene announced that he was ready to launch a consumer cooperative movement and wanted Bergengren to head it up at a much greater salary than CUNA could pay. The directors elected Bergengren without a negative vote. Doig was elected secretary and Clarke treasurer by acclamation.[9]

Much of the discussion at the first directors' meeting centered around the question of financing CUNA. This whole matter was closely connected with the question of borrowers' protection insurance. Bergengren accused those who wanted to charge borrowers a premium of wanting to make a profit in order to support both state leagues and the national association. Doig supported Bergengren's view, and argued that "the cost of the National Association should be financed by dues—entirely by dues." The emphasis should be on service, not on profits, Doig said.

But all credit union leaders agreed that insurance was absolutely necessary to protect credit unions and the families of borrowers. Indeed, some state leagues were already doing this business. Earl Rentfro pointed out that during 1934 such policies carried by the Missouri league had paid out over $5,000 on thirty-one deaths of borrowers. He explained that, "we've had deaths occur here that have brought this home to us, where the treasurer of the credit union, where the reserve fund was too small, had to go out and collect from co-signers on notes who couldn't buy shoes for their children." Charles Hyland of Wisconsin declared that there was a great demand in Wisconsin for borrowers' insurance and that if CUNA did not establish a program, several credit unions in his state were going to band together to make arrangements for their own. Other directors also voiced support for borrowers' insurance. It became clear at the meeting that not only were borrowers' protection plans already in operation, but that most credit union spokesmen felt a need for such a service. Therefore, the directors voted to endorse the principle that

[9] *Ibid.*, pp. 13–15.

CUNA establish its own insurance program, and instructed the executive committee to set up such a plan within six months.[10]

The directors also discussed other possible sources of service and potential profits. They voted to establish a department of supplies to begin functioning when CUNA opened its offices, and referred the questions of establishing a bonding department and a mutual life insurance company, which Bergengren said contained "much more of importance for credit union people than any other subject," to the executive committee.[11] *The Bridge* also offered a potential source of revenue. Claude Orchard believed that the magazine should not only make profits for CUNA but should cover cooperative activities everywhere. "In this manner," he said, "we can take the leadership in the whole cooperative movement which we ought to take and which we must take." Doig, however, again asserted that CUNA should not be associated with any profit-making ventures.

But it was the question of assessing dues as a way to finance the association which set off the real struggle in Kansas City. To Bergengren, Doig, and their supporters, dues provided the fairest and best way to get the necessary money. They were philosophically and practically opposed to relying on profits from CUNA services. The idea of profits in a cooperative venture was both repugnant and contradictory to them. On the other hand Helman of New York and O'Shaughnessy of Illinois argued that most of the funds for CUNA's budget should come from profit-making service departments and that dues be levied only to make up the difference between earned income and expenditures. They did not object to all dues, but insisted that such dues should be small and only supplementary to profits derived from CUNA services. States such as Illinois and New York, they said, would pay a disproportionate amount of the expenses of the national association if CUNA were financed by dues, because those states had the largest memberships. Nevertheless, Doig moved to fix the dues at ten cents per member annually. Helman warned that if the motion passed, New York "should have to withdraw, not because we want to, but because it would become financially imperative that we withdraw." Following additional discussion, the directors voted to levy dues of ten cents for each credit union member.

The total budget for the first year called for expenditures of $58,000. The directors had earlier voted to accept the first year subsidy from the Twentieth Century Fund of $25,000, of which $2,500 had already been

10 *Ibid.*, pp. 25–37.
11 *Ibid.*, pp. 21, 39–43.

expended to pay the expenses of the directors for attending the board meeting. Included in the expected revenue was $8,500 from printing and supplies, leaving $27,000 to be raised from dues. This budget was accepted, with Illinois and New York casting two votes each in opposition, while New Jersey cast its one vote against acceptance.[12]

Having at least temporarily settled the financial matters, the directors created an Organization and Contact Department to assist those leagues that requested help in organizing new credit unions, but left such matters as central banking, auditing, bonding, and statistics for future discussion.[13] The directors voted to incorporate CUNA as a nonprofit organization, leaving to the executive committee the question of how to incorporate the organization's service agencies.

Bergengren told the directors that plans had been made to continue to operate the extension bureau in Boston for a few months, but that a decision needed to be made for a permanent location for CUNA. Filene spoke in favor of Madison, Wisconsin, because it had "an atmosphere of democracy and research." Bergengren also favored Madison. A committee appointed to study the matter reported that Kansas City and Indianapolis had some support, but that it recommended Madison. On the basis of the committee's recommendation, the directors unanimously approved Madison for the new headquarters.[14]

The executive committee which consisted of the president, secretary, treasurer, and district vice-presidents met during the first annual meeting. But it conducted little business. Almost immediately Doig raised the question as to whether he should be a member of the committee since he was a paid employee of CUNA. Bergengren objected to excluding employees, because he did not think the movement "should emasculate any phase of the credit union movement at this stage by establishing any arbitrary rules that because a man is identified in any productive capacity he shall be excluded from constructive work on the Executive Committee." Orchard, however, asserted that Doig's views were sound and the members of the committee agreed, although they deferred the decision until the next meeting.[15]

The executive committee also established the salary scale for CUNA employees. Bergengren insisted that, even though his salary would not be paid out of CUNA revenue, as a precedent the amount should be a part

[12] *Ibid.*, pp. 45–52.
[13] *Ibid.*, pp. 22–25.
[14] *Ibid.*, pp. 55–56, 18–20, 68–70.
[15] Minutes, Executive Committee, CUNA, Jan. 27–29, 1935, p. 1.

of the budget. The committee set the managing director's salary at $15,000 a year, that of the assistant managing director at $3,600, manager of the printing and supply department at $5,000, and a total of $12,500 for other personnel. A committee was established to investigate setting up a borrowers' insurance plan, with immediate contracts to be placed with the Missouri league which was already handling business for the Arkansas and Texas credit unions. Filene and Orchard were appointed to push for federal legislation which would permit organizing a national clearinghouse to facilitate interstate credit union lending. Finally, the committee voted to vest all of its powers between quarterly meetings in the managing director, although Orchard suggested that Bergengren consult with directors and executive committee members as much as possible.[16]

Although the first meeting of the board of directors accomplished a great deal toward making necessary arrangements to begin the operation of CUNA, it did not solve the outstanding differences within the movement. Indeed, discussions at Kansas City tended to widen the conflicts. The Massachusetts league met on March 16, 1935, and again voted not to affiliate with the new association. In September, William H. Wellen, president of the league, informed delegates to the annual meeting, which included visitors from New York and New Jersey, that CUNA did not deserve the confidence of credit unionists in the United States. Nevertheless, he hoped that changes could be made in the constitution and bylaws so that all credit unions could subscribe to the association.

Not only did the leaders of the Massachusetts Credit Union League dislike CUNA's constitution and bylaws, they strongly objected to Bergengren's organization of a rival state league. To widen the split even farther, Bergengren informed the old Massachusetts league that the cost of supplies would be raised 10 percent above the prices paid by members of CUNA. Wellen objected to this tactic, and claimed that Bergengren had adopted this policy "to inconvenience the directors of our league by forcing us to increase the cost of supplies to our individual credit unions." The Massachusetts league withstood this pressure, however, and arranged with a local printer to supply business forms at prices the league had formerly paid CUNEB.[17]

The New York situation presented even greater difficulties for Bergengren and CUNA. Nat Helman, league attorney, had warned the CUNA

[16] Ibid., pp. 3–9.

[17] "Address of President William H. Wellen at the First Annual Convention of the Credit Union League of Massachusetts," New Bedford, Mass., Sept. 21, 1935.

directors at their first meeting that if the dues structure and league representation on the board were not altered, the New York league would withdraw its affiliation. When no changes were forthcoming, the New York league dropped its membership in CUNA. There were leaders in the state, such as Harold Winchester, who favored remaining in the association, and they continued to work for an accommodation. Both Bergengren and Doig visited New York in an effort to get friendly credit unions to bring pressure on league leadership to affiliate with CUNA. Doig also proselytized in upstate New York, where he found credit union leaders willing to organize an independent league to represent credit unions in the Albany-Buffalo area. He initially advised them against such independent action, however, and told CUNA's executive committee that if he and Bergengren could go into New York they would be successful in organizing a new league which would join CUNA and begin paying dues in 1936.

Bergengren asked the executive committee for permission to hold meetings in New York and present the case of the national association, leaving it to the credit unions to decide what action to take in regard to affiliating with CUNA. At the Napanoch convention of the New York league in June, 1935, he offered a resolution to the leadership which would have placed the league on record as being in sympathy with the national association and agreeing to cooperate with CUNA in presenting both sides of the argument over dues. If a majority of credit unions in the state subsequently voted to affiliate with CUNA, the league would not stand in their way, and that group of credit unions would elect national directors without forming a rival state league. The league directors, however, insisted upon adding a paragraph to the resolution, stating that "irrespective of the development or outcome of such campaign, it [the national association] will not organize or attempt to organize, or in any way sponsor the organization of any other League or Association of Credit Unions in New York State." Bergengren rejected that restriction. In September the executive committee decided that if the New York league did not accept the Napanoch proposal by October 15, 1935, it would allow Bergengren to hold meetings in New York and to assist those credit unions which desired to affiliate with CUNA.[18]

Meanwhile, on October 11, Helman and Edward A. Norman, president of the New York league, presented their grievances to Evans Clark

[18] Harold P. Winchester to Filene, April 6, 1935; Minutes, Executive Committee, CUNA, Sept. 28–29, 1935, pp. 19–21, 25.

and Percy Brown. At first Clark concluded that the only action he could take was to present the problem to the executive committee of the Twentieth Century Fund. Upon reflection, however, he concluded that the "present violent opposition to the Association and Bergengren on the part of a large proportion of the credit unions in New York and Massachusetts . . . is a far more serious matter for the movement as a whole and the Fund than Bergengren is willing to admit." Moreover, Clark concluded that he "ought to do what I can as an individual to get the maximum number of credit unions in New York State into the Association with the minimum of hard feeling and of future trouble." [19]

On October 16, Bergengren conferred with Clark about the controversy. The following day Clark urged Bergengren to abandon any idea of organizing a dual league in New York and to postpone any trips into the state to induce individual credit unions to join the national association, at least until November 1. Bergengren seemed to approve Clark's proposals, provided the leaders of the league would "step out of the picture entirely and do nothing to interrupt our meeting or interfere with them . . . ." He wondered, however, "whether the New York League is really worth salvaging." The next day, Bergengren again wrote Clark, warning that if Helman and Norman continued to work against the national association, they would compel him to organize a new league.[20]

Clark worked assiduously to keep Bergengren from taking precipitate action, and told him on October 21 that if action were delayed until November 11, he believed that he could extract a promise from Helman and Norman to refrain from opposition to Bergengren's meetings. Bergengren agreed to wait only until November 1.[21] By October 30, Clark had drafted an agreement to be submitted to both sides. Both parties would agree that there was a desire for the New York league to affiliate with CUNA, and that no dual league should be formed in the state. Moreover, they agreed that they would seek an amendment to the by-laws "which will make control of the Association proportionate to the geographical distribution of membership." The agreement itself provided for representatives of CUNA to hold meetings with credit unions in New York to present the case for the national association, without interference or expressions of oppositions from league officials. Any group of credit unions that decided to affiliate with the national association would com-

[19] Clark to Brown, Oct. 23, 1935.
[20] Clark to Bergengren, Oct. 17, 1935; Bergengren to Clark, Oct. 18 and Oct. 19, 1935.
[21] Clark to Bergengren, Oct. 21, 1935; Bergengren to Clark, Oct. 21, 1935.

prise a group "exclusively for the one purpose, *as a group*, of the collection of dues and the election of directors to the National Association." [22]

Clark forwarded the agreement to Rolf Nugent of the Russell Sage Foundation, who was acting as go-between for the New York league. Clark told Nugent that Bergengren had agreed to "live up to every word of the agreement." Clark expressed the hope that the league would not expect Bergengren to promote membership in the league at the meetings to be held, just as he did not expect the league to promote membership in CUNA.[23]

On November 1, Nugent rejected the proposal on behalf of the New York league. He insisted that the agreement be amended to bind the national association not to accept any credit union that did not belong to the state league. On the question of representation on the national board, he wanted voting to be commensurate with the assessment of dues, that vice-presidents should be entitled to an additional vote in the executive committee for each 50,000 credit union members in the area he represented, and that the vice-presidents should be elected by directors from the areas represented and not by the entire board. Nugent agreed that this proposition offered little compromise, but "our conviction has become even more firm that the structure of the National Association needs complete revision." [24]

Percy Brown discussed the matter fully with Filene who concluded that Clark should continue to work for a compromise. Accordingly, Clark conferred again with Bergengren and Doig and persuaded them to agree to follow the "letter and spirit" of the proposed agreement, even though their New York opponents would not.[25] Meanwhile, however, Doig held meetings in upstate New York, provoking an angry response from Nugent. He warned Clark that "any effort to alienate New York credit unions will be to put in motion the procedure for forming a competing national association." Such a dual national organization, Nugent said, would succeed even if it were only an "alliance of the New York and Massachusetts Leagues." [26]

Bergengren remained basically conciliatory, saying that he favored

[22] "Suggestions for Agreement between Representatives of the New York State Credit Union League and the Credit Union National Association," Oct. 30, 1935, Russell Sage Collection.

[23] Clark to Rolf Nugent, Oct. 31, 1935, Russell Sage Collection.

[24] Nugent to Clark, Nov. 1, 1935, Russell Sage Collection.

[25] Brown to Clark, Nov. 6, 1935, Filene Correspondence; Clark to Nugent, Nov. 6, 1935. Russell Sage Collection.

[26] Nugent to Clark, Nov. 14, 1935, Russell Sage Collection.

amendments which would allow representation on CUNA's board of directors on the basis of credit union membership. At the February, 1936, meeting of the executive committee, he told the officers that such an amendment, along with one providing for election of vice-presidents by districts rather than from the board as a whole, would probably help solve the New York difficulties, although he doubted that the latter amendment would be approved by the directors. He still expressed pessimism about the New York league's affiliation, however, because of its position on dues. Bergengren also favored an amendment allowing individual credit unions to affiliate with CUNA, and Evans Clark, who was present at this meeting, endorsed such a proposal.[27]

When the directors met the next day, they voted to amend the bylaws to allow any two or more credit unions in a state to join the national association if there were no league in the state or if the existing league had not affiliated with CUNA. When the number of credit unions thus affiliated reached ten, they would be permitted to elect a national director. At the same time, they approved another amendment which allowed a league to elect one director for each 15,000 credit union members, with a limit of five directors from any one state.[28]

At the May meeting of the executive committee, ten individual credit unions from upstate New York were admitted to membership in the national association. Bergengren reported that he had informed the New York league of the amendments adopted in February, and that he had subsequently held a conference with Edward Norman, president of the league, in the office of Evans Clark. Since that time, the New York league had sent a questionnaire to all its members proposing affiliation with CUNA if the national association would agree not to admit any individual credit union to membership which was not a member of the league; and secondly, that only such members of the league as wished to pay dues would be eligible to vote for national directors.[29]

The willingness on the part of CUNA to meet some of the objections of the New York league leaders, together with the threat of creating a dual organization in New York evidenced by the admission of ten individual credit unions to the association, brought the dispute to a head. In August, 1936, the executive committee met at Spider Lake, near Hayward, Wisconsin, to listen to a presentation by Helman and John J. Ammering, another member of the New York league committee. Hel-

[27] Minutes, Executive Committee, CUNA, Feb. 9, 1936, pp. 36–37.

[28] Minutes, Directors, CUNA, Feb. 10, 1936, pp. 88–92.

[29] Minutes, Executive Committee, CUNA, May 9–10, 1936, pp. 48, 50–51.

man admitted at the outset that the major difference between the league and CUNA had been dues. Other points of contention had been very real, he said, but would not have kept New York out of the national association. Since many misunderstandings had been cleared up through conferences, Helman announced that the New York league was now ready to make application for affiliation with CUNA.

As in the past, however, Helman immediately placed reservations on the application. Most important, he said, was that New York's "budget at the present time does not permit our completely obligating ourselves to pay the dues which we would be required to pay under normal circumstances . . . . We would be required to pay $5,000; that is far in excess of our treasury and far in excess of our budget." Helman said that the league's directors proposed to pay CUNA in dues all that could be collected from credit union members. The second reservation was that CUNA had to agree not to accept membership from any credit union not a member of the league. For its part, the league would agree to urge all credit unions in the state to affiliate with the national association. It was clear that Helman was proposing that, while the New York league should be accepted in membership by CUNA, its dues would be assessed only upon members of those credit unions which elected to affiliate with CUNA. Therefore, while New York would be listed as affiliated with the national association, only a minority of credit unions might in fact be contributing members. Helman agreed, however, that only those credit unions paying national dues would participate in electing national directors, and he also conceded that individual credit unions already affiliated with CUNA but not with the league could likewise participate in such elections. Moreover, he pledged the cooperation of the league in urging all credit unions to affiliate, and pledged not to accept for league membership any new credit union that did not affiliate with CUNA.

After hearing lengthy discussion of New York's proposal, the executive committee appointed a committee of five officers to consider the application of the New York league and to report back the next day. The committee recommended that the application be accepted, but insisted that it be an "unconditional" one. It recommended further that if the New York league did not complete its formal application within a "reasonable" time, a "rump" group organized by John Wanhope should be given membership in CUNA. After amending the report to allow forty-five days as "reasonable," the executive committee approved the report and Helman filed an unofficial application for membership. Before the next meeting of the executive committee, the New York league completed its formal membership procedures and was admitted to the national association.[30]

As if CUNA did not have enough difficulty in Massachusetts and New York, strong opposition also existed in Illinois. The problem there was closely associated with the league's insurance business. The Illinois league had established its own Death Loss Prevention Fund which insured loans in the event of the death of borrowers. Bergengren claimed that the league charged the same premiums as private companies, thus giving no advantages to members. Moreover, he believed that it was unfair for borrowers, through their insurance premiums, to provide most of the league's support, while making investors "a preferred class of capitalists whose investments are guaranteed by over-charging borrowers who are already paying too much." Bergengren charged that exorbitant profits were being made on the sales of insurance, and reported that one large Chicago credit union was paying about $11,000 a year for premiums while its total losses had been $1,300. Bergengren also saw league profits as a threat to CUNA. With sufficient money earned on insurance policies, state leagues might decide that they had no need for a national association and its services. Besides the differences over insurance, CUNA's dues policy also continued to create opposition in Illinois.

By the summer of 1935, an impasse had been reached between the national association and the leaders of the Illinois league, especially O'Shaughnessy and Sol Cohen, head of the Chicago Post Office Credit Union. Several Illinois directors friendly to CUNA and its management forced the calling of a league director's meeting on July 28. At the opening session, Ralph Long moved that all officers of the league and the two national directors be asked to submit their resignations. Although the motion carried, the officers refused to resign. A second motion was then passed which directed that the assessed national dues which had been withheld because of the dispute be paid immediately. O'Shaughnessy had no recourse but to direct the treasurer to send the league's check to CUNA's treasurer. The next regular meeting of the league directors convened on August 18 and there fifteen directors voted to remove the president, vice-president and the two national directors from office. Only six directors voted against the motion, including O'Shaughnessy and Cohen.

At a meeting of CUNA's executive committee the following month, the national association's officers ratified the action of the Illinois league in

[30] *Ibid.*, Aug. 5–8, 1936, pp. 77–91; *ibid.*, Nov. 6–7, 1936, p. 99.

removing O'Shaughnessy and A. Wanner as national directors and commended the new Illinois directors, Pressley D. Holmes, William Maguire, and Ralph G. Long. But there was no reconciliation. The Illinois dissidents withdrew from the league and organized a rival group known as the Credit Union Associates, or the Forum Group. The credit unions belonging to the forum were mainly located in Chicago and had a total membership of 13,510 with assets of $1,470,430, which represented larger totals than those of credit unions represented by the successful directors.[31] This split in the Illinois movement continues, but has not proved as divisive or harmful as the division in Massachusetts.

Thus during the first months of CUNA's existence, internal dissensions plagued the credit union movement. The controversies over representation and dues, difficulties between some of the state leagues and CUNA, the interference by the national association in state league activities, and even the formation of some dual leagues, all indicated that much remained to be done to establish a unified, genuinely cooperative type of credit union movement. Another problem for CUNA was that a majority of credit unions did not belong to any league. For example, of the 168 credit unions in Iowa by the spring of 1935, only 71 belonged to the league; in Wisconsin of the 312 credit unions, 114 belonged. The figures for Tennessee were 29 of 76, for New Jersey 18 of 45, and for Michigan 13 of 65.[32]

To meet this problem, Bergengren and Doig spent much of their time between the first board of directors meeting in January and the midsummer of 1935 traveling around the country to persuade credit unions to affiliate with their state leagues, and then to urge the leagues to pay their national dues. The bylaws had explicitly forbidden the national association to begin functioning until one-half of the assessed dues were in the treasury. Meanwhile, the movement continued to be directed and financed by the extension bureau from Boston. Despite the unfavorable prospect that these dues would be received, the CUNA directors had also approved Bergengren's request to transfer the offices from Boston to Madison by September 1.[33]

Bergengren's strategy, therefore, was to rely upon the voluntary payment of dues and to take whatever amounts the state leagues were willing

[31] *Credit Union Forum*, I (Dec., 1935); also see John L. Kelly to Jerry K. Burns, Nov. 11, 1968.

[32] Bergengren, "Status of League Development as of March 25, 1935"; Bergengren, "Report of the Managing Director," May 19, 1935.

[33] Bergengren, "Status of Organization Program re National Association," May 31, 1935.

and able to contribute. By May 15, 1935, when one-half of the dues were required to be paid, twenty-one leagues had paid $8,540 of the $13,500 expected. Twelve other leagues had pledged to pay their dues, including Illinois which had already voted to do so. The four leagues paying the largest dues from a high of $1,480 to a low of $1,000, were Missouri, Minnesota, Massachusetts, and Wisconsin. The remainder of the leagues, with two exceptions, paid dues of less than $500.[34] Even though the directors voted at the first national board meeting that dues for the second half of the year might be waived if not needed, the executive committee at its September, 1935, meeting decided to collect the balance of league dues.[35] By that month the CUNA treasury contained almost $20,000, with over $9,000 still to come from the Twentieth Century Fund.[36] The decision to collect the remainder of the dues for 1935 would hopefully add an additional $13,500. In any event, Claude Clarke, the treasurer, reported that the 1935 budget would allow for a $10,000 surplus.[37]

Although Bergengren, as managing director of CUNA, was faced with a multitude of problems during the first year after the Estes Park meeting, he managed to close out the Credit Union National Extension Bureau in Boston and open up the headquarters of the Credit Union National Association in Madison, Wisconsin. On July 22, 1935, he notified all leagues of the "honorable conclusion" of CUNEB's work. Meanwhile, in May the executive committee of CUNA had met in Madison and approved a lease on what Bergengren called "an old mansion house" at 142 East Gilman Street. This building had three floors and a basement. Bergengren put the printing and supplies department in the basement, while he located the general offices on the first two floors. The upper story was used for storage. There were two extra rooms and a bath on the second floor, which were rented to Agnes Gartland and two other employees who moved from Boston. CUNA paid $2,500 a year rent for these quarters, which included the services of a caretaker.

Bergengren, his son Roy, and Tom Doig spent most of August converting this former student boardinghouse into suitable offices. The headquarters building was promptly dubbed Raiffeisen House. The

---

[34] Bergengren, "Present Status of Credit Union Movement—re Leagues and Dues," May 31, 1935.

[35] Minutes, Executive Committee, CUNA, Sept., 1935, p. 28.

[36] Bergengren, Managing Director's Quarterly Report to Executive Committee, Sept. 25, 1935.

[37] Minutes, Executive Committee, CUNA, Feb., 1936, pp. 79–80.

initial staff consisted of Bergengren as managing director; Doig, who was in charge of the Organization and Contact Department; Earl Rentfro, who headed the Loan Protection Insurance Department; Agnes Gartland, who was secretary to Bergengren and temporary head of the Printing and Supply Department; a shipping clerk and multilith operator, a bookkeeper, and two stenographers. With this staff of seven, some printing equipment and furniture moved from Boston and a small amount purchased in Madison, CUNA opened for business on September 1.

So, despite the difficulties of getting CUNA organized, Bergengren was able to get the association established and operating in its new home on schedule. During the little more than a year between the Estes Park meeting and the establishment of the CUNA office in Madison, he had worked skillfully and patiently among the conflicting groups. He had gotten credit union members to at least begin supporting their national association, but he refrained from insisting on immediate and full compliance with the bylaws when it came to dues payments. To have done so might have split the organization irrevocably. Bergengren showed a practical flexibility, and patiently negotiated the differences between such important state leagues as New York and Illinois and CUNA. By 1937, only the old Massachusetts league remained outside the national association.

Bergengren could look back with pride and satisfaction over the period since 1921 when, without much knowledge of credit unions or experience in organizational work, he had begun to build a national cooperative credit movement. When the Credit Union National Extension Bureau had been organized, only three states had effective credit union laws and there were only 199 credit unions in the entire United States. During the next fourteen years, thirty-eight states passed credit union laws, and Congress enacted a law for the District of Columbia, as well as a general federal credit union act. By 1935 there were 3,600 credit unions in the country, with approximately 750,000 members. The number of credit unions was increasing by about 100 per month, while membership was growing at the rate of 6,000 weekly. On the basis of this growth, Bergengren and other credit union enthusiasts believed that the best days for cooperative credit were still ahead.

CHAPTER X

Expanding Credit Unionism, 1935–37

THE ORGANIZATION OF CUNA, with its growing support from the nation's credit unions, opened up the way for the association to undertake additional services and activities which greatly promoted the movement. Among the most important of these services was the establishment of an insurance company which Bergengren described as marking "a new epoch in the history of the credit union movement . . . ." [1] Formation of the insurance company, however, created considerable strife and controversy. The difficulties centered around the question, to what extent should the national association be financed from insurance revenues? More important in the long run was the relationship of the insurance company to CUNA and to the credit union movement as a whole. If the insurance company established its own organization and developed millions of dollars in assets, there was a possibility that it would assume an independent existence outside the control of CUNA.

Bergengren had been interested in providing insurance for credit union members since the early 1920s, and by the time CUNA was organized, several state leagues, most notably Illinois and Missouri, had contracts with private insurance companies to insure the unpaid balances of loans. The national board of directors endorsed the principle of establishing an insurance company at its first meeting in January, 1935, and instructed the executive committee to work out the details. [2] Bergengren told Filene early in March that a CUNA-owned company could provide low-cost, nonprofit insurance for loan protection, and should eventually broaden its activities into a "truly mutual non-profit cooperative life insurance company, modeled on savings bank life insurance . . . ." As had been true in supplying credit, the credit unions could provide a cooperative insurance service that the private sector had neglected. This, Bergengren

[1] Bergengren, *Crusade*, p. 258.
[2] Minutes, CUNA Directors, Jan., 1935, p. 39.

said, would be another genuine service.[3] The executive committee finally decided to establish the CUNA Mutual Insurance Society. Bergengren had already arranged a $25,000 loan from Filene to provide the required capital.

Initially, CUNA Mutual handled only borrowers' protection insurance. The executive committee decided that insurance would be sold by the society directly to credit unions, but that no effort would be made to sell protection in those states where the leagues were presently deriving revenue from their own sales, unless, that is, the leagues requested it.[4] Filene proposed that the cost of borrowers' protection policies should be paid by the credit unions instead of the borrower. However, the executive committee voted to postpone a decision on this matter.

The board of directors of CUNA Mutual held its first meeting on May 20, 1935. Filene was elected president; Bergengren, vice-president and general manager; Doig, second vice-president; Rentfro, secretary; and Hyland, treasurer. Filling out the board were Clarke, Edward L. Shanney of Massachusetts, John L. Moore of California, Hubert M. Rhodes of North Carolina and Claude Orchard. With the addition of Hyland, this board was identical to the executive committee of CUNA.[5] Moreover, the close connection between the two organizations is further demonstrated by the fact that at first CUNA provided both offices and operating expenses for the society.

Incorporation of the CUNA Mutual Society under Wisconsin law was completed by September, 1935, and the firm began to write insurance. Earl Rentfro was named manager and he conducted the society's business in offices on the second floor of Raiffeisen House. The most serious problem facing the society during its early months was how to comply with the various state insurance laws. While in most cases insurance could be sold by mail, different procedures had to be followed from those required by Wisconsin. Another problem was how to assess the costs of the premiums. Nevertheless, Bergengren wrote Filene in September that these problems were being worked out and, when they were, "I am satisfied that the CUNA Mutual Society will develop very rapidly and that it will inevitably lead us into the broad fields of life insurance two or three years from now." Meanwhile, according to Bergengren, the very organization of CUNA Mutual had "caused the other companies writing loan

[3] Bergengren to Filene, Mar. 6, 1935.

[4] Minutes, CUNA Executive Committee, May, 1935, p. 13.

[5] CUNA Mutual Insurance Society, "Summary of Action at the First Meeting of the Board of Directors of the CUNA Mutual Society," May 20, 1935.

protection insurance to halve their rates, and we have already broken up the racket which the CUNA Mutual Society was organized to eliminate." [6]

The society grew rapidly from its modest beginnings. Rentfro reported in September that the society had written $193,000 worth of insurance covering 1,669 loans made by 205 credit unions.[7] In October the first claim arrived in Madison. Although it amounted to only $40, Bergengren did not know from what funds to pay it. (This revealed the officers' lack of knowledge and experience in managing the society.) Therefore, he hurried over to the insurance commissioner's office and asked if the claim could be paid from the $25,000 in the bank! When he was told that the society could not impair its capital, he borrowed an additional $10,000 for operating purposes.[8] By the end of 1936, 437 credit unions in thirty states were members of the society. A total of 23,000 loans were insured, with a total coverage of $2,425,000. The reserves of the society for payment of claims amounted to $11,000.[9]

As the society proved its success, there was the inevitable demand for broadening its services. The executive committee considered the matter of writing automobile insurance in August, 1936, but took no action. At the same meeting the question was raised as to whether the society should begin writing general life insurance. Both Rentfro and Bergengren thought it was too early to begin such a business. However, the directors decided to experiment with life insurance by providing coverage for officers and families of CUNA, CUNA Mutual, and for employees of state leagues.[10]

At the final meeting of CUNA's executive committee in 1937, Rentfro reported that the society's membership had grown from 825 member credit unions in January to 1,281 in September. On September 30, loan coverage had reached more than $18,000,000, and premium receipts were up from $7,000 in January to $13,000 nine months later. The assets of the society stood at $86,000. The unassigned surplus amounted to $5,400, which allowed a patronage dividend to participating credit unions of 6 percent. Many credit unions were now using a "constant

[6] Minutes, CUNA Mutual Society, Sept. 28, 1935, unpaged; Bergengren to Filene, Sept. 27, 1935.

[7] Minutes, CUNA Executive Committee, Sept., 1935, p. 26.

[8] Bergengren, *Crusade*, p. 260.

[9] Minutes, CUNA Directors, Feb. 10, 1936, p. 80; Minutes, CUNA Executive Committee, Aug., 1936, p. 69; Nov., 1936, p. 99.

[10] Minutes, CUNA Executive Committee, Aug., 1936, p. 92-93; Benjamin F. Hillebrand to Filene, July 28, 1936.

coverage" policy which automatically insured all loans. Even though an ordinary life insurance policy was now available to those who wished it, only thirty-seven members had purchased it. Rentfro concluded that such a policy did not appeal to credit union members and that if any popular plan were to be put into effect, "it must be done by a method never yet used." He therefore recommended that for the present the maximum amount of life insurance be reduced from $5,000 to $2,000, which was the limit for loan protection. One plan he suggested was for a policy that would cover both loans and share accounts of credit union members.[11]

With the increasing success of the society a problem arose in regard to the relationship between CUNA and its affiliates. Although the insurance commissioner of Wisconsin criticized the complete identification of the society with the national association, the executive committee wanted to control all of CUNA's credit union enterprises. Claude Clarke, attorney and director of CUNA Mutual, stressed the importance of checking the tendency of establishing affiliates "separate and apart" from the movement's general association. He therefore offered the following resolution, which the executive committee and directors of CUNA Mutual approved:

> Be it resolved that the CUNA Mutual Society, by reason of the condition and circumstances giving rise to its organization, is and at all times should be recognized as, an affiliate of the Credit Union National Association so far as conformable to law, and that it is not an independent insurance company for profit; that in this relationship, its central purpose and method of operation shall be such as are in accordance with and amenable to the central purpose and ideals of the Credit Union National Association and that its business shall be so conducted as to contribute to the sum total of the benefits which CUNA is seeking to make available for the well-being of credit unions and their members.[12]

However definite this resolution may have seemed, it did not solve the problem of CUNA Mutual control which continued to plague the movement for years.

Although the CUNA Mutual Society generated more enthusiasm and support among credit union leaders than other activities of the national association, at their first meeting the directors voted to establish a Department of Supplies. This department would supply credit unions with bookkeeping and promotional forms just as the old extension bureau's

[11] Earl Rentfro to CUNA Executive Committee, Nov. 9, 1937.
[12] Minutes, CUNA Executive Committee, April, 1937, p. 113.

League Central Committee had done. The executive committee incorporated the printing and supply business under Wisconsin's cooperative society law, with membership consisting of state leagues, CUNA, and CUNA Mutual. Subsequently, the name was changed to CUNA Supply Cooperative, and the new organization began business on July 1, 1936.[13]

The question of the relationship of CUNA Supply Cooperative to the national association, as well as to individual credit unions and to leagues, developed early. Credit union leaders recognized that they not only provided a needed service at lower costs, they also induced credit unions to affiliate with their state leagues because of the 20 percent discount offered to member credit unions. Although CUNA Supply sold its merchandise to unaffiliated credit unions, it used the discount to emphasize the advantages of affiliation.[14] Also the problem arose as to whether the cooperative would assume a life of its own or would always remain an instrument of the national association. As had been true of CUNA Mutual Society, Claude Clarke insisted that the executive committee or the directors should form the "controlling group" of CUNA Supply Cooperative. This would provide a kind of interlocking directorate. Clarke's recommendation was approved in 1936. The first board of directors of the cooperative were all from CUNA's management or board of directors, including Bert Beales, who became manager.[15]

A number of problems faced the new cooperative. There was the matter of setting the proper level of prices to meet competition, supplying the forms and equipment needed by credit union societies, and collecting accounts receivable. The supply cooperative met these problems as quickly and efficiently as possible. Within six months the cooperative's sales averaged $6,500 to $7,000 a month and it had reduced prices 10 percent. It also bought new equipment which permitted the specialized printing required by credit unions. The net worth of the business increased from $9,700 in September, 1935, to $29,800 in April, 1937. By the fall of 1937, the cooperative had a surplus of $30,000, after having paid patronage dividends of 4 percent to member leagues.[16]

[13] Minutes, CUNA Directors, Jan., 1935, p. 21; Minutes, CUNA Executive Committee, Sept., 1935, pp. 24–25; Feb., 1936, p. 42.

[14] Minutes, CUNA Executive Committee, Nov., 1936, p. 99.

[15] Minutes, CUNA Directors, Feb., 1936, pp. 92–93; "An Accounting by the Office Staff and Affiliates of CUNA," prepared for the Third Annual Meeting of CUNA, April 7–10, 1937, p. 11.

[16] Minutes, CUNA Executive Committee, Sept., 1935, p. 26; "An Accounting by the Office Staff and Affiliates of CUNA," p. 11; Report of CUNA Managing Director, Sept. 18, 1937, p. 3.

Bergengren had proposed at the first meeting of CUNA's directors that the executive committee be empowered to consider some form of central bonding service for credit unions.[17] Both state and federal credit union laws required the bonding of credit union treasurers and other officials who handled money. A major problem facing credit unions, however, was that bonding companies determined their rates on the basis of "actuarial" experience. Bergengren argued that credit union personnel had a far better record of honesty and faithful performance than those of other financial institutions, but this, he claimed, was ignored by the rating companies.[18] Therefore, he contracted with a bonding company to provide a master bond at CUNA headquarters, from which credit unions could apply for their own faithful-performance bonds. This service began in February, 1937, and by April some 400 credit union treasurers were bonded in the amount of $800,000. By September, over 800 credit unions were being served by the central bond, with total coverage of nearly $1.5 million. In addition, a central burglary policy was being written for 60 credit unions with coverage of about $45,000.[19]

One activity which elicited more enthusiasm than any other from Bergengren was the re-establishment of *The Bridge* as the official voice of the credit union movement. The magazine had been suspended in August, 1934, for lack of money. At their first meeting, however, CUNA's directors held a long discussion regarding *The Bridge*. No one questioned the desirability of supporting such a publication, but differences of opinion existed as to whether it should be a profit-making venture. Both Bergengren and Filene predicted that large profits could be expected from advertising revenue. In January, 1936, the magazine resumed publication and the executive committee decided that any profits should be distributed to state leagues as patronage dividends, after 10 percent had been set aside for CUNA for "handling charges." [20]

By November, 1936, almost 22,000 subscriptions had come in, and Bergengren reported that with 50,000 subscriptions the magazine could be published without advertising. He decided also that any state which had as many as 2,500 subscriptions would be entitled to submit copy for

[17] Minutes, CUNA Directors, Jan., 1935, p. 43.

[18] Bergengren, *Crusade*, pp. 262–63.

[19] "An Accounting by the Office Staff and Affiliates of CUNA," p. 11; Report of CUNA Managing Director, Sept. 18, 1937.

[20] Minutes, CUNA Directors, Jan., 1935, p. 40; Minutes, CUNA Executive Committee, Sept., 1935, p. 28.

a four-page insert that would deal exclusively with credit union activities in that state. The following spring circulation had reached 40,000, but the magazine still operated at a deficit.[21] In 1936, Bergengren had donated $5,000 of his own salary to meet publication expenses and expected to do the same during 1937, with the hope that the magazine could become self-sustaining in 1938.[22]

Despite *The Bridge*'s financial plight, Bergengren was determined to make it a national publication with mass circulation rather than a small house organ.[23] He wanted to publish a journal that "would eventually reach into millions of credit union homes and be interesting to all members of the credit union family, men, women, children of whatever ages." He assumed that credit union members and their families were "first of all, people, and interested in everything which interested people." Moreover, he told the leaders of the movement that, "we are trying to bind the whole credit union movement together, to inspire it, to promote the best possible operating practices, to have a magazine rather than a house organ, to make it interesting, inspirational and the real voice of the credit union movement in the United States." [24]

By late 1937 Bergengren declared that *The Bridge* had become the most "bothersome" problem of the movement, costing about $40,000 a year to publish, while subscriptions, at fifty cents per year, brought in only $20,000. Doig began to solicit subscriptions during his organizational trips and during the summer of 1937 the number of subscribers rose from 35,000 to 50,000, with 75 credit unions subscribing for their entire memberships.[25] However, no large advertising revenue could be expected until *The Bridge* had a minimum of 100,000 subscriptions. As *The Bridge*'s deficits mounted, Bergengren stubbornly retained his faith and hope that either the movement would subsidize the publication, or that circulation would reach the point where advertising would begin to provide sufficient revenue. Other credit union leaders did not share Bergengren's enthusiasm for a national magazine, particularly when it ran ever more deeply into debt. Moreover, his handling of *The Bridge* caused disenchantment with his general management among some credit unionists. Instead

[21] Minutes, CUNA Executive Committee, Nov., 1936, p. 100; "An Accounting by the Office Staff and Affiliates of CUNA," p. 9.

[22] Brown to Filene, Jan. 5, 1937.

[23] Minutes, CUNA Executive Committee, Aug., 1937, p. 123.

[24] Bergengren, *Crusade*, pp. 271–72; "An Accounting by the Office Staff and Affiliates of CUNA," p. 9.

[25] Report of CUNA Managing Director, Sept. 18, 1937.

of reducing the size, scope, and cost of the publication, however, Bergengren continued to present optimistic reports for the future, thereby damaging his credibility and leaving the problem unsolved.

Another useful service in which Filene was greatly interested and which was approved by the first board of directors was the establishment of a statistical department. Filene and other credit unionists had long been critical of Bergengren for spending so little time and effort gathering statistics about the movement. Filene continually insisted that no organization should operate "in the dark," not knowing exactly what was taking place or where current policies and practices were leading. However, it was many years before the national association employed highly trained personnel, including an economist, to engage in the type of research and record keeping, and to make prognostications about the future, which Filene believed so necessary.

Filene also was much concerned about a continuing and effective educational program. With the establishment of CUNA, he offered to help finance educational programs for credit union leaders, and the directors appointed a special committee, including Filene, to make the necessary plans. After almost three years, however, nothing had been done and Filene withdrew his offer of financial aid and resigned from the committee. Bergengren told Filene that he thought credit union education was of "first importance," but that too many other activities consumed the time and efforts of the staff. So important was this to Filene that he recommended setting up an education department in offices outside of Madison, where it would work independently of CUNA's management. Bergengren objected to this proposal, saying that it would violate the principles of the movement. Filene agreed to restore his pledge of financial support if an acceptable plan and budget were submitted, but Bergengren argued that it would be enough to sponsor a series of summer schools for credit union personnel.[26] But such schools were not then implemented.

However useful CUNA's centralized and auxiliary services may have been, the national association's primary responsibility was, as the bylaws stated, to "promote the organization of credit unions, under state and federal laws, both by direct effort and in cooperation with other agencies having a similar purpose." Accordingly, the board of directors, at its first meeting, created the Organization and Contact Department, with Doig as its head. Doig and his three field secretaries—Dora Maxwell,

[26] Bergengren to Percy Brown, May 26, 1937; Minutes, CUNA Executive Committee, Aug., 1937, p. 137; Nov., 1936, p. 99.

Hubert M. Rhodes, and Ralph C. Christie—along with Clifford O. Skorstad, who worked part-time, became the physical link between the national association and the credit unions and leagues throughout the country.[27] While Doig and his staff made the organization of individual credit unions one of their responsibilities, they also promoted CUNA Mutual insurance, collected national dues, and generally represented CUNA in the field.

But the Organization and Contact Department organized relatively few new credit unions. Most of this work was done by the Credit Union Division of the Farm Credit Administration, the agency charged with administering the federal credit union law. Even before Claude Orchard formally joined the Credit Union Section, and prior to the Estes Park meeting, he recommended that the FCA should "actively encourage the organization of Credit Unions, both State and Federal, the type of charter to be determined by the wish of the Credit Union itself, in the light of the cost of organization and of operation and the workability of the State Law involved." Thus, Orchard, like Bergengren, viewed the Credit Union Section of the FCA as an integral part of the general credit union movement, with the federal law to be used as an instrument to promote credit unions where no state law existed and where state laws were inferior to the national statute.[28]

When Orchard began work in Washington on August 20, 1934, his office consisted of one room, a few filing cabinets, and three employees. He immediately began to recruit field "investigators" to organize and supervise new credit unions. Orchard had met many of his new employees on organizational tours for Armour and Company. Among his most effective organizers were Henry Peterson, who had been active in farm cooperatives around Dodge City, Kansas; J. E. Blomgren, former treasurer of a credit union in a school supply company in Wisconsin; Howard Stamm, who had been a post office employee in Red Bank, New Jersey; Oppie King, who was treasurer of a credit union for Armour employees at St. Joseph, Missouri; and Herb Ingalls, who served as treasurer of a small American Legion post. At the beginning there was no civil service examination required for Credit Union Section employees; so Orchard established as a condition of employment prior experience in organizing at least six credit unions. While some of the new field men had already organized more credit unions than that as vol-

[27] Minutes, CUNA Directors, Jan., 1935, p. 22; advertisement in *The Bridge* (Sept., 1936), back cover.

[28] Orchard to Emmerich, July 27, 1934; Emmerich to Orchard, July 30, 1934.

unteers, others had to go out and organize their six before they could be employed. By late 1935, Orchard had nineteen men working in the field, organizing and supervising credit unions.[29]

Orchard's section organized its first credit union in Senator Morris Sheppard's home town of Texarkana, Texas. An attorney there suggested this as a way to honor the author of the federal credit union law. Accordingly, a federal charter was granted to the Morris Sheppard Texarkana Federal Credit Union on October 1, 1934.[30] The next month the first federal charter issued to a farmers' group went to the Duval (Florida) Farmers' Federal Credit Union. By the end of 1934, after only three months of operation, federal charters had been issued to seventy-eight credit unions in twenty-two states.[31]

During the last part of 1934 and throughout 1935, the federal section organized far more credit unions than those formed under state laws. By the end of 1935, 906 federal credit unions had been chartered by the FCA.[32] This record not only demonstrated the value of the federal law, but indicated what an energetic organizing staff could do. As Bergengren wrote Filene: "We did a pretty good trick for the credit union movement in the United States when we got Senate Bill 1639 enacted." At the same time Bergengren realized the dangers of relying too heavily on the federal government for organizational services. Although he predicted that the staff of the federal section would increase to forty or fifty field men, and that the number of credit unions would increase rapidly in the following months, he warned that if the political climate of the country became more conservative, Congress might "do away with all the agencies created by this Administration regardless of their merit." For this reason, he insisted upon developing a strong organization department within CUNA. [33]

There was also great concern on the part of many leaders that federally chartered credit unions might not integrate into the national movement. Filene warned Bergengren of this possibility early in 1935, and Bergengren assured him that every effort was being made to prevent any division between credit unions organized under state and federal law. He

[29] "Early Days of the Federal Credit Union Program," transcript of a tape-recorded conversation between Claude Orchard, J. E. Blomgren, W. E. Allen, and J. Dean Gannon, June, 1964, pp. 19–38.

[30] Sheppard to Orchard, Aug. 2, 1934; *Cooperative Savings with Federal Credit Unions,* I (Jan., 1935), 5.

[31] *Cooperative Saving with Federal Credit Unions,* I (Jan., 1935), 5.

[32] Bergengren, *Crusade,* p. 263.

[33] Bergengren to Filene, Mar. 30, 1935.

consistently urged state leaders to concentrate on bringing federal credit unions into their leagues. There were reports, however, that federal credit unions were reluctant to affiliate. In Pennsylvania, for example, where the state law was weak and inadequate, more federal credit unions were organized than in any other state, with over eighty in the Pittsburgh area alone. There, the credit unions banded into a local chapter and then refused to affiliate with the state league. Developments of this kind distressed league officials, and they searched for answers to the problem, but there was no way to force a credit union to affiliate with the state organization. Nevertheless by the late summer of 1936, Doig reported that the situation had greatly improved.[34]

The rapid advance of federal credit unions was not lost on President Roosevelt and New Dealers in Washington. Replying to an official of the Associated Retail Credit Men and Credit Bureau of St. Louis who suggested that the government guarantee loans at low interest rates through established lending agencies to "employed and honest persons" to liquidate debts, President Roosevelt pointed out that credit unions were "rapidly providing an orderly method for the liquidation of the small debts which honest families have accumulated while out of employment, as well as providing for emergency credit of the same character in normal times."[35] In mid-1936, Frederic C. Howe of the Consumers' Council informed Roosevelt that "no cooperative institution awakens the interest as does the credit union," and recommended that the government publicize the organization. Roosevelt immediately suggested to the secretary of the treasury that publicity be given credit unions, adding: "They are popular."[36]

The federal government soon had an opportunity to prove its friendship to the credit union movement. Early in 1936 a representative of the comptroller general's office was visiting Oakland, California, and in the federal building he noticed that one room was occupied by a credit union with a postal employee in charge. Although he would have found similar situations at most major post offices in the country, he reported his discovery to the comptroller who searched the federal statutes to see if federal facilities and employees could be legally used in this way. The comptroller notified James Farley, postmaster general, on April 29, 1936,

---

[34] Minutes, Executive Committee, Aug., 1936, pp. 64–66.

[35] A. J. Bruse to President Franklin D. Roosevelt, June 8, 1935; Roosevelt to Kruse, June 25, 1935, OF3035, Roosevelt Papers.

[36] Frederic C. Howe to Roosevelt, June 29, 1936, PPF3702, Roosevelt Papers; Roosevelt, Memorandum for the Secretary of the Treasury, July 2, 1936, OF3035, Roosevelt Papers.

that he could find no such authorization. Again in November the comptroller informed the Post Office Department that such use of federal buildings was illegal. At that point the postmaster general was forced to notify all post offices of this ruling, although he set no date for compliance.[37]

Almost immediately postal employees and other credit unionists sent a barrage of letters and telegrams to congressmen and administration officials. For example, the president of the St. Paul, Minnesota, post office employees' credit union wrote to Senator Ernest Lundeen that if the order were upheld, the credit union would be forced to find new quarters that would provide the security, perhaps even with armed guards, that banks possessed. Such a move, he said, would be both inconvenient and costly. He therefore asked the senator to request President Roosevelt to issue an executive order staying the ruling until postal credit unions could persuade Congress to enact legislation legalizing the traditional practice of providing space for credit unions consisting of federal employees. This request was endorsed by the attorney general of Minnesota in a letter sent directly to Roosevelt.[38] Upon hearing about the problem, Bergengren hurried to Washington to talk with Senator Sheppard and other friends of the movement.

In December, 1936, the National Legislative Council of Federal Employee Organizations urged the president to support legislation allowing space in federal buildings for credit union activities. Congressman Melvin J. Maas of Minnesota informed Roosevelt that he believed such legislation would be forthcoming.[39] Early in January, 1937, Senator Sheppard asked Roosevelt to solve the problem by issuing an executive order allowing the use of federal space. While Roosevelt did not favor Sheppard's proposal, he did set the date for compliance with the removal order on June 1, 1937, some five months hence. This delay gave Bergengren and Sheppard time to seek a legislative remedy.[40]

Roosevelt was sympathetic to the postal credit unions, telling Farley that he did not want "to throw out the Credit Unions." Farley told the president that in spite of the published deadline for compliance, the Post

[37] JMD [Jesse M. Donaldson], First Assistant Postmaster General, to Farley, Jan. 4, 1937, OF3035, Roosevelt Papers.

[38] G. A. Schulte to Senator Ernest Lundeen, Dec. 9, 1936; Attorney General (Minnesota) Harry H. Peterson to Roosevelt, Dec. 11, 1936, OF3035, Roosevelt Papers.

[39] National Legislative Council of Federal Employee Organizations to Roosevelt, Dec. 15, 1936; Congressman Melvin J. Maas to Roosevelt, Dec. 15, 1936, OF3035, Roosevelt Papers.

[40] Sheppard to Roosevelt, Jan. 5, 1937, OF3035, Roosevelt Papers; Bergengren, *Crusade*, p. 288.

Office Department would not enforce the ruling even then; "in other words," he said, "we will let it ride along until such time that we have an opportunity to adjust the situation, because as I understood from my conversation with you, you are in sympathy with the Credit Unions, and you want the Post Office Department to assist if we can possibly do so." [41] Meanwhile, Representative John S. Cochran of Missouri and Senator Sheppard introduced bills in Congress to allow rent-free space in federal buildings to credit unions made up of federal employees. The House bill passed on July 1, after a supporting speech from Representative John McCormick of Massachusetts, and the Senate acted the next day. With support from the FCA, the Treasury Department, and the Bureau of the Budget, Roosevelt signed the measure into law on July 9, 1937. [42]

Bergengren played a major part in getting the space bill enacted. He made no less than six trips to Washington and spent most of his time during the summer of 1937 working on the bill. Although the movement had other bills pending during the same period, he considered the space legislation of greatest importance. As he later said, "we are conservatively saving credit unions of Federal employees a quarter of a million dollars annually in estimated rentals—more than four and a half times our national budget." His work was even more important, he believed, because passage of the bill made federal credit unions "thoroughly conscious of the fact that they are a part of CUNA and that their real protection and cooperation will come rather from the National Association than from Washington." [43] Bergengren wanted to emphasize that there was no conflict in the movement between federal and state credit unions, and that the movement's guiding force was not in FCA headquarters in Washington but at Raiffeisen House in Madison.

Despite its early organizational success, the federal Credit Union Section's work in this field began to decline in 1936 for two reasons. In the first place, the Bureau of the Budget informed FCA officials that the federal credit union law did not justify or permit "cold canvassing." This meant that Credit Union Section field men had no authorization to go before groups and urge them to set up a credit union. For a government agency to encourage the organization of a financial concern over which that agency would later have the responsibility for supervision and ex-

---

[41] Roosevelt to Farley, Jan. 11, 1937; Farley to Roosevelt, Jan. 19, 1937, OF3035, Roosevelt Papers.

[42] Bergengren, *Crusade,* pp. 288–89; Croteau, "The Federal Credit Union System," p. 5.

[43] Report of CUNA Managing Director, Sept. 18, 1937, pp. 1–2; Bergengren to Percy Brown, telegram, July 3, 1937.

amination smacked of a conflict of interest. A second problem arose within FCA itself. The field representatives of the Credit Union Section had followed the practice, endorsed and encouraged by CUNA, of organizing credit unions under state rather than federal law where such action seemed most desirable. In 1936, the chief examiner of the FCA decided that since these state credit unions had been organized by employees of the FCA, they should be examined by his office. In conducting those examinations, he found that shortages existed in two of them. Believing that he should protect the FCA, the chief examiner recommended curtailing the organizational activities of the Credit Union Section, particularly as they related to the organization of state-chartered credit unions.

Rather quickly, therefore, Governor Myers of the FCA began limiting the activities of the Credit Union Section. Fieldmen were still able to assist groups to organize a credit union if they received a specific request, but otherwise they were limited to supervisory work. Orchard opposed these restrictions and concluded that most FCA officials were not really sympathetic to the credit union movement. According to Orchard, examiners were generally critical of credit union practices, while they did nothing to help credit unions correct their shortcomings.[44] Publicly, Bergengren continued to praise the administration of the federal law, but he privately resented the FCA's opposition to organizational work. This is not hard to understand because by the middle of 1937 approximately one-third of all credit unions in the country had federal charters.[45]

The decrease of organizational activity by federal representatives placed additional burdens on CUNA. Although the Organization and Contact Department had helped to organize a number of individual credit unions, it had emphasized the creation of strong state leagues which would assure support for the national association. Besides appropriating additional funds for organizational work, Bergengren relied on his earlier practices of staging contests with cash prizes to those credit unionists who organized the most credit unions.

Despite previously discouraging experiences, CUNA devoted considerable attention to organizing credit unions among farmers. This old interest of Bergengren's was renewed after so many rural banks failed during the early days of the depression. Clifford Skorstad, who was

---

[44] "Early Days of the Federal Credit Union Program," pp. 49–51.
[45] Bergengren to Brown, May 26, 1937.

primarily responsible for rural credit union development, became convinced that credit unions should make their services more appealing to farmers by providing some sort of withdrawal plan, but he opposed checking accounts. Doig also objected to combining credit union with banking functions.

On March 21, 1936, Bergengren met with farm leaders in Illinois to consider the problem of rural credit unions. One of the main problems which participants recognized was that farmers did not have regular incomes, and that credit unions lacked checking facilities. Rentfro suggested that CUNA concentrate on community-type credit unions in rural areas, but Filene objected because he believed that community credit unions extended membership to many persons not in sympathy with the plight of the small farmer and the wage earner. Throughout 1936 CUNA officials continued to search for ways to form and operate successful rural credit unions, but they experienced little success.

The entire rural credit union movement was brought into focus in November, 1936, when E. C. Johnson, a University of Minnesota economist, published an article, "Rural Cooperative Credit Unions" in the *Journal of Farm Economics*. Johnson observed that not over 5 percent of the approximately 5,100 credit unions in the United States were serving farmers. He saw three reasons why rural credit unions were not more widespread. First, credit unions, for the most part, made small personal loans, while farmers needed larger sums for production purposes. Secondly, most rural communities had banking and credit facilities which had been organized to meet farmer needs. In the third place, the credit union movement had expended less effort to organize in rural areas than in urban centers. Johnson conceded that credit unions would probably benefit "croppers or tenants with limited capital on small farms who have been dependent largely upon merchants and landlords for credit and have paid high rates of interest for borrowed capital," but he did not hold out much hope that traditional credit unions could solve the needs of the majority of farmers.[46]

In surveying twenty-five rural credit unions, most of which were located in the Middle West, Johnson found that eleven were serving members of farmers' cooperative marketing or purchasing associations, seven were organized among farmers in a single county, one was a parish credit union, and six were community credit unions. Membership ranged from 23 to 364, with an average of 111 members per association. Assets of

[46] E. C. Johnson, "Rural Cooperative Credit Unions," *Journal of Farm Economics,* XVIII (Nov., 1936).

most of these societies were small, and their loans averaged only $8,483 per credit union. Johnson revealed what many credit union leaders already knew—farmers faced different credit problems from those of urban wage earners who had regular incomes and who borrowed money for small personal purchases. Despite the meager achievements in forming rural credit unions, it was several years before Bergengren and other leaders abandoned their hopes and plans for a viable rural credit union movement.

If CUNA failed to establish credit unions among farmers, it could boast of remarkable success in urban areas. During the national association's first three years, or up to early 1938, the number of credit unions increased from 2,450 to 6,219.[47] As mentioned above, the Credit Union Section of the FCA was responsible for much of that increase. Moreover, federal organizers went into areas not previously canvassed. For example, the first credit union established on United States soil outside of the continental limits began operation in September, 1936. Organized by an FCA field man, the credit union served 550 public school teachers in Hilo, Hawaii. Only a year later, there were 50 credit unions in Hawaii, with over 9,000 members. [48]

Even more significant was the continued growth of the credit union movement in Canada, a development in which Bergengren had a great interest. Earlier he had been instrumental in organizing a credit union in Ontario, and had later aided in the Antigonish movement which secured the passage of a credit union law in Nova Scotia. In July, 1936, Bergengren attended a meeting of the Nova Scotia league, which adopted a resolution calling for some sort of affiliation with CUNA. The next month the executive committee voted to accept the Nova Scotia league as an "international associate member" which entitled the league to a fraternal delegate without a vote and exempting it from dues payments for one year.[49] The same year credit union laws were adopted in New Brunswick and on Prince Edward Island, and supporters began a movement to revive the languishing Ontario law.[50] By the end of the year 1937, there were 441 credit unions in Canada, with over 77,000 members, and both Manitoba and Saskatchewan had new laws. With the admis-

[47] "Relative Development of State and Federal Chartered Credit Unions, 1925–1950," reprint from *Monthly Labor Review* (Nov., 1951).

[48] *The Bridge* (Sept., 1936), p. 31; Bergengren, *Crusade*, p. 297.

[49] Minutes, CUNA Executive Committee, Aug., 1936, p. 63.

[50] Bergengren, *Crusade*, p. 276.

sion of the Nova Scotia league as a fraternal member of CUNA, the national association became international in scope.[51]

The experience of particular credit unions was becoming impressive. By March, 1936, Armour and Company employee credit unions contained over 22,000 members, had $1.25 million in assets, and had made loans up to that date of almost $7 million. There were twenty-four credit unions among Sears-Roebuck and Company employees, with 7,982 members, and those in the U.S. Steel Corporation's mills numbered almost 23,000 members. The Indiana Farm Bureau Federation had succeeded in organizing thirty-two credit unions with 23,000 members. A credit union served employees of the United States Senate, and Senator Morris Sheppard served as a member of its supervisory committee. Another credit union at the movie studios of Twentieth Century-Fox had over 1,000 members.[52] By the end of 1937 there was scarcely any aspect of American economic, social, or political life not touched in some way by the credit union movement.

While the number, assets, and loans of individual credit unions continued to grow during the first three years of CUNA's existence, the national association's major concern was persuading credit unions to affiliate with their state leagues. The Organization and Contact Department spent most of its time and effort organizing, strengthening, and securing national dues from state leagues. When the department did undertake individual organization, it was usually done in order to establish enough credit unions in a state so that a league could be formed.

Even after moving the national headquarters to Madison, Bergengren retained an office in Boston which he left in charge of Dora Maxwell. Her task was to build up the CUNA-affiliated Massachusetts league, to work for the loyalty of both the New York and New Jersey leagues, and to try to develop vigorous leadership in Pennsylvania. Early in February, 1936, Doig proposed that his department concentrate its work in states that were closest to having self-sustaining leagues, such as Wisconsin with 400 credit unions, Pennsylvania with 200, Ohio with 171, Texas with 140, Indiana with 125, and California with 125. Throughout the years of 1936 and 1937, leagues continued to be organized and to affiliate with CUNA. During the first year leagues from Connecticut, Florida, Idaho, and Maine were admitted as members, while the next year Hawaii, New Hampshire, West Virginia, North Dakota, and Montana were added.

[51] *Ibid.*, p. 297; "Canada Credit Union Statistics, 1920–1951," typescript in BMML.
[52] Bergengren, *Crusade*, p. 276.

The number of leagues affiliated with CUNA thus grew from thirty-five at the end of 1935 to forty-four by the close of 1937.[53]

The major problem facing state leagues was the lack of financial resources to employ a full-time managing director, open an office, and provide operational services to credit union members. In order to remedy this situation, CUNA's executive committee decided in 1936 to insist that all new state leagues institute annual dues schedules of one-half of one percent of their member credit unions' assets.[54] This amount would enable the league to become self-sustaining and provide the money required by the national association. At the time only eight affiliated leagues, plus the unaffiliated Massachusetts league, employed full-time managing directors and could be called self-sustaining. These were New York, Illinois, California, Minnesota, Ohio, Missouri, Indiana, Michigan, and Massachusetts. Bergengren urged a number of other states which had several hundred credit unions each to employ managing directors, but they did not do so.

The relationship between the national organization and the state leagues was much more congenial while the leagues remained relatively small and financially weak. In spite of the severe difficulties which CUNA experienced in its early days with the strong leagues in New York, Massachusetts, and Illinois, CUNA and its staff were looked upon as the experts and directors of the movement. Yet, CUNA officials were employees of the movement, which in effect meant of the state leagues. Moreover, since credit unions and their organizations operated under state or federal laws, it was difficult for CUNA to make policies that directed the methods and procedures of operation in each state. Even the national directors and the executive committee of CUNA generally could only recommend policies and procedures to individual credit unions and leagues. The Madison office had to depend on persuasion, not force.

Nevertheless, the board of directors attempted to set some uniform standards of good practice for all credit unions. It voted, for example, that no commissions for any services be paid to any credit union member or employee, and that all compensation be in the form of salary or wages. The directors later instructed the executive committee to make a study of salaries being paid to credit union treasurers, managing directors, and other personnel of leagues, and the employees of CUNA, then to work

[53] Minutes, CUNA Directors, Feb., 1936, p. 76, 84; Minutes, CUNA Executive Committee, Nov., 1936, p. 100; April, 1937, p. 114; Nov., 1937, p. 153.

[54] Minutes, CUNA Executive Committee, Aug., 1936, p. 66.

out a uniform salary schedule for the movement. Subsequently, the executive committee recommended that all clerical help in credit union leagues and CUNA receive a salary 10 percent above the average salaries in their vicinity for similar services. They also recommended that 40 percent of the gross income of a credit union be used for expenses, including dues, salaries, and insurance premiums. Maximum salaries were recommended for league managing directors of $5,000 in states with a population of more than 4 million down to $3,600 in states with less than 2 million. Maximum salaries for CUNA management were set at $10,000 for the managing director, $8,500 for the assistant managing director, $7,500 for a department head, and $5,000 for field secretaries.[55]

The board of directors also attempted to establish uniform practices in the payment of dividends. Doig suggested early in 1936 that the directors recommend to all credit unions that dividends be limited to 6 percent. He believed that it was bad for credit unions to concentrate on raising their dividends, and that there was greater danger of credit unions being taxed if they paid out excessive amounts. In 1936 the executive committee considered recommending that dividends be limited to 5 percent. When one director said that CUNA had no business advising credit unions on this matter, Doig retorted that the directors should at least have the courage to go on record for sound credit union practices. The directors finally voted to recommend that dividends should not exceed 6 percent, although it suggested a 5 percent maximum as being more suitable.[56]

Bergengren, his staff, and members of the board of directors realized that since affiliation by individual credit unions with state leagues, and the state leagues with CUNA, was entirely voluntary, constant education of credit union members and league officials about the value of a national association was necessary. One area in which CUNA alone acted for all credit unions in the country was the matter of getting federal legislation. Not only did CUNA continually seek to improve existing laws, it had to guard against unfavorable legislation. Passage of a law to allow credit unions of federal employees to use federal facilities rent free was a case in point.

Another goal which required legislative action was the creation of a central discount agency or central bank. Bergengren had long favored such an agency, and at its first meeting the CUNA directors passed a resolution directing the executive committee to prepare legislation per-

[55] Minutes, CUNA Directors, Feb., 1936, p. 93, 96; April, 1937, p. 113.
[56] Ibid., Feb., 1936, pp. 93–94.

mitting the organization of a central bank in each state for credit unions and their officers, and the establishment of a national central bank to serve the state agencies. State central banks were to serve as "clearing-houses" for credit unions with surplus funds to lend and those which needed to borrow additional money. The national central bank would serve the various state banks. In September, 1935, the executive committee appointed a committee to work with officials of the FCA to prepare a bill for introduction during the Seventy-fourth Congress. This measure would provide for organizing central banks in each state to serve federal credit unions, but with a provision that state-chartered credit unions were eligible for membership. Then there was to be a federally controlled central agency for all of the state banks.[57]

The FCA had earlier received a request from President Roosevelt to investigate the desirability of such agencies. After surveying 1,080 credit unions, the FCA found that, while 317 of them had postponed action on loan applications because money was not available, only 106 loan applications had been rejected outright for the same reason. Moreover, 182 credit unions reported they had borrowed $453,500 during 1934, with over 91 percent coming fully or partially from commercial banks. Only 14 credit unions reported they had attempted to borrow and had been refused. The FCA concluded that there was no real need for legislation allowing central banks to serve credit unions, although 867 societies had indicated that they favored making it possible for credit unions with surpluses to make loans to other credit unions.[58] Nevertheless, the FCA had no objection to CUNA seeking legislation for state and central banks. Senator Sheppard introduced two bills in 1936, one allowing the organization of central credit unions and the other permitting federal credit unions to lend money to other credit unions up to 25 percent of their capital and surplus. The Senate passed the investment bill, but the House of Representatives took no action. During the next session of Congress, however, Sheppard's bill allowing federal credit unions to lend money to other credit unions passed, with a new amendment allowing those credit unions also to invest in federally chartered savings and loan associations.[59] Establishment of central credit unions remained an unsettled question.

[57] *Ibid.*, Jan., 1935, pp. 23–24; Minutes, CUNA Executive Committee, Jan., 1935, p. 5; Sept., 1935, p. 19.

[58] Myers to Roosevelt, July 2, 1935, OF3035, Roosevelt Papers.

[59] Minutes, CUNA Executive Committee, May, 1936, p. 56; Croteau, "The Federal Credit Union System," pp. 2–5.

Taxation of credit unions was a matter of supreme importance to the credit union movement. Bergengren had stoutly resisted attempts by state legislatures to impose what he considered "prohibitory" or "confiscatory" taxes on cooperative credit institutions. Sometimes he had succeeded and at times he had failed. In any event, credit unionists argued that their societies were cooperative institutions, and, like other cooperatives, should not be taxed like profit-making corporations. Their main claim was that cooperative credit unions made no profits, but returned their savings or earnings to the shareholders who in turn paid personal income taxes on the dividends.[60] While taking this stand publicly, Bergengren told CUNA's executive committee that he doubted if credit unions could escape all taxation, particularly when some societies paid high dividends. Filene remained firm in opposing all attempts by state or federal governments to tax credit unions, and Orchard agreed with him.

The original federal law did not include exemption of credit unions from federal taxation. Indeed, states were free to tax federal credit unions up to the maximum rates levied on similar banking institutions. Since federal credit unions were prohibited from accepting deposits, they had a very high percentage of share capital in relation to total assets. States commonly taxed banking institutions on the basis of share capital, thus placing a "discriminatory" burden on credit unions. In 1936, Senator Sheppard introduced a bill to prohibit all federal, state, and local taxation of federal credit unions which was not based on real or tangible personal property. That bill, however, died in committee.[61] During the next session of Congress, Sheppard reintroduced his bill; passing both houses, it was signed by President Roosevelt on December 6, 1937. Federal credit unions were now exempt from taxation except on real and tangible property. The new law permitted the taxing of members upon shares held in any federal credit union, but limited the tax to the rate imposed upon holdings in similar cooperative organizations. This law was a major accomplishment for the movement, and CUNA's Hubert Rhodes played a major part in its enactment.[62]

Also in 1937 Senator Sheppard introduced a bill which reduced the examination fees for small credit unions. The federal credit union law permitted the governor of the Farm Credit Administration to establish a

---

[60] CUNA International, Washington Office, "The Credit Union Tax Exemption, A Legislative History," Aug., 1965, p. 3.

[61] *Ibid.*, pp. 1–2.

[62] *Ibid.*; Sheppard to Roosevelt, Dec. 2, 1937, OF3035, Roosevelt Papers.

scale of fees to cover the expense of conducting the examinations. Leaders of the movement argued that such fees were prohibitory when applied to newly organized credit unions and those with small assets. Sheppard's bill, amending the original act, provided that the fee schedule should take into account the ability of the credit union to pay. Thus, larger credit unions were expected to provide the actual cost of an examination, while smaller credit unions would pay less. In effect, the bill allowed an indirect federal subsidy to new and small credit unions. It became law on December 6.[63]

In numerous ways then, CUNA proved to be a valuable asset to the movement. And such successes as those in Congress were necessary in order to convince credit unions and their state leagues of the national association's value. Support by the state leagues meant payment of adequate dues to finance CUNA. But the question of dues prompted long, lively discussion at each annual meeting of the board of directors. Very often that controversy divided the directors into warring camps, with representatives of the larger, older leagues on one side, and spokesmen of the smaller, newer leagues on the other. Discussion of dues schedules often provoked discussion of the proper role of CUNA, as opposed to the functions of individual credit unions and their state leagues. Questions such as "Should CUNA be engaged in certain costly activities?" or "Has the CUNA staff spent its resources wisely?" were often asked during these debates.

As explained earlier, the dues issue, along with other matters, caused a serious split in CUNA during its early existence. By 1937 CUNA adopted a budget of $72,975. Of this amount, the directors anticipated $53,475 from dues, $15,000 from the Twentieth Century Fund subsidy, and the balance from surplus and rental income. Although some directors urged that dues be fixed at five cents per member, the ten-cent figure was retained. Also they continued the $5,000 maximum due from any state.[64]

Despite some controversy over dues, there was a general spirit of harmony in the national association during its early years. When Filene told the directors in 1936 that he would not be a candidate for re-election as president of CUNA, the directors immediately elected Claude Clarke of Ohio by acclamation. For district vice-presidents to serve on the executive committee, Rhodes, Shanney, and Moore were re-elected, while

[63] Croteau, "The Federal Credit Union System," pp. 4–5; Sheppard to Roosevelt, Dec. 2, 1937, OF3035, Roosevelt Papers.

[64] Minutes, CUNA Directors, April, 1937, p. 125–28.

Pressley D. Holmes replaced Orchard, who no longer lived in the north central district. Hyland was re-elected treasurer and Doig, secretary, although he resigned so that Orchard could be given an official post and remain on the executive committee. Within four months, however, Orchard resigned as secretary, and was replaced by Doig, because CUNA was seeking federal legislation and FCA regulations prohibited its employees from engaging in lobbying. The directors re-elected Clarke president in 1937, although they adopted a two-year limitation for that office at the same time. The vice-presidents remained the same, with the exception of Garfield Seibert of Kentucky, who replaced Rhodes. Once again Doig left the office of secretary and was replaced by Joseph DeRamus of Illinois.[65] Whatever differences may have existed, unity prevailed in the election of officers.

However, conflicts developed early among the CUNA staff, mainly between Bergengren and his chief assistant, Tom Doig. Bergengren was re-elected managing director without difficulty each year, although he regularly went through the ceremony of offering his resignation. Bergengren retained the confidence of most of the directors, and complaints against his administration did not extend much beyond the deficits being incurred by *The Bridge*. By 1937, however, there were strong indications that Doig, supported by Charles Hyland, was becoming restive under Bergengren's firm authority in managing the CUNA office.

When the executive committee met in April, 1937, Hyland proposed that a definite amount of money be set aside for the Organization and Contact Department, that Doig be allowed to spend it as he saw fit, and that Doig should approve all expenses charged to his department's account. Hyland's proposal stemmed from Bergengren's practice of charging his own and others' travel to Doig's department. Bergengren opposed Hyland's motion and the other directors supported him. Doig then proposed that his department be abolished, but again Bergengren objected, saying that he intended to recommend that Doig be made assistant managing director. The executive committee did agree to a separate budget for the department and ordered that accounts be kept in such a way that the committee would know if any money were spent that had not been approved by Doig. The executive committee also named Doig assistant managing director. But this did not end the controversy between Bergengren and Doig. A few months later Doig complained that his de-

[65] *Ibid.*, Feb., 1936, pp. 77, 80, 88; Minutes, CUNA Executive Committee, May, 1936, p. 46; Minutes, CUNA Directors, April, 1937, pp. 117, 121.

partment had overspent its travel budget by $700, because Bergengren had charged his own travel to that account.[66]

By November, 1937, Bergengren was complaining about Doig to the executive committee. He warned that the Organization and Contact Department, like CUNA Mutual and CUNA Supply, must remain under the control of the managing director or it would become a "menace" to the movement. There was, he said, a lack of "relationship between the department and the National Association," and unless a firm and defined relationship were quickly established, two managing directors might develop. Doig retorted that he had not asked to head the department, and "didn't care if he remained there." Moreover, he said that final authority rested with Bergengren so there was no reason to argue about the matter. It had become clear, however, that a major source of the difference between Bergengren and Doig centered around the managing director's proposal to hire field representatives to work with state leagues, but keeping them independent of Doig's department. Bergengren urged the executive committee to define the scope of activities for the Organization and Contact Department but the committee took no action. Consequently, the difficulties between Bergengren and Doig continued to fester.[67]

Filene was aware of the personnel problems, as he continued his close association with the credit union movement after his year as president of CUNA. At the same time, however, he became increasingly interested in other projects. One of these was the creation of a chain of cooperative department stores throughout the United States. He believed that credit unions could play a vital part in the plan for cooperative stores if their members formed local cooperative groups and purchased the shares to provide the necessary capital. But neither CUNA nor individual credit union leaders showed any enthusiasm for joining Filene in the Consumer Distribution Corporation movement. When Filene wrote B. F. Hillebrandt in the summer of 1936 about starting a cooperative store in Kansas City or Minneapolis, Hillebrandt replied that while he favored the principle, it was probably unwise for credit unions to associate themselves officially with cooperative stores. In November, 1936, Bergengren devoted an article in *The Bridge* to the question. He wrote that he had been asked recently if there was any effort, direct or indirect, on the part of CUNA or any league, to promote or finance cooperative stores, factories, light, oil, power, or telephone companies. "The unqualified answer," he said, "is 'NO!' " Although he had worked closely with Filene on the co-

---

[66] Minutes, CUNA Executive Committee, April, 1937, p. 110; Aug., 1937, p. 124.

[67] *Ibid.*, Nov., 1937, pp. 156–57.

operative stores project, Bergengren said that credit unions were "sticking strictly to their job." [68] Consequently, Filene's plan for cooperation between credit unions and cooperative stores came to nothing.

Another favorite scheme advanced by Filene called for a program of "socialized medicine." Early in 1936 Bergengren told the CUNA directors that the Twentieth Century Fund had a department for furthering group medicine and it seemed that credit unions were the logical groups to form the nucleus for instituting health care plans on a cooperative level. Filene argued that it was important for credit unions to become involved in this project because such a large percentage of credit union loans went for medical care of members. The directors charged the executive committee to cooperate with the fund. The next year, after hearing a report on a group medical plan used by the Standard Oil Company (N.J.) in Louisiana, the executive committee passed a resolution in favor of group medicine, and appointed a committee to develop some concrete proposal. Soon afterward, Filene gave $5,000 to CUNA so that it could demonstrate in a practical way how a group medical plan could work.[69] Again, however, nothing was done.

Filene was constantly thinking of ways and working on plans which he believed would help the average man and strengthen the American economic and political system. He had become so much a part of the credit union movement that the announcement of his death in September, 1937, was a severe shock to his many friends and acquaintances. In July he had sailed for Europe on the S.S. *Normandie*, but he soon became ill and died at the American Hospital in Paris on September 26 at the age of seventy-seven. In compliance with his wishes, his ashes were scattered on the Charles River in Boston.[70]

Messages of condolence poured into Filene's Boston home, not only from businessmen and industrialists, but from such leaders as John L. Lewis and Norman Thomas. President Franklin D. Roosevelt wrote:

It is not individual persons but the people as a whole who were closest to the heart of this unique personality. Mr. Filene was, however, more than a champion of popular rights. He was a prophet who perceived the true meaning of these changing times. He was an analyst who was able, by mathematical calculation, to make plain to us that our modern mechanism of abundance cannot be kept in operation

[68] *The Bridge* (Nov., 1936), p. 30.

[69] Minutes, CUNA Directors, Feb., 1936, pp. 78–79; Minutes, CUNA Executive Committee, April, 1937, p. 117, and Aug., 1937, p. 131.

[70] Bergengren, *Crusade*, p. 298; Filene to Bergengren, July 17, 1937.

unless the masses of our people are enabled to live abundantly. His democracy was, therefore, more than a tradition. His liberalism was more than a formula. His faith was more than a mere assent to principles which have proved to be tried and true. He did not repudiate the past, after the fashion of some reformers, nor did he repudiate the future after the fashion of those who fear reform. He believed in learning and searching out the ways of human progress.[71]

Bergengren was "completely surprised and profoundly shocked" by the news of Filene's death. But, he knew that Filene would not appreciate any of his friends wasting much time in personal grief. As Bergengren wrote, Filene would say impatiently: "Bergengren, there is a lot of credit union work to be done today—don't mope." Bergengren held a deep affection for Filene despite the fact that, as he wrote Percy Brown, "Mr. Filene seemed to take a delight in making our lives utterly miserable almost every time we came in personal contact with him . . . ." While Bergengren would miss Filene, he was determined to use his death to advance the credit union movement: "I feel that he will become the great tradition in the credit union movement and that now that his life is concluded, his influence uniting a credit union family may be even more profoundly useful than was his immediate participation in our affairs." [72]

In line with this thinking, Bergengren decided to hold a series of memorial credit union meetings around the country. Between October 16 and December 20, some thirty-one gatherings were held all the way from Washington, D.C., to Los Angeles. The theme was the same everywhere. As Bergengren told credit unionists, Filene had left them an "extraordinary legacy," and they had "the privilege of carrying the credit union work forward and accomplishing with it all of those extraordinary objectives which Mr. Filene so anticipated. He becomes our priceless tradition." [73] This attempt by Bergengren to capitalize on Filene's death brought criticism from Lillian Schoedler, one of Filene's close aides. She resented Bergengren's emphasis upon Filene's credit union work and the neglect of his other accomplishments. The memorial meetings, she wrote, were "a little premature, and if I may speak frankly, perhaps selfish and inconsiderate and ill-advised on the part of the Credit Unions, if they had Mr. Filene's best interests at heart, to capitalize for *themselves alone* on something which could equally well be used, and better

[71] Bergengren, *Crusade*, pp. 301–2.

[72] Bergengren to Brown, Sept. 27, 1937.

[73] Bergengren to All National Directors, Managing Directors, and State League Presidents, Sept. 29, 1937. For account of the Filene memorial meetings see Bergengren, *Crusade*, pp. 302–4.

be used, to advance and promote *all* of Mr. Filene's ideals and work instead of just their little corner of it." [74] When a member of the executive committee proposed changing the name of CUNA headquarters in Madison from Raiffeisen House to Filene House, Bergengren objected, saying that, "although Mr. Filene had done much for the credit union movement, it did not compare with the work of Mr. Raiffeisen." Nevertheless, as Bergengren wrote later, "after Filene's death nothing was quite the same." [75]

In many ways Filene had been the "heart" of the credit union movement. He provided inspiration, guidance and, most important, the necessary financial support. Yet, as Bergengren later wrote: "Filene never, to my knowledge, organized a credit union. No laws can be traced to his authorship. The mechanics of the leagues and the National Association concerned him only in a broad way. He equipped and financed the Crusade. Without the war chest, our battle could not have been won. Much more than that, he rode at the head of the Crusade, on a snow-white charger, cheering us on to follow his lead to the great glory which he could see quite beyond the sight of ordinary mortals." [76]

This sentimental assessment belied some of the struggles between the two men, although from the beginning of their association the quarrels and differences had almost always been over means and not ends. Filene played a decreasing role in the affairs of the movement after the organization of CUNA, but during the year of his presidency, he participated actively in the work of the movement and refused to consider himself a figurehead or "honorary" president. Because of growing ill health, however, he often missed meetings of the executive committee after the middle of 1936.

Although Filene had lived a long and fruitful life, he had experienced many frustrations and failures. His plans for turning his department store into an employee-owned business, the work of the Twentieth Century Fund, the attempt to set up cooperative department stores, and even the credit union movement had either failed or had not met his expectations. Shortly before his death, he wrote that any biography written about him should be entitled "The Life of an Unsuccessful Millionaire." But this was self-denigration, not an objective self-evaluation.

Whatever his other achievements, Filene considered the development of the credit union movement as his greatest accomplishment. He viewed

---

[74] Schoedler to Bergengren, Nov. 8, 1937.
[75] Minutes, CUNA Executive Committee, Nov., 1937, p. 162; Bergengren, *Crusade*, p. 299.
[76] Bergengren, *Crusade*, p. 299.

credit unions as agencies to protect and strengthen American democracy. The most "basic and valuable projects for the prevention of the business, economic and social evils that threaten our democracy," he wrote, "are Credit Unions and Consumer Cooperatives." Then he added: "Into this work I have put most of my thought and time. These projects, I feel, are so basically important that if I had life to start over again, I would again devote most of my thinking and work for the common good to forwarding and promoting them . . . ." Credit unions, he said, "are the schools for the masses so that they may be educated to establish financial democracy for themselves and free their jobs and themselves from the absolute control of those who have need and are using money solely for their own profit, without the requisite understanding that they have no right to use money except for the common good and social interest of all the people, and that the wholly selfish use of it will bring with it radical movements, revolution and war . . . ." Filene, then, saw the credit union movement as one of the nation's institutions which would contribute to political stability by meeting the needs of the masses. He was so convinced of credit unions' economic and social worth that he urged his executors and trustees to use most of his fortune to promote them and consumer cooperatives.[77]

During his last days, Filene expressed deep concern over the place which he would eventually hold in the history of the credit union movement. He sometimes chided Bergengren for the way the managing director presented him in credit union literature. He also engaged in a lengthy controversy with Felix Vorenberg about their relative roles in founding credit unionism in the United States.[78] Whatever his position in history, even before his death Filene was considered the "founder" and "father" of the movement. His picture hung on the office walls of many credit unions. He was the subject of constant tributes, and audiences listened raptly to his discussions of ways and means to achieve economic democracy in America.

Filene was not so much the founder of credit unionism in the United States as he was its supporter and sustainer. More than any other man, he brought the movement to the place where it could be self-sufficient. His death, then, ended one era, while the memory of his life and work provided the strength and inspiration for those who continued to work for his principles and ideals.

---

[77] Edward A. Filene, "Dictation by Edward A. Filene Concerning His Work and Objectives," New York, May 19, 1937, typescript.

[78] Lillian Schoedler to Filene, Mar. 28, 1937. Filene's comment written in margin of *ibid.*

CHAPTER XI

The Search for Stability and Progress, 1937–41

DURING FILENE'S LIFETIME, most credit unionists looked upon CUNA and the organized movement as his creation, and, since Bergengren was viewed as Filene's agent, the managing director's power was seldom questioned. But between Filene's death and American entry into World War II, CUNA went through a series of "growing pains." New leaders emerged who often challenged Bergengren's position and decisions, and controversies arose over basic policies and their administration. An especially difficult matter was that of keeping the CUNA Mutual Insurance Society under the direction and control of the national association. The administrative confusion and serious internal conflicts indicated that the once tightly knit and relatively simple movement had become complicated and diffuse, and that new methods had to be found to promote continued growth and to administer the whole structure.

One of Bergengren's difficulties stemmed from his management of *The Bridge*. Not only was the magazine operating at a large deficit, but some directors attacked Bergengren for nepotism when he hired his son Roy as "managing editor." [1] By the spring of 1938, *The Bridge*, in spite of a circulation of 114,000, was about $30,000 in debt. In April, Charles Hyland proposed that an advisory committee be appointed to determine the policies and content of the magazine. Bergengren objected to such a move and argued that what was really needed was sufficient money to publish an outstanding journal. He refused to apologize for the publication and appealed to the directors to have faith in him. If they gave him support Bergengren promised to make *The Bridge* into the movement's greatest asset. [2] But six months later the financial situation had worsened

[1] Minutes, CUNA Executive Committee, April, 1938, p. 170; Nov., 1938, p. 260; interview with Roy F. Bergengren, Jr., Madison, Wis.

[2] Minutes, CUNA Executive Committee, April, 1938, p. 177; Minutes, CUNA Directors, pp. 196–97.

to the point where *The Bridge's* deficit had risen to $45,000 and the executive committee at its meeting in November removed Bergengren as editor and replaced him with Joseph DeRamus, the managing director of the Illinois league.[3]

His removal as editor of *The Bridge* deeply distressed Bergengren. He had founded the magazine and it had become his major interest. He blamed CUNA's president, P. D. Holmes, and Doig for the executive committee's action. Bergengren feared that *The Bridge* would be turned into a "typical house organ" rather than continue as a spokesman for the broader cooperative movement. He believed that such a possibility was a serious mistake.[4]

Another internal difficulty was the continued strained relationship between Bergengren and Doig. Their controversies were often played out in executive committee meetings. As head of the Organization and Contact Department, Doig was in a similar position to Bergengren during the 1920s in that he was the most "visible" representative of credit unionism. His work took him into virtually every state, and as the movement grew and new leaders emerged, Doig came to know them well, whereas Bergengren's contacts in the field were more casual and impersonal. Doig also supervised the largest number of CUNA employees and controlled the biggest segment of the budget. Given these conditions, it was natural for Doig to want greater freedom from Bergengren's control so that he could make the necessary decisions and take actions which he thought were in the best interest of credit union expansion. Moreover, there was a degree of personal rivalry between the two men. Bergengren, in many ways, represented the pioneering stages of the movement, while Doig was the young, vigorous representative of the more recent developments. Bergengren had brought Doig into the movement and taught him the basic principles of credit union organization, but Doig was no longer a student who paid homage to his mentor.

During 1938, Bergengren and Doig quarreled when Doig announced that he expected to have charge of hiring all personnel in his department. Bergengren quickly reminded Doig that the bylaws gave that responsibility to the managing director. Later in the year Bergengren criticized Doig for making his departmental reports directly to the executive committee rather than channeling them through his office. Doig retorted that he did not object to this procedure, providing the managing director sub-

---

[3] Minutes, CUNA Executive Committee, Aug., 1938, pp. 195–96; Nov., 1938, pp. 47–84.

[4] Bergengren to James W. Brown, Nov. 21, 1938; Bergengren to the Credit Union Leadership, Dec. 15, 1938.

mitted the reports without alteration. Bergengren also complained that Doig did not keep him informed on the activities of the Organization and Contact Department.

At the meeting of the executive committee in November, 1938, Doig declared that if the committee did not approve the way he was handling his department, it should remove him. He reminded the committee that field work had become CUNA's main activity, and, since the editorship of *The Bridge* had been taken from Bergengren, the managing director had little to do besides meddle in Doig's department. While Bergengren attempted to be conciliatory, Doig insisted that if he were not given full authority over his department, he would resign.[5] At this point Percy Brown stepped into the quarrel. Saying that both men "have been highly regarded by the Credit Union Movement for recognized conspicuous contribution," Brown appealed to the executive committee not to air the differences between Bergengren and Doig because it would lead to breaches that could never be healed. Brown expressed the hope that neither Bergengren nor Doig would become so emotional that they would issue threats or ultimatums. This counsel temporarily quieted the controversy, but the basic differences were as great as ever.

A further source of growing dissatisfaction with Bergengren was his independent course in handling the financial affairs of CUNA. Earlier Doig had charged Bergengren with disregarding proper budgetary practices. Then, in April, 1938, Bergengren persuaded the board of directors to designate 1938 as Filene Year and to use the occasion to raise money to build a Filene Memorial Building to house the offices of the association. Four months later he reported to the executive committee that he had taken an option for CUNA on some property in Madison on which to construct such a building, plus additional land across the street adjacent to Lake Mendota. Both President Holmes and William Pratt, a vice-president from Pennsylvania, objected to Bergengren's action and insisted that it should not be repeated. Bergengren's unauthorized expenditure prompted the executive committee to limit his authority to sign checks. Bergengren strongly objected, saying that such action implied dishonesty on his part and was "a personal insult." Nevertheless, Doig's name was added to that of Bergengren as being authorized to countersign checks issued by the treasurer.[6]

Percy Brown concluded that CUNA was violating a number of sound

---

[5] Minutes, CUNA Executive Committee, April, 1938, pp. 167–68; Nov., 1938, pp. 216–30.

[6] Minutes, CUNA Directors, April, 1938, pp. 193–94; Minutes, CUNA Executive Committee, Aug., 1938, p. 211, 219, 35–36.

business practices and procedures. He believed that all personnel should report to the executive committee through the managing director, but he objected to the comptroller and the treasurer being the same person. Finally, Brown suggested that a special committee be appointed to study the organizational structure of CUNA and make recommendations for its reform. The executive committee had decided to appoint a special budget committee to prepare the 1939 budget in advance of the next annual meeting; so it instructed that committee to carry out Brown's suggestions.[7]

Bergengren informed Brown that he would do his best to iron out all difficulties before the board meeting in May, 1939. Yet, he said, "certain very well defined differences of thinking" were developing. This was particularly true in regard to ideas expressed in *The Bridge* which he identified with Joseph DeRamus. "We shall have to decide," he wrote, "whether the thinking DeRamus gave voice to—that the credit union is nothing but a personnel activity in industry and that we must be governed by the thinking of industrialism—or my growing conviction that the credit union is part of the cooperative movement . . . is to prevail. In the end we must stand with cooperation." In regard to operating procedures, Bergengren admitted that he had operated in a loose and free-wheeling fashion and that he would change his ways. He attributed his rather careless administrative practices to habits developed when Filene was alive and when he "always spent his [Filene's] money as though I were spending my own." Bergengren recognized, however, that "we are now operating the National Association as a real democracy," but "as the hired man of the democracy, I find it difficult to make some of the necessary adjustments."[8]

A majority of the executive committee, however, believed that Bergengren could not make those "readjustments" quickly enough or was unable to make them at all. When the special budget committee met in Chicago on January 8, 1939, several directors began a move which they hoped would lead to replacing Bergengren as general manager. The growing differences between Bergengren and the executive committee received a full airing. Indeed, the pressure against the managing director became so strong that, in order to avoid a cleavage in the movement, Bergengren said he was willing to resign. He mentioned the possibility of going to Canada to organize provincial leagues. But if he did leave CUNA, he wanted the title "managing director emeritus." After further

[7] Minutes, CUNA Executive Committee, Nov., 1938, pp. 174–75, 179.
[8] Bergengren to Brown, Nov. 27, 1938; Bergengren to Parke S. Hyde, Jan. 5, 1939.

discussion and an attack on Bergengren by DeRamus, the budget committee voted unanimously to urge the full executive committee to recommend to the board of directors that Bergengren be made managing director emeritus and assigned to credit union work in Canada.[9]

But Bergengren was not serious about resigning. He was playing for time. He knew that if he could present his case to the full board of directors at its May meeting only three months away, he could win any fight against the unfriendly executive committee. When the executive committee met in February, 1939, he made it clear that he did not intend to resign and that he had suggested this course the month before out of "desperation." Bergengren insisted that many of the allegations against him and his administration of CUNA were untrue, and that the entire controversy should be settled by the full board of directors.[10]

Faced with Bergengren's determination to stay on, the executive committee tried another approach. It recommended an amendment to the bylaws giving the committee full power to employ and to discharge the managing director. Bergengren heatedly objected to such a move, claiming that this would simply "make another employee out of him . . . . If you do not like him, get rid of him, and get a managing director who will do what you want him to do." When Hillebrandt proposed that they designate Bergengren as managing director emeritus, Bergengren exploded: "You have no managing director emeritus, and as far as I am concerned you will not get one." Harold Moses admitted, however, that unless Bergengren were provided for, the bylaw amendment could not be passed at the directors' meeting. Only J. C. Howell allied himself with Bergengren, calling the proposals "in mighty poor taste," and warning the committee that it had better wait until it saw what the directors did "before you provide flowers for the funeral." Nevertheless, the executive committee voted, with the exception of Howell, to present the amendments to the directors.[11]

The proposed amendments to the bylaws were drawn up by a special committee. When they were sent to Bergengren so that his office could print and distribute them in preparation for the board meeting, he told his friend Parke Hyde that the executive committee had "practically constituted itself into a Constitutional Convention" to relegate him to

---

[9] Minutes, CUNA Special Budget Committee, Jan. 8, 1939, unpaged; Percy S. Brown, "Analysis of Organization Problems of Credit Union National Association" (Report for Executive Committee of CUNA, Feb. 6, 1939).

[10] Minutes, CUNA Executive Committee, Feb., 1939, pp. 152–55.

[11] *Ibid.*, pp. 298–310.

private life, "with three cheers and by legislative enactment." He thought, however, that the directors would "laugh it off the docket," and he hoped that they would also "elect a real credit union leader to be President and another one to be Treasurer." Bergengren had heard, however, that "Holmes is through and that the plot is to elect Bill Reid and to dispose of me." [12]

By the time of the annual meeting in May the situation within CUNA was extremely tense. The executive committee met for three days before the actual gathering of the board and there were numerous angry exchanges. DeRamus resigned as editor of *The Bridge,* charging that he had received no cooperation from Bergengren, and that the managing director had told credit unionists around the country that the magazine was "rotten and ruined." Moreover, DeRamus accused Howell of writing letters depicting him as "a plotter and conniver." Reid denounced the continuation of the Filene Memorial Fund Drive and the talk that credit unions might embark on plans for cooperative purchasing. Bergengren, showing his old self-assurance, retorted that the solicitation of donations for the Filene memorial was the first time CUNA had engaged in such an activity, and that money paid for *Bridge* subscriptions were for "value received." I have kept my mouth shut about *The Bridge,*" he said. "We could have had a *Bridge* if we had guts." After further exchanges during which Reid told Bergengren that he "had been sitting around here doing nothing," Bergengren concluded: "We will settle at the national board who is the managing director." [13]

The board of directors convened with an air of excitement. The annual report of the president, usually duplicated and given to the delegates upon their arrival, was delivered orally by Holmes who said that he was "greatly perplexed as to what my report should contain and just how far I should go in laying before you the problems that have been encountered this past year." To remain silent, Holmes said, would indicate that he condoned what had been done; on the other hand, he hestitated to present a long, detailed account of what he and the executive committee considered to be serious problems. Therefore, he had decided to discuss in a general way the major difficulties facing the movement.

Holmes reported that 1,070 new credit unions had been organized during 1938, admittedly an appreciable number, but he believed that much more could have been done if there had been "complete harmony"

[12] Bergengren to Hyde [n.d.], 1939.
[13] Minutes, CUNA Executive Committee, May, 1939, pp. 13, 36–56.

within the association. He criticized the excessive amount of time spent in trying to get bonding rates reduced, saying that management should have devoted its time and efforts to more pressing problems. Holmes also thought that CUNA Supply had not moved quickly enough to provide the specialized forms desired by credit unions. Furthermore, the national association had failed to encourage local credit union chapters but had left them "to drift and get on as best they could." While favoring the Filene Memorial Fund, Holmes complained that the cost had risen from the original proposal of $150,000 accepted by the board, to $250,000, and recently Madison newspapers announced that $500,000 would be raised to build headquarters in that city. Holmes asserted that the question facing the directors was, "*where* our headquarters are to be located and if *now* is the time to proceed with this campaign." Finally, he reported that CUNA had entered the current fiscal year with a $48,000 deficit, of which all but about $1,000 had been incurred by *The Bridge*. Another pressing problem was the matter of incorporation. Although Bergengren had incorporated CUNA in 1936 as a nonprofit corporation, CUNA was actually operating as a "voluntary association," because neither the directors nor the state leagues had ever ratified the original incorporation papers. Thus, there were technically two legal entities. This placed CUNA in a most peculiar situation. The fault, Holmes said, rested on the management.

Holmes made it clear that he believed Bergengren was inefficient and uncooperative. In some cases he had ignored the directives of the board and of the executive committee, and in other instances he had taken unauthorized actions or misrepresented situations. Neither Bergengren nor any other member of the staff, according to Holmes, appeared "thoroughly familiar with accounting practices," which contributed to the current deficit. Holmes's report detailed the problems of the association and charged Bergengren as being mainly responsible for them. He called upon the directors to remedy the situation by approving the by-law amendments authorizing the executive committee to name the managing director.

Bergengren fell back on history, emotion, and idealism to defend his position before the board. He reviewed his contributions to the movement after joining Filene in 1920, made generous references to credit union leaders, and met the vexing problem of *The Bridge* head on by saying that "it was a major contribution and worth probably all that it cost." Bergengren denied or minimized the charges leveled by Holmes and concluded:

As I look back over the years I know that I have done my level best in your service. Satisfied? No. We have made a fair quota of mistakes which humans always have and always will make. Less probably than a half dozen of the men and women I see about me were in the credit union movement when Mr. Filene and I organized the Bureau in 1921 when there were 190 credit unions and three or four workable laws. I can see now nearly 8,000 credit unions and their two million members; what is infinitely more important, I can envision the thirty million members we will one day have in a hundred thousand credit unions. I see many, many good men harnessed to our work; I see 3,000 Federal credit unions and appreciate the fine leadership they are bringing to us and I can remember the day when I landed in Washington with the draft for a Federal law in my pocket, wondering just where to start on the long journey which led eventually to its triumphant enactment. I recall the Estes Park meeting and review all that has happened since, mistakes and all, and do not read failure in it. I look into the hearts of all of you, who love the credit union as I do and who give it the same sort of service I have tried to give it and I appreciate that there was a first day when I first met almost everyone of you. When the credit union first came into your life, it was a day to remember and a day to celebrate.

Bergengren asked the directors not to approve the amendment naming him managing director emeritus because he would not accept the position. He was standing for re-election he said, and "I hope that I may continue to serve you." [14]

Bergengren's fight with the executive committee ended in a kind of draw. The board unanimously re-elected him managing director, but the directors also adopted an amendment giving the executive committee power "to suspend or remove the managing director" for cause, but only after specified charges had been preferred and a proper hearing held. Another amendment, however, favored Bergengren in that it placed all departments under the "complete supervision" of the managing director. The directors gave Bergengren another "victory" when they voted to make Madison the permanent home of the association and reaffirmed their decision to continue the campaign to raise money to construct an office building there.[15] Thus, while the directors supported Bergengren, they somewhat paradoxically elected an executive committee which was not strongly pro-Bergengren.

Although Bergengren was able to maintain his position and leadership in the credit union movement through World War II, criticisms of his

[14] Report of CUNA Managing Director and Report of CUNA President, for Fifth Annual Meeting, Credit Union National Association, New York City, May 11–13, 1939, *passim.*
[15] Minutes, CUNA Directors, May, 1939, pp. 41–66, 170–80, 182–85, 191–94.

administration continued. During the summer of 1940 the executive committee received a report of CUNA accounts from an outside auditor which revealed many discrepancies between it and Hyland's comptroller's report. William Reid, who had been elected CUNA president in 1939, compared the association's business practices to "the operation of a country cross-roads grocery store." Careless handling of bonding certificates, undeposited receipts, and other lax practices caused both critics and friends of Bergengren to agree that, despite his many talents, Bergengren knew little about administration or sound business practices.[16] Nevertheless, his strong majority on the board of directors assured him that he would continue in his position, at least for several years.

Dissatisfaction with Bergengren's leadership stemmed to a considerable extent from the normal "growing pains" of the national association. But further troubles developed over the relationship between CUNA and its affiliate, the CUNA Mutual Insurance Society. CUNA Mutual had grown at a rapid pace. By 1938, it had advanced to rank 305 in coverage among all of the nation's insurance companies, and it ranked 133 a year later. By December, 1941, the company had 5,300 participants, mainly credit unions, and insurance coverage in force totaling $106 million. During its first seven years CUNA Mutual had paid 9,152 claims amounting to $1.2 million. The firm's assets had reached $600,000 by 1941 and it had a surplus of some $330,000.[17] Indeed, this was a spectacular record.

The lifeblood of CUNA Mutual was its borrowers' protection policies. The first loan protection plan for CUNA Mutual called for writing policies for individual credit union borrowers who would pay the premiums. Bergengren and others criticized this practice because it placed the burden of paying insurance coverage entirely on the borrower who, they claimed, was placed in a different category from the investor. Moreover, with a staff of only two or three people, CUNA Mutual became involved in "a mass of accounting detail, until within a few months it seemed evident that in a short time the whole plan of loan protection would bog down from its own weight."[18]

To solve the problems presented by the original loan protection plan, CUNA Mutual devised what they called the AA plan, under which a credit union took out a "blanket" policy on the total amount of its monthly outstanding loan balance. This plan proved immensely popular

[16] Minutes, CUNA Executive Committee, May, 1940, pp. 31–77.

[17] Bergengren to CUNA Mutual Directors, Feb. 1, 1941, pp. 33.

[18] Rentfro to CUNA Directors, May 1, 1940, p. 1.

with credit unions, and by May, 1940, 93 percent of all credit unions were using this type of loan protection insurance. The cheaper costs of administering this plan reduced premium rates 24 percent by mid-1940.

Shortly after its organization, CUNA Mutual also developed a life-savings insurance plan. This, too, was a type of "blanket" policy for credit unions, and each credit union investor received insurance equal to the value of shares he held up to a maximum of $1,000.[19] According to Rentfro, this kind of policy was designed to encourage the 75 percent of credit union members who still only held the minimum $5 share in their credit unions to save more, the inducement being free insurance. Also such a plan provided some basic insurance for families who otherwise would have no insurance at all, or who paid the relatively high rates for ordinary coverage.[20] By the end of 1941, however, Bergengren reported that only 519 credit unions out of 10,000 had taken advantage of the life-savings insurance program. One reason was that federal credit unions were not permitted, under FCA regulations, to participate. Moreover, CUNA Mutual had adopted a regulation requiring a credit union to contract for loan protection insurance before it was eligible for life-savings insurance.[21]

From the time Bergengren first conceived of CUNA Mutual, he looked forward to the day when the credit union movement would handle substantially all the insurance needs of its members. In April, 1938, Rentfro suggested that only two steps were necessary to complete the service of CUNA Mutual: the creation of a renewable term policy so that credit unionists who wished to do so could immediately secure the maximum amount of coverage available, and another type of term insurance that would cover the unpaid balance on real estate loans.[22] These policies were soon added. Despite expanding insurance services, Bergengren was concerned over the small amount of life insurance sold. He suggested that CUNA Mutual should undertake an aggressive campaign to increase its life insurance business, or abandon it altogether. He warned that only the loan protection insurance was protecting the life insurance contracts and that the risks involved in so few policies was too great.[23] Rounding out

---

[19] *Ibid.,* p. 2.

[20] Minutes, CUNA Directors, April, 1938, p. 166.

[21] Report of CUNA Managing Director to the CUNA Mutual Directors, Dec. 2, 1941, p. 2.

[22] Minutes, CUNA Directors, April, 1938, p. 166.

[23] Bergengren, "CUNA Mutual Society: Analysis of Coverage in Force," May 1, 1939; Minutes, CUNA Executive Committee, Nov., 1938, pp. 148–50.

the insurance services of CUNA Mutual in the prewar years were group life insurance and single premium policies.

CUNA Mutual operated during its early years on a kind of trial and error basis. The unique role of the company in serving the needs of credit union members, plus its managerial inexperience, led the company into experiments that were perhaps unusual to regular insurance firms. In 1940 the commissioner of the Wisconsin Insurance Department concluded that "frequent rate reductions, high dividends, and ultra-liberal claim payments were not prudent insurance practices," and he began to invoke tighter regulation over the society.[24]

Since the selling of insurance was regarded as a service to credit unions, leaders of CUNA viewed it as an inducement to all credit unions to affiliate with their leagues and the national association. During 1939, however, a national director charged that he knew of twenty-nine credit unions which were receiving insurance coverage without belonging to their state leagues. The directors adopted a policy that required CUNA Mutual not only to cancel the coverage of those twenty-nine credit unions, but in the future to cancel promptly insurance contracts of credit unions which were not affiliated with their state league. A year later Rentfro reported that CUNA Mutual was attempting to follow that policy, although leagues were either slow in reporting or failed to report at all. [25]

The major problem that seemed to occupy the national association and CUNA Mutual during its early years was that of becoming qualified to sell insurance in every state. Requirements varied from place to place, but the main criterion for receiving a state license was generally that an insurance company have a stated amount of surplus and reserves. In the case of CUNA Mutual, which began with a borrowed capital of only $25,000, time was needed to build up reserves, especially when many credit union leaders wanted dividends to be kept high. Nevertheless, the society usually took the position that it was legal to sell insurance by mail in almost every state. Technically CUNA Mutual had no salesmen in the field, but looked upon every credit unionist as both salesman and consumer. Doig's Organization and Contact Department assumed the main responsibility for urging credit unions to use the society's services. Moreover, even though CUNA Mutual claimed to have no selling agencies in

[24] Rentfro to CUNA Directors, May 1, 1940, p. 3.
[25] Minutes, CUNA Directors, May, 1939, pp. 307–8; Minutes, CUNA Executive Committee, May, 1940, p. 168.

any state, individual credit unions and state leagues performed a type of agency function.

By the summer of 1940 CUNA Mutual had a surplus of $168,000 which qualified it to sell insurance in seven states.[26] Several state insurance departments were questioning CUNA Mutual's qualifications for doing business in their states, however, and in a few, insurance departments had warned the society not to do business until they became legally qualified.[27] As late as the spring of 1941, the society was seeking official sanction in such important credit union states as Michigan and California, where surplus requirements for an insurance company was $200,000. By the end of the year, CUNA Mutual still was only qualified in eight states and it was estimated that the society served less than one-half of all credit unions in the country.[28]

CUNA Mutual extended its insurance coverage to Canadian credit unions, but it ran into difficulty when the Dominion commissioner at Ottawa declared that one requirement for selling insurance in Canada was the deposit of $100,000 in cash or acceptable securities in a Canadian bank. CUNA Mutual was able to avoid this requirement temporarily, but early in 1941 only 53 Canadian credit unions had taken out insurance with CUNA Mutual.

The persistance of operational problems caused a number of CUNA directors to become critical of the society's management. They complained that many of the troubles resulted from the fact that CUNA Mutual officials ignored recommendations and direction of the parent body. The relationship between the two organizations became strained over the question of CUNA Mutual declaring dividends without consulting CUNA directors, and failure of Rentfro to provide CUNA's executive committee with adequate reports. In other words, the national association feared that CUNA Mutual was becoming too strong and independent. The critical issue, however, was whether or not the national association would be supported by revenues from its affiliates. At the time of CUNA's organization, those who favored financing the movement from dues won the day. But as financial difficulties increased, the question arose again as to how the subsidiaries could help CUNA. Although Rentfro told the executive committee as early as 1938 that CUNA Mutual's role in the credit movement was "to render a service to credit unions but not to contribute financial support to the move-

---

[26] Report of CUNA Managing Director, Aug. 27, 1940, p. 15.

[27] Minutes, CUNA Executive Committee, May, 1940, pp. 167–68.

[28] Bergengren to CUNA Mutual Directors, Dec. 2, 1941, p. 3.

ment," [29] in February, 1940, the executive committee notified the boards of both CUNA Mutual and CUNA Supply that they would be expected to help provide CUNA's annual budget. The committee told the society that it should pay $3,000 of Bergengren's salary, $2,000 of the expenses of the Organization and Contact Department, and $2,000 for office rent at Raiffeisen House. CUNA Supply's share of the budget would be somewhat less.[30] At the next meeting of the CUNA board of directors in May, President William Reid asserted that the time had come to decide whether or not CUNA was to be entirely financed by dues or partially supported by income from its affiliates. He indicated that he favored the latter, and that the recent assessments were a "slight step" in that direction.[31]

Conflict over management practices and financial support between CUNA and its insurance affiliate was exacerbated by the attitude of the Wisconsin Insurance Department. In 1938 an examiner from that department concluded his annual report on the society by saying:

> The interlocking directorates of the two organizations have placed the company under the domination of the Association. This set-up gives rise to two very serious dangers. In the first place, the desire of the Association group for abnormally low rates has manifest itself on more than one occasion, and, secondly, there may develop a disposition to encroach upon the funds of the company to subsidize the Association. Such a situation is repulsive to the writer's conception of the proper operation of a life insurance company. It is entirely foreign to Wisconsin standards for the conduct of the life insurance business. We therefore urgently recommend that immediate steps be taken to remedy this condition so that the company may fix its own rates and adopt its own policies free from the dominating influence of the Association group.

Two years later, the examiner repeated his criticism and added that "instead of ridding the company of the influence of the National Association in the interim between examinations, a program has been followed to increase the domination and to take additional funds from the company's treasury to pay salaries and expenses of officers of the Association." [32]

This attitude of the state insurance department held out the disturbing prospect of the insurance affiliate becoming completely independent

[29] Minutes, CUNA Executive Committee, May, 1940, pp. 166, 175; Aug., 1938, p. 228.
[30] *Ibid.*, Feb., 1940, p. 120.
[31] Report of CUNA President William Reid, May, 1940, p. 13.
[32] *Ibid.*, p. 9.

of CUNA. Fearing this trend, as mentioned earlier, the CUNA directors had adopted a resolution in the spring of 1937, which stated that there should be a close relationship between the two organizations. CUNA Mutual's own bylaws maintained the same position, but the company's management had to deal with the state insurance department,[33] which held a contrary view. In order to insure control over the insurance affiliate, George Jacobsen, a director from Minnesota, moved that CUNA Mutual enter into a contract which would turn over the management of the insurance business to the parent organization. This suggestion, along with others, prompted the directors to appoint a special committee to study the problem. The work of what came to be called "CUNA Mutual Control" fell mainly on Nat Helman, who had become CUNA's attorney. In February, 1940, Helman reported that Wisconsin laws prohibited following the Jacobsen suggestion. The executive committee discussed other possibilities, but took no action. Bergengren thought that while the matter was important, "there is no possibility of the CUNA Mutual getting out of control of the credit union movement, not any more than there is of the moon dropping to the earth." [34]

During the summer of 1940, Helman discussed various arrangements with the Wisconsin insurance commissioner which would assure CUNA control over its insurance affiliate. It became clear, however, that the commissioner wanted CUNA Mutual to be an independent company and operate like other insurance firms under Wisconsin law. It was his job, he told Helman, to see that insurance companies remained financially sound. Helman reminded the commissioner that CUNA Mutual was "created to serve the members and its success or failure depends on the operation of CUNA and it would seem that every effort should be made to maintain such control rather than discourage it." But the commissioner replied that the law did not recognize such a relationship, that they should be kept apart, and "each stand on their own merits." Helman concluded, therefore, that "there appears to be no possibility under the laws of Wisconsin in regard to mutual insurance companies that would show us another way out of the problem and it seems the problem must be solved by more drastic action than that which we have tried thus far." [35]

In late 1940 and early 1941 Bergengren and Helman explored other

---

[33] *Ibid.*, p. 8.

[34] Minutes, CUNA Directors, May, 1939, pp. 313, 314; Minutes, CUNA Executive Committee, pp. 43–46; Minutes, CUNA Directors, May, 1940, p. 215.

[35] Minutes, CUNA Executive Committee, Sept., 1940, pp. 36–38.

avenues which would keep CUNA Mutual under the national association's control. One special fear was that a large number of credit unionists holding individual life insurance policies might disaffiliate with their credit unions. Since, as a member of a mutual company, they could still vote, CUNA management worried about the possibility of electing CUNA Mutual officers who had little interest in the national association. They discussed getting a special law passed in the Wisconsin legislature, seeking incorporation in another state, and changing CUNA Mutual into a stock company. Finally, to try to get some concrete action, Helman's control committee and the CUNA Mutual bylaws committee met in Chicago in November, 1941. Claude Clarke, speaking for the insurance group, said that his committee had "no inherent or fundamental objections to the organization of a stock company." Thereafter Helman and Clarke worked out a mutually agreeable plan for the creation of a new stock company which they called the CUNA Life Insurance Company, with a capitalization of $250,000. The national association through stock holdings would maintain complete control over the new company. Its shares would be voted by the president of CUNA upon instructions from the board of directors, thus ensuring that only candidates for office favored by the national association would serve on the insurance company board.[36]

When the CUNA Mutual directors met the next month, they were faced with strong opposition to converting CUNA Mutual into a joint stock company, and they defeated a resolution favoring such action. Instead, the directors adopted a resolution which called for presenting the proposal to all policyholders and, if "substantial opposition" appeared, the whole matter would be referred back to CUNA's directors. A second resolution proposed by Bergengren was also passed. It called for CUNA Mutual to amend its bylaws so that its business would be confined to writing policies only for credit unions and that a life insurance company be organized on a stock basis under the complete control of CUNA to write individual life policies for credit union members. Finally, the CUNA Mutual directors agreed to continue to cooperate with CUNA in carrying out these plans.[37] Thus, nothing had really been settled, but the attack on Pearl Harbor postponed the search for a solution to the problem of the fundamental relationship between CUNA and its insurance affiliate.

[36] Proceedings of the Joint Meeting of Special Committees, CUNA and CUNA Mutual, Nov. 15–16, 1941, pp. 1 ff.
[37] Minutes, CUNA Mutual Directors, Dec., 1941, pp. 2–11.

The corporate organization of CUNA, and the matter of building a new headquarters in Madison, continued to cause difficulties within the national association. As mentioned earlier, on April 2, 1936, Bergengren called together five employees of CUNA in Madison to sign the articles of incorporation which supposedly converted CUNA from a voluntary association into a nonprofit corporation under the laws of Wisconsin. The five signatories adopted the constitution and bylaws adopted at Estes Park, accepted the thirty-six state leagues as members, and elected the executive committee already chosen by CUNA's directors as the officers of the corporation.[38] Although this was only a technicality, the directors of CUNA never formally voted to turn over its assets, liabilities, and membership to the new corporation. Moreover, some of the provisions of the constitution and bylaws conflicted with the requirements of the Wisconsin incorporation law.

By the time many directors became determined to incorporate CUNA properly, however, the matter had become complicated by the initiation of the Filene Memorial Fund campaign to raise money to build a permanent office building, and Bergengren's insistence that Madison be designated as the permanent headquarters. In April, 1938, the directors voted to make Madison the permanent site, providing that CUNA could be properly incorporated in Wisconsin.[39] By May, 1939, some $20,000 in cash and pledges had been raised for the Filene Memorial Fund, but further complications arose when the Madison credit union chapter promised an additional $20,000 if the headquarters were constructed in that city. Claude Clarke, who was chairman of the memorial fund campaign, recommended that CUNA as a voluntary association be dissolved and that it be legally changed to its existing nonprofit corporate status. The directors, however, postponed action on incorporation for one year, but on a roll call vote again designated Madison as the permanent site and authorized the executive committee to buy the land necessary for the construction of a building.[40]

Even though the board of directors had repeatedly expressed a preference for Madison, local citizens wanted further assurance. With the option running out on a choice site, the Madison credit union chapter purchased the land on January 6, 1940, and offered it to CUNA as a gift.

[38] Minutes, First Meeting of Members of Incorporated National Association, April, 1936, pp. 98a–98c; Report of CUNA Managing Director, May, 1939, p. 100.

[39] Minutes, CUNA Directors, April, 1938, pp. 190–91.

[40] Minutes, CUNA Executive Committee, May, 1939, pp. 36–40; Minutes, CUNA Directors, pp. 160–75, 194.

Although there was objection to accepting the land until they had settled the matter of proper incorporation, the directors voted to accept the offer in May.[41] This action supported Bergengren, who proposed constructing a three-story office building at a cost of $100,000, along with a "factory" to house the CUNA Supply Cooperative. A year later there was $79,000 on hand, $10,000 having come from CUNA Mutual to help erect the building in which its offices would also be housed.[42] The wartime scarcities, however, ended plans for immediate construction.

The question of to what extent CUNA should work closely with the rest of the nation's cooperative movement continued to cause differences and controversy within credit unionism. Bergengren maintained his earlier position that credit unions were the "financial arm of the cooperative movement," but many credit union leaders did not agree. They argued that a close identification with producer and consumer cooperatives would alienate businessmen who were friendly to credit unions but hostile to other aspects of cooperative enterprise. Nevertheless, by 1939, the relationship between the credit union and consumer cooperative movements became somewhat closer. In March CUNA became a "fraternal" member in the Cooperative League of the United States, and employees of consumer cooperatives organized an increasing number of credit unions. The Consumer Cooperative Association of Kansas City, the Farmers Union State Exchange of Omaha, and the Farmers Union Central Exchange of St. Paul passed resolutions recommending the organization of more credit unions among the employees of their member associations.[43]

Bergengren did not say so publicly, but he became more and more convinced that there "must be some reorganization of economic society on a cooperative basis." Several times he told his friends that "capitalism in most of its aspects has failed, and that in the long run we cannot develop economic democracy on the principle of dog eat dog and the theory that the shrewdest, the most unscrupulous, the smartest of our number, should survive at the expense of all of the rest of us." He insisted that he had no use for either fascism or communism, but believed in "demo-

---

[41] Report of CUNA President William Reid, May, 1940, pp. 5–8; pp. 10–11; Report of CUNA Managing Director, May, 1940, p. 3; Minutes, CUNA Directors, May, 1940, pp. 92–93, 171–80.

[42] Minutes, CUNA Executive Committee, Sept., 1940, p. 33; Minutes, CUNA Directors, May, 1941, pp. 15, 163; Minutes, CUNA Mutual Directors, Sept., 1941, p. 13.

[43] Minutes, CUNA Executive Committee, Nov., 1938, pp. 186–93; Feb., 1939, pp. 186–87; "Operations of Credit Unions in 1941," *Monthly Labor Review*, LV (Sept., 1942), 540–41.

cratic economics." That principle was not radical, he said, and cooperative effort must always be "sane and reasonable and efficient," proving
simply that the "principle of human brotherhood is a sound, workable
principle." But Bergengren did not press these ideas openly. His mere
suggestion that credit unions should get more fully involved in general
cooperative activities, brought opposition from many credit union spokesmen.[44]

Another problem within the credit union movement involved the relationship between CUNA and the Federal Credit Union Section of the
Farm Credit Administration. Although most leaders of CUNA believed
that the FCA was helpful to the larger movement, some CUNA officials
were critical of the FCA. Initially, the federal office had helped to organize hundreds of credit unions, and by June, 1941, the seventh anniversary of passage of the national law, 4,570 federal charters had been
granted, covering more than one million members.[45] But after 1937 the
rate of growth had been slower because FCA ruled that its employees
could not take the initiative in forming new societies.

This change of policy regarding organization of new credit unions did
not distress Bergengren and other credit union leaders greatly because
they believed that most organizational work should be done by the state
leagues and the national office. What did annoy them, however, was the
Federal Credit Union Section's increasing emphasis upon regulation.
Bergengren charged in 1938 that FCA turned practically every question
over to its legal department, which was unfriendly to credit unionism.
Moreover, federal examinations tended to "oversupervise" federally
chartered societies.[46] Some CUNA leaders also objected to the FCA ruling that federal credit unions could not buy life-savings insurance from
CUNA Mutual, that they could not purchase subscriptions to *The Bridge*
even for officers, that the legal division established security requirements
for loans rather than leaving that function to the local credit committees,
and that FCA had failed to encourage the newly formed credit unions to
become members of the state leagues.[47] There were also complaints that

[44] Bergengren to James W. Brown, Oct. 6, 1939; Bergengren to Parke S. Hyde, Nov. 2,
1938.

[45] Otto Wilson, "Six Years with Federal Credit Unions," *The Bridge* (Oct., 1940), p. 220;
Howard Mace, "The Federal Section," *The Bridge* (Aug., 1941), p. 188; Bergengren to John H.
Fahey, Dec. 9, 1940.

[46] Bergengren to Fahey, Dec. 9, 1940; Minutes, CUNA Executive Committee, Aug., 1938,
p. 194.

[47] A. W. Thomas, unpublished manuscript of editorial, n.d.; Minutes, CUNA Executive
Committee, Nov., 1938, pp. 119–20.

the FCA had wrongly turned down applications for charters. Dora Maxwell reported in 1939 that applications from a small group of farmers in Maryland and from fishermen in Maine had been rejected because the prospective organizers were "too poor." [48] Bergengren once remarked in the presence of FCA personnel that the agency had shown no enthusiasm for organizing rural credit unions.[49] These issues led Earl Rentfro to complain that the FCA had become "almost another credit union movement," while the board of directors of the New Jersey league passed a resolution calling for the removal of the Credit Union Section from the FCA and the creation of an independent agency to administer the law.[50]

Bergengren went to Washington in July, 1938, to confer with Governor Myers about the problems and complaints. They reached an agreement whereby a group from CUNA, called the Contact Committee, would meet with representatives of the Farm Credit Administration to try to reconcile their differences. Meetings were held in September and November, 1938. But these conferences helped very little. The FCA did agree to send a representative to meet with any group about to form a credit union, providing the agency had a specific request, but generally the FCA did not change its current administrative policies. The refusal of FCA officials to notify the state league when a new credit union had been organized was especially irritating to Bergengren. The federal agency held that such action would be a concession to CUNA, while Bergengren complained that the FCA's ruling exceeded the intent of the law, thus "confusing themselves with Congress." He believed that there would be "a political fight sooner or later as to what their [FCA's] powers are."[51] But the coming of the war diverted attention from the growing demand in CUNA that the federal law be administered more liberally, or even by a different agency.

The various difficulties which faced CUNA in the pre–World War II years did not measurably retard the national association's primary goal of extending credit union services to all people in the United States. By 1939 CUNA operated on a budget of about $85,000 a year and, with the assistance of some state leagues, carried on a fairly effective organizational campaign. The results were most encouraging. During the five

[48] Minutes, CUNA Executive Committee, May, 1939, p. 23.

[49] *Ibid.*, May, 1940, pp. 93–96.

[50] A. W. Thomas, editorial, n.d.; Minutes, CUNA Executive Committee, Nov., 1938, pp. 107–8; Bergengren to A. W. Thomas, June 23, 1938; Thomas to P. D. Holmes, July 29, 1938; Henry Stricker to Thomas, July 12, 1938.

[51] Minutes, CUNA Executive Committee, April–May, 1941, pp. 87–91.

years from the end of 1936 to the close of 1941, the number of active credit unions nearly doubled, increasing from 5,241 to 9,891. Membership rose from 1,170,000 to 3,304,000 in the same period. Total assets nearly quadrupled, growing from $82,817,000 to $322,000,000. Loans also climbed rapidly, rising from $148,773,000 in 1939 to $219,856,000 in 1941.[52]

Despite this record, credit unions still handled only a very small percentage of the total installment credit business. In 1941 installment loans in the United States reached more than $6 billion. Of this amount, credit unions supplied only about 3.3 percent. However, the percentage provided by credit unions was increasing at a substantial rate. But the greatest increase in personal credit was being supplied by the commercial banks.

In the early days of credit union development commercial banks showed little interest in personal consumer credit, but by the late 1930s they were aggressively entering the small loan field. Instead of confining their participation in consumer credit to loans to personal finance and sales companies, and even to credit unions, the commercial banks set up personal and consumer loan departments, in order to handle this installment business directly. According to one authority, the movement toward direct consumer financing by commercial banks was "attributable largely to the need for an outlet for bank funds which may yield higher returns than are available in other fields." [53] It may have been that bankers were becoming concerned over the growing volume of credit union business. However, the banking journals in that period do not reflect any particular worry about credit union competition. In any event, by the end of 1938 at least 1,500 commercial banks were operating personal installment loan departments, most of which were established after 1931, and were serving more than one million people.

However good the credit union record was, it did not satisfy Bergengren. In December, 1938, he wrote that "at the present rate of progress it will take nearly a century to establish the number of credit unions needed for the service of the people of the United States." [54] In analyzing the task for credit unions two years later, he pointed out that while Madison was not an ideal field for organization because it was not an indus-

[52] CUNA, Research and Economics Department, *Consolidated State and Federal Reports* (n.d., mimeographed report).

[53] John M. Chapman and Associates, *Commercial Banks and Consumer Installment Credit* (New York: National Bureau of Economic Research, 1940), p. 3.

[54] Report of CUNA Managing Director, Dec. 15, 1938, p. 1.

trial city, there were 53 credit unions with memberships of 9,000 in a population of 70,000. Even by Madison standards, he wrote, on the basis of 140 million people in the United States, there should be 106,000 credit unions in the country with 2.5 million members, and billions of dollars in assets. "It is when we have reached that goal," he said, "that we may feel that we are beginning to reach our normal objectives." [55]

Credit unionists offered a variety of reasons as to why societies were not organized at a faster rate. Some charged that the curtailment of organizational work by the FCA was responsible. Members of the executive committee believed that the lack of harmony in the movement diverted energies that could have been spent in organizing credit unions. But CUNA management had always hoped that the primary responsibility for organizing new credit unions would be undertaken by the state leagues, not the national association. The development of state leagues, however, came slowly. By May, 1940, only twenty-two state leagues employed full-time, paid personnel. Even the most active leagues tended, according to Doig, "to employ people who do not cost them much in the way of remuneration and by so doing they naturally attract folks who do not have much organizing ability." [56]

As for his own Organization and Contact Department, Doig faced continuing problems. One of his greatest obstacles was the lack of money to employ more field representatives. By the spring of 1941, Doig had only four field men besides himself. Most of their time, however, was spent collecting national dues, attempting to create viable leagues, and speaking at innumerable meetings of leagues and chapters. In an attempt to promote the educational activities of the national association and to relieve the Organization and Contact Department of some of its responsibilities in that area, CUNA in 1941 employed J. Orrin Shipe, a credit union leader from Buffalo, New York, to head the education department after the Good Will Fund donated $5,000 for that purpose. Shipe had first joined CUNA's staff in 1939 as a field organizer. In addition to preparing promotional literature and addressing credit union groups, Shipe also became editor of *The Bridge*.[57]

The national association attempted several methods to promote credit union organization. Drawing on Filene's old insistence that the best results could be obtained through mass production of credit unions,

---

[55] *Ibid.*, Aug. 27, 1940, p. 12.

[56] Report of CUNA Organization and Contact Department, May 1, 1940, p. 2; April 15, 1941, p. 6.

[57] *Ibid.*, April 15, 1941, p. 6.

Doig's department created in 1940 the CUNA Organization Service. Dora Maxwell, who headed the project, was charged with contacting national organizations to develop "leads" about groups which might be interested in forming credit unions. Maxwell passed on whatever information she obtained to state leagues which, it was hoped, would do the actual organizational work. Miss Maxwell's contacts with such organizations as the National Education Association, the Municipal Finance Officers' Association, the International Ladies Garment Workers Union, Stouffers' Restaurant chain, and the Statler Hotel system produced some new credit unions.

A second project begun late in 1940 was the creation of Volunteer Organizers Clubs in a number of states. This project began when several state leagues appealed to CUNA for help in training credit unionists who wanted to devote some of their spare time to organizing new societies. Chapters in various cities were encouraged to form these clubs by persuading five to fifteen members to agree to spend an hour and a half for three successive evenings attending a "school" on organizing techniques taught by an experienced organizer. The first such "school" was conducted in East St. Louis, Illinois, in October, where ten persons met with Charles Hyland and Orrin Shipe.[58] Finally, Bergengren's older creation, the Founder's Club, an honorary organization for all those who had organized at least one credit union, continued to be active. In August, 1940, he reported that the club had 541 members.[59]

Membership in credit unions continued to come from employees of both private firms and government agencies. A survey of the types of credit unions organized by the Federal Credit Union Section up to the beginning of 1936 indicated that of 906 credit unions chartered, only 62 were organized among business and professional, cooperative, fraternal, religious, and trade union associations; 28, among rural and urban community groups; whereas 816 served wage-earner groups. As might be expected, the largest number comprised federal employees, with 133 credit unions, while in second place were 102 credit unions serving workers in the petroleum industry. Other occupational groups served by more than 25 credit unions each were those in public schools, meat packing, local government, public utilities, department stores, and railroads.[60] About the same distribution existed in state-chartered credit unions.

[58] Report of CUNA Assistant Managing Director, April 2, 1941, pp. 24–26.
[59] Report of CUNA Managing Director, Aug. 27, 1940, p. 2.
[60] *Cooperative Saving*, II (Jan., 1936), 8.

Employers were generally cooperative when organizers wanted to tell employees about the benefits of credit unions, or when employees themselves expressed interest in organizing a credit union. In some cases employers took the initiative in promoting credit unions to provide their workers with agencies of thrift and small loans because they thought that employee well-being made better workmen. Such employers generally provided office space for the credit union. In some cases, however, employers attempted to dominate the operation of the credit society in clear violation of good credit union principles, and occasionally credit unionists charged that some employers were "paternalistic in the extreme." During the early years of the New Deal, when organized labor received both favorable legislation and administration encouragement, some employers allowed or promoted credit unions as a means of allaying employee dissatisfaction and forestalling the organization of labor unions. Problems arose, however, when credit unions were formed without genuine employee support. For example, a large corporation in Detroit promoted a credit union among its employees, but it remained moribund for many months and was finally liquidated. A few years later, however, employees of the same manufacturer took the initiative in organizing a new credit union and it was soon established on a firm footing.[61]

There were often cases where antipathy toward labor unions caused employers to oppose credit unions because they misunderstood the nature of such organizations. A clothing manufacturer in Georgia called in federal credit union organizers and told them that his company was in favor of organizing a credit union for the employees provided the charter did not contain the word "union." When the federal organizers explained that this was not possible under the law, the officials tried to get a state charter. When that, too, proved impossible, they simply dropped the matter. Sometimes representatives of the Federal Credit Union Section discovered that employers unfriendly to the New Deal opposed credit unions because they thought that there might be political implications in endorsing them.[62]

A large new geographical field for organizing credit unions opened up during the late 1930s. In 1938 the provincial legislature of British Columbia joined the other Canadian provinces by enacting a credit union law. Although CUNA Mutual and CUNA Supply quickly extended their services to Canadian credit unions, the Organization and Contact Department was unable, with its limited financial resources and

[61] "Early Days of the Federal Credit Union Program," p. 46.
[62] *Ibid.*, p. 47.

personnel, to give much attention to Canada. Bergengren had been interested in Canadian development for many years, and he visited credit unions and leaders there whenever possible, frequently during his vacation. After one such trip in 1939, he reported that credit unions in Canada were not usually organized within potentially large industrial groups, and concluded that there would be "relatively few very large credit unions, outside the large cities." The most typical type of credit union, he predicted, would be among community groups and cooperative organizations. He noticed a growing relationship between credit unions and consumer cooperative organizations of all types. Overall, he envisioned the development of a strong movement in Canada, similar to that in the United States.[63]

There were 844 credit unions in Canada by the end of 1939, and during that year CUNA directors amended its constitution to permit the affiliation of provincial leagues. League development progressed slowly, however, and the next year some national directors moved to repeal the previous year's action and urged that Canadian leagues be made ineligible for membership in the national association. These directors were angry because Canadian credit unions were using the services of CUNA, but had not yet affiliated and begun paying dues. One director even expressed the opinion that as soon as the Canadian movement became "strong enough to be of value to us they will form a national association of their own and withdraw." Both Reid and Moses asserted that "you will find that Canada is for the Canadians and not for the United States." But Bergengren made an impassioned plea, urging the directors to defeat the motion, so that the movement could serve the "common interest of working people wherever they are," promote the "cordial relations between the two great democracies of the world," and prove that credit unionism was a "movement of the heart." On a roll call vote, the motion was defeated 54 to 36. Bergengren warned that league growth in Canada would proceed slowly, but no more so than had league development in the United States.[64] By the end of 1941, only the Nova Scotia and British Columbia leagues had affiliated with CUNA, but Canada was destined to play an important role in the later history of credit unionism.

During the four years before the United States entered World War II, credit unionism continued to grow and extend its services internationally, although at a pace considered too slow by some leaders. The real heart of the movement consisted of the thousands of individual credit

[63] Bergengren, "Canadian Credit Unions," ca. 1940, pp. 1–3.
[64] Minutes, CUNA Directors, May, 1940, pp. 84–89.

unions and their members in the United States, but the activities of the national association were crucial to the movement's over-all growth and development. Therefore, the problems within CUNA tended to reflect the difficulties within the movement. Nevertheless, the credit union movement had gone through depression, internal conflicts, and growing competition from small loan departments of commercial banks and had continued to gain strength. Perhaps it was a people's movement as Filene and Bergengren had said.

CHAPTER XII

The War Years

FRIDAY, December 5, 1941, was payday for employees of the Hawaiian Air Depot at Hickam Field on the island of Oahu. All that day and the next, members of the federal credit union came into its offices located in the corner of one of the large hangars and made share deposits and loan payments, leaving their passbooks for posting during the next few days. At noon on Saturday, the credit union treasurer deposited the $5,000 on hand. The next morning, from his home in Honolulu, he witnessed the Japanese air attack on Hickam Field. A former treasurer of the credit union, P. W. Eldred, lived nearer to the field. When he saw what was happening, he rushed for the credit union office to save the credit union records, but before he reached the hangar, bullets from a machine gun in an enemy plane had riddled his body. Moments later, a salvo of bombs destroyed the hangar. One bomb scored a direct hit on the credit union office, destroying over 90 percent of the passbooks.[1]

Although the Hawaiian Air Depot Federal Credit Union was the only American credit union ever to come under direct enemy attack, the credit union movement as a whole—like all other American institutions —was greatly affected by the second great world war of the century. The first reaction of credit unionism was to promise support for the American cause. "The credit union," Bergengren announced, "enlists for the duration of the war." The cartoonlike symbol of the movement, created by Boston newspaper cartoonist Joseph Stern, that showed a "little man" under an umbrella labeled "Credit Union," protecting him from rain drops called "hard times, sickness, and financial distress," gave way to a picture of the same "little man" in army uniform, with a rifle over his shoulder and the umbrella folded and propped up in the corner. A new credit union poster announced the wartime objectives of the movement. They included winning the war; cooperating in "the sale and purchase of war fund securities"; continuing "every possible service to our members consistent with the national program"; expanding the "growth of

[1] Bergengren, *Crusade*, pp. 352–54.

credit unions"; and helping "members accumulate savings, that they may have vitally needed financial resources when the war is over." [2]

Even before the United States became involved in the conflict, the national association emphasized its eagerness to cooperate fully in the preparedness efforts. Accordingly, by September, 1941, the Treasury Department informed CUNA that all credit unions had been designated as agents for the sale of United States Savings Bonds.[3] CUNA issued promotional literature, urging credit union members to invest at least 10 percent of their incomes in war bonds. However, CUNA discouraged credit unions from making loans for the purchase of bonds. Neither did credit unions want members to withdraw money from their share accounts for bond purchases. Such action might force credit unions to liquidate because of inadequate capital. Moreover, many credit unions invested a percentage of their assets in government bonds, and if too many members requested withdrawals, the credit union would have to redeem its bonds to meet the demands of withdrawals. In that case credit unions would provide no additional funds for the war effort.[4]

Credit unions, along with other financial institutions, were affected by wartime credit regulations. With increasing incomes and the rising demand for consumer goods, there was a serious threat of inflation. Therefore, President Roosevelt issued an executive order in the summer of 1941 to regulate consumer credit. In accordance with that order, the board of governors of the Federal Reserve System issued Regulation W prescribing the terms upon which installment sales and loans could be made. Regulation W restricted the amount of credit that might be granted, and it limited the time for repaying loans.[5]

The effects of Regulation W were felt almost at once. A month after the restrictions went into effect, a credit union treasurer reported that loans had been only half as much in September as in the month before. As credit union loans fell, CUNA Mutual's insurance coverage also declined. Between September 1 and November 1, 1941, eighty-one new credit unions were organized, indicating that the decline in insurance coverage was due to the drop in loans. By the spring of 1943 Bergengren reported privately that the restrictions had reduced normal loans about

[2] *Ibid.*, p. 329; Bergengren to Members of the National Board, Dec. 22, 1941.

[3] Minutes, CUNA Executive Committee, Sept., 1941, p. 10.

[4] See *The Bridge* (May, 1942), pp. 103–5, 113.

[5] Board of Governors of the Federal Reserve System, *The Federal Reserve System, Purposes and Functions* (Washington, D. C.: Government Printing Office, 1954), pp. 60–61.

50 percent, while CUNA Mutual protection had declined nearly 30 percent.[6]

CUNA officials moved quickly to bolster the spirit of credit unionists around the country. They emphasized that credit unions should not expect business as usual during wartime, and urged local officers to meet the challenge by improving their services. The major stress was on *thrift*. Besides helping the war effort through bond purchases, credit union leaders argued that savings would provide money for postwar purchases. While the emphasis was on promoting maximum savings rather than loans, credit union officials emphasized that loans to refinance home loan mortgages, to pay for education and medical expenses were advisable. "When in doubt," CUNA told credit committees, "don't decide against the loan." [7]

President Reid spoke frankly to the directors at their meeting in May, 1942. "Until recently, we have had business fairly falling into our lap," he said. "It has come too easily. No real ingenuity was needed . . . . The justification for our existence is that we can and should furnish services that banks can but won't. If we carry on in the same conservative way banks do, it's time we shut up shop." Then, he expressed the idea that credit unions had paid "too much attention" to dividends.

A credit union more interested in dividends than helping people get over financial difficulties might well take stock of itself. . . . We . . . are now faced with the job of selling the Credit Union services. All the financial ailments of our people are still present. They can't be legislated away. It is our job to help these people . . . . The lending of money for the purchase of cars and other durable goods was an easy way to invest Credit Union funds. Since that medium for lending money has gone, many Credit Unions seem to want to drift. They don't want to be bothered with $50 or $100 loans for remedial purposes. It now means five or ten loans where one was made before to put the same amount of money to work.[8]

Reid was not only reacting to problems created by war but to some of the general trends within the movement. He was really saying that credit unions, at least some of them, had given up their emphasis upon service. Rather, he said, there was a tendency for credit unions to emulate ordinary commercial consumer credit companies, and abandon the "provident and remedial" loans stressed by the founders of cooperative

[6] Bergengren to Parke S. Hyde, Mar. 31, 1943.

[7] "The Credit Union in War Times," circular issued by CUNA, ca. Feb., 1942.

[8] Minutes, CUNA Directors, May, 1942, pp. 27–28.

credit. Reid was among the first of the credit union pioneers to face up to this problem openly and frankly.

The CUNA Mutual Insurance Society also stressed the necessity for obtaining new business. Bergengren told the society's directors that in seven years of operation only 3,796 credit unions out of the 10,000 in existence were policy owners of the society. He emphasized that the 62 percent of all credit unions that did not use CUNA Mutual's services "constitutes a field for normal and proper expansion." Earl Rentfro echoed Bergengren's challenge by saying: "With a field wide open for development, we should approach the problem of decreasing coverage with optimism and confidence in the service we have to render." [9]

If the business of individual credit unions diminished because of war, one way to keep advancing the movement was to increase the number of credit unions. As part of CUNA's "war program," Bergengren recommended that organizational efforts be increased, and the executive committee concurred. President Reid, however, believed that the current level of organization was high enough because the field force was unable to service the new credit unions, including the training of personnel. Another director warned that organization of credit unions in defense plants might lead to numerous postwar liquidations which would give the movement a "black eye." "I think we ought to stabilize our present credit unions as much as possible," he said, "and be very cautious in the formation of new ones to see that those that are organized now will be a permanent organization." Nevertheless, it was clear that a moratorium on organization would bring stagnation.[10]

The major organizational problem continued to be the lack of adequate personnel, both at the state and national levels. The old experienced organizers—Bergengren, Doig, and Dora Maxwell—were so involved in administrative work that they no longer carried on organizational activities. CUNA's field force consisted of only Hubert Rhodes, Clifford Skorstad, and Charles Eikel. But even they organized very few new credit unions. They spent most of their time attending meetings of state leagues, local chapters, and speaking before groups of credit unionists.[11] During the fiscal year ending on February 28, 1942, 1,093 credit

---

[9] Bergengren to Directors of the CUNA Mutual Insurance Society, Feb. 6, 1942; Rentfro to Directors of the CUNA Mutual Insurance Society, Feb. 9, 1942.

[10] Minutes, CUNA Executive Committee, Jan. 1942, pp. 70–77.

[11] *Ibid.*, pp. 81–87.

unions had been organized in the United States, compared to 1,306 the previous year, a decrease of 16 percent.[12] In other words, the decline had set in even before the United States entered the war.

Some of the factors responsible for this drop included the inadequacy of the field force, and the fact that the Federal Credit Union Section no longer actively encouraged organization. Moreover, Doig suggested that state league directors were instructing their managing directors "to give more attention to servicing existing credit unions" than to organizing new ones.[13] When the paid personnel failed to organize many credit unions, the CUNA executive committee urged that a "corps of voluntary organizers" be utilized, and that leagues add credit union organizers to their staffs as rapidly as possible. Early in 1942 CUNA announced another organization campaign to emphasize "that the organization of more new credit unions is our greatest internal need." To credit union leaders such as William Reid and Claude Clarke, the encouragement of volunteers as organizers was essential not only for practical reasons but also because they believed volunteers conformed more closely to original credit union philosophy. [14]

At the beginning of 1943 there were only forty-three more credit unions than there had been a year earlier.[15] The small increase was due not only to poor organizational success, but to the growing number of liquidations. Early in the war there was a tendency for credit unions to disband "because of fear of the future." Bergengren argued that the job of the leadership was "to preach the certainty of the successful outcome of this war, and the certainty further that the credit union movement will come through it with colors flying." [16] However, talk could not cure the problems which went beyond a crisis in confidence. Some credit unions were finding it more and more difficult to succeed under wartime conditions and, as Bergengren admitted in 1942, there had been "an exceptional number of liquidations . . . ." The executive committee urged credit unions to make every effort to prevent liquidations and advised any society that contemplated liquidation to consult its chapter, league, and CUNA before taking such action. [17]

[12] Annual Report of the Assistant Managing Director to the Managing Director, April 14, 1942, p. 6A.

[13] *Ibid.*

[14] Minutes, CUNA Executive Committee, Jan., 1942, pp. 87–90; "Prizes for Organization Activity," circular issued by CUNA, ca. Feb., 1942.

[15] Bergengren to Parke S. Hyde, Mar. 31, 1943.

[16] Bergengren to Hubert M. Rhodes, Feb. 20, 1942.

[17] Annual Report of the Managing Director, May 9, 1942; Minutes, CUNA Executive Committee, May, 1942, p. 219.

While CUNA worked hard to avoid them, liquidations grew at a rapid pace. Between March 1, 1944, and February 28, 1945, 360 credit unions began business, while 407 ceased operations. The only consolation in those figures was that most liquidated credit unions were the "smallest and weakest," and that losses to credit union shareholders were either nonexistent or very small.[18]

The credit union movement suffered much more from war than it had from depression. Of the credit unions operating during the depression years, 93.6 percent survived. One report concluded that "credit unions had the maximum capacity for survival . . . 26 of every 27 credit unions in operation in 1929 were still going in 1936." [19] The number of credit unions during wartime, however, decreased from 9,891 at the end of 1941 to 8,683 by December 1945, while membership dropped from 3,304,390 to 2,842,989. During those years, personal income of Americans rose from $96 billion to $191 billion and personal savings from $11 billion to $29.6 billion, but savings in credit unions increased from only $303 to $369 million. This modest increase actually represented a decline in the percentage of personal savings (from .62 percent to .10 percent) held by credit unions as opposed to other financial institutions. Regulation W also had its effect on loans, because during the war loans outstanding for all credit unions declined from around $220 million to $128 million. Moreover, there was a scarcity of consumer goods which eliminated the need for many traditional credit union loans. The only real increase in credit union business was in total assets, which rose from over $322 million to $434 million.[20]

Although most credit unions that liquidated did so voluntarily, there was also an increase in defalcations which forced some societies to close their doors. Any defalcation caused great distress to credit union leaders because it shattered their claim that credit unionists were somehow more honest than employees of other financial concerns. Even when liquidation resulted from poor management rather than dishonesty, it tarnished the claim that the average credit unionist could successfully operate such a simple business. In any event, Bergengren argued that losses could be reduced if the supervisory committees in each credit union performed their jobs better, and if the state supervisory agency conducted thorough audits. But he admitted that closer supervision and stricter audits alone

[18] Annual Reports of the Managing Director, May 11, 1946, and May 1, 1951.

[19] Bergengren, *Crusade,* p. 331.

[20] *Credit Union Yearbook, 1968* (Madison, Wis.: CUNA, 1968), table 13, p. 37, table 14, p. 38, and table 15, p. 39.

would not solve the problem. In 1942 he reported that two defalcations had come in states with "the most adequate and severe" examinations. To put defalcations in perspective, he insisted that credit unions would occasionally be victims of the "natural born looter," just as were banks.[21]

Defalcation was tied closely to the bonding business carried on by CUNA. By March 1, 1942, coverage of 4,755 credit unions provided through the national association totaled almost $14 million. Increasing losses brought the inevitable notice from the bonding company that premiums must be increased. This dismayed Bergengren, who had worked hard to obtain a low rate and to reduce it continually. A representative of the bonding company, however, told the CUNA executive committee in January, 1943, that during 1942 claims for excess coverage had exceeded premiums and that the loss ratio on primary bond premiums was unfavorable to the company. The bonding company spokesman rejected arguments by Reid and Bergengren that the firm should not base its action on one year's experience and asserted that recent defalcations in credit unions had caused "panic" in the bonding business. The dire concern of company investigators, he said, centered around the fact that these credit unions' books had not been properly audited for months, or even years, and that the records had been poorly kept. Unless CUNA engaged in a strong educational effort to "bring these people up short with the realization that they are handling other people's money," he warned "you will see rates doubled, or quadrupled in the next few years, and we may not be able to carry this business at all. . . ."[22]

At the next executive committee meeting in May, a bonding company representative declared that "during the past year fraud, embezzlement and missappropriation of credit union funds has developed into almost epidemic proportions." During the first four months of 1943, he said, seventy-eight losses on primary bonds had been reported, sixty-three of which were estimated to total over $51,000. The company anticipated a loss ratio of 80 percent for the year and an over-all loss ratio since the plan had been instituted of 72 percent, a figure totally unsatisfactory to the company.[23]

The firm's spokesman admitted that abnormal conditions played a role in these losses. He cited "days of rapid change, unprecedented personnel turnover, the disparity between wages and the rising costs of living and the distractions and pressure and demands of war on the home

[21] Minutes, CUNA Executive Committee, May, 1942, pp. 194–97.
[22] Ibid., Jan., 1943, pp. 166–74.
[23] Ibid., May, 1943, pp. 46–48.

front," as reasons for credit union problems. But he also said that conditions within the movement contributed to defalcations. He listed these as: "(1) Hopelessly unfit or lackadaisical internal control or supervision; (2) Niggardly scope of outside (independent) audits or examinations; (3) Perfunctory check of details instead of alert and responsible scrutiny of records; (4) Lack of knowledge and instruction to supervisory committees as to recognized method of auditing procedure; (5) Failure to select proper personnel on supervisory committees or appraise them of their duties and responsibilities; (6) Failure of the Board of Directors to keep themselves current on the internal affairs of the credit union." [24] These were severe indictments and they stung members of the executive committee. But even the most efficient operation of credit unions could not guarantee against defalcation as had happened in Kentucky, where a credit union treasurer had embezzled $22,000 of the $25,000 in assets. Thus the national association became rudely aware that dishonesty, even among credit unionists, was a problem that had to be faced, and that providing bonds for credit unions was one of the most valuable services CUNA could render.

One of the most encouraging aspects of credit unionism during the war years was the steady growth of societies in Canada. In 1940 there were 1,167 credit unions in that country, with assets of $25 million, serving over 200,000 members. By the end of the war the number of credit unions had nearly doubled, increasing to 2,219, while membership stood at 590,000 and assets at almost $126 million. The organizational trophy awarded by CUNA was won by the Alberta league in 1943 and by the Saskatchewan league in 1944, while the individual volunteer organizer's prize went to Harry Finch of Windsor, Ontario, in the latter year.[25]

League development in Canada, however, came slowly and caused some CUNA directors to question whether or not CUNA should make much effort to extend its services north of the border. Bergengren always insisted, however, that the admission of Canada to the national association was one of the most statesmanlike steps the organization had ever taken. The problem of affiliating with CUNA stemmed from the Canadian contention that the leagues in Canada could not afford the dues. But there were also other difficulties in New Brunswick, for example, where a split occurred between the English- and French-speaking credit unionists. This led to the secession of the French group from the New

[24] *Ibid.*, pp. 47–49.
[25] Doig to the National Board, May, 29 1945.

Brunswick league in 1945 and the establishment of a dual league. Nevertheless, by the end of 1944, eight Canadian leagues were represented in the national association.[26] One Canadian director, Angus B. Mac-Donald, became treasurer of CUNA and one of its leaders.

CUNA extended its services to Canada as far as its resources allowed. CUNA Mutual Insurance was popular from the beginning, although CUNA Supply did little business in the provinces. Both Bergengren and Doig made occasional trips to Canada, usually to address large meetings and to assist newly organized leagues. William B. Tenney, a field man for the Organization and Contact Department, was assigned to the provinces of British Columbia and Alberta, along with his northwestern territory in the United States. In 1941, for example, he spent six days in British Columbia, and conducted a total of 26 meetings, "ranging from conferences with one or two persons to general meetings of some hundred persons." [27] One problem with the French-speaking credit unions in New Brunswick, however, was their demand for an organizer who spoke their language. In 1943, C. Gordon Smith, a pioneer leader in the Ontario league, was appointed as Canadian agent for CUNA Mutual. Not until 1946, however, did CUNA open an office in Canada under the direction of a Canadian.[28]

CUNA's increased attention to credit unionism north of the border did not prevent Canadians from considering the organization of their own national association. Angus MacDonald told the CUNA executive committee in May, 1943, that "we have domestic problems of our own," and they can only be taken care of at our own meetings. "We have the matter of taxation and dividends at the present time and we have a regulation similar to your regulation W and we find it very important at the present time to discuss these domestic problems and take action on them." MacDonald insisted that such a move should not be considered as a threat to CUNA, because a Canadian association would not compete in "any particular field that is now covered by CUNA. As far as I can see, there is a need for us to get together once in awhile and discuss our own problems and use all of the facilities and the advantages that CUNA has to offer." [29] These conversations reflected another problem which the movement had to face in the future.

---

[26] Bergengren to Directors, Aug. 10, 1944; *Maritime Co-operator* (June 15, 1954), p. 5.

[27] William B. Tenney, "Credit Unions in the Northwest," *The Bridge* (Feb., 1942), pp. 38–39.

[28] Annual Report of the Managing Director, May 11, 1946.

[29] Minutes, CUNA Executive Committee, May, 1943, pp. 143–50.

Another phase of the growing world-wide credit union movement occurred in the Philippine Islands. It was there that Filene had recommended the establishment of credit unions to President Theodore Roosevelt as early as 1907. Although nothing was done, interest in credit unions did not die. Over the years both Filene and Bergengren had received occasional inquiries from the Philippines about the credit union movement. Then, in the late 1930s, the Reverend Allen R. Huber, an American missionary with the Philippine Federation of Christian Churches, organized some thirty credit unions even though the islands had no enabling legislation. When the Japanese captured Manila, they threw the Reverend Huber into a prison camp and the movement languished.[30]

From the 1920s onward Bergengren occasionally received letters or personal calls from foreign visitors who had heard about credit unions and wanted more information on how to introduce them into their own countries. During 1939, for example, he reported Australian and Jamaican visitors, and a letter from Siam, all seeking aid in establishing credit unions.[31] During World War II CUNA also began receiving requests for help and information from people in various South American countries. Dora Maxwell suggested to the executive committee that perhaps CUNA should offer its services through the offices of Nelson Rockefeller, the coordinator of Inter-American Affairs, so that "we will be really thinking in terms of building an international cooperative Credit Union." One director objected, however, declaring that CUNA had already extended its operations into Canada. William Reid abruptly ended the discussion by saying: "I think we should follow up what we have started here in this country. We have not got the help to do anything else." [32] So while the vision of credit unionism was international, the practical situation dictated that organizational work be concentrated in the United States.

One of the problems facing CUNA was the lack of sympathy for the movement among Farm Credit Administration officials, even including a number of those within the Credit Union Section. Orchard fought a running battle with the FCA's legal and examining divisions, spending "a considerable amount of money undoing damage" which, according to him, "should never have been done." To make matters worse, Governor Black ignored Orchard. "I had tried to make appointments to discuss

---

[30] Bergengren, *Crusade,* pp. 194, 317–18.
[31] *Ibid.,* p. 324.
[32] Minutes, CUNA Executive Committee, May, 1943, pp. 102–3.

our work with him," Orchard said, "but he would not see me."[33] Moreover, many FCA officials directly charged with supervising the Credit Union Section were more than indifferent to the movement; they were openly hostile.

On April 23, 1942, the Bureau of the Budget forwarded a draft of an executive order to the attorney general providing for the transfer of all duties, records, and personnel of the Credit Union Section from the FCA to the Federal Deposit Insurance Corporation. The bureau notified President Roosevelt that the reason for the transfer was that the activities of the section had "no relationship to the basic functions of the FCA . . . ." Roosevelt signed the executive order on April 27. The reaction in the FCA, according to Orchard, was "good riddance." [34]

Before the physical transfer took place, a number of meetings were held between personnel in the Credit Union Section and officials of FDIC. Orchard and his colleagues attempted to inform the FDIC representatives about the "peculiar, . . . factors that needed to be considered in the economical and proper work of chartering, supervising, and examining Federal credit unions." Once again, however, they found that FDIC examiners, whose work with banks was vastly different, "failed to show any enthusiasm for the new child which had been placed under their wing." [35]

CUNA's early relations with the FDIC were indeed difficult. Administratively the new arrangement seemed cumbersome and inefficient. The section was immediately decentralized, and officials assigned a field man to each of the regional offices of the FDIC. All correspondence from the section to its field men had to be addressed to the FDIC examiners, who then issued orders and instructions to the field force. Moreover, all such letters had to be signed by the chief examiner in Washington.[36] There were also long delays between the application and granting of charters. Bergengren charged that the FDIC was unduly stringent in its chartering procedures.

The national association wasted little time in determining whether the FDIC would be friendlier than the FCA had been in regard to its proposals on policy, operation, and legislation. Doig visited FDIC officials

[33] "Early Days of the Federal Credit Union Program," pp. 50, 6.

[34] Harold D. Smith, director of the Bureau of the Budget, to the Attorney General, April 23, 1942; Smith to Roosevelt, April 23, 1942; M. H. McIntyre to Smith, April 28, 1942, Roosevelt Papers; "Early Days of the Federal Credit Union Program," p. 62.

[35] "Early Days of the Federal Credit Union Program," p. 63.

[36] Ibid.

late in 1942 and requested that the agency reverse the FCA rule that federal credit unions were ineligible for CUNA Mutual's life-savings insurance. They denied this request. He also asked that deposit insurance be extended to federal credit unions, but was told that the law did not permit such coverage. Finally, he asked if the FDIC would support an amendment to the federal law to allow officers of federal credit unions to borrow from their own societies, but this proposal, too, was rejected. Nevertheless, following a meeting between representatives of CUNA and the FDIC in July, 1942, the CUNA committee left the session convinced "that the relationship between the FDIC and the Credit Union National Association would be fine for the credit union movement." [37]

But within weeks that opinion changed, and CUNA President R. A. West told the executive committee "that we are very much of an orphan in the Federal Depository [sic] Insurance Corporation and that steps must be taken to relieve this situation as quickly as possible." A major source of conflict continued to be the prohibition against life-savings insurance, but the FDIC had also opposed proposed amendments to the federal law, writing their sponsor, Senator Robert F. Wagner of New York: "We think they are not important enough for a Congress to consider during war times." When CUNA proposed that the law be extended to the Canal Zone, where credit unions were already being organized, the FDIC opposed such an extension on the grounds that it could not properly supervise even all of the credit unions in the United States and Hawaii.[38] The relations between the District of Columbia Credit Union League and the FDIC became so strained that Representative Patman and Senator Capper introduced a bill to transfer the administration of the Credit Union Section to the Federal Home Loan Bank. However, Congress took no action.

During the war years CUNA did not devote much effort to obtaining new credit union legislation. The national association recognized that Congress had little time or disposition to consider routine legislative proposals. CUNA's last legislative victory before 1945 came in June, 1940, when an amendment to the federal law raised from $50 to $100 the maximum unsecured loan which federal credit unions could make. This was only a partial victory as the movement had sought a maximum of $300. A number of other amendments, mainly clarifying the original act, were

[37] Minutes, CUNA Executive Committee, Jan., 1943, p. 57; Minutes, CUNA Directors, May, 1943, pp. 112–15.
[38] Minutes, CUNA Executive Committee, Sept., 1943, pp. 4, 108–22.

offered during the war years, but most of them failed to even receive a committee hearing.[39]

With the death of Morris Sheppard, credit unionists needed another friend in Congress. Both Wright Patman and Senator Wagner proved to be strong friends of the movement, but by the end of the war Congressman Jerry Voorhis of California had emerged as one of credit unionism's most reliable friends in Congress. Yet, no one up to this time could wield influence on behalf of credit unions equal to that of the former Texas senator.

By 1942, CUNA officials recognized that so far as legislative action was concerned it "was not getting the job done" with the national association's current methods. The association had a legislative committee to recommend legislation, but the contacts with individual congressmen were generally left to Bergengren or Doig. To meet the problem of representation in Washington, the midwestern caucus of CUNA directors asked the national association in May, 1942, to establish a Washington legislative office.[40] At the next meeting of the committee, Nat Helman, CUNA's general counsel and member of the legislative committee, said that although the legislative committee had urged greater contacts with congressmen, it did not want such an office set up, because "we do not want our organization labelled as a lobbying organization . . . ." [41] By the end of the war, Doig was visiting Washington periodically to call upon congressmen, taking Hubert Rhodes with him so that he, too, could gain experience. Doig thought that these contacts, together with aid from the "folks back home," could "strengthen our position" in the capital.[42] However, CUNA did not then establish any regular office in Washington.

Throughout the war period, the over-all strength of the national association grew as more state and Canadian leagues became affiliated with CUNA. By the spring of 1942, there were forty-eight affiliated leagues, representing forty-three states, the District of Columbia, Hawaii, and three Canadian provinces. In addition, individual credit unions from Vermont, Delaware, Nevada, New Mexico, and Wyoming, the Canal Zone, and five provinces in Canada were affiliated with CUNA. Two years later the number of affiliated leagues stood at fifty-three, with all

[39] Croteau, "The Federal Credit Union System," p. 5.
[40] Minutes, CUNA Executive Committee, May, 1942, p. 207.
[41] *Ibid.*, Sept., 1942, p. 159.
[42] Doig to National Board, May 29, 1945.

the additions coming from Canada. A survey conducted by CUNA in 1942 revealed that there were 204 active credit union chapters in the United States.[43] Twenty-seven state leagues employed full-time field representatives.[44]

Due to wartime travel and convention restrictions, a number of state leagues cut back or eliminated their annual meetings. Bergengren encouraged all leagues to continue their state conventions because he believed that such state-wide gatherings were needed to see credit unionism through the emergency. He also worked hard to persuade leagues not to slacken their efforts because of the war. Bergengren emphasized the example of Illinois, which in 1942 adopted a $50,000 annual budget without any "discussion of retrenchment or curtailing their activities . . . ."[45] He was distressed by what he considered the inclination of newly employed managing directors to rent an office, stock supplies, and wait for business. He believed that a new league executive should "keep his office in his hat for a considerable period," and devote his energies to organizing new credit unions, to visiting existing societies, to bringing credit unions into the league, and to improving the services of local credit unions and the league. "There is something almost fatal about an office," he concluded. "A man in an office can find innumerable reasons for staying there, and what we need in the credit union right now is men in the field."[46] In order to maintain as much supervision and direction of the movement as possible, CUNA's executive committee continued its quarterly meetings during the war, as well as the annual gathering of the board of directors. In 1945, however, the federal War Conventions Committee turned down CUNA's request for the annual board meeting.

The conflicting views among the state leagues as to basic policies and operational procedures of the national association continued to be apparent in the debates over CUNA's budget and dues schedule. These struggles intensified during the war years because of the financial difficulties experienced by the state leagues. Much of the dissension occurred between the big, wealthier leagues, and the small, poorer ones. The stronger state leagues which had large memberships continued to

[43] Annual Report of Managing Director, May 9, 1942; Bergengren to CUNA Directors, Aug. 10, 1944.

[44] Annual Report of Assistant Managing Director to the Managing Director, April 14, 1942.

[45] Bergengren to Hubert M. Rhodes, Feb. 20, 1942.

[46] *Ibid.,* Jan. 15, 1942.

resent supplying so much of CUNA's budget through the assessment of membership dues. In 1942 the board of directors fixed dues at seven cents per member for the next year with a maximum of $5,000 for any league.[47] Karl Guenther, a member of the dues committee from Michigan, unsuccessfully opposed this arrangement at the board meeting and frankly alluded to what he considered the factions in the credit union movement. He even accused President Reid of packing the dues committee so that the national association's revenues could be maintained at the expense of the state leagues.[48]

The dues issue produced a crisis in 1943 following a controversy over whether CUNA would supply the Michigan state league with certain financial information. When the league did not receive what it considered a proper response, it remitted only $1,000 of its assessed dues of $5,000 to the national association. Bergengren quickly moved to smooth over the difficulty, but just before the annual meeting it appeared that the Michigan league might withdraw from affiliation with CUNA. This, however, was averted. Nevertheless, conditions continued to be strained between some of the strong state leagues and CUNA.[49] By 1945 the national association was operating on a budget of some $122,000, mostly derived from dues.

Because of the opposition to what some credit union leaders considered high dues payments, there was constant pressure on the Madison office to reduce its operating expenses. But the national association had influential supporters who believed that there should be little or no retrenchment in the association's activities. Not wanting to cut CUNA's budget, one Missouri director said: "We are investing in the future." He argued that weaker credit union states had lost their managing directors and only CUNA was able to "keep up the life that has been born and nurtured" in those areas.[50]

Bergengren told his friend Parke Hyde that criticism by some CUNA directors reflected a lack of confidence in the staff. But it was not, Bergengren wrote, a lack of efficiency that created problems but the loss of personnel to military services. By August, 1944, there had been an 87 percent turnover in the staff at Raiffeisen House. In 1945, for example, Orrin Shipe, director of the education department, was inducted into the

[47] Minutes, CUNA Executive Committee, May, 1942, p. 233.

[48] Minutes, CUNA Directors, May, 1942, pp. 197–203.

[49] *Ibid.,* Jan., 1943, pp. 142–51; J. C. Howell to Bergengren, Dec. 28, 1942; Bergengren to Howell, May 3, 1943.

[50] Minutes, CUNA Directors, May, 1944, pp. 81–222, for entire debate.

armed forces, and Doig reported that employees in CUNA's executive offices had been reduced from eight to four.[51]

The election of officers in 1942 also revealed deep divisions within the movement. Reid was unanimously re-elected president, and Harold Schroeder was again named secretary. But on a close vote of 57 to 49, G. V. Carroll of Texas defeated the incumbent treasurer, Dr. A. G. Weidler of Berea College. Weidler refused to make the usual formal gesture of a defeated candidate by moving that the election be made unanimous. "There is no use saying there is unity when there is not," he added, "and I of all persons would not want to be under the suspicion of lending any seeming consent to any so-called Hitlerism." Weidler further charged that his defeat had been engineered by CUNA's staff, and that he had seen "a good deal of jubilation when the election was announced." Not only had the staff been active politically at the meeting, he said, but many credit unionists from several states had told him that the staff frequently engaged in political activities in their states. A director from Minnesota then offered a resolution that, in effect, instructed the employees of CUNA to stay out of national association politics, but his motion was tabled.[52]

When it came time to elect President Reid's successor in May, 1943, Karl Little of Utah was the first name placed in nomination. His supporters reminded the directors that all previous presidents of CUNA had come from the larger states of the East and the Midwest, and that it was time to give consideration to the smaller states of the West and the South. However, the presidency went to R. A. ("Doc") West of Illinois, a man characterized by his supporters as not being committed "in any way to any individual or group." Little then moved that the vote be made unanimous, because he said that a talk with West the night before revealed that their ideals and principles were similar.[53] But before Reid left office he talked frankly to the annual convention delegates. "If we want to stop our backward movement, we will be required to do some things that will not be popular with some people. Our revenues are falling so we must cut expenditures. Hence, we must reorganize our administrative structure if we want to prevent the whole structure from falling apart. We cannot wait until the war is over. We cannot continue any longer to blame the war and Regulation W for our setbacks." [54]

[51] Bergengren to Hyde, Mar. 17, 1944; Bergengren to Directors, Aug. 10, 1944.
[52] Minutes, CUNA Directors, May, 1942, pp. 212–33, pp. 276–78.
[53] *Ibid.*, pp. 141–47.
[54] *Ibid.*, p. 39.

Not only did the war produce stress and strain within credit unionism, it delayed a major CUNA project—the construction of an office building and memorial to Filene. In January, 1942, Claude Clarke reported that the Filene Memorial Fund stood at $151,000. Although some preliminary plans for the building had been prepared, Bergengren announced that construction would have to be postponed because of war restrictions.[55] The old problem of *The Bridge,* however, was finally solved. In 1941, the publication's debt stood at almost $19,000; one year later, through careful management and a circulation of 25,000, the debt was reduced to only $3,000. Most of the editorial work had fallen to Shipe, but with his increasing duties as head of the educational department, Richard Giles was named as assistant editor. In September, 1943, Howard Custer was appointed editor.

CUNA's two affiliates were hard hit by war. The CUNA Supply Cooperative, however, suffered most. Less than a year after Pearl Harbor, some 80 percent of its male employees were in the armed forces, including the assistant manager, the accountant, several of the shipping room clerks, and the most skilled machine operators. In addition, paper shortages and rationing hampered the operations of CUNA Supply. Business dropped off until in January, 1943, the directors of CUNA Supply recommended dissolving the cooperative. But CUNA's directors opposed such action and they continued to operate the supply business.[56]

Like CUNA Supply, the CUNA Mutual Insurance Society was hard hit by the war. Its total insurance coverage, including loan protection, life-savings, and individual insurance policies, stood at $106.7 million in September, 1941. Each year saw a drop in that coverage to a low of $77.7 million in February, 1944. The next year, however, coverage improved and one year later it stood at $91.4 million. The society's assets increased from $607,000 in 1942 to $850,000 in 1945, while its surplus rose from $339,000 to $504,000 in the same period. By March 1, 1944, CUNA Mutual had paid $276,000 to its members in patronage dividends.[57]

The CUNA board of directors continued its search for a way to insure control of its insurance subsidiary. The CUNA proposal that the Mutual Insurance Society be reorganized as a stock company controlled by the

[55] Minutes, CUNA Executive Committee, Jan., 1942, p. 126; Minutes, CUNA Directors, May, 1942, p. 177.

[56] Minutes, CUNA Executive Committee, Jan., 1943, pp. 206–10.

[57] Figures compiled from annual reports and minutes of the CUNA Executive Committee and Board of Directors during the years from 1942 through 1945, all of which are cited above.

national association was rejected by the CUNA Mutual directors just before Pearl Harbor. Claude Clarke, chairman of the CUNA Mutual Control Committee, reported this action to the executive committee in January, 1942, which in turn decided to take the entire question to CUNA's directors.[58]

In May, 1942, the directors voted to issue a report to all member credit unions, outlining the long controversy between CUNA and CUNA Mutual. It was hoped that feedback from leaders in the movement would be useful in making any decisions. Meanwhile, however, both CUNA and CUNA Mutual agreed on one reform. As mentioned earlier, one of the reasons given by CUNA's executive committee for the necessity of safeguards to insure continued control of its subsidiary was that holders of individual life insurance policies might withdraw from their credit unions but still be allowed to vote for society directors, thus possibly electing directors who had no connection with the movement at all. Working through the Wisconsin league, CUNA and its insurance affiliate sponsored a bill in the 1943 legislature that would set up area meetings of CUNA Mutual policyholders. At these meetings the policyholders would designate delegates to attend the annual CUNA Mutual meeting to represent them. If a policyholder attended the area meeting, he was bound by the decisions reached. If he did not attend, he was still free to attend the annual meeting in Madison, but all voting by mail would be eliminated. After the bill became law, the CUNA Mutual board amended its bylaws to conform with the new practice.[59]

Bergengren believed that the new system of representation was "much more democratic than our present provision for a voting right in the individual policyholder, which right he can never effectively exercise."[60] The policyholder meetings were held in 117 locations around the country in 1944 and, in most cases, CUNA directors were chosen to represent their areas. Again, Bergengren asserted that this was "the longest step ever taken in the matter of putting mutuality into a mutual insurance company," and that great progress had been made "in making truly cooperative and democratic the control of our society."[61]

The change in representation did not provide the "control" over CUNA Mutual envisioned by many leaders of the national association. The

[58] Minutes, CUNA Executive Committee, Jan., 1942, pp. 232–76.

[59] *Ibid.*, Sept., 1942, pp. 112–13; May, 1943, pp. 9–10; Annual Report of the Managing Director, May 13, 1944, p. 17.

[60] Bergengren to J. C. Howell, May 19, 1943.

[61] Annual Report of the Managing Director, May 13, 1944, p. 17.

CUNA board and the executive committee had never dictated policy to the CUNA Mutual board, although there had usually been enough overlapping of membership to provide influence. By late 1943, however, Harold Moses, a CUNA director from Louisiana, pointed out that "up to this year we used to have some interlocking between the Executive Committee and the Board by some members sitting on both of them which we have not got this year . . . ." [62] Although all members of the CUNA Mutual board were credit unionists, most took a highly independent attitude toward the "parent" organization. This resulted partly from the fact that they knew the law made the company separate and distinct from CUNA, a fact which the insurance commissioner frequently brought to their attention. Also they intended to resist the pressure from the national association to enlarge its financial support of CUNA.

In May, 1944, CUNA's executive committee met with the CUNA Mutual directors to, in the words of CUNA President West, "work out and put on a business basis the connection of CUNA with their affiliates." West asked CUNA Mutual to agree to pay 2 percent of its gross premium dividends each year for the services the national association rendered to the society to replace the "lump sums" contributed in the past. Edward Shanney, the president of CUNA Mutual and a CUNA director, asserted that the state law restricted the money which the insurance society could pay to another organization. While the insurance commissioner had agreed that CUNA Mutual could pay fees for certain contracted work, each contract, he told Shanney, must be specific and not simply a general contract "for services rendered."

Shanney said that CUNA Mutual was agreeable to enlarging its board membership to eleven and to specifying that the additional member should always be the president of CUNA. While he would not agree to pay the 2 percent assessment, the insurance company was prepared to pay for rent, utilities, the part-time services of the managing director, the dissemination of literature, and the full-time services of a field representative. Shanney believed that payment for these services would equal the 2 percent, although he rejected the principle of a percentage assessment.

Reid said that the reason for paying a CUNA field man to handle all the insurance business was that the Wisconsin insurance commissioner had criticized the use of Doig for promoting this business on a part-time basis. An executive committee member criticized the employment of a field man concerned exclusively with insurance, saying that it was only a

[62] Minutes, CUNA Executive Committee, Sept., 1943, p. 52.

first step to asking for six and then eight such employees. "When you do that," he added, "you are establishing two distinct organizations; you are creating two distinct field forces, and what you will do will be to create antagonism, or what you might do is to cause a rift in the structure through an action of this description."

Reid insisted that the main unsolved issue was to what extent CUNA Mutual would support CUNA. He reminded the directors that credit unions already paid dues to the national association for the services it provided, including the advertising and sales of insurance. Reid concluded by saying that "the National Association should carry its own self by its dues. . . ." After the usual reminders from executive committee members that CUNA Mutual would not exist without CUNA and charges that CUNA Mutual had become a "money-making institution," the CUNA directors agreed to accept $9,000 from CUNA Mutual but refused to transfer a field man to its exclusive use.[63]

When the executive committee met in March, 1945, it again searched for ways to bring about closer cooperation between CUNA and its affiliate, but the gap between the two groups was widening rather than becoming narrower. In order to meet criticism of the insurance commissioner of Massachusetts, who held that CUNA Mutual was illegally dominated by CUNA, the executive committee drafted a statement which, in effect, asserted the independence of the two organizations.[64] This acknowledgment, however, did not end the question of the relationship between the two agencies, and if anything, the suspicions, the quarrels, and the bitterness only increased during the postwar years.

Although it did not come as a surprise, Bergengren's departure from CUNA was the most dramatic event in the credit union movement during the war period. He had earlier survived an attempt by the executive committee to remove him from office, largely because he retained the respect and affection of most national directors. But as time passed, Bergengren played a smaller and smaller role in administering the national office. Even his friends concluded that although he was a superb propagandist, organizer, and inspirational leader, he was not a particularly good administrator. In effect, then, Bergengren became a sort of elder statesman in the last years of his administration. By the early 1940s Tom Doig managed most of the important affairs of CUNA. The growing changes are reflected in the annual reports. Bergengren's contribu-

[63] Proceedings of the Joint Session of CUNA Executive Committee and CUNA Mutual Directors, Madison, Wisconsin, May 10, 1944, *passim.*
[64] *Ibid.,* May 12, 1945, pp. 31–33.

tions were largely reviews of the history and philosophy of the movement, while Doig's reports dealt with facts, figures, and pragmatic suggestions for action. Moreover, the executive committee increasingly asserted its rights and obligations in setting all policies for the management of the national association.

In 1941 at the annual meeting in Jacksonville, Florida, the board, to Bergengren's surprise, honored him for his twenty years' service, and Doig made a warm and generous speech praising his long efforts.[65] In his memoirs Bergengren looked back upon the Jacksonville meeting as the end of his crusade. The movement, he wrote, "had then reached the edge of maturity. Neither Filene, who had gone to his reward after making the credit union movement possible in the United States, nor I, who had designed the legal structure and helped to give his dream reality, fitted normally into the next step. That involved the complete democratization of cooperative credit in North America."[66]

At that time, however, Bergengren did not indicate that he no longer was the real head of the movement. In March, 1943, for example, he wrote a friend that he had under control "some of the difficulties which have come out of so much political manipulation in the past . . . ." A short time later when West succeeded Reid to the presidency, Bergengren told another friend that he thought the election "very wholesome," because a faction in the organization had tried to determine the election in advance and had failed.[67] At the next meeting of the executive committee he did not sound like an official contemplating either voluntary or forced retirement: "We have had splendid harmony and we have made splendid progress, and I want to say for management how much we appreciate the leadership that President West has given to us."[68]

But Bergengren's time of crisis had arrived. In September, 1944, the executive committee met in closed session at Kansas City. Edward Shanney, president of CUNA Mutual, an invited guest, and Karl Little, president of CUNA Supply, were also present. Neither Bergengren, Doig, nor any other staff member was in the room. Without any preliminaries, President West said that he had left the last annual meeting convinced that CUNA had not been developing as it should because of Bergengren's mismanagement. He charged that there was discord, confusion, and lack of direction at Raiffeisen House, and that the managing director must be

[65] Bergengren, *Crusade*, pp. 347–50.
[66] *Ibid.*, p. 351.
[67] Bergengren to J. C. Howell, May 19, 1943.
[68] Proceedings of CUNA Executive Committee, Sept., 1943, p. 293.

replaced. The heads of the national association's two major affiliates joined in the criticism of Bergengren. Shanney explained that CUNA Mutual had drawn further and further away from CUNA because Bergengren was not qualified "to conduct a large enterprise in the strictest sense from a business standpoint." Little also criticized Bergengren for trying to bypass the manager of CUNA Supply and for dealing directly with employees, for misrepresenting aspects of the cooperative's operations, and for incurring financial obligations without the board's authorization. "He has done so many things that I am perfectly frank with you, gentlemen, that the CUNA Supply Cooperative cannot operate under the present management we have in Madison today . . . ."

West recognized that firing Bergengren would arouse opposition throughout credit unionism. However, he told the executive committee that it must come to a unanimous decision and then carry it out "regardless of public opinion from our membership." The only voice raised in Bergengren's defense was that of Harold E. Latham of North Carolina. He charged that by stripping Bergengren of his duties and powers, the executive committee had not given him a fair chance to prove his administrative abilities. Moreover, he declared that, while only one other person in North Carolina knew about Bergengren as a manager, every credit unionist was aware of his "inspirational speeches and the building up of the enthusiasm and the urging of the furtherance of the movement." Latham argued that those qualities were more necessary in the future than "the action of the business management or mismanagement that may occur at the home office, serious as it may be and annoying as it may be." While CUNA could employ business managers, Latham concluded, it could not "hire enthusiasm," and Bergengren's "enthusiasm and his interest and his inspiration has covered this continent too damned well to dispose of it with a snap of the fingers." The question seemed to be whether the movement's greatest need was good business management or inspiration. The majority of the executive committee was obviously ready to opt for improved management.

Following a lunch break, the executive committee appointed West, MacDonald, and Ammering to talk with Bergengren and urge him to resign. To ease his exit, the delegation was authorized to offer Bergengren a position of promotional advisor at a salary of $5,000 a year. Some directors thought that the proposed salary was too high, but West, somewhat cynically, said that he would support the figure because Bergengren had "a lot of friends and a lot of people who love him and we can afford to spend a few dollars of the Credit Union National Association money to satisfy those people and we are doing him a little better than average and I think it is money well spent."

The three-man group then visited Bergengren for fifteen minutes in his hotel room and explained the decision of the executive committee. After hearing the proposal, Bergengren said that it was not logical or fair, but that he had known such action was coming. He admitted some of his difficulties, but explained that he did not think it would be "proper" for him to continue as an advisor. "Under no circumstances," he added, "would he work under Tom Doig." Seeing that he had no other practical choice, Bergengren assured the executive committee that he would resign on January 1. The three-month interim would give him time to find another job and "to step out most gracefully." The executive committee thereupon postponed formal action until its next meeting and agreed to say publicly only that the management question had been discussed.[69] The executive committee had agreed, however, that Doig would become CUNA's new managing director when Bergengren stepped down. Doig told the committee that "I know that I can do the job, . . . and I think I am entitled to a chance at it."

Following this confrontation, Bergengren tried to explain his position without revealing fully what had happened at Kansas City. To one close associate he wrote that he contemplated "retiring" at the end of the year. He explained to another friend in a somewhat colored account that the executive committee had suggested that he retire after the annual meeting in May, 1945, and take a semihonorary position. Bergengren said that he had "made a sort of dicker" with the committee that he would "string along" until May and then refuse to be a candidate for re-election. He would not, he said, take any lesser job with CUNA.[70]

Meanwhile, Bergengren became increasingly committed to the larger cooperative movement. He expressed concern that there seemed to be two "fairly-well defined concepts" within the movement. "One group," he wrote, "thinks of the credit union as a personnel activity in industry. As such, it takes care of the short-term-credit problem of employees on a humane basis, and performs a useful function which is appreciated by both employee and employers. The other concept is that cooperation is a sort of circle made up of segments, and that the credit union is one of the segments, and therefore a part of the cooperative whole."[71] He be-

---

[69] Proceedings of the Quarterly Meeting, Credit Union National Association, Executive Session, Kansas City, Missouri, Sept. 24, 1944, *passim.*

[70] J. C. Howell to Bergengren, Dec. 18, 1944; Bergengren to James W. Brown, Dec. 4, 1944.

[71] Bergengren to James W. Brown, Sept. 29, 1944.

lieved the second position was the sound one. Bergengren further revealed his fundamental interest in cooperation when he wrote a letter of recommendation for Orrin Shipe, who was then under consideration for a position with the Council for Cooperative Development. Bergengren wrote that Shipe was "very much in earnest, sound in his cooperative approach and would be very valuable if, later on, we get at the organization of credit unions within consumer cooperatives and of other credit unions which may form the financial basis for other cooperatives in the consumer field." [72]

Bergengren hoped to find future work in the cooperative movement. He suggested to officials of the Edward A. Filene Good Will Fund, where he served on the board of directors, that the fund might employ him "in a somewhat free-lance capacity within the cooperative movement . . . ." He proposed that he work with credit union leaders in channeling their accumulated funds into cooperative enterprises. He also proposed a college to educate young men and women in cooperative ideals, recommended that extension courses be set up to train employees of cooperative stores, and suggested that he could promote the organization of cooperative stores, radio stations, newspapers, and central banks. Bergengren also favored "organizing a new type of credit union which would be, from the outset, oriented to the development of consumer cooperatives as its objective." The new organization could be used to carry credit unions to Jamaica, British Honduras, New Zealand, Australia, and England, making Filene's legacy "a factor in the good neighbor policy . . . ."

Bergengren had become especially interested in extending credit unions and other cooperatives among southern blacks. His concern had been heightened after learning about a credit union operating among Negro farmers in North Carolina. He hoped that this kind of organization would serve as a prototype of "the utilization of cooperation to so improve the economic lot of the Negro" to the end of solving all the economic problems of the nation. [73]

Bergengren, members of his family, and some of his friends thought that this vital interest in cooperative activity had much to do with his ultimate removal. In January, 1945, he told a friend that his insistence that credit unions were a part of the larger cooperative movement was "not overly popular with some of our leaders who are so identified with their own industrial organizations that they build their economic think-

[72] Bergengren to R. L. Trevenfels, Nov. 10, 1944.

[73] Bergengren, "Notes re a Tentative Plan of Work for the Good Will Fund," typescript, n.d.; Bergengren to James W. Brown, Sept. 29, 1944.

ing around loyalty to the system which provides the pay check." [74] This was not a new issue. James W. Brown reminded Bergengren of 1936 when *The Bridge* carried a picture of a cooperative store, and many leaders "wanted to hang you for a communist and a wrecker of the private profit system." [75] Bergengren later identified West as being in the "industrial" camp, although he concluded that he thought the CUNA president was "honest in his opposition to cooperative effort; he is simply unable to understand what is going on." [76]

Early in 1945 Bergengren wrote West that he would not be a candidate for re-election as managing director at the May meeting, but that he wished to remain in office until that time. But when the executive committee met in March, 1945, Bergengren implied that he was still undecided as to whether he should resign. Disgusted at Bergengren's evasiveness and indecision, John Eidam moved that he be dismissed immediately but with full salary until the end of the year. Bergengren then said that he would accept the position of promotional advisor, but he asked to retain his title of managing director until the annual meeting in May. Eidam withdrew his motion, but by the next morning he thought better of his action and again moved that Bergengren be dismissed forthwith and given the promotional position at a salary of $5,000 a year. The motion was approved unanimously. Doig was then elected managing director at a salary of $7,500. [77]

Bergengren, however, did not give up his fight. He again presented his case in a report to the board of directors as he had done in the past. Soon protests from credit unionists began to pour into West's home. Unfortunately for Bergengren, wartime restrictions prohibited CUNA's annual meeting, so he had no forum for appeal. The directors did not have an opportunity to give Bergengren's removal a full review until May, 1946. Several directors then attempted to vote Bergengren some kind of permanent honorarium or pension, but this was defeated. The most that the directors would do was to name him *managing director emeritus*. Many of Bergengren's friends were highly incensed by the board's action. There was even talk in some state leagues of withdrawing from the national association. Dismissing Bergengren, said C. E. Michaels of Alabama, "is not going to bring about peace and harmony." The Hawaii league warned West that it was "very much concerned over the undemocratic

[74] Bergengren to Brown, Jan. 3, 1945.
[75] Brown to Bergengren, Oct. 23, 1946.
[76] Bergengren to Parke S. Hyde, May 1, 1947.
[77] Minutes, CUNA Executive Committee, Mar., 1945, pp. 5–38.

tendencies within the Credit Union National Association. We are afraid, if the present trend continues, that CUNA will eventually be dominated by a comparatively few individuals, instead of being representative of the entire credit union movement." [78]

Clearly embittered and deeply hurt, Bergengren concealed his feelings from all except his family and a few close personal friends. Publicly, he wished the movement nothing but success and, as he wrote, "I am through with CUNA but am not through with the credit union." Those he held responsible for his demise would "one day learn how to think straight and there will be new men come along who will get the notion of the credit union as a cause, almost as a religion, because it has to do essentially with the humanities." [79] He made no public criticism of any person connected with his removal, and his memoirs written a few years later gave ample credit to those he considered friend and foe. The movement, to Bergengren, was more important than personalities.

Thus ended another chapter in credit union history. Although Bergengren always considered credit unionism a mass movement which had been built by the thousands of volunteers, it is difficult to exaggerate his personal contributions. He took over a small, weak, moribund organization in 1920 when it appeared that no one else was interested in, or cared about, its success, and developed it into a viable instrument to help solve the credit needs of people with small and moderate incomes. With an evangelical zeal he helped secure the passage of forty-five state credit union laws and the federal credit union act, organized scores of credit unions, wrote seven books and numerous articles on credit unions, made hundreds of speeches, introduced credit unions of the type found in the United States into Canada, personally organized the Estes Park meeting out of which the national association developed, conceived and helped to organize the CUNA Mutual Insurance Society and CUNA Supply Cooperative, and then played a major role in getting the national organization into successful operation. Throughout all of his activities, he always left a little of his own dedication and philosophy wherever he went.

Soon after Bergengren left office, he and his wife moved to a new home, which he described as "a little farm on a pleasant Vermont hillside." [80] His connection with the credit union movement did not end, for he continued to write, to speak, and to observe the progress of CUNA.

[78] Minutes, CUNA Directors, May, 1946, pp. 23–55, 161, 220–21.

[79] Bergengren to J. C. Howell, n.d.

[80] Bergengren, *Crusade*, p. 354.

Moreover, he spent the remainder of his life promoting credit unionism in Vermont, among Negroes in North Carolina, and in the other countries of the world. Many credit union leaders from the past and the future visited his home in Montpelier to discuss credit union philosophy, and he traveled widely to spread his ideas to others. Later he appeared before the CUNA directors in a successful appeal for the organization to extend its services to all parts of the world. But in 1945, with the world war ending, CUNA at last came under new leadership.

CHAPTER XIII

The Postwar Decade

In 1945, at the end of World War II, the American credit union movement was thirty-six years old. It had shown rather steady progress until 1941, but during the war years the number of credit union members, the number of societies, and the amount of loans all declined substantially. These conditions indicate the damaging effect of wartime conditions. Only in total assets did credit unions experience significant gains. Moreover, CUNA Mutual insurance coverage dropped drastically, and the CUNA Supply Cooperative was on the verge of going out of business. Serious problems for the movement had also arisen over the number of liquidations and defalcations. While the movement had progressed rapidly during the economic depression of the 1930s, the war of the early 1940s had brought retrogression.[1]

Nevertheless, most members of CUNA's executive committee believed that the postwar years would bring renewed opportunities for credit unions. To be properly prepared for the anticipated expansion was one of the main reasons for the executive committee's determination to place the national association under new management, to reorganize the work at headquarters, and to restore the old relationship between CUNA and its affiliates. At the March, 1945, meeting when Doig replaced Bergengren, the executive committee voted to restore all powers to the managing director and to request that CUNA Mutual and CUNA Supply do the same. In addition, President West reported that a caucus of representatives of the three organizations had recommended that the affiliates work more closely with CUNA, and that CUNA Supply be disbanded and its assets turned over to CUNA with no changes in operation. The executive committee also voted to work for a merger of the CUNA Mutual board of directors and its own body. In closing the meeting, West said: "I want to say that we have entered into a new era of management and I hope that the cooperation and coordination will prove beyond a doubt very successful . . . ." Two months later West visited Madison and talked with

---

[1] *International Credit Union Yearbook, 1968* (Madison, Wis.: CUNA, 1968), table 13, p. 37, and table 18, p. 42.

CUNA personnel. He found "improvement in the condition of the office, both physically and apparently the mental attitude." [2] In 1946 West reported to the board of directors that, "to the best of my judgment National Headquarters has never before enjoyed the fellowship, the willingness to do and above all that outstanding spirit of cooperation that now exists." [3]

By that time Earl Rentfro had retired as head of CUNA Mutual, and Doig had indeed become the managing director of the total operations. His full control of the national office was subject only to the cooperation of the CUNA Mutual directors and to the directions from CUNA's executive committee. Of the original "big four" CUNA employees only Doig and Hyland remained, although Dora Maxwell rejoined the Madison office as director of the Organization and Education Department. After returning from the armed forces, William Tenney was employed as Maxwell's assistant, but Orrin Shipe did not then return to CUNA, choosing to accept other employment. [4] Although CUNA's operation was somewhat shorthanded immediately after the war, it continued to perform the services desired by most credit unions.

The decade following the war saw dramatic recovery and great advancement of the movement. The greatest progress, however, came after 1950. In the immediate postwar period advances were slow. Almost a year after V-J Day, Doig reported that "the trend is still downward as to numbers of credit unions organized and those liquidated." [5] In 1947, however, he was able to report that "for the first time in several years we have shown an increase in the total number of credit unions in operation." During 1946, 552 credit unions were organized, while liquidations numbered 524. This was not a very impressive record, except when it is compared to 1945. In that year liquidations nearly doubled the number of new societies organized. At the close of 1946 there were 11,602 credit unions in the United States and Canada, an increase of only 110 over the previous year. [6]

In order to stimulate the organization of credit unions, CUNA continued to sponsor contests, awarding a trophy to the state league that organized the most new credit unions and a cash prize to the individual

[2] Minutes, CUNA Executive Committee, Mar., 1945, pp. 36–39, 58; May, 1945, pp. 10–11.

[3] Report of CUNA President R. A. West to Board of Directors, May 11, 1946.

[4] Annual Report of the Managing Director, May 11, 1946, p. 4.

[5] *Ibid.,* p. 1.

[6]*Ibid.,* May 10, 1947, pp. 1–2.

volunteer who formed the largest number. In addition, members of the board of directors were encouraged to form new societies. To stimulate interest in organizational activity, the CUNA directors set a goal for the nation and quotas for each district and each league. From 1946 through 1949, the national goal was 1,000 new credit unions a year, but they raised the number to 2,000 by 1953. The earlier goal was not reached until 1949, when 1,039 credit unions were organized.[7]

The corner had been turned, and Doig announced during the summer of 1950 that during April alone 143 credit unions, the largest number organized in any month since June, 1941, had been formed. In 1951, 1,215 credit unions were organized, and only Prince Edward Island in Canada failed to report a new credit union. Moreover, the Illinois, Michigan, and Ontario leagues each reported organizing more than 100 credit unions, the first time in ten years that any league had reached that figure. By 1952 CUNA reported the formation of 1,733 credit unions, the highest total ever recorded in a single year up to that time.[8] The following year 2,098 credit unions were organized, and 2,107, in 1954; but during 1955 newly formed societies dropped to 1,804. The number of credit unions almost doubled in the United States between 1945 and 1955, rising from 8,683 to 16,201; membership trebled, from 2.8 million to 8.1 million; outstanding loans rose from $369 million to $1.9 billion; and assets increased from $434 million to $2.7 billion. Not only were credit unions getting much more numerous, they were becoming larger in order to provide for the credit needs of a public starved for consumer goods. By 1955 credit unions were providing nearly 6 percent of the installment credit in the United States. Meanwhile, the number of credit unions in Canada had grown to 4,100 by 1956, a net gain of almost 2,000 since the end of the war, with a membership of 1.7 million, assets of $652,000, and outstanding loans of $372 million.[9]

Although the organization of new credit unions took place in every state, there was a change in the relative standing of the state leagues. Comparing the total number of credit unions in the ten top league jurisdictions in 1948 and 1954, Illinois remained in first place, but Massachusetts and Missouri moved out of the elite group. They were replaced by Ontario and Michigan. Older traditional leading states, such as Ohio,

---

[7] Information about each year's organizing contests can be found in the Annual Reports from 1946 to 1956.

[8] Annual Report, May 5, 1950, p. 2; May 8, 1952, p. 17; April 14, 1953, p. 11.

[9] *International Credit Union Yearbook, 1968,* table 13, p. 37 and table 18, p. 42.

New York, Pennsylvania, and Wisconsin declined in relative strength. The over-all situation in 1954 is revealed in the table below.[10] The

RELATIVE STANDING OF TOP TEN LEAGUES
(In Total Number of Credit Unions)

1943		1948		1954	
League	Credit Unions	League	Credit Unions	League	Credit Unions
Illinois	840	Illinois	865	Illinois	1413
New York	823	New York	768	Quebec	1203
Ohio	670	Quebec	765	California	1112
Pennsylvania	638	Pennsylvania	623	Ontario	1090
Quebec	610	Ohio	597	New York	995
Wisconsin	598	Wisconsin	544	Texas	883
Massachusetts	563	Massachusetts	543	Ohio	862
California	473	California	520	Pennsylvania	862
Texas	414	Missouri	384	Michigan	820
Missouri	398	Texas	379	Wisconsin	687

organization of new credit unions, however, showed a fairly consistent and even growth as is demonstrated in the table below.

ORGANIZATION OF CREDIT UNIONS BY CUNA DISTRICTS

District	1946 New Credit Unions	1953 New Credit Unions	% of Increase
Canadian	90	312	347
Northeastern	66	218	330
Eastern	74	243	328
Midwestern	48	164	341
Central	106	398	375
Southern	102	469	460
Western	80	294	367

While the organizational efforts of volunteer credit unionists accounted for significant gains in the number of credit unions, better-staffed state leagues also contributed. In 1946, for example, only twenty-four leagues had full-time field men available to organize new credit unions, and

[10] Report prepared by CUNA's Organization and Education Committee, 1954, typescript, unpaged.

only a few of them had more than one such employee. By 1954, forty-seven leagues employed field men and twenty-six of them had more than one.[11]

The Organization and Contact Department of CUNA, which had been renamed the Organization and Education Department, accounted directly for few of the new credit unions. The war had reduced Doig's force of field men from a high of six to only two in 1947. Both of these employees were located in the Midwest. In May Doig asked the executive committee to allow him to employ four additional organizers, but the committee took no action after failing to see where it could get $26,000 for salaries.[12]

Since field men had traditionally publicized and sold CUNA Mutual insurance, the understaffed condition of the Organization and Education Department was intolerable to the society's directors. Therefore, they decided to employ two field men for CUNA Mutual and so informed the CUNA executive committee in August, 1947. The only question raised by a member of the committee was whether the new field men could organize credit unions as well as promote insurance sales. The insurance society's spokesman replied that the field men would be under Doig's control and would thus carry out his directions. CUNA's executive committee then unanimously approved the new field representatives. Doig announced that he had re-employed J. Orrin Shipe, "an experienced man" who had been editor of *The Bridge*. "He has now worked with the general cooperative movement and is well known around the country," Doig explained, "and he is a salesman." [13]

At the next directors' meeting, representatives of several of the larger leagues suggested, in the absence of greater expenditures for field men, that CUNA concentrate its activities on states that could not afford field representatives. The Illinois league, for example, even offered the services of four field men and fifty voluntary organizers to work in other states.[14] At a joint meeting of the CUNA executive committee and the CUNA Mutual directors in August, 1948, the two bodies agreed that CUNA's remaining field men be transferred to the CUNA Mutual payroll.[15] Given their unwillingness to find the funds to support a field force, few questions were raised by CUNA directors at the time, but by the annual

[11] Report of Charles F. Eikel, Jr., assistant managing director, May, 1954, p. 6.
[12] Minutes, CUNA Executive Committee, May, 1947, pp. 16–22.
[13] Minutes, CUNA–CUNA Mutual Joint Meeting, Aug., 1947, pp. 34–36.
[14] Minutes, CUNA Directors, May, 1948, pp. 244–51.
[15] Minutes, CUNA–CUNA Mutual Joint Meeting, Aug., 1948, pp. 31–32.

meeting in 1950, the board of directors voted to study means by which all employees could be transferred back to the CUNA payroll, and that CUNA Mutual find some other way of paying for the services it received. But it soon became clear that the state insurance commissioner would not permit CUNA Mutual to allocate large sums of money to CUNA, even for services it performed for the insurance society. Consequently, CUNA's board of directors continued to seek a solution for this problem.[16]

By May, 1954, the credit union movement had developed the largest field staff in its history. CUNA employed J. C. French in the Southeast, C. Gail Keeton in the Midwest, Donald Smith in Canada, and James Yates in the Northeast. CUNA Mutual employed Charles Compton in the Midwest, Willard Johnson in the East, Hasell Hood in the South, T. E. Davis in the West, and Henry Timme as a "general utility" field man. CUNA Mutual also paid half the salaries and expenses of Clifford O. Skorstad, director of the Organization and Education Department, and J. W. Burns, assistant manager of CUNA's Canadian office. In addition CUNA Mutual had embarked upon a large nationwide radio and magazine advertising campaign, and employed eight field men, including Dora Maxwell, to follow up organization leads gained from that advertising.[17]

The field staff, now numbering nineteen persons, provided a wide variety of services. During 1953, for example, the field force operated in forty-five states, Hawaii, and nine Canadian provinces. They organized 419 credit unions, sold 638 insurance contracts, and convinced 320 credit unions to affiliate with their respective state leagues. They also sold over 1,700 subscriptions to *The Bridge,* and 355 surety bonds. In addition they attended scores of credit union meetings of local organizations, chapters, and leagues and contacted thousands of local and league officials. Fieldmen met with different groups to explain the credit union movement. For example, Skorstad attended the Southern Hosiery Manufacturers' Association convention, which later carried a favorable article on credit unions in its trade journal. He also attended the Catholic Rural Life Conference in Minnesota and several district cooperative conferences in Wisconsin. Gail Keeton accompanied the president of the National Farmers' Union to a series of meetings in South Dakota. Colleges and universities also enlisted field men to speak before meetings and regular

[16] Minutes, CUNA Directors, May, 1950, p. 93; May, 1951, pp. 88–91.
[17] Report of C. F. Eikel, Jr., assistant managing director, May, 1954, p. 11.

classes about the credit union movement, while various civic organizations invited CUNA representatives to luncheon and dinner meetings for short addresses.[18] Altogether, the activities of the field force fulfilled Filene's early expectations of mass-producing credit unions. But it also proved Bergengren correct, that money was needed to employ enough personnel to make the contacts with groups and organizations which were in a position to spread credit unionism. That money, however, came increasingly from CUNA Mutual and not from the national association, and this fact produced increasing difficulties between the two organizations.

By the late 1940s the movement turned to a more extensive advertising and public relations program to promote credit unionism. Previously, public relations work had been carried on by the most informal methods. Then CUNA directors instructed their president Gurden Farr to proclaim October 21, 1948, as the first annual Credit Union Day to celebrate the one-hundredth anniversary of the founding of credit unions and to use that occasion to launch a fund-raising campaign for publicity work. The campaign was named the Public Relations, Organization and Publicity Program, commonly called POP. Numerous meetings were held around the country, resulting in free publicity in many newspapers. On the same day, October 21, of the following year there were many more meetings and Doig reported that they resulted in the organization "of a good many credit unions, increased membership in credit unions, new league members. and increased revenue to both the leagues and the National Association." [19]

In February 1952, CUNA's executive committee decided to establish a public relations department as a jointly supported activity of CUNA, CUNA Mutual, and CUNA Supply, with the first two organizations furnishing $10,000 and the latter contributing $5,000 each year.[20] The department was set up on September 1, 1952, under the direction of Charles F. Eikel, Jr., a former CUNA field man. The objectives of the new department were to inform people about credit unions, and to seek active public support for the movement. It disseminated promotional literature, distributed news releases for radio, television, and newspapers, and pre-

[18] *Ibid.,* pp. 9–12.
[19] Annual Report, May 14, 1949, p. 2; May 5, 1950, pp. 9–10.
[20] *Ibid.,* May 8, 1952, p. 20.

pared fifteen-minute radio scripts, magazine articles, and study kits for high school classes.[21]

In its second year, Eikel reported that the public relations department was "working with a growing circle of influential people and agencies that knew about, appreciate and support credit union development," including "national and international leaders of community, industry, labor, church, government, columnists, newspaper and magazine editors, radio and TV commentators, and governmental legislators and administrators."[22] When attacks on the tax exempt status of cooperatives increased, the movement stepped up its public relations activities. During 1955 the budget of the department increased to $86,000.[23]

While public relations had always been a part of the credit union movement, advertising was something new. CUNA Mutual inaugurated a radio and magazine advertising campaign in January, 1952, sponsoring radio programs by news commentator Gabriel Heatter in the United States and by actor Lorne Greene in Canada. Commercials carried on these programs publicized both the credit union movement and the insurance services of CUNA Mutual, and within a few weeks they brought 27,000 inquiries about credit unions. In addition, CUNA received hundreds of requests for information as a result of advertisements in such national magazines as *Newsweek, U.S. News, Nation's Business,* and *Business Week*. The leads received from letters of inquiry were passed along to state and provincial leagues for follow-up, and by May, 1952, the organization of thirty-three credit unions could be attributed directly to this advertising.[24] Credit unions already in operation also benefited.

Not all credit union leaders believed that large sums should be spent on advertising. On one occasion the western district conference of CUNA directors called for the complete termination of the advertising program and the diversion of funds to other movement activities.[25] From the sidelines, Bergengren concluded that the money spent on advertising had produced scant results and that if he had initiated such a program when he was managing director he would have been "halved, quartered and burned."[26] CUNA's management, however, defended the advertising program, arguing that it had resulted in the organization of more credit

[21] Report of C. F. Eikel, Jr., assistant managing director, May, 1954, p. 12; Annual Report, April 24, 1953, p. 10.

[22] Report of C. F. Eikel, Jr., May, 1954, p. 12.

[23] Annual Report, April 20, 1956.

[24] *Ibid.,* May 8, 1952, p. 24.

[25] Minutes, CUNA Directors, May, 1953, pp. 216–17.

[26] Bergengren to J. C. Howell, Nov. 30, 1953.

unions, as well as an increase in the number of CUNA Mutual contracts sold. In addition, Doig pointed out other intangible benefits: "In America nothing succeeds like success. A national radio program is an indication of successful operation. It brings tremendous prestige."[27] Since the entire cost of advertising was being borne by CUNA Mutual, many CUNA directors feared that this was just another abdication by the national organization to its subsidiary. Therefore, the CUNA directors voted at their annual meeting in May, 1954, to continue advertising but to shift the cost to CUNA as soon as possible. To prepare for this change, the directors voted to create an Advertising and Promotion Service Department. Finally, the directors expressed the view that radio advertising should be dropped for the increasingly popular medium of television.[28]

Doig reported the following year that a television program for the United States and Canada would cost about $1 million a year, a sum far beyond the ability of CUNA and CUNA Mutual together to pay. He also announced that since CUNA Mutual had discovered that it could not sponsor a radio program in a state where it was not qualified to do business, the radio program was being dropped altogether in favor of continuing magazine advertisements. The latter was budgeted at $593,000 of which CUNA would pay only $22,000. CUNA had, however, carried out the director's instructions by creating the Advertising and Promotion Service Department, managed by J. Orrin Shipe, with Richard Giles as copy chief. This new department produced promotional literature and advertisements for the various activities of CUNA, state leagues, and individual credit unions.[29]

After eighteen months of operation the advertising department reported that it had spent most of its time working with individual credit unions, chapters, and leagues. The department had developed a variety of advertising and promotional materials "in all price brackets to meet all credit union advertising programs that will run around the calendar." The increased need of credit unions for such promotion stemmed, in part, from the "heavy advertising of savings and loan associations, banks, automobile dealers" and other competitors in the consumer credit field. When the department was set up, the directors loaned it $40,000, but insisted that it become self-supporting and repay the loan. During its first year of operation, the department charged customers on an hourly

[27] Annual Report, April 24, 1953.
[28] Minutes, CUNA Directors, May, 1954, pp. 49–53.
[29] Annual Report, April 29, 1955, pp. 3–5.

basis and did a gross business of $103,000, using only $15,000 of the loan and showing a profit of $2,355.[30]

Closely related to the major advertising and public relations work was the decision by a joint meeting of the three CUNA societies to pay a Hollywood film company to produce a movie about the need of average wage earners for credit union services. The film was completed early in 1953 at a cost of about $100,000. It was expected that this amount would gradually be recovered by the sale of copies to state leagues. Like the money spent on advertising, some credit unionists strongly objected to such an expenditure. Nevertheless, by the end of 1955, there were 347 prints of the movie in circulation; leagues, chapters, credit unions, and cooperative organizations owned 214 copies, while 100 were being used by a commercial company. That company, upon payment by the movement of $6.00 a screening, took the film to "theatreless, TV-less" rural towns where it was shown outdoors. During the summer of 1955, there were 688 showings of the film to over 225,000 persons in eleven states. In addition another commercial firm, at a cost of $2.75 a showing, took the film to numerous industrial concerns, schools, churches, and civic clubs which reached over 65,000 persons in thirty-eight states in about six months. Numerous television stations also carried the film as free "filler" between their regular programming.[31]

During the postwar decade, *The Bridge* found favor with an increasing number of credit unionists, particularly since the staggering debt of the early years had been eliminated and the magazine operated on a self-sustaining basis. By April, 1952, circulation stood at 23,000 and the publication enjoyed a surplus of over $6,500. The following year a new feature was added called the "Family Credit Union Digest," which carried stories from readers "based on real life experiences to reveal current family finance problems, finance costs, the treatment by creditors based on family experiences, and how such problems are solved." The magazine added an additional section in January, 1954, called the "Newsletter" which contained short articles on current economic trends, federal credit union legislation, and news items on the movement. Although Doig estimated that 200,000 directors and committeemen still did not receive CUNA's most important publication in 1955, circulation had reached over 33,000.[32]

[30] *Ibid.,* April 20, 1956, pp. 25–28.

[31] *Ibid.,* April 24, 1953, p. 6; April 20, 1956, pp. 6–7.

[32] *Ibid.,* May 8, 1952, p. 12; May 9, 1954, pp. 9–10; April 29, 1955, p. 13.

The general revival of the credit union movement after the war, supported by a greatly increased public relations and advertising program, stimulated all phases of credit union activity. The CUNA Supply Cooperative, which seemed in danger of being disbanded during the war, showed an amazing recovery in the postwar years. Even though the affiliate was plagued by shortages of paper and other supplies, its business totaled $147,000 during 1946, an increase of 66 percent in one year. In 1948 CUNA Supply extended its operations to Canada and its total business continued to expand. The year 1951 was a major turning point in the supply cooperative's history. That year sales reached $395,000 and net profits were $44,458. This, according to CUNA's management, was the most successful in the affiliate's history. By 1955 sales had risen to over $700,000, with net proceeds of over $47,000.[33] There was no longer any question of discontinuing the services of the CUNA Supply Cooperative.

Two other subsidiaries of the national association gained strength in the postwar decade. In 1944 the CUNA board of directors decided to require the CUNA bonding service to become financially self-supporting, just like CUNA Mutual and CUNA Supply.[34] Soon thereafter, the board created a department called the CUNA Insurance Research Division to handle that business. At the same time, both primary and excess bond purchases were transferred to one company, Lumbermen's Mutual, a nonbureau member. The number of credit unions availing themselves of this protection rose from 1,500 in 1945 to 10,340 in 1954. By 1955, 14,500 credit unions were purchasing bonds through the national association, but losses were a problem. During just the last quarter of the year the bonding carrier lost over $204,000 which was 65 percent of the earned premium.[35]

CUNA also began providing automobile insurance through a private company in January, 1949, with individual credit unions receiving a service fee for handling applications.[36] By 1955, credit unions in twenty-eight states, Alaska, and four Canadian provinces were using this service, although three years earlier the Texas Credit Union League had organized its own casualty insurance company. CUNA management warned credit unions not to accept income from the sale of automobile insurance,

[33] *Ibid.*, May 10, 1947, p. 8; May 14, 1949, p. 7; May 8, 1952, p. 12; April 20, 1956, p. 29.
[34] *Ibid.*, May 11, 1946, p. 7.
[35] *Ibid.*, May 5, 1954, pp. 7–8; April 20, 1956, p. 9.
[36] *Ibid.*, May 14, 1949, p. 2.

however, as such profits would jeopardize the tax exempt status of those organizations. At any rate, by 1955 credit unions using the automobile insurance program paid premiums of over $2 million.[37]

A most spectacular development was the rapid growth of the CUNA Mutual Insurance Society. Tied as it was to the general expansion of credit unions, insurance coverage declined drastically during the war years. But even so, by the end of 1945 coverage stood at $90 million. Life-savings insurance accounted for $26.5 million, loan protection $61 million, and renewed sales of individual policies for $3.8 million. The society boasted that it was "one of the fastest growing life insurance companies in the world" after only ten years of operation, having "set the standard of service to credit unions insofar as low rates, broad coverage and prompt payment of claims is concerned." CUNA Mutual claimed over three times the necessary legal reserves, and proudly stated that it still returned eighty-nine cents of every premium dollar to policyholders in claims' payments, dividends, or reserves. The next year, insurance coverage increased 45 percent, when total coverage jumped to $130 million.[38]

The decision of CUNA Mutual to enter fully into the individual life insurance business proved an important boost for the society, but in May, 1948, the supervisory agency for federal credit unions lifted its long ban against federal credit unions purchasing life-savings insurance. These two decisions allowed CUNA Mutual to amass a total coverage of $231 million by May, 1948. The following year coverage jumped to $291 million, which made CUNA Mutual the eighty-second largest insurance company in North America based on coverage. In 1950 CUNA Mutual issued its annual report which it called "Fifteen Years of Building." It pointed out that during those fifteen years, the number of contracts had risen from 370 to 18,657, assets from $36,000 to $2.6 million, and that dividends had totaled more than $2 million. Over 45,000 credit union families had received $8.5 million in claims' payments. By March 31, 1952, coverage had risen to $816 million, and Doig ascribed the great increases to the advertising campaigns and to the zealous promotion of CUNA and league field men.[39]

Records continued to be broken almost weekly, and in mid-October, 1952, CUNA Mutual coverage reached the billion-dollar mark for the

[37] *Ibid.,* April 29, 1955, p. 17; April 20, 1956, p. 28.

[38] *Ibid.,* May 11, 1946, p. 9; May 10, 1947, p. 1.

[39] *Ibid.,* July 29, 1948, p. 11; May 14, 1949, p. 7; CUNA Mutual Insurance Society, "Fifteen Years of Building," 1950 Annual Report (Madison, 1951); Annual Report, May 8, 1952, p. 11.

first time, an increase of $300 million in 1952 alone. This momentum produced even greater increases, as the months of January and February, 1953, alone produced over $35 million of additional coverage *each month*. The end of the year recorded an annual increase of almost a half-billion dollars, and CUNA Mutual jumped in rank among all insurance companies from forty-fourth to thirty-sixth. Moreover, dividends to members increased $1 million over 1952's record-breaking total of $2.5 million. In his annual report for 1955, Doig proudly reported that "with coverage approaching two billion dollars, your life insurance company stands among the top twenty companies on the North American continent by coverage in force, a record-shattering achievement in the short span of twenty years." [40] Truly, this performance was a remarkable business achievement. But it was accompanied by fears on the part of many credit union leaders that the insurance company would eventually eclipse other aspects of the movement. Increasingly, the question was being raised about the relationship between the parent organization and its subsidiary.

The tremendous growth of the national association's activities, including the introduction of new departments for advertising, education, public relations, and statistics, required additional personnel and larger quarters. The Filene Memorial Fund contained $150,000 at the outbreak of war, but building construction could not proceed. By 1946, however, Doig was emphasizing the need for a new and more functional home for CUNA and its subsidiaries. The three organizations appointed members of a joint committee that recommended a building committee to plan for the erection of a headquarters building. This committee suggested to the CUNA directors at their May, 1947, meeting that Filene House be constructed with the funds available from the Filene memorial, plus a similar amount from CUNA Mutual and $50,000 from CUNA Supply, making a total of $350,000 available for the project. The directors accepted the recommendations of the building committee. [41]

Architectural plans were presented to the CUNA directors in May, 1949, and they agreed to go ahead with construction on the site purchased earlier. The result was a modern, functional building, with no expensive frills, on a beautiful site overlooking Lake Mendota in Madison. Through a sustained effort by credit union leaders around the country and their political allies, President Harry S. Truman attended

[40] Annual Report, April 24, 1953, p. 6; May 5, 1954, p. 23; April 29, 1955, p. 12.
[41] *Ibid.*, May 10, 1947, p. 6; Minutes, CUNA Directors, May, 1947, pp. 70–88.

the dedication ceremonies. Perhaps the highlight of the ceremonies, however, was Roy F. Bergengren's address, dedicating the building to Filene and, in his memory, to "Tolerance—Brotherhood—Friendship—Service —Hope." [42]

Despite progress at every level of operation, the credit union movement continued to be plagued by internal difficulties. As in the past, some of the controversy revolved around the question of dues to support CUNA's many activities. Doig recommended to the executive committee early in 1946 that the dues schedule for 1947 be retained at six cents per member, with a maximum of $6,000 for any one league. The dues committee brought in a budget based upon those dues. Harold Moses, a vice-president from Louisiana, objected to the budget of just under $100,000 as being inadequate. He complained that CUNA had "steadily decreased our budget for the past few years and if we are to operate effectively, then the only thing to do is to face that matter squarely and propose a budget to permit us to operate effectively." Doig agreed that it had been foolish to reduce dues in the first place, but warned that state leagues had already based their own budgets on the expectation that dues would be retained at their present level.[43] When the directors met in May they retained the recommended dues schedule.

Even by not expanding the field force, CUNA ended the fiscal year of 1946 with a deficit of over $7,000. Once again the issue was raised about CUNA Mutual's contribution to CUNA's operating expenses. A policyholders' meeting in the northeastern district voted to recommend that the society pay $50,000 a year to CUNA "for services rendered" during 1948 and 1949, and that CUNA dues be reduced to 4.5 cents per member. But the society's directors insisted that the Wisconsin insurance commissioner would not allow such an expenditure. CUNA's directors adopted a slightly larger budget of $124,000 with individual dues remaining at 6 cents per member but raised the maximum to $7,000 for any state league in 1948.[44] Those dues brought in $119,000, the largest amount ever received by CUNA in a single year. Inflation, higher costs, and increased activities by CUNA, however, allowed little of the increased revenue to be spent on field services. Instead, two of CUNA's field men were transferred to the payroll of CUNA Mutual, which also agreed to pay half the managing director's salary, half the salary of the

[42] Annual Report, May 14, 1949, p. 2; *Connecticut Credit Union News,* XII (June, 1950), 1–4.

[43] Minutes, CUNA Executive Committee, 1946, pp. 5, 26–32.

[44] *Ibid.,* May, 1947, pp. 128–29; Minutes, CUNA Directors, May, 1947, p. 14, 188, 210, 230.

manager of the Canadian office, and half the salary of Charles Eikel, the assistant managing director.[45]

Some CUNA directors recognized the consequences of the prospect of having no field force of its own, and therefore supported increased dues for the fiscal year 1949. Although there was general agreement that the individual dues rate should be raised by one-half cent per member, a proposal to raise the maximum was again opposed by representatives of the large leagues. Nevertheless, the maximum for any league was raised by $500. The following year the executive committee again recommended that dues be increased, but the directors retained the 1949 schedule.[46] It was clear that many credit union leaders wished to see CUNA regain control over the field men, but the directors refused to vote the necessary dues. The directors did approve a slightly higher budget of $157,000 for 1951 and a dues schedule of eight cents per member, with a maximum of $10,000. For the year 1952, the maximum alone was raised, but only by $1,000.[47]

By the time of the annual meeting in 1952, many leaders recognized that the movement was at a crucial juncture. A special dues committee reported that many league officials felt that promotional and organizational work could best be done at the state and provincial levels. Others believed, however, that CUNA was "becoming the weaker sister of a strong and aggressive CUNA Mutual Insurance Society." Still, the question uppermost in almost everyone's mind was "where are we going in the credit union movement." The dues committee said the question that must be faced immediately was: "Do we want a strong National Association with an ever-increasing budget . . . and with sufficient staff to cover all the programs necessary to keep this movement great, or do we want a national association that will be the only nominal head and guiding light of this movement operating on a limited budget, with impetus on strong leagues inadequately supported by national and international enterprises and defenses?" The answer supplied by the dues committee was that CUNA must advance on all fronts and this required more money. It recommended, therefore, that dues be raised to nine cents per member with maximums for any league of $13,000.

---

[45] Annual Report, May 14, 1949, p. 10; Minutes, CUNA–CUNA Mutual Joint Meeting, Aug., 1948, pp. 31–32.

[46] *Ibid.*; Minutes, CUNA Directors, May, 1948, pp. 105–6; May, 1949, pp. 82–87, 105.

[47] *Ibid.*, May, 1950, pp. 58 and 66; May, 1951, pp. 38–43.

This recommendation set off another debate. After considerable controversy, pressure from the smaller states produced a compromise, which resulted in raising per capita dues to nine cents per member and setting a maximum assessment at $15,000.[48] In 1953 and 1954 there was discussion of a sliding dues scale to be set on the basis of membership and the number of field men employed by a league. The board passed a resolution in 1953 setting the dues at a high of nine cents per member for a league with no field men, down to five cents per member for a league with five or more field men. The idea was, of course, that the more field men a league employed, the less it would require CUNA services. In 1954 the directors adopted the same dues schedule for 1955 without debate, and it seemed that a satisfactory formula for supporting CUNA had at last been found. In fiscal 1955 CUNA's budget was $316,000.[49]

A controversy sometimes accompanied the annual election of CUNA officers, but the directors generally achieved a surprising unanimity at their meetings even if it took some behind-the-scenes "politicking." Much of this harmony could be traced to the method of electing vice-presidents to represent the nine CUNA districts. Directors in district caucuses chose nominees for these positions and it was in the caucuses, not at the public directors' meetings, that conflicts were settled and compromises reached. Generally, the election of the president reflected a consensus for the policies which had evolved over the years. Following the end of R. A. West's terms in 1947, John Eidam and Gurden P. Farr were nominated for the highest office, with Farr being elected by a vote of 80 to 34. The following year Farr was re-elected without opposition. In 1949, however, the directors chose Eidam and by tradition he was re-elected unanimously for the following year. Marion Gregory of Illinois was chosen president in 1951 and 1952. In 1953 there was again a presidential race, with H. B. Yates of Texas defeating Paul Deaton of Ohio by a large majority. As was usual however, Yates was re-elected the following year with no opposition. Not until 1955, after the relationship between CUNA and CUNA Mutual became severely strained, was an election fought out along fundamental lines. In that year John L. Moore of California, who had been a member of the CUNA Mutual board since 1935 and had served as its president from 1939 to 1943, was nominated for president of the national association. His opponent was Melvin H. Widerman of Maryland. The director who placed Widerman's name in nomination

[48] *Ibid.,* May, 1952, pp. 28–36, and 36–70.
[49] *Ibid.,* May, 1953, pp. 110–32; May, 1954, p. 24.

told his colleagues that if they were satisfied with the way Yates had led the association for two years, they should vote for Widerman. He was elected by a vote of 101 to 72, rejecting any increasing control by CUNA Mutual.[50]

Following Bergengren's dismissal there was a general stability in the operation of the Madison headquarters. In 1947 Doig finally filled the position of assistant managing director. He chose Charles Eikel of Louisiana for the post, passing over Hubert Rhodes and Clifford Skorstad, who were senior in service to Eikel, but more advanced in age.[51] As early as 1952 there were discussions about Doig's successor as managing director, mainly because of his failing health. In 1954 the executive committee gave him a leave of absence and required that he take a complete physical examination by a physician selected by the president of CUNA. In the interim, Eikel became acting managing director. These administrative changes, however, did not interfere with CUNA's continued progress.[52]

One development which bothered some leaders of the organized credit union movement was the emergence of an organization representing the paid personnel of state leagues. In 1949 a group of league managing directors organized the National Association of Managing Directors. The organization met for several days before the annual CUNA directors' meeting, with some forty managing directors and field men in attendance. The following year fifty members attended. James Barry, NAMD president, told the directors that as the credit union movement had developed, fewer employees of the leagues were serving as directors or in any policy-making positions. Yet, he said, league personnel were responsible for executing those policies. Therefore, NAMD declared its intention of expressing its views on CUNA's administration and policies by presenting resolutions to the board of directors. Demonstrating their cooperation, both the management and officers of CUNA met with NAMD to discuss matters of common concern.[53]

When the annual meeting of CUNA convened in 1953, however,

[50] Minutes, CUNA Directors, May, 1949, pp. 61–71; May,1947, p. 101; May, 1948, p. 59; May, 1949, p. 56; May, 1950, p. 123; May, 1951, p. 61; May, 1952, p. 132; May, 1953, p. 36; May, 1954, p. 216; May, 1955, pp. 23–37.

[51] Minutes, CUNA–CUNA Mutual Joint Meeting, Feb., 1947, pp. 25–26. Bergengren believed that Doig preferred Dora Maxwell to Eikel. See Bergengren to Gartland, Feb. 20, 1947.

[52] Minutes, CUNA Executive Committee, Feb., 1954, p. 102; Minutes, CUNA–CUNA Mutual Joint Session, Aug., 1954, pp. 19–40.

[53] Minutes, CUNA Directors, May, 1950, pp. 18–20; May, 1951, p. 93.

NAMD became more outspoken regarding policies of the national association. A resolution presented by the league employees called for a better defined relationship between CUNA and the leagues, especially in the area of field services. The NAMD resolution asked the board of directors to appoint a special committee "to study, reevaluate and recommend policy governing field services of CUNA" in the "interest of closer cooperation, harmony and efficiency of service . . . ." The CUNA directors approved the resolution, although Gurden Farr, chairman of the Resolutions Committee, objected to receiving resolutions from "our hired personnel." A majority of the directors, however, voted to continue to receive such resolutions in the future.[54]

A few months later, a representative of NAMD attacked the practices of the CUNA Mutual Insurance Society, charging that it used its money and power to manipulate the credit union movement. Leaders of CUNA Mutual lost no time in counterattacking. A representative of the California league objected to NAMD's "constant attempt . . . to come in here and try to create discord amongst our organization . . . ."[55] On the other hand, spokesmen for the National Association of Managing Directors tended to curry favor with CUNA officials and therefore did not incur their opposition to any significant extent.

The rise of a professional managerial group within the credit union movement indicated that the original principle of volunteerism was fast passing from the scene. Most leaders still professed to follow this idea but many credit unions were becoming too large and their operations too complicated to rely on anything but trained personnel. Once the movement required professional management and employed hundreds and even thousands of people, the professionals developed a self-interest in credit unionism because it provided their livelihood. The managers of large credit unions and league managers were, therefore, no longer willing to place the direction of the movement entirely in the hands of people who devoted only a limited amount of time to credit union business.

Credit union leaders realized that as the movement grew and issues became more complex, the executive committee and board of directors must spend more time considering the various pressing matters facing the movement. In 1947, the directors voted to establish a standing committee to carry on a continuing study of the total program of the national association and from time to time report its findings and recommenda-

[54] Ibid., May, 1953, pp. 273, 295–99.
[55] Minutes, CUNA Executive Committee, Nov., 1953, p. 42; Nov., 1954, pp. 55–65.

tions to the directors. The Policy and Planning Committee met for the first time in August, 1950, and it submitted a preliminary report to the board of directors the following May. The report reaffirmed the objectives already adopted by the directors. These included the increase of credit unions from the existing 12,000 to a minimum of 100,000; the creation of a central discount bank; an effective public relations program; a sustained radio advertising program; and the creation of health insurance through CUNA Mutual. The committee also recommended a more efficient educational program in schools and colleges, as well as among credit union members, and it urged all leagues to develop to the point where they could employ managing directors and field men. The committee urged CUNA to develop a statistical and reference department, and recommended that CUNA Supply increase its services to members.[56]

By the early 1950s a number of circumstances caused movement leaders to begin re-examining the philosophy and objectives of credit unionism. For some, the assumption by CUNA Mutual of financial responsibility for field representatives led them to believe that CUNA had departed from one of its most basic functions. Others became fearful of the increasing hostility toward the movement shown by commercial banks, small loan companies, and individual business firms. In May, 1952, Paul Deaton, chairman of the Dues Committee, argued for more financial support for CUNA. "The bigger this movement grows, the more involved it will become with problems that cross league boundaries, internal problems of growth and external problems of public relations." A major danger facing the movement, Deaton said, was that some credit unions were losing sight of their original purposes. "They operate as a cross between a bank and a loan company. The members' welfare and benefit is not their chief purpose. This trend has started in many cases because of bigness of the individual credit union, but mostly it has started because of the turnover in the Boards of Directors of credit unions. We find many credit unions that have none of the original Board left and somehow we have neglected to tell these new directors about the purpose of the credit union movement." Therefore, he concluded, "to maintain and return to our ideals, our principles and aims, the Credit Union National Association must be strong and it must be independent."[57]

The executive committee directed Doig to prepare a statement of the basic purposes and objectives of CUNA late in 1954, and early the fol-

[56] Minutes, CUNA Directors, May, 1947, pp. 270–71; Report of CUNA Planning Committee, May, 1951.

[57] Minutes, CUNA Directors, May, 1952, pp. 29–32.

lowing year he issued his report. Generally, he restated the purposes and objective as set forth in CUNA's articles of incorporation and bylaws. Then he attached to his report a compilation of the "Policies of CUNA," [58] which had evolved since the organization was founded. Doig reaffirmed these principles on behalf of the management. The "Policies of CUNA" which had been amended and approved in May, 1953, stated that CUNA's objectives were to encourage "cooperative pooling and use of credit and financial resources of average salaried and income groups," to stimulate thrift, to provide "loan facilities at the lowest possible rates" and to combat usury. A broader goal was to promote the equality of man and to "afford all persons an opportunity to have a direct voice in the control of all public, financial and economic affairs."

To achieve these goals CUNA had to be constantly on the watch to prevent what it considered unfavorable federal legislation. The establishment of a CUNA office in the nation's capital indicated the increased importance attached to affairs in Washington. Doig chose Hubert Rhodes to head the office, as well as to act as managing director of the District of Columbia league. Rhodes assumed his duties on September 1, 1946. The next month he registered under the federal lobbying act. It was not long before the *Congressional Quarterly* commented that CUNA maintained "an active and effective set-up at Washington," and that Rhodes was "regarded as one of the most effective lobbyists in the co-op movement." [59] Rhodes was an effective representative for credit unionism, although nonpartisan good will toward cooperative consumer credit in Washington made his work easier.

CUNA continued to regard the supervision of federal credit unions as a crucial concern. Credit union leaders were never very happy with FDIC supervision, but in February, 1946, Doig recommended that the Federal Credit Union Section remain in that agency. On June 6, however, an audit report of FDIC to Congress indicated "that the supervision and examination of Federal Credit Unions was an extraneous function of the Corporation," and that these activities had resulted in a deficit of almost $475,000 through June 30, 1945. The FDIC suggested an increase in examination fees, and the addition of other supervision charges.[60] At its meeting in November, the executive committee reviewed

[58] Doig to National Directors, Jan. 10, 1955; and "Policies of CUNA," established by the National Directors, Credit Union National Association, and amended to May, 1953.

[59] *Congressional Quarterly*, XI (Nov. 13, 1953), 1327.

[60] Report of the Federal Supervision Committee to the National Board of CUNA, May 1, 1947.

the FDIC report and appointed a committee composed of William Reid, William P. Mallard, and Leonard R. Nixon to consider whether federal credit union administration should be continued in the FDIC, and, if not, what other federal agency could provide the best supervision. They were also to look into adjustments in the examination and supervision of fees. The committee went to Washington in November, 1946, to consult with officials of the FDIC, the Bureau of the Budget, and the Federal Security Administration. As a result of these conferences, the CUNA committee decided to work for a transfer of the Credit Union Section to the FSA, which had responsibility for the social security program. Rhodes so informed James E. Webb, director of the Bureau of the Budget, adding that the committee believed "that the things which the Federal Security Agency are now doing have for their purpose an improvement in the security and economic status of people and the work which the Federal Credit Union Section is doing falls into that general pattern." Webb replied that his office was considering the matter.[61]

Rhodes continued to contact congressmen and other federal officials, while the CUNA committee drafted a bill to transfer the administration of federal credit unions to the FSA, but redesignating the section as a Bureau of Federal Credit Unions.[62] Complications immediately arose. The previous year, President Truman had presented Congress with a federal reorganization plan, which permanently assigned the FCUS to the FDIC. Although the bill did not pass in 1946, Truman presented another plan on May 1, 1947, again assigning the administration of FCUS to the FDIC. The CUNA board of directors discussed these events a few days later, and decided to seek a meeting with Truman to enlist his support for a transfer to FSA. "We do not only want this transfer to avoid the increased cost in examination," Nixon asserted, "but we want the transfer to an organization which is more familiar with the science of human relations, shall we say, and we might be looked upon with more favor in the development of Federal credit unions."

Rhodes persuaded Congressman Wright Patman of Texas to take up the credit union cause, since Jerry Voorhis of California, who had emerged as the "champion" of the movement during the war years, had lost his congressional seat. Patman wrote Truman on May 2 suggesting the transfer to the FSA, but the Budget Bureau Director Webb replied

61 Rhodes to Webb, Dec. 18, 1946; Webb to Rhodes, Jan. 14, 1947.

62 Report of the Federal Supervision Committee, May 1, 1947; includes attached copy of draft bill.

that the decision had been made to leave the FCUS in the FDIC.[63] Despite a bleak outlook, a few weeks later Rhodes informed Patman that CUNA still wanted to make a major effort to transfer the FCUS to the Federal Security Administration. Meanwhile, CUNA prompted a flood of telegrams to President Truman protesting the decision not to move the Federal Credit Union Section out of the FDIC. According to members of the CUNA committee, the telegrams "caused quite a stir in Washington." In July the CUNA committee met with officials of the Bureau of the Budget and the FDIC, along with several congressmen, and again asked for support for the transfer.[64] Soon things began to change. In February, 1948, Senator Raymond E. Baldwin introduced a transfer bill, which moved rapidly and smoothly through committee and both houses of Congress. Truman signed it into law on June 29, 1948.

On June 29, 1948, Maple T. Harl, chairman of the FDIC, wrote all officers of federal credit unions about the impending administrative change. The transfer to the Federal Security Agency took place one month later. The old Credit Union Section became the Bureau of Federal Credit Unions, and was assigned to the Social Security Administration. Orchard became head of the bureau, and Joseph E. Blomgren was appointed deputy director.[65]

For over a year the relationship between CUNA and the new federal agency proved to be better than that which had existed with the FDIC. But the old question of financing the supervision and examination of federal credit unions soon proved to be a divisive issue. In 1950 when it appeared that the bureau's budget request would not be approved, Orchard and his colleagues increased its fees for examination. This action brought an immediate protest from CUNA, which believed that it would result in a "test of strength" between the bureau and the credit union movement. A special CUNA committee, established to study the matter, concluded that since the bureau was the only agency within the Social Security Administration with any potential income, the tendency would be for Congress to insist that it pay its own way. There was also criticism of Orchard for taking action without consulting leaders of the national movement. "The present difference[s] . . . [are] nothing more

---

[63] Webb to Patman, May 19, 1947; Matthew J. Connelly to Patman, May 29, 1947.

[64] Matthew J. Connelly to Farr, June 3, 1947; Rhodes to Patman, June 12, 1947; Minutes, CUNA Directors, May, 1948, pp. 115–17.

[65] Maple T. Harl to Officers, Directors, and Committeemen of Federal Credit Unions, June 29, 1948.

than a clash between democracy and bureaucracy," the report concluded.[66]

Orchard defended his action, however, and reminded Doig that he was acting under instructions from the Bureau of the Budget and from committees of both houses of Congress. Unless the policy was changed, Orchard wrote, the bureau "must consistently and persistently move toward a more nearly self-supporting" status.[67] This was not convincing to the CUNA board, however, and its members lobbied to maintain examination and supervision fees at existing levels and to increase federal appropriations for the bureau's work. This caused such a strain between CUNA and Orchard's agency, that Orchard even declined to attend CUNA's annual meeting in 1951.[68]

In April, 1952, Congress amended the Federal Credit Union Act and increased supervision fees paid by federally chartered credit unions. Three years later fees were again raised, although by that time CUNA officials accepted the move without much complaint. Doig informed movement leaders that since Congress had granted pay raises to federal employees, they must expect fee increases.[69] However, by the mid-1950s, the old complaints about the bureau had not been eliminated. Charles Eikel, CUNA's assistant managing director, told Rhodes that the bureau had "unlimited power," but that the executive committee might soon "take a notion to attempt to place a limitation" on that power.[70]

While these controversies stemmed from CUNA's belief that high fees charged by the bureau might hamper credit union development, there was another matter of great concern. CUNA had always considered itself the national leader, protector, and sustainer of credit unionism. If it could not successfully influence the Federal Credit Union Bureau, many credit unions and their leagues might decide that CUNA was ineffective and not worth supporting. Already there was support for independent organizations of federal credit unions, partly at least because the national association had not been able to obtain deposit insurance and central banks.

[66] Thomas Doig, "Policy of Credit Union National Association Regarding Fees Charged Federal Credit Unions for Examination and Supervision," Aug. 30, 1950; and Memorandum prepared by John E. Eidam, n.d.; Herbert B. Yates, Memorandum re Federal Credit Union Problem, Oct. 25, 1950.

[67] Orchard to Doig, Feb. 1, 1951.

[68] *Ibid.*, April 25, 1951.

[69] Orchard to Presidents of All Federal Credit Unions, Dec. 29, 1952; and Doig to All Managing Directors and National Directors, July 15, 1955.

[70] Eikel to Rhodes, Dec. 20, 1955.

Nevertheless, CUNA was reasonably successful in preventing the passage of unfavorable legislation and in obtaining laws that it wanted. CUNA generally opposed credit controls exercised by the Federal Reserve Board during the postwar years, and worked for the repeal of Regulation W. Congress retained credit controls until mid-1949, and after the onset of the Korean War extended them. CUNA continued to lobby for exemption from such controls. As its president, Gurden Farr, wrote the chairman of the Banking and Currency Committee in the summer of 1949: "Credit unions operate under Federal or State authority for supervision and we deem that sufficient. We believe consumer credit controls are unnecessary, that they favor the financially well-to-do and discriminate against those who are without such means and that they should be terminated. Credit unions create their own capital through savings of members and make loans only to members. They do not contribute to inflationary pressures." After continuing controls through the Korean War, Congress repealed the Federal Reserve's authority over consumer credit in June, 1952.[71]

The major legislative objective sought by CUNA during the decade following World War II, but without success, was the establishment of a central bank system for credit unions. Bergengren and Filene had discussed this matter as early as the 1920s. The need for central banks was based upon the idea that credit unions should not have to rely on commercial banks for funds which they had to borrow. The original federal credit union bill had even proposed that credit unions participate in the Federal Reserve System, but that provision had been eliminated. In May 1950 the CUNA board of directors voted to sponsor legislation establishing a Federal Credit Union Bank system, with a national control bank and seven regional banks. Such a system, it was argued, would allow credit unions to borrow in times of heavy loan demands and would aid newer credit unions in making more initial loans than permitted by their share deposits. It was not until 1951 that such a bill was introduced, but the legislation did not gain approval.[72]

The failure of CUNA to get central banking facilities caused some unrest among federal credit union members, but the question of deposit insurance for credit union shares produced a much greater controversy.

[71] Board of Governors, *Federal Reserve System,* pp. 61–62; Rhodes to Doig, July 31, 1947, and Dec. 3, 1947; Gurden P. Farr to Burnet R. Maybank, May 12, 1949.

[72] Minutes, CUNA Directors, May, 1950, pp. 24a–24c; May, 1951, p. 84; Croteau, "The Federal Credit Union System," pp. 6–7; and John E. Roe to Doig, Feb. 1, 1955.

Some of the demand for such insurance stemmed from the rising number of defalcations during the war. A bill guaranteeing credit union shares and deposits was introduced in Congress in 1947, but the CUNA board of directors strongly opposed it. A majority of directors believed that the problem of credit union losses should be handled through proper bonding of officials and closer internal and external supervision. Nevertheless, congressmen introduced similar legislation in several succeeding congresses. Since CUNA remained adamant in its opposition, a group of federal credit union leaders met in Kansas City early in 1954 and decided to form an association known as the American Association of Federal Credit Unions, to push for deposit insurance and a central bank system. This move worried CUNA officials, but since a federal deposit insurance law would apply only to federally chartered credit unions, H. B. Yates, a CUNA director from Texas, warned that it would "split the movement in two parts." In addition, Bergengren wrote Eikel from his Vermont home that "the enactment of such legislation, in my judgment, would be an almost fatal blow to the credit union movement as we have developed it." [73]

CUNA's opposition to deposit insurance was enough to kill all such bills introduced in Congress. There was some talk of the national association setting up its own corporation to insure share holdings. Meanwhile, CUNA urged state leagues to see that the legal requirements for bonding officials was complied with, and that bond requirements be raised. In 1954 CUNA President Herbert Yates announced that the "clamor for deposit insurance for credit unions has died down," but he warned, "as soon as another large credit union embezzlement hits the headlines, it will probably be renewed." [74]

CUNA leaders considered the concerted effort to remove the tax exempt status from cooperatives as the most dangerous attack on the movement in the early 1950s. Following World War II, with the national debt at an all-time high, and with increasing inflation and demands for tax relief, many congressmen began to look for sources of additional money. To place an income tax on cooperatives seemed to be one untapped source of revenue. Lawmakers were urged by business groups hostile to cooperatives to close what they called tax loopholes which, critics charged, gave cooperatives an unfair competitive advantage. The

[73] Minutes, CUNA Directors, May, 1947, p. 268; Minutes, CUNA Executive Committee, Feb. 13, 1954, pp. 46–53; Bergengren to Eikel, Mar. 24, 1954.

[74] Doig to All League Presidents and Managing Directors, Oct. 5, 1954.

two principal organizations which attacked the tax exempt status of cooperatives were the National Tax Equality Association and the National Associated Businessmen, Inc. NTEA had been organized in 1943, and its first president was Ben C. McCabe, head of the International Elevator Company of Minneapolis. Both organizations raised funds from businessmen and hired public relations firms to disseminate thousands of pieces of "educational" literature which were hostile to cooperatives of all types.

These organizations initially devoted most of their efforts against various types of farmers' cooperatives. Leaders of the credit union movement realized, however, that any legislation that permitted taxation of producer and consumer cooperatives would undoubtedly be applied to credit unions. Yet CUNA was slow to take any public position on this obvious threat, preferring to let other national cooperative organizations lead the fight against any revision of the tax laws. As early as the spring of 1945, however, Nat Helman warned CUNA's executive committee that the time was fast approaching when CUNA would have to act rather than rely on others to fight its battles.[75]

In January, 1951, Congressman Noah Mason of Illinois introduced a bill in the House of Representatives which would have repealed that portion of the federal credit union law exempting credit unions from payment of income taxes. Rhodes appeared before the House Ways and Means Committee and requested that the tax status of credit unions not be changed. At the same time, CUNA learned that many state legislatures, and even some city governments, had proposed various types of taxes on credit unions. Congress did vote to tax savings and loan associations, mutual banks, and some other types of cooperatives in 1951, but credit unions escaped the law's provisions.[76]

At this point, CUNA moved decisively to formulate its stand against taxation. Most leaders of the credit union movement insisted that credit unions should not pay regular corporate income taxes because as cooperatives they made no profit in the ordinary sense. All so-called profits or savings were returned to the members who in turn paid the regular personal income tax. Moreover, CUNA officials argued that credit unions were voluntary associations performing a public service

[75] H. B. Yates, secretary of CUNA, "The National Tax Equality Association," report, ca. 1951; *Congressional Quarterly, Weekly Report*, XI (Nov. 13, 1953), 1323–42; Minutes, CUNA Executive Committee, Mar., 1945, p. 7.

[76] Doig to CUNA Executive Committee, May 1, 1951, pp. 5–6.

and not seeking profit. Credit unionists were able to convince Congress in 1951 of their public service, nonprofit status.[77]

Nevertheless, threatening tax measures continued to appear in Congress. In 1953 Mason introduced another measure and Representative Clifford Davis of Tennessee sponsored an additional bill. Both of these measures would have taxed credit unions rather heavily, and CUNA again fought them vigorously. CUNA generated a heavy mail from credit union members, local societies, and state leagues to congressmen and senators. In September, 1954, Eikel wrote all league managing directors, reminding them that congressmen were then at home campaigning for re-election. "NOW is the time to find out just where they stand on credit unions," he wrote. He urged local credit union leaders to meet with their representatives and explain the position of credit unions on the matter of taxation. "Remember, in most districts," he explained, "the vote of the credit union members could decide the election. DON'T USE THIS AS A THREAT. IT NEVER WORKS. But tactfully explain who you represent and the number of members involved." [78] Many state league officials and local credit unionists complied with CUNA's advice. At the same time, national association officials continued to lobby in Washington. As a result, the movement successfully resisted the move to tax credit unions.

The attacks on CUNA by NTEA and the threat of unfavorable legislation prompted the national association to become much more concerned with its public relations. This necessity, in turn, led to a reassessment of the movement and the formulation of broad policies, not only to guide the new leaders entering the movement, but also to present to the general public. In May, 1953, CUNA President Marion Gregory pointed out that the NTEA attacks, the proposed taxation legislation, and the publicity given to credit union defalcations in newspapers, indicated "that an increasing number of people and organizations are becoming increasingly concerned about our growth." He asserted that "now is zero hour to us. Behind us is little more than preparation. Ahead of us is our place in the sun, or relative oblivion." [79]

NTEA not only hoped to influence congressmen in Washington, it also

[77] Doig to CUNA National Directors, May 8, 1952, pp. 20–21.

[78] *Ibid.*, April 24, 1953, pp. 3–4; Eikel to CUNA National Directors, May 5, 1954; Eikel to League Managing Directors, Sept. 24, 1954; Minutes, CUNA Executive Committee, May, 1955, pp. 24–28; Marion F. Gregory to Doig, Memorandum re Report on Meeting with Marion B. Folsom, undersecretary of the treasury, re Possible Federal Taxation of Credit Unions, May 27, 1955.

[79] Minutes, CUNA Directors, May, 1953, pp. 10–11.

worked to persuade bankers, businessmen, and industrialists that credit unions offered unfair competition to traditional American business enterprises. As a result, many industrialists began to question whether they were contributing to "socialism" in America by providing free office space and other facilities to employee credit unions. As credit unions grew larger many bankers began to question what they considered a "protected" status. The American Bankers' Association openly questioned the movement in the pages of *Banking* magazine. And, as might be expected, small loan companies supported the opponents of credit unions, although they usually stayed in the background because of the special interest nature of their opposition. In general, industrial leaders received letters from credit union opponents that asked: "Are you fighting to maintain the free enterprise, capitalistic system in this country on one hand and on the other hand fostering a socialistic, tax-exempt credit union that is working to destroy our capitalistic system?"

CUNA staff members worked assiduously to counteract this type of criticism. They visited officials of the ABA, the National Association of Manufacturers, the Canadian Bankers' Association, the Household Finance Corporation, and similar organizations. They wrote thousands of letters to businessmen, and published huge quantities of brochures explaining the movement. The letters and brochures denied the charges that credit unions were socialistic, arguing that they were "neither government-owned or controlled." "All members of credit unions are stockholders and they operate strictly to serve their own membership and are actually capitalistic institutions in the truest tradition of free enterprise," Gregory emphasized in a letter to the editor of *Banking*. CUNA's efforts met with success. Officials of both ABA and NAM agreed that their organizations would take no official stand against credit unions, although certain of their members might do so. In addition, CUNA was able to secure endorsements from several major corporations such as Marathon Oil, Monsanto Chemical, the New York Central System, and North Central Airlines. Although attacks on credit unions did not cease during the 1950s, CUNA was able to forestall a united front from businessmen and their organizations which might have led to the passage of harmful legislation.[80]

Probably the most important step taken by the Credit Union National

---

[80] Doig to CUNA National Directors, April 29, 1955; H. B. Yates to CUNA National Directors, April 20, 1956; Gregory to Doig, confidential report, Oct. 13, 1954; Gregory to William R. Kuhns, Aug. 6, 1954.

Association in the postwar decade was the establishment of its World Extension Division to propagandize for, and assist in, developing a worldwide credit union movement. This step resulted from a long concern for expanding credit unions outside the United States. As early as the 1920s, Bergengren had corresponded with persons from many countries who were interested in the movement, he occasionally entertained foreign visitors in his office, and *The Bridge* went to a number of persons in foreign countries. CUNA's activities in Canada were a natural extension of the movement on the North American continent. In addition, by 1953 the movement had spread to Puerto Rico, Jamaica, and the Dominican Republic, all of which were represented on the board of directors.[81] Moreover, credit union development was taking place in South America outside the sponsorship of CUNA. In British Honduras, for example, a Jesuit priest, Father Marion M. Ganey, organized the first credit union in the village of Punta Gorda in 1943. Three years later, the governor of the colony urged Ganey to devote his time to organizing credit unions throughout the country, and with the permission of his bishop Ganey was relieved of his regular missionary duties for that purpose. By 1953 Father Ganey had organized twenty-two credit unions and a league. That year he moved to Fiji in the Pacific at the request of its governor to begin the credit union movement there.[82]

The immediate cause of CUNA's entry into activities outside the United States was the cold war. After World War II the nation began competing with the Soviet Union for the allegiance of war-torn countries of Europe and newly emancipated colonial areas of Asia and Africa. In May, 1953, the CUNA directors adopted a resolution which read: "That CUNA shall undertake to influence increasingly the growth of international understanding and peace through participation in international programs with constructive, self-help objectives related to ours, such as Mutual Security Administration's Point IV Program, CARE and UNESCO. Management is specifically authorized to enlist CUNA as a sponsoring member of CARE and as a participant in Point IV and UNESCO conferences to which it may be invited."

At the same time, CUNA directors resolved "that the Credit Union National Association formulate now a plan that would expand and utilize credit unionism on a world-wide basis as one of the tools to win perma-

[81] Minutes, CUNA Directors, May, 1953, p. 3.

[82] Rev. Marion M. Ganey, S.J., adviser to the Fiji and Western Samoa Credit Union Leagues, A Report to Andrew Gerakas, United Nations senior development economist, n.d.

nent world peace and to solicit the aid of the United States Government in the promotion of the plan." This resolution was passed on to the Planning Committee to devise a scheme for implementation. That committee reported to the executive committee at its meeting in November, 1953, "that the credit union movement as we know it on this continent should eventually cover the entire world, and it is the feeling of the committee that this could best be done through the formation of a world credit union extension department in the National Association at Madison." The Planning Committee recommended that such a department be headed, initially, by one person who would handle inquiries from abroad, but that eventually a staff be employed to do actual organizing work in other countries. Finally, the committee reminded the directors that the work must be budgeted. They cautioned the directors, however, that CUNA should move slowly in the foreign field, because "if we try to force ourselves down the throats of some of the other peoples of the world, they might resent it." [83]

Within the next few months, CUNA representatives met with officials of the Foreign Operations Administration of the United States Department of State, and the United Nations. Both agencies were friendly to CUNA's proposals for the extension of credit unions to provide a "self-help program to give people a simple low-cost credit plan as the basis of their economy in economically under-developed areas of the world." Both asserted, however, that they only offered help to countries which had made direct requests for assistance. CUNA officials decided, therefore, that the first step was to develop an interest in credit unions throughout the world. The national association prepared information kits for dissemination through the Foreign Operations Administration, the Food and Agriculture Organization of the United Nations, the Economic and Social Council of the United Nations, and the International Labour Office. In addition, the FOA brought two Filipinos to the United States for training in the organization and operation of credit unions so that they might carry on such work in their homeland. [84]

The board of directors appointed a Foreign Credit Union Study Committee which invited Bergengren to speak to the executive committee in May, 1954. Bergengren recounted his long interest in expanding credit unionism throughout the world, but said that he had recently concluded

[83] Minutes, CUNA Executive Committee, Nov., 1953, pp. 94–95; Eikel to CUNA National Directors, May 5, 1954.

[84] Eikel to CUNA National Directors, May 5, 1954.

"that if you are going to have a decent life in any country, it has to be based upon a decent economic condition; also that you cannot save the soul of a man whose stomach is empty and you have got to go into these countries and do what you can to help build these people and build them economically." [85]

When the board of directors met two days later, CUNA president H. B. Yates told the delegates in his opening address that CUNA should join in the fight for democracy by helping to prevent poorer nations from turning to communism. "Usury in all its worst forms is found in all of these undeveloped countries," he said, and CUNA "is the only organization in the world that has the technicians to fight usury successfully." He concluded his remarks by saying:

One of the greatest dangers to democracy is the unequal distribution of wealth. The great chasm between the rich and the poor among individuals, as well as nations, causes distrust, dissatisfaction and trouble. The credit union movement helps to permanently solve this problem of unequal distribution by enabling man to help himself and permanently improve his condition. When man is able to help himself, character is strengthened and improvement is permanent. When man is aided only by gifts and subsidies, character is weakened, self respect is lost and no problem is solved, since relief is only temporary aid and giving must be continued. The credit union movement is a foundation stone of democracy today.

After Yates finished, the Planning Committee repeated its recommendations made earlier to the executive committee. As to financing a world extension project, it recommended the use of $35,000 of unappropriated surplus, plus an appropriation of $15,000 from the regular budget. The committee also suggested that the new program be named the CUNA Overseas program (COP), with the World Extension Division to be its administrative arm. The directors promptly approved these recommendations, except for the financial suggestions. Later Bergengren addressed the directors, telling them that he had come to this meeting in spite of poor health, because he hoped to persuade them to establish the overseas program "as my last contribution to the credit union movement." After an eloquent appeal for financing, the directors voted the $50,000 recommended by the Planning Committee.[86]

WED began operations on October 18, 1954, under the direction of Hans Thunell, a former official of CARE. Within a few weeks he left to return to CARE and was replaced by Olaf Spetland, who assumed his

[85] Minutes, CUNA Executive Committee, May, 1954, pp. 50–51.
[86] Minutes, CUNA Directors, pp. 5–7, 47–49, 52, 76–77, 207–15.

duties on May 1, 1955. Meanwhile, credit union literature was being sent to most governments of the world, and FOA had mailed information to all of its foreign mission chiefs. CUNA officials believed that they had established a good working relationship with FOA, and expected assistance from that agency. FOA was particularly helpful, for example, in Marion Gregory's visit to Mexico in March, 1955. Gregory discovered that a law already permitted the organization of credit societies known as *Union[es] de Credito,* although these agencies served mainly businessmen, small industrial concerns, and farmers. Moreover, they were not cooperatives in the strict sense. He found that individuals typically were forced to borrow from town moneylenders at rates of 10 percent a week. He learned that two Catholic priests had organized some sixty *Cajas Populares,* or People's Banks, although they did not have any legal status. Therefore, the main difficulty in CUNA's entering Mexico for organizing work was the absence of permissive legislation. Through the good offices of FOA and CARE, Gregory was able to discuss the need for such a law with the associate director of the Bank of Mexico, the president of the Mexican Banking Commission, the president of the Chamber of Industries of Mexico, and other government and business officials. All of them expressed interest in credit unions and many promised support in securing needed legislation.

CUNA also continued to assist in training representatives from other countries brought to the United States under the auspices of FOA. These included persons from Trinidad and Tobago and India, as well as the associate of Father Ganey in Fiji, Joane Naisara. Contacts with many organizations that worked in the foreign field were also made, including the Pan American Union, the Food and Agriculture Organization, the World Literacy Committee, World Neighbors, Inc., and the World Council of Churches. Several meetings were held with W. R. Hudgens of the International Development Services who carried the credit union idea to Peru. Within a short time WED had contacted individuals in nearly forty countries, and had submitted a detailed plan for establishing credit unions in Vietnam.[87]

After one full year of work, WED announced that it had received approximately three hundred letters from eighty-two countries and territories. As a result of such contacts, credit unions had been organized in New Zealand, the Philippines, India, Nigeria, and Guatemala. In addition, government agencies had sent to Madison for training, ranging from one day to three weeks, sixty-five individuals from twenty-two

[87] Doig to CUNA National Directors, April 29, 1955, pp. 1–3.

countries. In direct contact work, CUNA decided to concentrate on Latin America. In the fall of 1955 Spetland and Carlos Matos, a CUNA director from Puerto Rico, spent two months visiting with government leaders, businessmen, and others. As a result a credit union law for Peru was drafted and a number of experimental credit unions organized. In March, 1956, CUNA appointed Jose Arroyo of Puerto Rico as the CUNA representative in Latin America. In the Caribbean region, CUNA gave assistance to functioning leagues in Jamaica and Trinidad, and helped to organize leagues in the Dominican Republic and British Honduras. To pursue these activities, CUNA not only increased its appropriation, but several credit union leagues, particularly the Illinois league, made voluntary contributions to the program. Increasingly, CUNA translated its literature into other languages, and representatives of the movement appeared at international conferences and in the capitals of the world.[88]

In a basic sense the credit union movement was beginning all over again. It was returning to its first principles. In the United States, credit unions had come to serve mainly the stable, wage-earning and professional employees, those who used the credit union not only for emergencies but for ordinary consumer purchases. Credit unions still served their original "provident" purposes, but the meaning of "productive" had changed. In working with peoples in underdeveloped nations, however, the old needs for eliminating usury, providing facilities for savings, and accumulating those savings to lend money at low rates of interest so that farmers could buy basic tools or farm animals, or urban dwellers could go into small businesses for themselves, harkened back to the earliest cooperative credit principles. For many credit unionists in the United States this prospect rekindled the old idealistic zeal with which they had first entered the movement. And it came at a time when many were questioning whether credit unions had become simply another type of commercial venture in an affluent society.

[88] Yates to CUNA National Directors, April 20, 1956, pp. 22–25.

CHAPTER XIV

Credit Unionism in Maturity

A REVIEW OF the credit union movement between 1955 and 1970 reveals the growing strength and maturation of cooperative credit in the United States. To be sure, old problems and controversies persisted, but projects that had only been dreams of the movement's pioneers became realities in those years. Credit unions developed new and imaginative programs and services that enabled them to assume a growing role in financing the needs of a consumer-oriented society. While many of the new services resembled those employed by commercial rivals, cooperative credit institutions insisted that they remained true to their original philosophy and practices. For example, the creation of the World Extension Division by CUNA represented a bold step in enlarging the services of cooperative credit.

The expansion of credit unionism to all parts of the world was a victory for the movement's "pioneers." But just as there were those who had argued in the 1940s that the movement needed new leadership to carry credit unions beyond the methods of the 1920s and 1930s, so by the 1950s there were others who believed that new management was essential if credit unionism were to meet the challenges of the future. But the question was, what should be the orientation of the new leadership?

When Doig retired as managing director in 1955, CUNA's executive committee promptly elected H. B. Yates, former CUNA president, as his successor to serve on a temporary basis. This action brought an immediate protest from leaders of CUNA Mutual, and shattered the uneasy truce that had existed between CUNA and the insurance society for a decade. The CUNA Mutual board of directors favored Charles Eikel, Doig's assistant managing director, who had recently been given temporary authority to manage the insurance company. Relations between CUNA and its affiliate had improved under Doig's general management, and leaders of CUNA Mutual looked to Eikel as the person who would finally cement the relationship between CUNA and its affiliate. Some CUNA leaders, however, believed that Eikel was too "insurance-minded" and unresponsive to the CUNA executive committee to be managing director of the national association. Moreover, the CUNA directors insisted that only they had the ultimate authority to designate who would be managing director. Therefore, the executive committee had acted with almost no consultation with leaders of CUNA Mutual, who claimed that under the law its board of directors had sole responsibility for choosing a manager of its affairs.[1] This fight over who should be managing director contributed to what seemed would be an irreparable split between CUNA and the insurance company.

Within weeks after Yates's election, two events exacerbated the conflict within the organization. CUNA and its two affiliates had engaged a Chicago management consulting firm to study the operations of the national offices and to make recommendations for improvements. The report was highly critical of many aspects of the national association's management and staff. It concluded that, for the most part, department heads possessed "no outstanding ability, education or experience to merit the salaries they received." Moreover, management had failed "to establish real leadership and coordination in organization, education, public relations, world extension, and a media such as *The Bridge* to keep its membership enthused and advised of real progress within the organization." The consultants recommended that the managing director should "be a good organizer, [and] have good business and financial experience." It also suggested that a new constitution be drafted to define the roles of CUNA, CUNA Mutual, and CUNA Supply Cooperative in order to reduce misunderstandings which were likely to become greater. There was a danger, the report said, "of losing sight of the fact that the Credit Union National Association is expected to provide service, leadership and protection of a quality which will unify the credit union movement and keep it growing." In January, 1956, Yates announced that many of the recommendations of the management consultants would be implemented, although he stressed that they would be primarily in program rather than personnel changes. The major decision was to appoint J. Orrin Shipe as development manager. He was to be directly responsible to the managing director for the operation of all major CUNA departments. Shipe was given control over department heads, authority to make "personnel adjustments," and was expected to coordinate all efforts for increasing the functions and efficiency of CUNA.[2]

The other unsettling event was a suit filed in the United States District Court by a group of credit unionists against the board of directors of CUNA Mutual, charging it with illegally promoting candidates for its

[1] Proceedings of the CUNA Executive Committee, Nov. 12, 1955.

[2] Minutes, CUNA Directors, May, 1956, pp. 64–106; H. B. Yates, "A Progress Report," Jan. 16, 1956.

board and also attempting to influence elections of CUNA's directors. In hearings on a request for a preliminary restraining order in May, 1956, Federal Judge Patrick T. Stone concluded that the laws of Wisconsin allowed a mutual insurance company to use its funds to promote the election of candidates for its board. The following December formal hearings began, but after the plaintiffs completed their testimony, Judge Stone called both sides into his chambers and advised them to drop the suit. He agreed that employees of CUNA Mutual had acted improperly by meddling in the politics of CUNA elections, but CUNA Mutual's directors had assured the judge that such practices would be halted. Therefore, Stone commended the leaders of both organizations for their services to credit unionism and insisted that no good purpose could be served by continuing the case. Both parties agreed.[3]

CUNA's board of directors met in May, 1956, with the management consultant's report and the court suit fresh in mind. The board promptly re-elected Melvin H. Widerman president over John L. Moore of California, who was a member of CUNA Mutual's board of directors. This reflected the directors' determination to keep the leadership of CUNA in the hands of a man fully committed to the national association. The remainder of the officers were also "CUNA men," and were elected over those identified with the insurance society. Moreover, the CUNA directors generally endorsed the management consultant's report. When the executive committee assembled, it once again elected Yates as managing director, and Yates promptly appointed Shipe as his assistant.[4]

During the following months, controversy continued at CUNA's Madison headquarters. In August, Yates announced that several key staff members had resigned "in a surprise move." In addition to secretaries and a field representative, the list included W. B. Tenney, manager of the Education Department; Vaughn E. Liscum, assistant comptroller; Clifford O. Skorstad, manager of the Organization Department; Marion F. Gregory, director of public relations; and C. Gail Keeton, director of the Legal and Legislative Department. A few days after Yates's announcement, these employees issued a joint statement, blaming Yates and Shipe for their dissatisfaction, and concluding that "the people who left CUNA did not do so to satisfy their personal desires; they left because they were thoroughly disappointed and concerned about the sad

---

[3] U. S. District Court for the Western District of Wisconsin, Civil Action File No. 2792 (1956); Glenn D. Roberts, attorney for CUNA Mutual, to the Policyholders of CUNA Mutual Insurance Society, Feb. 15, 1957.

[4] Minutes, CUNA Directors, May, 1956, pp. 154, 158–99; Minutes, CUNA–CUNA Mutual Joint Meeting, May, 1956, pp. 36–56.

state of affairs in the Credit Union National Association." [5] Some people drew other conclusions, however, as several of the disaffected employees, including all of the above, found new positions with CUNA Mutual.

Conditions within the national organization continued to deteriorate. Several days before the staff resignations, a local sheriff served an eviction notice on Yates, giving him until August 9 to vacate his office. The original order had been signed by Eikel, who subsequently informed Yates that he could continue to occupy the office if CUNA would pay the insurance company $75 a month rental. Although Filene House had been built with $158,000 contributed by credit unionists to the Filene Memorial Building Fund, the lack of adequate financing and legal requirements had given CUNA Mutual eventual control over most of the building, including all entrances to the building, the heating plant, the stair wells, the cafeteria, and the managing director's office. The year before, CUNA Mutual had offered to sell its portion of the building to CUNA so as to construct a building of its own, but no action had been taken.[6] The eviction notice, therefore, reflected pressure upon CUNA to assume ownership of the entire building, as well as the extreme disharmony within the association.

Opportunity for improving the situation seemed to have developed by the fall of 1956, when CUNA Mutual finally agreed to an earlier proposal to participate in the search for a new managing director acceptable to both sides. A selection committee, composed of two members each from the CUNA executive committee and the CUNA Mutual board of directors, plus two "neutral" members acceptable to both sides, began the search. By October W. O. Knight, Jr., chairman of the committee, announced that both sides had submitted lists of candidates and several meetings had been held, but that no agreement could be reached. Knight announced, therefore, that for the first time, there was strong feeling that the two organizations had become large enough to warrant separate executive heads, but as an alternative one person might be chosen as "an overall public relations personage, someone who would represent all segments of the movement effectively at the highest levels," with the actual management left to separate executives. When the two bodies held a joint meeting the following month, it was clear that CUNA wanted its own managing director, while CUNA Mutual preferred a common managing director. The problem was, however, that the insurance affiliate insisted on Charles Eikel. After lengthy and acrimonious exchanges and

[5] H. B. Yates to CUNA National Directors, Aug. 16, 1956; M. F. Gregory and Others to CUNA National Directors, Aug. 22, 1956.

[6] "The Ownership of Filene House," Aug. 10, 1956.

a long recess for private consultations, the joint committee agreed that J. Deane Gannon, who had succeeded Claude Orchard as director of the Bureau of Federal Credit Unions, should be asked to become managing director of the national association.[7]

Meanwhile the state leagues had become deeply concerned over the conflict within the movement, and their spokesmen believed that Gannon's appointment would help heal the divisions. Representatives from thirty-seven state leagues had even called a special meeting to discuss the crisis. Most of those who participated were relative newcomers to the movement, and they viewed the situation without the inherited prejudices and assumptions of the past. A spokesman for the league representatives reported to the joint committee that they were convinced that if a managing director were not appointed at once, "CUNA will fall apart." They also warned that a second national association might emerge from the disunity, and that already some leagues were discussing withholding national dues until a solution was found. If this occurred, they concluded, there would "be widespread cancellations of CUNA Mutual policies," and that insurance competitors would begin to make inroads among credit unions. The league representatives recommended that policyholders in CUNA Mutual be given the sole right to amend the bylaws of the insurance society, that no personnel paid by a league should be eligible to hold policy-making positions at the national level, that all directors of CUNA Mutual be members of the CUNA board of directors, and that a single managing director for all affiliates be selected, with an assistant managing director for each.[8]

The choice of Gannon by the joint committee, therefore, reflected growing grass-roots unrest with the state of affairs in the association. CUNA's executive committee met immediately after the joint committee made its decision and offered the position to Gannon, who was present at the time. Gannon expressed his appreciation and interest, but gave no immediate answer. He wanted a management contract. But the executive committee was unwilling to agree to this demand. Two weeks later he rejected the offer. In February, 1957, after some further contacts with Gannon, the CUNA executive committee elected H. Vance Austin, manager of the Colorado Rural Electric Association.[9]

[7] W. O. Knight, Jr. to CUNA National Directors, Oct. 15, 1956; Proceedings of the CUNA–CUNA Mutual Joint Meeting, Nov., 1956, pp. 35 ff.

[8] Proceedings of CUNA–CUNA Mutual, *ibid.,* pp. 19–25.

[9] *Ibid.,* pp. 101–4; J. Deane Gannon to M. H. Widerman, Nov. 26, 1956; Widerman to CUNA National Directors, Dec. 3, 1956; Proceedings of CUNA Executive Committee, Feb., 1957, pp. 76–80.

The press release announcing the election of Austin as managing director of the national association and CUNA Supply Cooperative did not mention CUNA Mutual. Austin seemed a good choice for managing director, because he had not been involved in the quarrels within the credit union movement. He had become interested in cooperative credit while practicing law in Sterling, Colorado, and had helped form a credit union there in 1938, of which he became the first treasurer. He later became a director of the Colorado Credit Union League. Austin was a credit union "volunteer" in the strictest sense, devoting his vocational life to law and, since 1949, to the Rural Electric Association. That same year he was elected a regent of the University of Colorado, and he had been active in many community affairs. Despite Austin's apparent neutrality, CUNA Mutual decided that Charles Eikel would remain as its chief executive officer. This completed the split in management which was formally acknowledged at the joint meeting in May, 1957, when Knight announced that CUNA intended to retain Austin in office and was not asking CUNA Mutual to endorse his election. Both president Knight of CUNA and Harold Moses, president of CUNA Mutual, agreed that separate executive heads were now necessary and they expressed the hope that Austin and Eikel would work together for the common good of the two organizations.[10]

Recognition of the status quo in management did not eliminate the differences between CUNA and CUNA Mutual. In an effort to establish clear lines of function and authority, a special committee drafted a "code" to define the "duties, purposes and classification of areas of operations of the several organizations [CUNA, CUNA Mutual and CUNA Supply Cooperative] to further promote the progressive, harmonious and successful unification of services to credit union members." Adopted by CUNA's board of directors in May, 1957, this code failed, as had past efforts, to bring agreement over operations and organization.[11]

Besides its relationship to the national association, CUNA Mutual had some particular problems of its own. Most state leagues looked upon CUNA Mutual as a service affiliate, and they expected the society to provide the best insurance at the lowest possible prices. Moreover, since CUNA Mutual had for many years sold insurance only to league-affiliated credit unions, state leagues held out the benefits of low-cost insurance as a primary reason why individual credit unions should take out league membership. Another policy that began seriously to affect CUNA

[10] CUNA, News Release, Feb. 9, 1957, Proceedings of CUNA–CUNA Mutual Joint Meeting, May, 1957, pp. 68–69.
[11] Proceedings of CUNA Directors, May, 1957, pp. 292–95.

Mutual was the cooperative principle that insurance rates should be the same for all credit unions, regardless of their loss experiences. Earlier, when there were few large credit unions, the principle of share and share alike was generally supported. But as the nation became dotted with credit unions that had millions of dollars of assets and local officers of those credit unions realized that loan protection and life-savings insurance premiums represented their second highest administrative expenses, they argued that low-risk credit unions should receive lower premium rates.

This problem for the movement became greater when commercial insurance companies began actively to seek the insurance business of credit unions. In the fall of 1957 Harold Moses warned that some 60 percent of the credit unions that dropped CUNA Mutual services also discontinued their league membership in the same year. This, he said, was a serious matter. CUNA President W. O. Knight saw the problem in a different light. He asserted that outside competition was really "a very embarrassing situation for CUNA Mutual, because as it looses its biggest credit unions, its income is of course reduced and its dividends must also be reduced." Knight concluded that "CUNA Mutual today is in the same position that CUNA Supply has experienced for many years—it is up against price competition, and it is trying to avoid facing price competition by talking about loyalty and harmony." [12]

CUNA Mutual held firm on its equalized premium schedules, but sought to meet the growing outside competition through other devices. In 1957 the society inaugurated a Policy Owners' Representative Program (POR) in which chapter and league representatives of policyholders were brought to Madison to learn of the company's aims and policies. That same year the society embarked on a vigorous promotional program by adding twenty-one new field representatives to its payroll. Eikel insisted that every one of his field force was "imbued with the credit union spirit and philosophy and ideals." [13] Nevertheless, some credit unionists interpreted these moves as an intention by CUNA Mutual to take an independent course; others charged that the company was more interested in selling insurance than in the over-all development of credit unionism.

This may have been partly true, but the main task of a mutual insurance company was to grow and provide more services. But CUNA Mu-

[12] Proceedings of CUNA–CUNA Mutual Joint Meeting, Nov., 1957, pp. 14–15; W. O. Knight, Jr., typescripts of draft speeches, ca. 1957.

[13] Julius Stone, Report of First Annual League Area Representatives Conference, Madison, Wisconsin, Dec. 4–7, 1957 (Feb., 1958); Proceedings of CUNA–CUNA Mutual Joint Meeting, Feb., 1958, p. 42.

tual's growth required the expansion of the movement as a whole, and clearly officers of the society believed that CUNA was no longer capable of promoting vigorous growth. Therefore, CUNA Mutual gradually assumed many functions that CUNA performed, and in the society's view, poorly. The society held educational meetings, distributed literature by the ton, sponsored advertising, assisted league personnel with their problems, and even assisted in organizing new credit unions. Increasingly, CUNA officials condemned the insurance affiliate for attempting to become the national organization, but more often the charge was made that CUNA Mutual now made all its policy and operational decisions without consultation with the "organized" movement.

The full dimension of the problem facing CUNA Mutual came in 1959 when the Oregon league arranged with a private company not related to the league to supply the insurance services needed by its credit unions. Even more challenging was the decision by the Michigan league to acquire its own insurance company to supplant CUNA Mutual altogether. The insurance society promptly demanded that CUNA take action against the Oregon and Michigan leagues. But the executive committee reminded the society that the leagues had been complaining about CUNA Mutual's programs and that the insurance company had failed to meet competition. CUNA Mutual, therefore, announced a policy of selling insurance to nonleague credit unions in states where leagues had officially or tacitly encouraged a competitive company. CUNA's directors condemned this action, but CUNA Mutual declared that it would only revert to its former policy when the leagues restored CUNA Mutual as the sole league-sponsored insurance company.[14]

The split in the credit union movement hit a new high in 1959 and 1960. CUNA Mutual reversed its plans to construct an office building on land owned by the national association, arguing that there was not enough property to meet building and parking needs. Instead CUNA Mutual purchased eighteen acres across town in Madison on which to construct a new office building. At the same time, the society held out the possibility that CUNA and CUNA Supply might want to construct new buildings for themselves at that location in the future.[15] With a minimum of protest from CUNA, the society carried out its plans and dedicated a spacious, modern office building during the annual meeting in May, 1960.

---

[14] Proceedings of CUNA–CUNA Mutual Joint Meeting, Nov., 1958, pp. 70–72; Feb. 5, 1959, pp. 39–47; Minutes, CUNA Directors, May, 1960, p. 35.

[15] Charles F. Eikel, Jr., to Board of Directors of CUNA Mutual Insurance Society, Aug. 8, 1958.

The major crisis, however, came when CUNA Mutual announced that it intended to organize a new insurance company to handle property and casualty insurance. At an emergency meeting of the CUNA executive committee in December, 1959, President Julius Stone denounced the move for having been taken without consulting the organized movement. Stone asserted that such action was only the latest in a pattern of decisions by the society that "made CUNA Mutual more independent of the credit union movement," and "revealed a new operating philosophy, which is that, 'whatever is good for CUNA Mutual is good for the movement' . . . ." Moreover, Stone pointed out that the insurance company knew that the CUNA Insurance Services Committee was engaged in a study to determine whether the national association should acquire its own bonding and automobile casualty company. Finally, he questioned whether CUNA Mutual should consider such a step at a time when it had many problems with its present services. The executive committee instructed its Insurance Services Committee to continue its studies and requested CUNA Mutual to delay any decision in the matter until after CUNA's board met in May, 1960.[16]

When the CUNA Mutual directors gathered in February, 1960, they took no final action, but they did not accede to the executive committee's request for postponement until May. The next day, Stone told his executive committee that the society had "taken a long, long step in the direction of severing its relationship with the credit union movement." Stone recommended that the Insurance Services Committee intensify its studies of casualty and surety insurance so that it would have a proposal ready for the directors in May. More dramatic, however, was Stone's suggestion that the same committee have a proposal ready for CUNA to establish its own life insurance services, "should the movement find itself without the services of a facility for providing credit life insurance" as of the May meeting. Whether Stone actually believed that there was danger of a complete separation of CUNA from CUNA Mutual, or whether he was simply trying to pressure CUNA Mutual to abandon its plans to handle property and casualty coverage, he had thrown down the gauntlet.[17]

Three days before the CUNA board of directors met, the joint committee engaged in full-scale debate over the issues which divided them. Stone said that the question was not whether either organization should establish a casualty company, because CUNA saw no need for one and did not think CUNA Mutual was prepared to enter the field. He also

[16] Proceedings of CUNA Executive Committee, Dec., 1959, pp. 5–81.
[17] *Ibid.*, Feb., 1960, pp. 5–16.

said that there was no question as to whether CUNA was going to enter the life insurance business; it had no plans to do so and had only begun such a study "in the event that CUNA Mutual leaves." Nor was there any question about whether CUNA could legally control CUNA Mutual, because the law would not allow it. Stone asserted that CUNA had not asked for control, but "we have asked for participation." "It is not a question of one group controlling another group," he said. "It is a question of free discussion, free debate, carefully established voting rights, parliamentary procedures clearly spelled out, fair play and majority rule." Stone echoed the attitudes of leaders of the past when he reminded CUNA Mutual officials that the policyholders of CUNA Mutual were not the organized credit union movement. Both Joseph S. DeRamus and CUNA Mutual's President J. D. Nelson MacDonald replied to Stone's statement. They explained that CUNA Mutual had done nothing to harm the over-all credit union movement and that its policies represented the will of its policyholders. "We will not be browbeaten into actions that are contrary to our best judgment, or that are contrary to the laws under which we operate," MacDonald concluded.[18]

The CUNA directors met in May, 1960, in an atmosphere of crisis. Almost immediately representatives of the Ohio and New York leagues announced that they would withhold their dues until the crisis within the movement was settled. A resolution from the Ohio league denounced the "struggle for power," which would only lead "to the ultimate disintegration and collapse of our credit union movement." The New York league objected to the action by Stone and the executive committee as "closely approaching a 'rule or ruin' position." Following further discussion of insurance matters, the Insurance Services Committee recommended that neither CUNA nor CUNA Mutual establish bonding, casualty or property insurance programs, and that CUNA not consider entering the life insurance business. The directors approved the report, although they refused to include CUNA Mutual in the prohibition against organizing a surety and casualty company. In addition, when they approved the provision prohibiting CUNA from handling life insurance, they added "that CUNA reaffirm its endorsement of the CUNA Mutual Insurance Society as the credit union life insurance company of the organization." Almost immediately, MacDonald announced that the CUNA Mutual directors had just met and decided to form a general insurance company. Much discussion followed that announcement, and resolutions were introduced that criticized various CUNA Mutual policies

[18] Proceedings of CUNA–CUNA Mutual Joint Meeting, May, 1960, pp. 4–27.

and practices. But it was clear that a majority of directors wanted more cooperation between the two organizations, not a complete separation.[19]

As the movement moved into the 1960s, the open fights between supporters of the two organizations tended to be muted, although they colored almost every policy decision and activity within credit unionism. Loyalties were strong on both sides, and they were felt in local credit unions, state leagues, and officials on the national level. As Jack Dublin, both a participant in, and scholar of, credit union affairs, concluded: "In both factions there was genuine concern for the preservation and advancement of an enterprise—be it CUNA or CUNA Mutual—to which many people have selflessly devoted themselves, a cause for which they could fight with self-righteous conviction. Personal ambitions, human weaknesses, vested interests and the power that goes with money all played a part in the struggle."[20] Before 1965 most elections for positions on CUNA's executive committee were contested according to those loyalties, but by that time a smoothly functioning organization made up of CUNA-oriented state leaders and top CUNA management officials had clearly established the point that if CUNA Mutual could not be controlled by CUNA, the reverse would not occur.[21]

Despite the time and energy devoted to internecine struggles, steady progress occurred in extending credit union services to the people of the world. By 1958, CUNA's World Extension Department included a director, an assistant director, and field representatives for Latin America and the Caribbean. That same year, fifty-two different countries and territories in all six continents, the Caribbean, and the Pacific had been assisted by the WED, and as a result 104 credit unions were directly organized and many others came into existence as a result of volunteer activity. Several federal and international agencies, as well as WED,

[19] Minutes, CUNA Directors, May, 1960, pp. 2–4, 16, 44–52.

[20] Jack Dublin, *Credit Unions: Theory and Practice* (Detroit: Wayne State University Press, 1966), p. 163.

[21] For nominations and elections for CUNA officers, see Minutes of CUNA Directors for years 1957 through 1965. For activities of the CUNA "machine," see L. R. Nixon to Members of the Strategy Committee, Oct. 25, 1962, and Harold B. Carpenter to All Concerned, Subject: Unofficial Committee on Politics of CUNA (COPOC), Oct. 25, 1963. In a revealing memorandum following the May, 1964, elections, an unidentified member of the unofficial committee thanked the participants of COPOC on behalf of its candidates. He concluded: "Many have interpreted the outcome of the recent meetings as meaning simply: that CUNA directors should run CUNA and CUNA Mutual persons should run CUNA Mutual. It would be foolhardy to become overconfident since the other side will not lay down in their efforts to continually harass and sabotage any national program. From time to time, these letters will continue in an effort to keep you up-to-date on exactly what is going on" (May 15, 1964).

continued to sponsor the training of individuals at Filene House. During 1957, for example, sixty-three persons from countries such as Chile, Peru, Australia, Indonesia, Korea, Nigeria, and Thailand spent from a day or two to six months in Madison, learning about credit union philosophy and practices. CUNA representatives themselves became familiar figures throughout the world as they offered credit unionism as one method by which people in underdeveloped nations might improve their economic condition.[22]

The work of world extension was financed in part by CUNA, but the federal government, the United Nations, philanthropic bodies, and state leagues provided additional funds. The Illinois league, in particular, gave strong support to overseas activities. By 1959 the director of WED reported that the point had been reached "where credit unions have proven themselves adaptable to all economic levels anywhere in the world and have become a definite factor in the raising of the standards of living in developing countries." A Filipino credit union leader wrote: "I personally believe strongly that CUNA's entry in the Philippine credit union field will be the first non-governmental assistance that the American people will give to the Filipino people based on the principle of cooperation and self-help."[23]

By 1960 CUNA was sponsoring training conferences and seminars in many parts of the world. One of those was held in Chile, where thirty-seven credit union leaders from Peru, Argentina, Paraguay, and Chile spent twelve days at a conference cosponsored by CUNA, the Pan American Union, the University of Chile, and the Chilean Federation of Credit Unions. The WED's Caribbean fieldman, A. A. Bailey, conducted a series of short courses for credit unionists in Dominica, Trinidad, and British Guiana. CUNA also stepped up its efforts to translate credit union literature into other languages. In February, 1961, WED reported that in six months ninety-seven new credit unions had been organized, including societies in Ireland, Spain, India, New South Wales, and Australia.[24]

This rapid world-wide expansion naturally brought problems to CUNA. In a lengthy report prepared in 1961, the WED listed ten specific matters of concern. Among these were a lack of education among prospective members of credit unions; the failure of most countries to

---

[22] Report to the International Credit Union Study Committee from the CUNA World Extension Department, May, 1958.

[23] *Ibid.*, Feb. 5, 1959, p. 2; Aug., 1959, p. 2.

[24] *Ibid.*, Feb., 1960, pp. 1–2; Feb. 7, 1961, p. 1.

enact legislation recognizing credit unions; the scarcity of proper banking facilities, necessitating credit union treasurers to keep money in their
homes without proper safeguards; the difficulty of obtaining surety bonds
for officers of these new credit unions; the "lack of familiarity with the
democratic method of running an organization," which caused members
to mistrust their elected officers; and the low income of most members in
underdeveloped countries. All of these factors, the report said, hampered
credit union development.[25]

In spite of the difficulties, CUNA continued to emphasize its overseas
activities. By May, 1961, individuals, credit unions, and state leagues had
contributed over $30,000 to the work of WED, and that same year
CUNA signed a contract with the Agency for International Development
to undertake further credit union work. In 1962 the Saskatchewan Credit
Union League contributed $14,000 to aid credit union development in
Tanganyika. CUNA itself allocated $123,500 to WED in 1964, which
was 9.5 percent of its total budget. The Michigan league contributed
$20,000 for work in Africa. These funds allowed CUNA to appoint a
number of national and local personnel in Latin America and to open a
Far East office in Manila. In Fiji, Father Marion Ganey opened a credit
union training school, which he named in honor of Bergengren. In the
summer of 1962, three members of the CUNA staff participated in the
training of Peace Corps volunteers, who subsequently began to organize
several types of village cooperatives in Chile. By the summer of 1963,
there were approximately 3,600 credit unions outside North America,
with an aggregate membership of 750,000 and assets of $50 million.[26]

As a result of the work of the World Extension Department, assisted by
AID, the Peace Corps, and local volunteers, world-wide credit unionism
grew at an amazing pace. In 1956 CUNA had hired its first South American representative with headquarters in Lima, Peru. By 1966 recognition of the need for credit unions was so widespread in Latin America
that a Latin American Regional Office was opened under the CUNA-
AID program. No longer alone as a sponsoring agency, CUNA had been
joined by the West German Bishops' Fund, the Raiffeisen Organization
of the Netherlands and other cooperative, religious, governmental, and
international organizations. By 1969, there were over 4,000 credit unions

[25] "Problems Facing the Overseas Activities of the World Extension Department," April 26,
1961.

[26] Special Report from the World Extension Department to the International Credit Union
Study Committee, May 4, 1961; Report of the International Credit Union Study Committee,
May, 1962; Report of WED, May, 1963, pp. 6–7; Report of the Planning Committee, May,
1963.

and related societies in Latin America and about 1,200 in Africa. Altogether outside of the Americas, it was estimated that there were over 26,000 credit unions.[27]

The expansion of credit unions in the underdeveloped countries resembled the early history of cooperative credit in Europe, Canada, and the United States. People in small towns and villages pooled their meager resources and extended low-cost credit for "provident and productive" purposes. In an African village, a tribesman was able to put a permanent roof on his cottage; in an Asian city a credit union member was able to buy an automobile and become a self-employed taxicab driver; in Great Britain the secretary of a member of Parliament, who could not obtain credit at a bank, was able to purchase household goods for her new home. In Latin America, credit unions enabled villagers to obtain chickens or livestock or to purchase farm implements, and in Ghana a cooperative for fishermen became a reality.

The development of credit unionism outside North America naturally raised the question of the relationship between these new credit unions and CUNA. In 1958 credit union leagues in Chile, British Guiana, and Trinidad were admitted to CUNA membership. At the same time there were already leagues in New South Wales and Fiji, but the CUNA bylaws specified that only leagues in the Western Hemisphere were eligible for membership. That year, however, the bylaws were amended to make possible the membership of any league in the world. A parallel development occurred in 1958 when WED and the St. George's College Extension School of Jamaica assisted in the organization of the West Indian Confederation of Credit Unions, encompassing the credit unions of Jamaica, British Guiana, Saint Lucia, Saint Vincent, Trinidad, Dominica, and Grenada. The next year the Peruvian credit union league was admitted to CUNA. Soon new leagues existed in Ireland and the Philippines.[28]

A question still remained as to how these leagues fit into CUNA's organizational structure. As early as 1958, the International Credit Union Study Committee considered two approaches to the problem. One solution was for each country to form its own national association which would become, along with the United States and Canada, members in a world federation of credit unions. The other approach, which the com-

---

[27] Report of CUNA International World Extension Department, May, 1966; *International Credit Union Yearbook, 1970* (Madison, Wis.: CUNA, 1970), pp. 4, 8.

[28] Report to the International Credit Union Study Committee from the CUNA World Extension Department, May, 1958, p. 1; Minutes, CUNA Executive Committee, Aug., 1959, p. 8.

mittee finally recommended, was that leagues should be taken into CUNA because national organizations had not yet developed to a point where they could be self-supporting. In order to give new leagues representation on the executive committee, the board created a twelfth district. By 1960, District 12 encompassed the leagues of British Guiana, British Honduras, Chile, Fiji, Jamaica, New South Wales, Peru, and Trinidad, and its vice-president was Father John P. Sullivan, pioneer credit unionist in the Caribbean.[29]

Meanwhile, some credit union leaders believed that CUNA was devoting too much time and effort to the international aspects of credit unions and neglecting the national responsibilities. They opposed membership for new foreign leagues. At the annual meeting in May, 1960, the board of directors defeated a resolution calling for amendments to the bylaws that would have kept non–United States leagues from voting or interfering in the "internal affairs" of the United States leagues. It later tabled another resolution that would have limited membership in CUNA to leagues in the United States and its possessions. Many credit union leaders thought that a satisfactory solution had been found when Canada set up its own national association, while still retaining its affiliation with CUNA. As a Missouri director said, the development in Canada would be followed by "another area fully developed that would like to do business in its own way without hearing so much of us American lawyers yelling and shouting. They will do it quietly in their own way, but the format must be set up and it takes time to do these things thoroughly . . . ."[30]

There were still those who objected to the increased role of foreign leagues. A director from the District of Columbia league agreed that CUNA had played a necessary role in introducing credit unionism into other countries, but that once that was accomplished, CUNA should say to them, "you run it your way in your country and we will run it our way in our country." John L. Moore, a pioneer credit unionist from California, wrote upon his retirement as a CUNA director in 1961, that unless an "international" association was established immediately, United States credit unionists must "proceed forthwith to organize an association to take care of the 'National' affairs and interests of the credit unions of this Country."[31]

[29] Proceedings of CUNA Directors, May, 1958, pp. 329–30; Minutes, International Credit Union Study Committee, Feb. 10, 1960, pp. 1–2.

[30] Minutes, CUNA Directors, May, 1960, pp. 457, 492–94; May, 1961, pp. 44–45, 405–11.

[31] *Ibid.;* Report of John L. Moore, National Director, to Board of Directors, California Credit Union League, Nov. 3, 1961.

These pressures prompted CUNA officials to hasten plans for a new organizational structure. In May, 1962, the Planning Committee proposed the creation of an international organization, but when action on the proposal did not come quickly enough, a number of CUNA directors joined the National Committee for the Formation of an Association of United States Credit Union Leagues. This committee did not seek disaffiliation from CUNA, but only wanted a separate organization for United States leagues to deal with purely domestic matters, while remaining in an international federation that would deal with larger concerns.[32]

At its annual meeting in May, 1964, the board of directors approved the establishment of an international association with national forums operating within that structure. The following year, the name of the Credit Union National Association, Inc., was changed to CUNA International, Inc. In addition, separate forums for the United States and Canada held their first meetings, as did the District 12 Forum, which included all other affiliated leagues. The general meeting of the directors thereafter took on the air of a federation, to which propositions regarding the world-wide movement came from the three forums.[33] Purely national business was conducted in the forums. Thus, the movement devised a structure that permitted the special problems of the United States and Canada to be decided by leaders in those countries. At the same time these mature organizations could assist in the development of new credit unions elsewhere throughout the world. Few persons doubted, however, that continuous attention would have to be given to national and international structures in the future.

Kenneth Marin served as the last president of the national association and as the first president of CUNA International. The first chairman of the United States Forum was R. C. Morgan of Texas. James M. Davidson of Ontario became the first chairman of the Canadian National Forum, while Father Daniel McLellan became chairman of the District 12 Forum. The true internationality of the credit union movement was symbolized the following year, when A. R. Glen of British Columbia became the first president of CUNA chosen from outside the United States. During his first address, however, he charged the executive committee with reconsidering the entire organizational structure of CUNA International, "leading toward a more effective recognition of its inter-

[32] Report of the Planning Committee, May, 1962, pp. 2–8; Abridged Minutes, CUNA Directors, May, 1963, p. 32; National Committee to U. S. League Presidents, Dec. 8, 1963.

[33] Report of the Special Districts Structure Committee; Minutes, CUNA Directors, May, 1964, pp. 34–41; May, 1965, p. 24.

national characteristics and the desirability of national credit union affairs being guided and administered by the various national groups insofar as this is practicable." [34] As Filene and CUNEB had played their pioneer roles in launching the credit union movement in the United States only to turn its direction over to grass-roots leadership, so now was CUNA learning that the child it had brought into the world demanded a larger role in shaping its own destiny.

A second major development that revealed the movement's adherence to its basic philosophy was the directors' decision in 1958 to launch a continuous study of the problems of low income groups in the United States. After several conferences between CUNA and league officials, and representatives of inner city and minority groups, CUNA decided to establish demonstration credit unions among the poor. The directors also planned to bring representatives of low income groups to Madison for training to prepare them to work in their own communities. By May, 1961, the Organization Department had set up its first two demonstration projects for the Spanish-speaking poor in Nebraska and Texas.[35]

Progress in this area of service, however, was slight until 1964, when the growing nationwide concern with the plight of the poor led to a spate of publicity, congressional investigations, and a federal program dubbed as the War on Poverty. In May of that year, Orrin Shipe, now CUNA's managing director, told credit unionists that a "subject that lies close to my heart—because it gets us above the technical operations of credit unions and back to the true philosophy and idealism of our founders—is the credit union demonstration project for poor people you will be asked to consider here today." [36] The Planning Committee recommended the appropriation of $50,000 to begin demonstration projects in Chicago, Washington, and New York. There were some objections to the proposal, but the directors approved the new plan.[37]

Meanwhile, CUNA officials were also in close contact with government agencies, particularly with the Office of Economic Opportunity, which administered such War-on-Poverty programs as the Job Corps, the VISTA Volunteers, and the Community Action programs. R. Sargent Shriver, director of OEO, agreed that if credit unions were included as part of locally submitted Community Action Programs, his office

[34] Minutes, CUNA Directors, May, 1965, pp. 3, 7, 12, 14; Abridged Minutes, May, 1966, p. 20.

[35] Abridged Minutes, CUNA Directors, May, 1959, p. 13; Report of Managing Director, May, 1961, p. 4.

[36] Report of Managing Director, May, 1964, p. 4.

[37] Proceedings of CUNA Directors, May, 1964, pp. 26–27.

would cooperate with CUNA in their implementation.[38] By 1966 the OEO had granted CUNA $19,500 to pay the salary and expenses of one staff assistant "to step up efforts of CUNA in the utilization of credit unions as the consumer component in OEO's community action program." By that time there were demonstration credit unions in five locations. One of those in Chicago—the Pilsen Neighbors Federal Credit Union—was founded in 1964 in an area with a potential membership of 40,000, 60 percent of whom were Spanish speaking. By 1966 it had 511 members and assets of $59,000. The other Chicago demonstration credit union served the Prairie-Halsted Federated Churches, with an all-Negro membership of 344 and assets of $26,000. In 1965 a credit union was begun in an area embracing 15,000 Negroes, Latin Americans, and poor Anglo-Americans in Wilmington, Delaware.[39]

The CUNA-OEO plan anticipated transferring these demonstration credit unions to Community Action groups, but meanwhile it was thought that CUNA would gain valuable experience in developing societies among the poor. The national association discovered, however, that the old principle of developing a credit union by slowly accumulating savings from members and operating with volunteers was impractical for the development of low income groups. CUNA concluded that "low-income credit unions should be launched as full-time operations, complete with a paid manager and promotion programs." The manager's task was really to "run a 'money clinic.' His job is actually to teach economic illiterates, and to win their confidence. Volunteers in low-income groups have neither the skill nor the time for this essential service." CUNA officials found that, because these credit unions lent money to buy food or to make a small rent payment to save a family from eviction, delinquencies were high. In these communities the idea of building up a credit union slowly and patiently, "a dollar at a time," as some advocated, simply would not work. Credit unions in most low-income areas had to be subsidized by providing management, office space, and other overhead costs. Moreover, officials in the poverty program wanted credit unions "launched in full operation—perhaps even capitalized— ready to meet immediate needs which cannot wait." [40]

The development of credit unions among low-income groups became a cooperative effort. CUNA established an Economic Opportunity Department, headed by Robert M. Dolan, and a number of state leagues were also active in this field of service. In 1967 CUNA signed a contract with

[38] J. Orrin Shipe to R. Sargent Shriver, Jr., Oct. 28, 1964.
[39] CUNA, "Anti-Poverty Report, 1964–1966," n.d.
[40] Ibid.

OEO, under which the federal agency granted $180,000 to the national association to assist in providing five regional specialists for mobilizing the leagues to provide technical assistance to credit unions among the poor sponsored by OEO, and to evaluate the federally funded credit unions once they were in operation. The OEO also made grants to local Community Action Committees.[41]

Although credit unions in poverty areas grew slowly, many persons hoped for their success. An OEO official told one audience, for example, that credit unions were "an essential way to break the cycle of poverty, first because they meet one of the greatest needs of poor people by providing low-cost credit; second, because they represent an ideal example of what we mean by community action; and through a credit union, poor people learn how to work together to achieve something; they learn how to read an agreement and to make decisions." The chairman of the Chicago Congress on Racial Equality characterized credit unions as helping "to keep the money traveling in our community." In so doing, he added, "we are creating a new value system for our people. We are developing a new frame of reference, a new people-centered economic framework, a new morality." [42] However, this was more rhetoric than reality.

By October, 1968, there were 672 credit unions operating in recognized poverty areas, 245 of which were related to OEO Community Action programs. Four of the latter were designated as demonstration projects, each receiving over $100,000 in operational assistance. The OEO or private agencies subsidized ninety of them in amounts ranging from $10,000 to $30,000.[43] This class of credit unions, however, made but small gains in the last two years of the 1960s. Only seven of the 313 OEO-related credit unions had amassed total savings of $100,000 by 1969. Figures from all but 60 of the 313 credit unions revealed a total savings of over $4 million and membership of 87,000. The average shares per member were a mere $44. Shipe called credit unions for the poor "the biggest, toughest job the credit union movement has ever taken on. Yet no other organization can help the poor to help themselves like we can." [44]

Some credit union leagues actually stepped up their involvement in

[41] CUNA, "Frontline: News from the Credit Union War Against Poverty," Aug. 18 and Oct. 13, 1967.

[42] *Credit Union Magazine*, XXXII (Oct., 1967), 41; and "Frontline," Jan. 12, 1968, pp. 1 and 4.

[43] "Frontline," Oct. 15, 1968, p. 2, and Nov. 15, 1968, p. 1.

[44] *Ibid.*, June 13, 1969, p. 2; and CUNA "Briefs," Dec. 12, 1969, p. 1.

the low-income credit union field, but the pressures of inflation, the Vietnam war, traditional Republican budget-mindedness, and President Richard M. Nixon's skepticism about many of the Kennedy-Johnson social programs, combined to reduce support for continued federal funding of the OEO. Somewhat to the surprise of CUNA officials, the Nixon administration renewed and increased the OEO contract by $100,000, but it was permitted to expire in June, 1970. CUNA's Organization/ Limited Income Groups Department still functioned because it was financed by the national association, but the field staff was no longer available to assist the program.[45]

In the fall of 1970, CUNA appointed a special committee to assess the movement's efforts in the poverty field. It concluded that "the low-income credit union as such offers little or no opportunity for us to bring forth dynamic ways of improving in an outstanding manner our present approaches for bringing credit union services to poor people." While recognizing that some credit unions were rendering worth-while services to their members, it asserted that there were more "non-poor people than poor people who need but do not benefit from credit union benefits." The committee's only suggestion was that the OEO be approached to consider ways to "conserve" credit union services for existing organizations, but that no additional credit unions be organized among the hardcore poor until other plans could be developed.[46]

In contrast to the meager development of credit societies among low-income groups, there was an amazing growth of credit unions at American defense installations. Civilian employees and military officers received relatively good pay, and even the lower paid men in the ranks could save some money since the services provided their basic subsistence. Working through the Department of Defense, CUNA and state leagues expended a major effort to organize credit unions on domestic military bases in the 1950s and 1960s.[47] By the late 1960s there was also a growing interest in establishing credit unions at American military posts overseas. Since there were problems in chartering credit unions in foreign countries, the Department of Defense allowed existing credit unions to operate substations overseas. In 1968 the credit union at Barksdale Air Force Base began to open substations in the Philippines, while the Keesler Air Force Base credit union opened similar substations in Great Britain. Previously about

[45] "Frontline," July 18, 1969, p. 2, and Aug. 28, 1970, p. 1.
[46] Ibid., Nov. 25, 1970, p. 1.
[47] Report of the Defense Credit Union Council, May, 1964, p. 12.

a half-dozen stateside credit unions had begun suboffice operations on military bases in West Germany.[48] All told, at the end of 1969 there were 459 credit unions serving military and civilian personnel at defense installations, with 2,659,564 members and loans outstanding of $1.37 billion.[49] One of the outstanding credit unions in this category was that at Tinker Air Force Base near Oklahoma City. Organized in 1936 by seven civilian employees who each subscribed to one five-dollar share, it had become the tenth largest credit union in the world by 1970, with assets of over $43 million, and a full-time staff of 100, serving 40,000 members.[50]

Traditional credit unionism continued to develop throughout the 1960s, but at a rate hardly satisfying to most of the movement's leaders. In 1956 there were 17,256 credit unions with over 9 million members in the United States; by 1969 there were 23,761 societies and more than 21 million members. These were impressive gains, yet there was a decrease in the rate of organizing new credit unions. The last year in which the net increase in credit unions (the number of new credit unions organized, less the number liquidated or merged) exceeded 1,000 was 1956. Membership gains, however, were much more impressive as individual credit unions became larger. From 1956 through 1969, the number of credit unions in the United States increased 37 percent, but total membership grew by 138 percent.[51]

The slowdown in the organization of credit unions worried many leaders. CUNA President Melvin Widerman acknowledged the trend in 1956, and four years later, managing director Vance Austin told the board of directors, that "we have run out of easy ones to organize." [52] Moreover, CUNA found that it could no longer afford to provide field representatives to roam the country for "cold canvassing," while the federal bureau had much earlier given up that practice. By 1957 CUNA had no organizational representatives in the field at all. This situation resulted mainly from the insistence by state leagues that they assume responsibility for organizing new credit unions. CUNA, they said, should perform other functions. Although difficult to measure, it is probable, too, that the growing opposition to credit unions by bankers, small loan

[48] CUNA "Briefs," Nov. 8, 1968, p. 3.

[49] *Ibid.,* Sept. 25, 1970, p. 2.

[50] *Oklahoma Journal,* June 30, 1970.

[51] *International Credit Union Yearbook, 1970,* table 13, p. 37.

[52] Minutes, CUNA Directors, May, 1956, p. 8; and Abridged Minutes, CUNA Directors, May, 1960, p. 118.

companies, and industrialists had some impact on organizational efforts. The movement to extend "in-plant" banking to industrial firms also provided competition for credit unions. But mainly, the easy availability of credit to most American citizens, along with a decline in the zeal of credit union volunteers to extend the benefits of cooperative credit outside their own places of employment, slowed the rate of organization. To meet growing competition, leagues and CUNA itself concentrated more and more on consolidating smaller credit unions and in providing increasing services to their members.

The increase in the number of credit unions in Canada was also disappointing. In 1956 there were 4,258 Canadian credit unions, and only 284 more by 1969. Yet there was a great jump in membership in the same period, from 1,800,000 to 5,490,000.[53] The greatest gains world-wide came outside of the United States and Canada in countries where credit unions scarcely existed in 1954. By the fall of 1970, there were 1,795 credit unions in Africa, 16,827 in Asia, 848 in Australia, 610 in the Caribbean, 1,333 in Central America, 341 in Europe, 2,835 in South America, and 413 in the southwestern Pacific. Outside the pale of CUNA were the 25,845 Raiffeisen, Schulze-Delitzsch, and other cooperative credit societies, mainly in Europe. By that time there were 53,361 credit unions in the world. When the "related" cooperative credit societies were added, the total throughout the world reached 79,206.[54]

The great development of credit unionism resulted from more sustained and sophisticated advertising and promotion by credit unions, by the tightening of credit and increasing interest rates charged by other lending institutions, and by the increased availability of loan funds in the hands of credit unions. Yet money for lending was becoming a problem in some cases. In 1956, with personal savings in all United States financial institutions standing at $170.6 billion, credit unions held only $2.9 billion, or 1.7 percent. In 1969 total savings reached $491.2 billion, while the credit unions' share stood at $13.7 billion or 2.8 percent.[55] In 1964 CUNA leaders reported that during the previous year savings in credit unions had increased 14 percent, while lending jumped 16 percent. Shipe warned that if such a trend continued, the day would come "when we will run out of money for loans." But in general loans continued to grow

[53] *International Credit Union Yearbook, 1970*, table 15, p. 39.

[54] "Credit Union Count: Active Credit Unions Reported as of October 31, 1970," distributed with "Briefs."

[55] *International Credit Union Yearbook, 1970*, table 16, p. 40.

at a faster rate than savings.[56] Clearly the higher interest paid on savings by banks and other financial institutions, along with smaller savings by the typical credit union member because of inflation and increased consumption, were causing credit unions serious problems. This development also revealed that too many credit union members had come to look upon credit unions as simply convenient places for small loans, without a corresponding feeling that their credit union deserved support in the form of deposits.

These problems challenged the leagues and the national association to make important changes in their personnel, services, and programs. Perhaps the most striking developments came in state leagues, several of which moved into impressive office buildings of their own, employed large staffs, and operated programs and services parallel to those offered by CUNA. Directly representing the credit unions in their states —many of which had assets of millions of dollars—the leagues came to view CUNA as an organization that had to "deliver" substantial services in order to command their support. Most of them operated "stabilization funds" to assist credit unions in financial difficulty or to help liquidate credit unions with minimal losses to members. Some leagues sponsored central credit unions that while not acting as interlending agencies, allowed officers of member credit unions to borrow money for their own use. All engaged in a variety of services to their members, ranging from on-location consultation, to the sponsorship of educational conferences and schools, to advertising and promotion. The Michigan league owns its own life insurance company, while some leagues provide casualty and other types of insurance. By 1970, 91.5 percent of all credit unions in the United States were affiliated with their state leagues and with CUNA.[57]

CUNA's professional staff has been generally responsive to the needs of modern credit unions. Vance Austin introduced a wide variety of new programs. But he resigned in 1962 and was replaced by the assistant managing director, J. Orrin Shipe, who, unlike Austin, came from the ranks of the movement. In 1934, when he was only twenty-two, Shipe was working for an insurance company in Buffalo, New York, when he read a newspaper editorial about credit unions. He organized one for his fellow workers, and within five years had formed an additional forty to fifty credit unions in the state. In 1939 he joined CUNA as a fieldman in the Midwest, soon moving to Madison where he headed up the Education

[56] Report of Managing Director, May, 1964, pp. 1–2; "Briefs," Jan. 2, 1970, p. 1.
[57] "Briefs," Aug. 7, 1970, p. 4.

Department, edited *The Bridge,* and finally became assistant managing director.[58]

With the change in management, the directors began to re-evaluate CUNA's activities, with a view of eliminating unnecessary and unproductive functions, enlarging desirable programs, and planning entirely new services. They assigned this task to the Planning Committee, which issued its report in May, 1963. The study noted that over the years the leagues had developed programs and services parallel to those offered by CUNA. Therefore, the committee believed that some of CUNA's departments were becoming "superfluous as leagues assume the full responsibility in their own areas." Specifically, the Planning Committee recommended that CUNA introduce fewer new programs and services; that prospective programs receive more study before being inaugurated; that great care be taken to involve the leagues in the administration of programs; that consideration be given to consolidating some departments and programs; that CUNA programs and services be given more publicity; and that future planning include consideration of social and economic trends both within and without the movement before taking any action.[59]

There were few fundamental changes in CUNA's basic departmental structure or in the services it rendered as a result of the Planning Committee's report, although a decided shift of emphasis did result. Increasingly, specialized services in education, public relations, and technical services, as well as the traditional area of protecting and initiating federal legislation, were stressed. In 1954 CUNA sponsored its first School for Credit Union Personnel with the cooperation of the University of Wisconsin. Three years later, 123 professional credit union employees attended the school, 29 of whom were third-year students who "graduated" at the end of the summer session. In 1961 CUNA inaugurated a "graduate school," with 50 graduates of the School for Credit Union Personnel returning for further training.[60] CUNA's Education Department also conducted numerous highly specialized conferences and participated in league-sponsored educational efforts.

Various CUNA publications also served an educational and public relations function. *The Bridge,* whose name was changed to the *Credit*

[58] Abridged Minutes, CUNA Executive Committee, Nov., 1962, pp. 3–4; *Wisconsin State Journal,* Aug. 31, 1969.

[59] Report of the Planning Committee to the Members of the National Board, May, 1963; Abridged Minutes, CUNA Directors, May, 1963, pp. 6–7.

[60] Report of Managing Director, April 23, 1958, p. 8, and May, 1961, p. 5.

Union Magazine in 1963, became less of a general membership publication and more of an organ for the movement's leaders. After 1957 the magazine carried essentially three types of articles: those dealing with credit union operating problems, those on abuses in the field of consumer credit, and stories on related political, economic, and social trends. By 1968 the magazine's circulation exceeded 72,000. The Publications Department, under the direction of John Prindle, published *Everybody's Money,* a quarterly magazine begun in 1961 to provide information for consumers. It dealt with product comparison and safety, credit information, and rackets and frauds. By 1969 the circulation of this publication was two million copies.[61] The Public Relations Department, under the direction of Tom J. Hefter, issued a large number of specialized bulletins and pamphlets, as well as a weekly news report called *CUNA Briefs.* The department also provided articles for newspapers and magazines, teachers' manuals, movie and television films, promoted International Credit Union Day each year, and served in a consultative role for other CUNA departments and state leagues.

Closely allied to education and public relations was the work of the Research and Economics Department, which after 1960 was under the direction of Walter Polner, a trained economist. This department carried on basic research dealing with credit unions and their role in the national economy, as well as special economic studies on individual states. Much of the data collected was published each year in the *International Credit Union Yearbook,* a project of the Public Relations Department.

Other departments within CUNA by 1970 included a conference coordinator, who participated in the planning of all major conferences, meetings, and schools. The Insurance Services Department continued to offer fidelity bond service to credit unions, as well as chattel mortgage insurance, a group health program, and literature and consultative services to credit unions on loss prevention. The Organization/Limited Income Groups Department no longer directly organized individual credit unions, but like other CUNA departments, engaged in activities supplementing league organizational efforts. A Pension Plan Department provided retirement benefits to employees of CUNA, state leagues, and credit unions. A small Historical Projects Department headed by E. R. Brann maintained the Bergengren Memorial Museum Library which housed historical manuscripts and books of a technical and general nature, and also maintained displays of credit union memorabilia of interest to the many national and international visitors at Filene House. Another

---

[61] *Ibid.,* May, 1961; *Everybody's Money,* Aug., 1969.

extremely important office was that of comptroller, held since Charles Hyland's retirement in 1957 by John Brady.[62]

One important function of CUNA was that of representing the political interests of cooperative credit. The Washington office remained an effective instrument for contacts with federal officials, congressmen, and the Bureau of Federal Credit Unions. Hubert Rhodes remained CUNA's chief lobbyist in charge of that office until 1961 when he was forced to retire because of ill health. In 1956 CUNA organized its Legal and Legislative Department under the direction of David Weinberg. In 1961 Robert Davis was added to the department's staff as its League Legislative Specialist, to assist state leagues in protecting existing credit union laws and in initiating new and desirable legislation. The executive committee maintained both standing and *ad hoc* committees concerned with legislative affairs. In the mid-sixties CUNA's legal and legislative operations were further strengthened with establishment of a separate legal department under a general counsel, and the transferring to Washington of the entire Department of Legislation and Governmental Affairs, except for that section dealing with state legislation. Credit unionism continued to enjoy strong bipartisan support in Congress with Congressman Wright Patman of Texas and Senator John Sparkman of Alabama serving as strong spokesmen for the movement.[63]

Credit unions had to be constantly on guard against unfavorable legislation. The attack on the tax exempt status of credit unions continued throughout the 1960s as the National Tax Equality Association led the fight. Perhaps more disconcerting to the movement was the growing opposition of bankers. An article in the *American Banker* in 1956 which emphasized the great growth of credit unions after 1941, began: "It's better to be swallowed by a whale than nibbled to death by minnows. . . . This frame of mind is increasingly shared by bankers, who have watched with mounting concern the spawning of quasi-public-welfare units that have invaded financial feeding grounds hitherto allotted to chartered banks." The writer acknowledged that credit unions seem "so innocuous when evidenced in small, purely localized units," but they took on "vastly different character when they appear in town as major-sized competition with chartered bank services." [64] The Industrial Relations Division of

[62] For activities of CUNA departments, see their annual reports, issued yearly.

[63] Report of Managing Director, May, 1961, p. 10.

[64] R. E. Gormley, co-chairman of the Bankers Committee for Tax Equality, to "Dear Sir," June 12, 1956; and "Credit Unions, Their Growth Poses Questions," reprint from *American Banker* (May 17, 1956), circulated by the Bankers Committee for Tax Equality.

the National Association of Manufacturers reviewed the operation of credit unions in 1958, and urged management "to take a sober, second look at the operations of any credit union connected with the company." [65]

Vance Austin discussed the growing opposition to credit unions in 1960. He pointed out that competitors were trying to eliminate credit union competition by restricting the chartering of new credit unions, by removing the income tax exemption, and by persuading businessmen to reverse their approval of credit unions. Three years later, Orrin Shipe charged the American Bankers' Association with trying to obtain legislative restrictions against credit unions, which was the "first overt action taken by any responsible organization anywhere to attempt to determine our laws for us." [66] CUNA countered these attacks by attempting to persuade competitors that credit unions were desirable institutions that threatened no one except loan sharks, and by working effectively in Washington to stave off unfavorable legislation.

CUNA also sought new legislation that would strengthen federal credit union operations. In 1959, after a three-year campaign, CUNA succeeded in securing a complete revision of the federal law, the first major revision since its enactment in 1934. CUNA officials declared that the revised statute contained everything desired by the movement except a provision permitting a central bank.[67]

CUNA also played an important role in supporting the bill introduced in 1960 by Senator Paul Douglas, requiring all lending institutions to fully disclose their finance charges in terms of simple annual interest rates. Until the enactment of the so-called Truth-in-Lending Act in 1969, CUNA publicized and lobbied for the passage of this significant measure.[68] Other legislation important to credit unions included a 1970 law making share insurance up to $20,000 mandatory for federal credit unions and optional for state societies; the so-called omnibus bill of 1967 amending the federal credit union act so that credit committees could delegate their authority to a loan officer, and authorizing quarterly dividend payments and a full month's dividend credit for shares purchased and fully paid up during the first ten days of a month; in 1968 two addi-

---

[65] National Association of Manufacturers, Industrial Relations Division, "A Report to Management on Credit Unions," Aug., 1958.

[66] Report of Managing Director, May, 1960, p. 7, and May 10, 1963, p. 1.

[67] *Ibid.,* May 2, 1960, p. 5.

[68] Minutes, CUNA Directors, May, 1960, p. 496.

tional measures allowed payroll deductions for federal employees for credit union accounts; and a ten-year maturity limit on certain secured loans, an unsecured loan limit up to $2,500, and permission for federal credit unions to invest in state-chartered central credit unions.[69] Clearly, CUNA had a strong voice in legislative matters of interest and concern to credit unionism.

Perhaps the movement's most significant legislative victory was the passage of H.R. 2 in 1970, which created an independent supervisory agency for federal credit unions. Indeed, Shipe called the law the most important since the passage of the original federal act. The law transferred the existing Bureau of Federal Credit Unions to an autonomous agency known as the National Credit Union Administration. President Nixon appointed retired Marine Corps Lieutenant General Herman Nickerson, Jr., to the top administrative post, although CUNA preferred J. Deane Gannon. A National Credit Union Board was also to be appointed consisting of six persons, each representing one of the credit union regions. Its function was to "provide advice, counsel and guidance to the administrator with respect to matters of policy relating to the activities and functions of the Administration." CUNA immediately nominated a full slate to fill the posts.[70]

Equally significant for the organized credit union movement, CUNA itself underwent a significant restructuring in 1970. After several years of considering how to rationalize an organization directing world-wide credit union activities so there could be maximum self-determination by United States, Canadian, and other national credit union groups, the board of directors abolished CUNA International and organized the World Council of Credit Unions, Inc. The world council received title to Filene House and assumed control of two of the old association's departments—world extension and historical projects. It was decided that a delegates meeting would be held every three years. In the interim, a fifteen-man board of directors, representing the world-wide movement, would govern the affairs of the organization. The first president was CUNA International's past president, R. C. Robertson, while Shipe was chosen as the managing director.

A confederation of United States leagues, named the Credit Union National Association, Inc. (CUNA), was organized to replace the former United States Forum. It essentially maintained the structure it had de-

[69] *Federal Credit Union Observer,* I (July, 1968), 1–5.

[70] *Ibid.,* IV (April, 1970), 1–7; *Credit Union Magazine,* XXXV (June, 1970), 4; CUNA Public Relations Department, *Washington News* (Sept. 11, 1970), pp. 1–2.

veloped under the old association, with three "table" officers and nine vice-presidents representing the other districts. Wilfred S. MacKinnon of Texas became the first president, and Shipe was named managing director. The Credit Union National Association shared Filene House with the world council. The Canadian leagues also organized the National Association of Canadian Credit Unions, while the Australian leagues formed the Australian Federation of Credit Union Leagues. For the time being, the Overseas National Forum, divided into its English-speaking and Spanish-speaking subsections continued as a part of the world council, but there was little doubt that additional national confederations would one day take their place in the world-wide organization. For the time being, as well, it was clear that the United States association would continue to operate most of the services it had in the past, as well as providing services to other confederations on a cost basis.[71]

Thus, credit unionism moved into the 1970s, operating with a new federal agency and a greatly revised organizational structure. Modernization of operating methods was also being implemented. The absence of share insurance in the past had led many state leagues to establish "stabilization" programs to channel funds into credit unions that were in financial difficulty or to aid societies to liquidate with minimal losses. In 1962 CUNA established the CUNA Stabilization Program, Inc., with many state leagues as members.[72] Similarly, with the great technological advances made in the field of data processing, several state leagues set up centralized computer services for their members. In 1969 CUNA, CUNA Mutual, and several leagues incorporated the CUNADATA Corporation which aimed eventually to provide "a complete, unified computer accounting system for U.S. credit unions." It announced as its first undertaking the supply of so-called software, or computer programming that would be followed by the purchasing of supplies on a national basis.[73]

Perhaps the most ambitious undertaking by the movement was the formation in 1966 of the ICU Services Corporation to provide credit unions with the most up-to-date techniques "for the generation of funds, transfer, and lending or allocation as the needs of the individual credit unions and their members dictate." Such a role, the Planning Committee concluded, required "the ability to create new kinds of money-type instruments and to manage their use." There was much discussion in

[71] *Credit Union Magazine,* XXXV (June, 1970), 4–7; "Briefs," May 22, 1970 and Aug. 7, 1970.

[72] Report of Managing Director, May, 1962, p. 3.

[73] "Briefs," Nov. 21, 1969, p. 1.

the movement about modern society moving into a "cashless, checkless" economy. No one was certain about what services the corporation would eventually offer, but it first supplied credit unions with money orders and traveler's checks for sales to members. Soon thereafter it initiated an investment program, where credit unions with surplus funds could invest them by means of a trust arrangement in U.S. government securities. Most recently, ICU Services became a clearinghouse to facilitate inter-lending between credit unions and to tap the public money market through the issuance of commercial paper. Other projects considered were establishing lines of credit for members and a world-wide credit card. The services corporation, indeed, offered the movement an almost unlimited number of possible services to keep credit unions abreast of developments in the modern consumer economy.[74]

Thus, as the credit union movement reached its age of maturity, it found that the philosophy of cooperative credit was still sound, but that its methods must change with the times. Looking to the future and po-tential members, the movement developed a variety of programs designed to tell the credit union story to the youth of America. Realizing that the close personal relationship of members had broken down in a complex society and that one's fellow members no longer knew or particularly cared about the individual problems of others, the movement ventured into the field of family financial counseling.[75] Realizing, too, that the small credit union, while still performing a useful function, could not provide the myriad of services or successfully compete with other savings and lending institutions, CUNA began promoting service centers to provide various management and promotional services for groups of small credit unions. CUNA also recognized that smaller credit unions would perhaps be better off if they combined into larger institutions, or if the common bond were expanded so that different groups could form a single credit union.

Sometimes CUNA led in seeking new ways to serve credit union mem-bers, but at other times individual credit unions and leagues pushed and pulled it into new programs. Many leagues had large staffs and programs every bit as sophisticated as those in Madison. A growing number of credit unions had assets of millions of dollars and they, too, carried on a wide range of activities. By 1961 there were enough "million-dollar" credit unions under full-time professional management that a special

[74] Report of the Planning Committee, May, 1966, *passim;* "Briefs," June 21, 1968, p. 1; Oct. 18, 1968, p. 1; Oct. 30, 1970, p. 1.

[75] Report of Managing Director, May, 1961, p. 4.

program was developed, known as the Credit Union Executive Services Program (CUES), to provide an assortment of services and programs for the larger credit unions. In addition, the managers of those credit unions organized themselves into the CUES Managers' Society, later called the Credit Union Executives' Society.[76] Among the growing number of peripheral groups were such specialized organizations as the Congress of Central Credit Unions, organized in 1967 to promote and develop the expansion of central credit unions and to foster programs and policies for advancing their objectives. There was even an Association of State Credit Union Supervisers to deal with the problems and programs of government supervisors at the state level.[77] From every level, then, came proposals—and sometimes demands—for programs to meet the needs of modern credit unionism.

[76] Minutes, CUNA Directors, May, 1962, pp. 249–80.

[77] See, for example, the following articles in the *Credit Union Magazine:* R. C. Morgan and A. R. Glen, "Where We've Been . . . and Where We're Going" (April, 1970), pp. 30–34; Kenneth J. Marin, "Toward Credit Union 'Mercy Killing' " (June, 1968), p. 18; John McCullough, "Philosophy . . . and A Challenge," (May, 1968), pp. 37–39; Phillip Wilder, "Do We Have A 'Delicatessen' Image?" (Oct., 1969), p. 22.

CHAPTER XV

Looking Back and Ahead

BETWEEN 1909, when Desjardins and a few citizens formed the first credit union in the United States at Manchester, New Hampshire, and 1970, the number of credit unions increased from 1 to 23,400. By August, 1970, credit unions were providing $12.2 billion of installment credit in the United States, or about 12 percent of the total. This was an increase from only $590 million, or 4 percent, twenty years earlier. Another way to view the advancing role of credit unions is to compare their rate of growth with that of other financial institutions. While installment credit provided by commercial banks and consumer finance companies rose about seven times between 1950 and 1970, credit unions experienced a twentyfold increase. It was clearly evident by the 1960s that credit unions had become an important part of the nation's expanding consumer credit business. Millions of Americans looked to their credit unions as the natural place to invest their surplus funds and to borrow money for time purchases. Moreover, cooperative credit has become a world-wide development expanding to every continent.

These achievements, however, have come only after more than a half century of work and struggle. Beginning in Germany with Schulze-Delitzsch and Raiffeisen in the mid-nineteenth century, the movement spread to other parts of Europe, to Canada, and then to the United States. Following World War II cooperative credit societies developed throughout many parts of the underdeveloped world. Although credit unionism appeared in the United States during the Progressive movement in the early twentieth century, it never became a major progressive reform. The initial support for credit unions came mainly from philanthropic businessmen in the Boston area, the most important of whom was Edward A. Filene. He supported the movement generously until his death in 1937. At first Filene and a few of his friends attempted to promote the establishment of credit unions among various local groups which needed better credit facilities, but it was not until the organization of the Credit Union National Extension Bureau in 1921, and the employment of Roy Bergengren, that the movement made any significant headway. Bergengren undoubtedly did more than any other single individual to establish and develop credit unionism in the United States. His work, along with Filene's financial backing, shows what a few individuals can do if they have faith in a cause, commitment, and money, and if their cause fulfills a social and economic need.

Etched on the bust of Filene located in Filene House in Madison, Wisconsin, is the inscription, "Keep Purpose Constant Here." But the observer may wonder what was, and what continues to be, the purpose of cooperative credit. Are credit unions simply ordinary financial institutions, or are they different in purpose, spirit, and operation? And if they were distinctive in the past will they continue to be so in the future?

The credit union movement in the United States began on a note of high idealism. Its purpose was service, and, as Bergengren said, credit unions would prove "the practicality of the brotherhood of man." Indeed, Bergengren and other movement pioneers held deep religious values which emphasized service to one's fellow men. Bergengren liked to remind his listeners and readers that the movement's founders were a German Protestant (Raiffeisen), a French-Canadian Catholic (Desjardins), and an American Jew (Filene). According to the founders and early promoters, credit unions were to be agencies of humanitarian and philanthropic reform where people working together could meet their problems of credit.

Although cooperative in spirit and organization, the credit union movement was not anticapitalist. In its early development most loans were made for productive purposes and to help small businessmen and farmers reach economic independence. This was the goal of practical cooperation. What the founders of credit unionism hoped to do was to reduce the harsh and exploitive aspects of capitalism and to make the system work better for more people. Credit unionism was the type of reform which sought to bring the masses into the main stream of the economy by supplying one of their basic needs—credit. Moreover, the founders of credit unionism emphasized the importance of democratic control. In this respect, they stressed participation by all members. The true goal, then, was economic democracy through self-help.

At the same time credit unionism was basically a conservative force in American society. Both Bergengren and Filene argued that one of the main virtues of credit unions was their role in making employees more content and efficient, and less likely to accept any brand of radicalism. As Bergengren said repeatedly, wage workers without savings and credit were ideal prospects for "bolshevism." He believed that constitutional democracy was still on trial, and that helping people meet their credit needs would provide strength and stability to American institutions. This ideal continued to prevail long after Bergengren concluded his active leadership in the movement. One of the reasons advanced by credit union leaders in the 1950s for expanding cooperative credit to underdeveloped countries was, they said, to create a bulwark against communism.

In the early years of credit unionism there was a great deal of discussion about the benefits which cooperative credit could bring to the poor. However, by the very nature of credit unions their benefits were confined mainly to workers with jobs because a member had to have money to invest and means to repay his loans. This meant that credit unions had little to offer the hardcore, unemployed poor who did not need loans so much as grants or jobs. As early as the 1920s, Filene told Bergengren to quit wasting time trying to organize credit unions among poor Appalachian mountaineers and concentrate on workers in the industrial centers. The "Policies of CUNA" developed over a period of time and published in 1953 frankly stated that the purpose of the national association was to encourage "cooperative pooling and use of credit and financial resources of average salaried income groups." Thus credit unionism in the United States became principally a middle-class movement which provided loan and investment services for millions of wage and salary workers. Moreover, it had been shown as early as the 1920s that credit unions did not have much to offer farmers.

This does not mean that the credit union movement abandoned all attempts to help the poor. The development of credit unions after 1950 in many underdeveloped countries indicated the desire to assist people with very low incomes. Credit unions in the 1960s also sought to establish societies in the black ghettos where rates of unemployment were high and incomes low, as well as among Spanish-Americans and poor whites. While these were generally unsuccessful, even with federal aid, they demonstrate credit unionism's continued concern for the permanently poor. Managing Director J. Orrin Shipe told the CUNA International Board of Directors in May, 1968, that "I would hate to see credit unions become so soft and complacent that they are willing to serve only the more affluent members of our society." But credit unionists, like other Americans, discovered that the poverty which exists within a relatively complex and affluent economy is not susceptible to so simple a cure as credit unionism. Better education, medical care, housing, and jobs are the *sine qua non* for breaking the "culture of poverty." Nevertheless, the hope of meeting the needs of the poor lives on among credit unionists. In 1966 a Methodist minister and a Catholic priest in Richmond, Kentucky, organized a credit union at Eastern Kentucky University to meet the needs of people in the poverty-stricken surrounding area on the edge of Appalachia. But, for every case of this kind there were hundreds of credit unions serving factory workers, teachers, ministers, government employees, and others who had regular and adequate incomes.

From the outset credit unionism was people-oriented. Its founders deeply believed that organization and operation of credit unions should be done by volunteers. But this was practical only during the earlier phases of the movement. Although thousands of volunteers served, and continue to serve, as organizers and officers of credit societies, it became clear as early as 1920 that if cooperative credit were to become significant in the American economy, money, organization, and professional leadership were essential. Both Filene and Bergengren recognized this fact and together they provided these necessary ingredients for success. Organization of the national association in 1934 and the employment of a paid staff were further evidences of the need for professional direction and trained management. This same trend occurred in the state leagues and in individual credit unions. As the work of the leagues expanded, and as some credit unions became multimillion dollar institutions, paid management was an absolute requirement for successful operation. Consequently, over the years, as in Germany, credit unionism in the United States became more professionalized and less volunteeristic; more hardheaded and practical and less idealistic.

How should the credit union movement be evaluated in the midstream of its development? While any final judgment would be premature, some things seem clear. Credit unionism arose out of a felt need to provide credit at more reasonable rates of interest. In this credit unions have been successful. While cooperative credit did not eliminate all of the problems associated with loan sharks which preyed on small borrowers, it did help to greatly reduce the former abuses. Credit unions loaned money to millions of people at interest rates considerably below those charged by commercial lending agencies. Perhaps even more important was the fact that credit unions provided loans to people who had been denied credit of any kind except by the worst of the loan sharks. Although the evidence is unclear, competition from credit unions may have in some cases prompted banks and small loan companies to reduce their interest rates and to improve their installment loan services. Credit unions, moreover, gave many people a sense of pride and accomplishment by bringing them together through cooperative efforts to solve at least one of their crucial economic problems. Credit unions also added an important dimension to the world-wide cooperative movement.

Partly because of the growing size of credit unions and the rise of new leadership, some credit union spokesmen became deeply concerned over what they considered the tendency to depart from the original principles and purposes of cooperative credit and the rising business-orientation within the movement. Members of CUNA's board, the managing directors, and other officials regularly dealt with this question in the 1950s and 1960s. In 1952, Paul Deaton, chairman of CUNA's Dues Committee, said that some large credit unions were nothing but "a cross between a bank and a loan company." The new directors of many credit unions, he said, did not really understand the purposes of credit unions. Fifteen years later CUNA's Managing Director Shipe declared that it was essential for credit unionism to "keep its ideals above its financial statement."

These and other leaders had raised one of the most fundamental questions facing credit unionism. They were really asking whether the credit union movement would retain its original spirit of cooperation and service, or whether the large societies would forget the traditional people-orientation and concentrate on imitating other financial institutions handling installment financing. Something of a paradox existed by the 1960s. Could the original goals of service be squared with the modern demands for business efficiency? As credit unions become increasingly concerned with modern management techniques, electronic computations, and a wider variety of programs, will they lose their heritage which was concern for people? One thing seems clear in this regard—if credit unions do not meet the challenges of the modern economy they will be unable to compete and consequently they will have no heritage to preserve. The crucial question, then, is how to "keep up" in the business world and yet somehow maintain the original purposes and philosophy behind credit unionism. Unless this is done, credit unions will become just additional financial institutions and will deserve no more loyalty of members than the local bank or the small loan company.

The basic purpose of credit unionism, that is, the cooperative pooling of savings and the lending of money, remains the same as in the movement's beginning. The principles of self-help, cooperation, and democracy still rank high in the traditions and practices of credit unions. But silent and ritualistic tributes to Raiffeisen, Desjardins, Filene, and Bergengren at meetings of the board of directors will not maintain these principles in the future. The task of credit union leadership is to combine the principles of service and cooperation with the highest standards of business management. How the credit union leadership achieves this goal will determine the direction and tone of the movement during the last third of the twentieth century.

APPENDIX

Year	Number of Active Credit Unions	Number of Members	Shares and Deposits (Savings)	Loans Outstanding† to Members	Reserves	Assets
69	23,761*	21,630,958	$13,672,774,441	$12,942,433,595	$1,000,609,396	$15,867,683,572
68	23,406	20,264,487	12,323,735,152	11,284,057,909	861,317,431	14,209,972,929
67	23,049	19,070,072	11,323,563,525	9,876,815,058	779,007,206	12,775,299,851
66	22,686	17,897,351	10,106,473,629	9,093,129,509	677,904,383	11,605,503,953
65	22,119	16,753,106	9,248,865,386	8,095,443,809	589,512,465	10,552,125,323
64	21,807	15,619,210	8,241,615,640	7,046,016,021	510,318,443	9,360,818,386
63	21,369	14,586,988	7,166,397,511	6,170,577,360	441,453,778	8,130,655,890
62	20,951	13,762,047	6,331,180,434	5,476,668,785	381,298,538	7,186,213,145
61	20,615	12,882,793	5,635,808,585	4,817,635,085	325,657,500	6,382,517,938
60	20,047	12,037,533	4,974,580,218	4,377,305,517	272,284,887	5,653,475,890
59	19,452	11,262,581	4,436,396,254	3,707,712,487	232,207,013	5,024,163,414
58	18,838	10,431,606	3,869,853,889	3,078,287,068	197,694,237	4,345,513,247
57	18,203	9,819,452	3,381,850,852	2,778,305,187	165,257,432	3,813,447,173
56	17,256	9,061,339	2,914,121,390	2,326,167,885	136,520,194	3,270,944,723
55	16,201	8,153,641	2,446,846,375	1,933,886,150	109,932,462	2,743,441,284
54	15,073	7,355,642	2,039,294,483	1,552,050,289	91,068,892	2,270,354,609
53	13,703	6,635,543	1,688,329,872	1,307,502,648	75,053,792	1,895,106,600
52	12,291	5,888,287	1,355,820,077	985,044,812	66,572,058†	1,516,118,652
51	11,283	5,196,393	1,040,437,236*	747,084,026	59,426,468	1,198,327,876
50	10,591	4,610,278	850,488,875	679,864,572	52,074,361	1,005,475,598
49	9,924	4,090,721	702,989,666	515,824,566	43,239,509	827,088,969
45	8,683	2,842,989	369,122,697	127,903,039	24,416,088	434,622,487
42	9,767	3,144,603		148,771,572		340,347,742
41	9,891	3,304,390		219,855,642		322,214,816
40	9,023	2,826,612		190,250,726		253,149,629
39	7,964	2,309,183		148,773,153		193,599,722
37	6,105	1,538,177				116,337,733
36	5,241	1,170,445				82,817,246
35	3,372	641,797				50,336,168
34	2,489	427,097				40,212,112
29	974	264,908				
25	419	108,000				
21	190	72,310				
09	1					

* No statistics on deposits in state-chartered credit unions available before 1952.

† Due to past reporting system, some loans to other credit unions are included in data before 1960.

Source: Bureau of Labor Statistics, National Credit Union Administration, State Supervisory Agencies.

Bibliographical Note

THE PRINCIPAL sources for this book are located in the Bergengren Memorial Museum Library at Filene House in Madison, Wisconsin. The authors had complete and unrestricted access to these records. The most important collection of papers dealing with credit union history in the United States is that of Edward A. Filene. They contain voluminous correspondence files, bound copies of speeches, and scrapbooks. Besides the records dealing with credit unions, the Filene Papers contain materials relating to his personal and business affairs, as well as to his numerous public service projects. The other major manuscript collection is the correspondence of Roy F. Bergengren. Much of the Bergengren correspondence is intermingled with the Filene Papers. Unfortunately, there are no significant amounts of correspondence for other early credit union leaders such as Thomas Doig.

Other manuscript materials of utmost importance are the records of the Credit Union National Association and its successor, CUNA International. These include the minutes of the executive committee, the board of directors, the Joint Committee of CUNA and the CUNA Mutual Insurance Society. In addition there are correspondence files, reports by CUNA's managing director and president, and reports by various committees and departments. Files relating to state legislative campaigns, passage of the Federal Credit Union Act, the Estes Park meeting, activities of the Washington legislative office, the World Extension Department, and many other aspects of credit union history are also found in the Bergengren Memorial Museum Library. In short, there are abundant manuscript materials dealing with the history of credit unionism in the United States, and, for more recent years, cooperative credit throughout the world.

The Bergengren Memorial Museum Library has also acquired copies of unpublished documents from other collections which are vital to any study of credit union history. One of these collections is the correspondence of Alphonse Desjardins which deals with his earliest interests in cooperative credit. The original letters are in the *Archives de la Fédération des*

361

Caisses Populaires Desiardins in Quebec. The other collection is the corre-spondence of officials of the Russell Sage Foundation, copies of which were obtained from the Library of Congress. These files contain material on the foundation's relations with Desjardins, its work on behalf of uni-form small loan legislation, and the establishment of the credit union movement in New York.

The Bergengren Memorial Museum Library also houses large quan-tities of published material dealing with the history and operation of credit unions. One especially important source is the file of *The Bridge* which was published from 1924 to 1963 with the exception of 1934 to 1936. It was succeeded by the *Credit Union Magazine* in 1963. The Credit Union National Association also published many specialized newsletters, pamphlets, and reports which provide useful insights into the movement.

Although quite a number of popular, promotional-type books have been written on aspects of credit union development, there is a dearth of scholarly studies on cooperative credit. There are a few, however, that deserve attention. For works in English on the European background of cooperative credit, one should consult Henry W. Wolff's *People's Banks: A Record of Social and Economic Progress* (London: P. S. King & Co., 1919); Myron T. Herrick's *Rural Credits: Land and Cooperative* (New York: D. Ap-pleton & Co., 1914); and Donald S. Tucker's *The Evolution of People's Banks* (New York: Columbia University Press, 1922). The best account of Desjardins's work in Canada is Hector MacPherson's "Co-operative Credit Associations in the Province of Quebec" (Ph.D. dissertation, Uni-versity of Chicago, 1910).

The most comprehensive book on cooperative development in the United States is Joseph G. Knapp, *The Rise of American Cooperative Enter-prise, 1620–1920* (Danville, Ill.: Interstate Printers and Publishers, 1969). Roy F. Bergengren wrote a number of books dealing with cooperative credit in the United States, but the most useful is his *Crusade: The Fight for Economic Democracy in North America, 1921–1945* (New York: Exposition Press, 1952). Two recent works of a more specialized nature can be con-sulted with profit. Jack Dublin's *Credit Unions: Theory and Practice* (Detroit: Wayne State University Press, 1966), is a basic introduction to credit unionism and contains one chapter on the history of the movement. A more technical work is John T. Croteau's *The Economics of the Credit Union* (Detroit: Wayne State University Press, 1963).

The popular periodicals have carried relatively few articles on credit unions and their development. The mass-circulated magazines have published occasional articles on credit unions, but most of them are of little historical value. Anyone interested in seeing the type of articles which have appeared in American magazines on credit unions should consult the *Reader's Guide to Periodical Literature*. One valuable source of information, however, is the *Monthly Labor Review* which began publishing material on credit unions in the mid-1920s.

Besides the printed sources, the authors interviewed numerous credit union leaders who were, or had been, active in the development of cooperative credit. Not only did these interviews supply additional concrete information, but they helped the authors to see and feel the intense missionary spirit of the credit union pioneers.

Index